THE POLITICS OF
SOVIET AGRICULTURE, 1960-1970

THE POLITICS OF

SOVIET AGRICULTURE, 1960-1970

WERNER G. HAHN

THE JOHNS HOPKINS UNIVERSITY PRESS
BALTIMORE AND LONDON

The Johns Hopkins University Press, Baltimore, Maryland 21218
The Johns Hopkins University Press Ltd., London

Library of Congress Catalog Card Number 72-151
International Standard Book Number 0-8018-1359-X

Library of Congress Cataloging in Publication data
will be found on the last printed page of this book

"Look at the root!"

"No one can embrace the unembraceable."

—widely quoted aphorisms of the legendary Kozma Prutkov

CONTENTS

PREFACE

The objective of this book is to examine the agricultural issues over which Soviet leaders have been divided during the decade 1960–70. It does not encompass all agricultural policies or problems—only those which have given rise to disputes among prominent Soviet politicians. Nor does it encompass all political disputes—primarily only those involving agriculture. More comprehensive analyses of the economics of agriculture can be found in works by Naum Jasny, Roy Laird, Erich Strauss, and others, and more detailed or broad studies of the general political disputes are contained in the writings of Michel Tatu, Carl Linden, and Robert Conquest.

The study is divided into two parts: the era of Khrushchev's leadership (1960–64) and the reaction against Khrushchev's policies (mainly in 1965), and the post-Khrushchev leadership (1965–70). For the Khrushchev period this study leans more heavily on the intra-agricultural issues (agrotechniques, crops, organization) than on questions of priorities between industry and agriculture, questions of reform and de-Stalinization, etc., which have been well documented for the Khrushchev period in other works (Michel Tatu, Sidney Ploss, Carl Linden). Because of this and also because it deals with the least successful period of his rule, the portrait of Khrushchev is less flattering than that presented in some other studies.

For the Brezhnev period the priorities question has been central, consequently the material on this period is organized around the struggles over resources for agriculture. Because of the public reticence of Khrushchev's successors and because they have largely avoided interfering in technical agricultural questions, agricultural politics during this period are less complicated and can be covered in somewhat less space.

In writing a history of agricultural disputes, I hope to present a very pragmatic picture of how the Soviet political system functions—how programs develop and turn into policies, how Soviet politicians conduct their political struggles, and how policy disputes affect the personal fortunes of politicians and vice versa. In addition to exploring and unraveling the agricultural-political disputes and rivalries in Moscow, we will also observe the role played by territorial party organizations, their frequent close identification with individual leaders, their rivalry with other party machines, and—despite the centralized Soviet system—their ability to occasionally initiate policies and influence Moscow's actions or to evade Moscow's directives and partially implement their own preferences. (In regard to the latter point, one may cite the leaders of Belorussia, Lithuania, and Kurgan Oblast who suffered much abuse for their lack of cooperation in Khrushchev's agricultural campaigns, or, more recently, the Estonian leaders, who have repeatedly demonstrated a lack of enthusiasm for agricultural decisions pushed by the Politburo.)

We will also observe how agricultural scientists and farm leaders often form alliances with local party bosses who are on the lookout for new methods, the success of which will win them favor in Moscow. Some local party leaders have risen to top jobs in Moscow at least partly on the success of the agricultural innovations which they and their scientific protégés promoted (Orenburg First Secretary Voronov and his ally, Orenburg Agricultural Institute director Khayrullin; Altay First Secretary Pysin and Altay Agricultural Institute director Nalivayko). The rivalries between regional party machines and their patrons are sometimes matched by rivalries between agricultural institutes and scientists (for example, the Saratov Institute versus the Orenburg Institute in the Southeast Zone; the Omsk Institute versus Maltsev's farm in west Siberia), and scientists such as Nalivayko, Khayrullin, and Barayev have won high-level political support for their ideas during bitter agricultural disputes. Of course, the most prominent example of a scientist being raised up as a national authority is Lysenko, who collapsed into disgrace when his patron Khrushchev was overthrown.

My approach is to seek to identify individual leaders' positions on issues through careful study and comparison of their statements through the years, to identify the role of these leaders and their viewpoints in disputes and decisions, and to compare personnel shifts and career patterns with policy changes and political disputes.

For the benefit of both the general reader and the specialist I have included a number of aids and appendixes. Following this Preface is a simplified diagram of government and party organs to aid in visualizing the relationship between the government and party and between national, republic, provincial, and local levels. Following the diagram are maps of the European and Asian parts of the USSR to aid in locating the republics and provinces referred to in the text and also to identify the provinces where the campaign to cultivate virgin land had the greatest impact. Finally, there is a glossary of special terms (primarily names of Soviet organizations).

In the back of the book are a number of appendixes. For convenient reference, detailed charts of the membership of the Central Committee's Presidium (renamed the Politburo in 1966) and Secretariat are included in appendixes 1 and 2. For the serious student of Soviet politics I have included much hard-to-find information on less-public organizations and positions. Appendix 3 contains a detailed study of the Central Committee's Bureau for the RSFSR (which plays an important role in this history) in the form of a chart of membership and accompanying documentation. Unlike the Central Committee's Presidium (Politburo) and Secretariat, the Bureau was not formally elected at Central Committee plenums and the appointment and removal of members was rarely announced—hence determination of its membership and changes in membership require extensive research and collection of random press identifications. In appendixes 4 and 5 are charts of the heads of Central Committee sections and of Central Committee sections for the RSFSR during the period covered by this history. Since appointments and removals of these very important insiders are rarely reported in the press, I include a documentation of press identifications on their comings and goings. Appendix 6 presents a chart of editors of the key newspapers involved in this history (*Pravda, Izvestiya, Sovetskaya Rossiya, Selskaya Zhizn, Komsomolskaya Pravda*), since the editors of the leading Soviet newspapers are also rarely identified. An anonymous "editorial collegium" signs off these newspapers instead of the chief editor, so that changes in editorial leadership can go unnoticed for months, and if they are announced it is usually only later in the journalists' trade magazine *Zhurnalist*—with no indication of the precise date of the change. Even these inexact announcements were not made systematically prior to late 1965. A chart of the leaders of the USSR Agriculture Ministry for the period covered by this study is contained in Appendix 7. In lieu of a bibliography, I have listed the periodicals used as sources with a brief identification of each (Appendix 8). Finally, a name index is included for cross reference.

The source material for this study is almost exclusively the Soviet press. Among the more valuable sources are the post-Khrushchev *ocherki* (essays or sketches), by Leonid Ivanov, Yuriy Chernichenko, and others, giving probing analyses of agricultural problems and exposés of past misdeeds. The main non-official source is Soviet biologist Zhores Medvedev's remarkable writings on Lysenko, which circulated underground in the Soviet Union for a number of years and eventually were published in the West.

The bulk of the material on the Khrushchev era was compiled in 1968–70, although many episodes were initially researched earlier. The post-Khrushchev part was written in 1970–71 and includes material through December 1971, including the March–April 1971 24th Party Congress.

I wish to thank Mrs. Luba Richter for reading part of the original manuscript and making valuable suggestions.

SIMPLIFIED DIAGRAM OF THE HIERARCHICAL STRUCTURE OF GOVERNMENT AND PARTY ORGANS

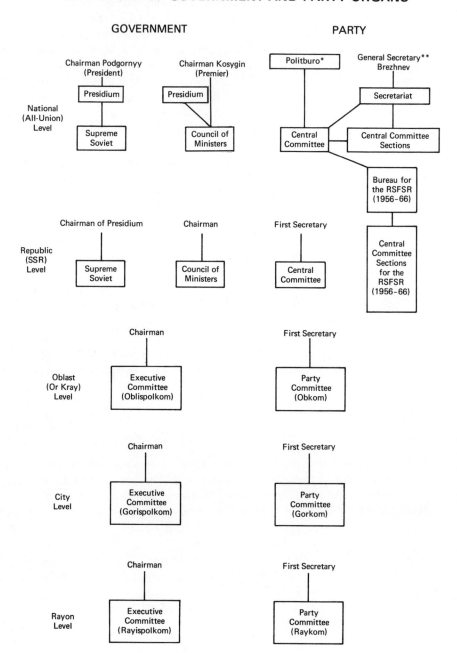

GOVERNMENT

PARTY

National (All-Union) Level

Chairman Podgornyy (President) — Presidium — Supreme Soviet

Chairman Kosygin (Premier) — Presidium — Council of Ministers

Politburo* — Central Committee

General Secretary** Brezhnev — Secretariat — Central Committee Sections

Bureau for the RSFSR (1956–66)

Republic (SSR) Level

Chairman of Presidium — Supreme Soviet

Chairman — Council of Ministers

First Secretary — Central Committee

Central Committee Sections for the RSFSR (1956–66)

Oblast (Or Kray) Level

Chairman — Executive Committee (Oblispolkom)

First Secretary — Party Committee (Obkom)

City Level

Chairman — Executive Committee (Gorispolkom)

First Secretary — Party Committee (Gorkom)

Rayon Level

Chairman — Executive Committee (Rayispolkom)

First Secretary — Party Committee (Raykom)

*Until 1966, this was named the Presidium.
**Until 1966, the title First Secretary was used.

European USSR

UKRAINIAN PROVINCES

1. CHERKASSY
2. CHERNIGOV
3. CHERNOVTSY
4. CRIMEA
5. DNEPROPETROVSK
6. DONETSK
7. IVANO-FRANKOVSK
8. KHARKOV
9. KHERSON
10. KHMELNITSKIY
11. KIEV
12. KIROVOGRAD
13. LUGANSK
14. LVOV
15. NIKOLAYEV
16. ODESSA
17. POLTAVA
18. ROVNO
19. SUMY
20. TERNOPOL
21. VINNITSA
22. VOLYN
23. ZAKARPATYE
24. ZAPOROZHE
25. ZHITOMIR

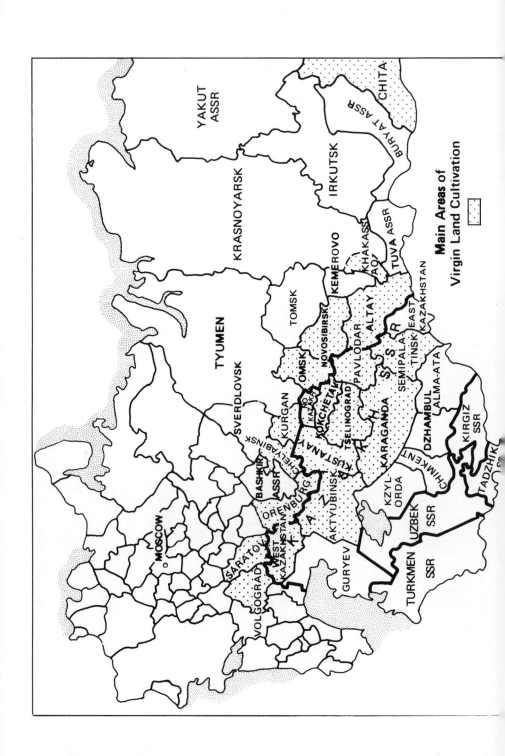

Main Areas of Virgin Land Cultivation

YAKUT ASSR

KRASNOYARSK

IRKUTSK

BURYAT ASSR

CHITA

TUVA ASSR

KHAKASS AO

KEMEROVO

ALTAY

TOMSK

NOVOSIBIRSK

PAVLODAR

EAST KAZAKHSTAN

SEMIPALATINSK

TYUMEN

OMSK

NO. KAZAKH.

KOKCHETAV

TSELINOGRAD

K A Z A K H   S. S. R.

KARAGANDA

ALMA-ATA

SVERDLOVSK

KURGAN

CHELYABINSK

KUSTANAY

DZHAMBUL

KIRGIZ SSR

BASHKIR ASSR

ORENBURG

AKTYUBINSK

CHIMKENT

TADZHIK SSR

MOSCOW

SARATOV

WEST KAZAKHSTAN

KZYL-ORDA

UZBEK SSR

VOLGOGRAD

GURYEV

TURKMEN SSR

GLOSSARY

Agitprop: The Propaganda and Agitation Section of the Central Committee (or of republic central committees or kray, oblast, city, or rayon committees).

Agricultural Equipment Association (Selkhoztekhnika): The organization established in 1961 to distribute agricultural equipment and spare parts to farms and to handle repair work.

Agrogorod ("agricultural town"): Khrushchev in 1951 proposed a plan to build new "agricultural towns" in order to raise rural living standards and improve farming efficiency.

Aktiv: the activists of a party or economic organization.

Apparatchik: Usually used to denote a worker of the party *apparat* (apparatus).

Bolshaya Sovetskaya Entsiklopediya: The Great Soviet Encyclopedia, 2nd edition.

Bureau for the RSFSR: The organ established to run the affairs of the biggest Soviet republic (all other republics are run by republic central committees). The Bureau had its own Central Committee sections for the RSFSR. Created by Khrushchev in 1956, it was abolished in 1966.

Cadre Sections: The organs supervising personnel matters and activities of lower party organs (in recent years referred to as party organs sections or party-organizational work sections).

CEMA (The Council of Economic Mutual Assistance): The organization for economic collaboration between the states of the Soviet bloc.

Fermy (farms): Livestock farms which comprise parts of kolkhozes or sovkhozes.

Gorispolkom: A city executive committee—the executive committee elected by a city soviet (its chairman is head of government for the city and is the formal equivalent of mayor).

Gorkom: A city party committee.

Gosbank: The State Bank.

Gosekonomsovet: The short-lived State Scientific and Economic Council of the Council of Ministers which shared Gosplan's planning functions.

Gosplan: The State Planning Committee.

Gosstroy: The State Committee for Construction Affairs.

Grassland system (travopolnaya sistema): The system developed by V. R. Vilyams to maintain soil fertility by use of grasses and fallow.

Intertilled system (propashnaya sistema): The system developed by the Altay Agricultural Institute based on use of corn and other intertilled crops.

Ispolkom: An executive committee of a local soviet.

KGB: The Committee of State Security (the secret police).

Kolkhoz: A collective farm.

Kolkhoznik: A member of a kolkhoz.

Komsomol: The Young Communist League.

Kray: A region (a territorial unit larger than an oblast).

Krayispolkom: A regional executive committee.

Kraykom: A regional party committee.

Kuban: Krasnodar Kray.

Link (zveno): A small team of farm workers (as opposed to big units—brigades). In this study we will mainly discuss a more recently developed form of links—the unregulated mechanized link (*beznaryadnoye mekhanizirovannoye zveno*)—a small team of tractor drivers which operates on a permanently assigned plot of land, without detailed work assignments and with its pay based considerably on final production results.

MVD: Ministry of Internal Affairs (earlier called NKVD).

Non-Chernozem Zone (Non-Black Earth Zone): This zone includes the Baltic Republics, Belorussia, and the central and northern parts of the RSFSR.

Obkom: A provincial party committee.

Oblast: A province.

Oblispolkom: A provincial executive committee.

Orgburo: The Central Committee's Organizational Bureau—abolished in 1952.

Politburo: The Central Committee's Political Bureau—abolished in 1952, restored in 1966.

Pood: A Russian unit of measurement equivalent to 16.3 kilograms. There are 61.04 poods in a ton.

Rayispolkom: A district executive committee.

Raykom: A district party committee.

Rayon: A district—a smaller unit than an oblast. In rural areas, the rayon is equivalent to a county and its leading organs exercise supervision over smaller towns. In large cities, the rayon is equivalent to a ward or borough (Moscow City currently has twenty-nine rayons).

RSFSR (The Russian Soviet Federated Socialist Republic): The largest Soviet republic, including about half the USSR's population.

Selkhoztekhnika (see Agricultural Equipment Association).

Shabashniki: Private construction workers.

Shablon: Stereotype; a standardized method or policy applied everywhere without regard for local conditions.

Sovetskaya Istoricheskaya Entsiklopediya: The Soviet Historical Encyclopedia.

Sovkhoz: A state farm.

Sovnarkhoz (Economic Council): These regional economic councils were established by Khrushchev in 1957, abolished in 1965.

SSR (Soviet Socialist Republic): The supposedly independent republics comprising the USSR (the Ukraine, Belorussia, Kazakhstan, etc.).

Supreme Soviet: The Soviet formal equivalent of a parliament.

TASS: Telegraph Agency of the Soviet Union.

Tsentralnaya usadba: The central farm of a sovkhoz.

Untethered method *(bezprivyaznaya sistema):* A method of handling livestock promoted by the Altay, Orenburg, and some other livestock raisers.

VASKhNIL: The All-Union Lenin Academy of Agricultural Sciences.

Yarovization or vernalization *(yarovizatsiya):* Lysenko's method of treating seeds.

Yelochka: The "Christmas tree" milking machine apparatus.

Znaniye Society: The All-Union Society for Spreading Political and Scientific Knowledge.

Zyab: Fall-plowed land.

THE POLITICS OF
SOVIET AGRICULTURE, 1960-1970

INTRODUCTION

The importance of agriculture in Soviet politics has been obvious ever since the public recognition of the agricultural crisis soon after Stalin's death. Stalin's first successor, Malenkov, resigned as premier in February 1955, confessing incompetence in agricultural leadership. Khrushchev, whose victory over Malenkov was greatly facilitated by the success of his agricultural initiatives, was himself overthrown in October 1964, after his leadership had been seriously undermined by the 1963 agricultural disaster. Like Khrushchev, Brezhnev's first initiative upon election as first secretary was to present a big program to solve the agricultural crisis, and his 1970-71 rise has been closely linked with the victory of the agriculture lobby in the resource struggle.

Stalin's successors inherited a countryside impoverished to build Soviet industry, grain production lagging behind demand, and a livestock sector weaker than before the 1917 revolution. Stalin in his last days not only refused to financially aid the farms but even sought to squeeze more money out of them, while Malenkov, who supervised agriculture, optimistically announced at the October 1952 party congress and again at the August 1953 Supreme Soviet session that the grain problem had been solved.

Yet only six months after Stalin's death, Khrushchev, at the same September 1953 Central Committee plenum which officially made him first secretary, directed the country's attention to the agricultural crisis and presented a program of financial aid and incentives for the farms: increased state investments, lower delivery quotas and higher purchase prices for livestock products—measures which, he said, would immediately raise kolkhoz income by many billions of rubles. Only months later, in a 22 January 1954 Note to the Central Committee Presidium, Khrushchev directly refuted Malenkov's claim to have solved the grain problem and revealed that in 1953, for the first time in years, so little grain was produced that the state had to take grain out of its reserves to feed the country. In contrast to Malenkov's ineffectual management of agriculture,

Khrushchev proposed a bold program to vastly expand grain production (and thereby also facilitate expanded livestock raising) quickly and relatively cheaply by sowing grain on millions of hectares of idle and virgin land and also by expanding the raising of corn.

Khrushchev's program was approved by a February–March 1954 Central Committee plenum—despite the skepticism and even opposition of most of his Presidium colleagues—and the virgin land adventure began. Aided by favorable conditions, his gamble paid off and grain production began to rise in the same year in the eastern farming areas.

After a 25–31 January 1955 plenum on livestock at which Khrushchev cited the improvements in agriculture resulting from his September 1953 and early 1954 initiatives, Malenkov resigned as premier, acknowledging his "guilt and responsibility for the unsatisfactory situation in agriculture," which had been previously under his leadership (*Pravda*, 9 February 1955). "Now," he noted, "as is known, a general program to overcome lagging in agriculture . . . has been worked out on the initiative and under the leadership of the Central Committee" (i.e., Khrushchev).

Khrushchev was further strengthened against his foes by the record harvest of 1956. Riding high on agricultural successes, in May 1957—just before the "Anti-Party Group's" final unsuccessful attempt to overthrow him—he rashly disregarded all economic advice and promised to catch up to the US in per capita production of meat, milk, and butter in the near future. Another bumper harvest in 1958 further led him, and others, into exaggerated expectations of future soaring triumphs. Especially characteristic of this attitude was the announced determination to overtake the US in meat production per capita and the irresponsible pledges to triple livestock production in one year and fulfill the seven-year plan in only two or three years.

At the same time that targets were raised, the resources allotted to agriculture were cut back. The seven-year plan drawn up in 1958 reduced expenditures for production of agricultural equipment, fertilizer, and other inputs. After rising in 1954 and 1955, agriculture's relative share of state investments declined.

But after reaching the peak of their success in 1958, Khrushchev's agricultural programs began to falter. He had begun his career as first secretary with programs to greatly increase production of grain and livestock products, but by late 1960 the main elements of these programs—the virgin land and meat campaigns—clearly had turned into fiascos.

After several years of heavy and careless exploitation, the productiveness of the fragile virgin land soil began falling and erosion and weeds became serious obstacles. In addition, the limitations of the short virgin land growing season became painfully evident in 1959, when huge areas of grain were not harvested before the snows arrived. By mid-1960 Soviet leaders were debating solutions to the new virgin lands problems, and the scientist Lysenko offered a new program involving earlier sowing to avoid harvest disasters like that of 1959.

The campaign to overtake the US in meat production per capita became a fiasco in late 1960, when it was revealed that Khrushchev's reckless prodding to unrealistically double and triple meat procurement had led local leaders into massive fraud. In late 1960 the scientists and political leaders of Orenburg and Altay provinces promoted new livestock methods and supposedly proved the superiority of corn and other intertilled crops as livestock fodder.

Like the original virgin land and meat campaigns, the new solutions seized upon by Khrushchev promised quick results with relatively little expense. Already at the December 1959 Central Committee plenum he had spoken of new "virgin lands the cultivation of which does not require expenditure of additional funds": bringing more land into production by ignoring crop rotations and planting clean fallow and grasslands and by replacing crops regarded as "less productive" (for example, oats) with "highly productive" crops (for instance, corn). The application of these measures on a massive scale was made possible in late 1960 by the Altay scientists' "proof" that corn (and other favorite Khrushchev crops) was nourishing fodder and replenished the soil as well as clean fallow and grasses.

Faced with persistent resistance to his methods for dealing with the serious agricultural problems, Khrushchev's interference in the most technical questions of agriculture and his insistence on mandatory stereotyped methods increased, miring politics in agriculture as never before and hobbling farmers with rigid prescriptions. The post-Khrushchev Soviet characterization of recent agricultural history breaks down the Khrushchev era into the "good" 1953-58 years when real progress was made and the "bad" 1959-64 years when subjectivism and wilfulness caused great harm and agricultural growth slowed. Making this distinction in his March 1965 Central Committee plenum report, Brezhnev noted that while agricultural production was supposed to grow by 70 percent during the 1959-65 seven-year plan, it actually grew only 10 percent (Stenographic record of the March 1965 Central Committee plenum, pp. 6-7).

However, Khrushchev's options were severely limited by lack of resources and his reliance on innovations in techniques and organization rather than new investment to raise agricultural production was not entirely voluntary. While he was able to force through his ideas on crops, agrotechniques, and reorganization (which did not unduly disturb the powerful entrenched interests of industry and defense), he was much less successful when proposing more investment in agriculture (which had to come from industry and defense). His earlier programs (for example, the virgin lands) had managed to avoid conflict with heavy industrial interests, but with millions of hectares of virgin lands already cultivated (and becoming exhausted) and with clean fallow and grass being drastically reduced, the possibilities for increasing production by extensive means dwindled and Khrushchev found it necessary to turn increasingly to intensive solutions requiring more investment—and to administrative reorganization.

In October 1960 Khrushchev proposed that some of the resources created by the large overfulfillment of industrial production plans in 1959 and 1960 be diverted to rescue the lagging agricultural sector which had been shortchanged to increase investment in industry. He managed to win a small increase for agriculture in 1961, but his conflict with the defenders of heavy industry (especially Kozlov and Suslov) sharpened and the need for money became increasingly pressing. As Khrushchev forced the abandonment of the grassland system—which replenished the soil without fertilizer—he became increasingly preoccupied with the need for huge amounts of chemical fertilizer which required big investments. However, his increasingly aggressive drive for more resources for agriculture (and consumer goods) in 1962, 1963, and 1964, and his radical 1962 reorganizations alienated broad and powerful segments of the party, government, and military. These factors, aided by disastrous agricultural and foreign policy reversals in 1962 and 1963, set the stage for his overthrow in October 1964, which apparently was triggered by still more plans for resource reallocation and administrative reorganization.

Nevertheless, while rejecting Khrushchev's big campaigns to massively reallocate industrial funds into chemical fertilizer production and other schemes, his successors recognized the obvious—that inputs had to be greatly increased if output was to rise. Since his successors have condemned and largely eschewed interference in agrotechniques and crops, conflicts in the post-Khrushchev period have centered more exclusively on the question of resources (Khrushchev's reorganization mania was condemned too, but there have also occasionally been long struggles over proposed reorganizations during the Brezhnev period).

Despite having more resources to work with than did Khrushchev, his successors have wound up squeezing out more for agriculture, mainly when confronted with crisis situations, while cutting back on agricultural investment when the situation eased and other sectors—consumer goods, defense, heavy industry— appeared in greater need of funds. Although the 1965-66 programs for greatly increased financial aid to farms, increased prices and other incentives, less interference, and large-scale investment in land improvement (irrigation and drainage) have greatly increased grain production during the 1966-70 five-year plan period, the programs were cut back financially after the 1966 record harvest and failed to reach their goals. Thus, a new big financial program to stimulate agriculture—especially livestock raising—had to be adopted in 1970, occasioning another struggle over resources in the 1971-75 five-year plan. As this study ends in 1970 and 1971, the country's attention once more is concentrated on agricultural problems and under Brezhnev's leadership the forces favoring agricultural interests have won a considerable political victory.

PART I

THE KHRUSHCHEV ERA

THE KHRUSHCHEV
ERA: 1960-1964

L ET US BEGIN at the turning point of the Khrushchev era—when the agricultural successes of 1953-58 began turning into the failures of 1959-64. In the wake of the 1959 agricultural failures and in the face of strengthened opposition in early 1960, Khrushchev found himself in specially urgent need of new programs which could bring quick, spectacular achievements. Characteristically taking the initiative, Khrushchev in mid- and late 1960 seized upon panaceas which suited his personal notions—poorly tested programs developed by scientists and politicians who sought to win his favor and personal power for themselves by promising big progress in meat and grain production. These were Lysenko's early sowing virgin lands program, the Altay intertilled system (*propashnaya sistema*), and Voronov's Orenburg system (Chapter I). After a long and bitter struggle, Khrushchev, using these pseudoscientific programs, achieved a major breakthrough for his ideas, overthrowing the old agricultural leadership and establishing a new team of agricultural leaders (Polyanskiy, Voronov, Lysenko, and Pysin). Following their victory, this new team in 1961 conducted the most extensive purge of the Khrushchev era and forced the most rigid stereotypes on Soviet agriculture (Chapter II).

However, Lysenko's early sowing soon proved unsuccessful, and within a year of the new team's ascension to power, it split. The virgin landers (led by Voronov and Pysin) with their intertilled system (based on corn) became dominant in 1962, displacing Polyanskiy and Lysenko (Chapter III). Khrushchev needed and favored both groups, backing the virgin landers' programs (the intertilled system, the Orenburg system and their livestock raising techniques) and virtually all Lysenko's programs (except for his unsuccessful virgin land early sowing program).

Political infighting intensified during 1962. A big agricultural reorganization in March 1962 brought confusion and unhappiness which were compounded by an even more thorough reorganization in November 1962. These reorganizations became major charges against Khrushchev when he was overthrown in 1964. Although Voronov clearly had gained from the March 1962 reorganization, he lost power in the November 1962 reorganization and followed Polyanskiy into eclipse (Chapter IV). Khrushchev then began forming a new team of agricultural leaders.

But shortly afterward, Khrushchev suffered the greatest agricultural setback of his reign: the massive 1963 crop failure, especially in the virgin lands, which forced the Soviet Union to buy grain abroad and which discredited the agrotechniques promoted by Khrushchev for the virgin lands and elsewhere (Chapter V). This led to intensified disagreements over agricultural techniques and over interference in agriculture. Apparently as a result of these disputes in the Presidium, Khrushchev began an attack on Voronov and his protégés, presumably aimed at ousting him from the leadership (Chapter VI). Khrushchev set a Central Committee plenum for November 1964, which was to resolve certain hotly debated issues—another reorganization of agricultural administration, specialization of livestock raising, and the need for clean fallow. This plenum presumably would provide an opportunity to strike at his foes in agriculture—Voronov and Polyanskiy. But the other leaders beat Khrushchev to the punch, removing him in October 1964. When the November 1964 plenum was held, it turned into a reversal of Khrushchev's November 1962 reorganization.

In addition to Khrushchev's unpopular reorganizations, his ill-advised interference in crop policies and agrotechniques, and his arbitrariness toward his associates, he also was done in by his irrational confidence in Lysenko and by his aggressive campaigns to shift resources to agriculture and consumer goods.

Although Khrushchev had fought some of Lysenko's main programs under Stalin and permitted Lysenko's dethronement after Stalin's death (Khrushchev foes Malenkov and Molotov were Lysenko's patrons), Lysenko was able to win Khrushchev's enthusiastic support in late 1958. One reason for Khrushchev's support (and also for Stalin's) was that Lysenko offered cheap solutions to agricultural problems. Khrushchev's backing was so strong that he himself attacked Lysenko's foes and drove many of them out of their jobs. He went to great lengths to cover up Lysenko's crimes during the Stalin era and even portrayed himself as an old friend and ally of Lysenko.[1] Lysenko's foes sought to split Khrushchev and Lysenko by dredging up Lysenko's past as the main obstacle to Khrushchev's favorite crop, corn, as well as his involvement in the Stalinist crimes being exposed by Khrushchev. But Khrushchev put his faith in Lysenko and his leadership was discredited by his support of Lysenko's irresponsible programs. Lysenko never was very popular and by early 1964 the tide of opposition to him was growing so strong that even Khrushchev could not stem

---

[1] Soviet biologist Zhores Medvedev even states that "Khrushchev gave Lysenko broad and concrete help somewhat more often than had Stalin" (see Zh. A. Medvedev's *The Rise and Fall of T. D. Lysenko* [New York: Columbia University Press, 1969], p. 196).

it. When Khrushchev was removed in October 1964, it is clear that his support of Lysenko was an important factor used against him.

A more positive role was played by Khrushchev in the resource question. However, he was less successful at pushing through his ideas on financial questions than on administrative reorganizations, crop structure, agrotechniques and even personnel changes. Khrushchev's agricultural programs were to a considerable extent substitutes for the huge investments needed by agriculture, but at the same time they could not be successful partly because they were not backed by the resources needed. Khrushchev recognized this and pushed more and more urgently for major reorientation of resources to ensure the success of his agricultural programs, but in so doing he antagonized the forces of heavy industry and defense, which controlled the lion's share of resources and which managed to withhold most of the funds he needed.

The fall of Khrushchev let loose the stored-up resentment of those who suffered from his policies or personal interference (Chapter VII). Yet the blame for failures fell unevenly. Voronov and Polyanskiy and their colleagues from the 1961-62 period largely escaped blame, while their rivals—Khrushchev's favorites in 1963-64—were dismissed. Still, Voronov and Polyanskiy had to take a back seat in 1965, as Khrushchev's foes in agriculture (in many cases also their own foes) rode the anti-Khrushchev wave.

CHAPTER I

KHRUSHCHEV'S STRUGGLE: 1960

As a result of serious agricultural setbacks and murky power struggles between Khrushchev's lieutenants and between Khrushchev and his lieutenants in 1959, he wound up seriously weakened by early 1960. His virgin land program was in disarray after the Kazakh harvest disaster had been exposed at the December 1959 Central Committee plenum, and in January 1960 two of Khrushchev's most loyal henchmen, Central Committee Secretary and heir apparent A. I. Kirichenko and Kazakh First Secretary N. I. Belyayev, were demoted. After the December 1959 plenum Khrushchev became uncharacteristically quiet on the subject of agriculture,[1] becoming immersed in foreign policy questions. Preoccupied with foreign travel and vacation rests between trips, he spent less than seventy-five days in Moscow in the eight months from mid-February to mid-October.[2]

Khrushchev's initiatives on improving relations with the US and reducing the size of the military stirred up sharp opposition in early 1960, and the position of his top foreign policy ally, First Deputy Premier A. I. Mikoyan, already showed signs of weakening in March and April. When Khrushchev's foreign policy appeared to suffer setbacks in early May (notably in the U-2 affair and the subsequent break-up of the Paris conference), Mikoyan, the foremost advocate of détente, went into decline, while conservative leaders M. A.

[1] Between his setback at the December 1959 plenum and his victory at the January 1961 plenum Khrushchev's most important public pronouncement on agriculture was his short talk with Kalinovka kolkhozniks in August 1960.

[2] He visited Indonesia, India, and Afghanistan 11 February–6 March; France 23 March–3 April; was on vacation on the Black Sea from at least 10 April until 30 April; was gone for the Paris conference 14–21 May; on vacation in early and mid-June (see *Pravda*, 11 and 13 June); was in Rumania 18–27 June; in Austria 30 June–8 July; on vacation 21 July–27 August; in Finland 1–6 September; and out of the country for the UN session 9 September–14 October.

Suslov and F. R. Kozlov rose.[3] At the 1 May 1960 parade, Central Committee Secretary Suslov and First Deputy Premier Kozlov ranked as Khrushchev's top deputies for the party and government, instead of Kirichenko and Mikoyan (Mikoyan dropped from his usual No. 3 position to No. 7, while Kirichenko disappeared from the leadership entirely). A 4 May 1960 Central Committee plenum removed Khrushchev allies Kirichenko and Belyayev from the Presidium, dropped five of the ten Central Committee secretaries and installed Kozlov as Central Committee secretary. At the same time, Khrushchev's sole remaining close protégé in the Secretariat, L. I. Brezhnev, was sidetracked into the ceremonial post of Soviet president and later (in July) also dropped from the Secretariat, leaving only Suslov and Kozlov and the less important Kuusinen and Mukhitdinov in the Secretariat with Khrushchev.

With the decline of Khrushchev and his closest allies, the power of Agriculture Minister V. V. Matskevich and RSFSR party chief A. B. Aristov rose in agriculture. Matskevich successfully blocked many favorite Khrushchev programs and disagreements between the two men developed into a large-scale struggle on a whole series of issues. Meanwhile, Aristov apparently began undermining RSFSR Premier D. S. Polyanskiy, who was one of Khrushchev's few close allies in the agricultural field. Aristov and Matskevich may have been encouraged by Khrushchev's foes Kozlov and Suslov; however, the relationship was not close, since neither Suslov nor Kozlov appeared seriously affected by the fall of Aristov and Matskevich at the end of 1960.

Meanwhile, in addition to the reversals in his virgin land project, by the summer and fall of 1960 Khrushchev's other main agricultural program—the campaign to catch up with the US in meat and milk production per capita—turned into a fiasco, culminating in the exposure of the Ryazan scandal and the apparent suicide of Ryazan leader and Khrushchev favorite A. N. Larionov.

By late summer of 1960 Khrushchev was faced with the urgent need to find some means to rescue his faltering agricultural programs and bolster his waning political power. His response was to seize the initiative in agriculture with panacea programs conveniently provided by T. D. Lysenko (the early sowing program for the virgin lands announced in mid-summer) and by opportunistic Altay and Orenburg scientists and politicians (the Altay intertilled system and the Orenburg farming system which became the objects of national attention in the fall of 1960).

After a protracted struggle, Khrushchev and his allies overcame their foes, and in late December 1960 and early January 1961 Matskevich and Aristov lost their powerful positions and were sent into exile. In fields other than agriculture, however, Khrushchev was not so successful at removing opposition, as Kozlov and Suslov continued in their leadership posts, often resisting his proposals.

---

[3] The signs of discord over the military cutback and détente and the indications of the diminished role of Mikoyan and Khrushchev and the rise of Suslov and Kozlov are explored in Michel Tatu's *Power in the Kremlin* (London, 1969).

Kirichenko's Fall

The year 1960 opened with the fall of Khrushchev's heir apparent and long-time protégé A. I. Kirichenko. Kirichenko had been the first Khrushchev protégé promoted to the Presidium (as candidate member in May 1953 and as full member in July 1955). In December 1957 he had surrendered his post as Ukrainian first secretary to become a Central Committee secretary in Moscow and, with Khrushchev's patronage, was quickly moved ahead of his seniors. At the 1958 May Day parade Kirichenko stood fourth (after First Secretary and Premier Khrushchev, President Voroshilov, and First Deputy Premier Mikoyan)—even ahead of senior Central Committee Secretary Suslov, implying that he now was de facto second secretary. On some occasions in 1958 (*Pravda*, 24 June and 30 June) Kirichenko and Mikoyan were pictured flanking Khrushchev—as his deputies for the party and for the government.

Kirichenko's spectacular rise surely generated friction and only months later he was visibly downgraded. At the 7 November 1958 parade he dropped to fourteenth place, even below Presidium candidate members Pospelov and Kosygin and only ahead of Presidium candidate member Polyanskiy (*Izvestiya*, 9 November 1958). What is more, he was the only Presidium member to suffer a significant decline in the comparison with the May Day parade standings. That this was not simply a fluke was indicated by the 7 November and 11 November 1958 *Izvestiya* pictures of other ceremonies where Kirichenko stood last on one end.

However, in December 1958 Kirichenko was restored to high ranking—although usually only as number five (behind Suslov instead of ahead of him)[4]—and at the January 1959 21st Party Congress he sat in the center, ahead of Suslov (*Izvestiya*, 28 January and 6 February 1959). On May Day 1959 Kirichenko again stood fifth (after Khrushchev, Voroshilov, Mikoyan, and Suslov).

After intense maneuvering in mid-1959 Kirichenko slipped to 7th place at the November 1959 parade and was replaced as number five by Kozlov.[5] When May Day 1960 rolled around, Kirichenko was not even among the leaders reviewing the parade[6] and was removed as Central Committee secretary and Presidium member three days later.

Kirichenko's downfall appears to have been the result of his having alienated many other leaders by his spearheading of Khrushchev's policies and drive for more power and also by his own power plays as Khrushchev's favorite. In addition to his obvious rivalry with Suslov for the status of second secretary, his activities in the field of cadres and agriculture appeared to infringe on the spheres

---

[4] See *Pravda* for 8 December, 23 December, and 28 December 1958.

[5] *Pravda*, 8 November 1959. Kirichenko also ranked low in the 7 November and 13 November *Pravda* pictures and in virtually all pictures thereafter.

[6] Although he was in Moscow and was reported attending a reception on 3 May (*Pravda*, 4 May 1960).

of his fellow Central Committee secretaries N. G. Ignatov (the secretary in charge of agriculture) and A. B. Aristov (the secretary in charge of RSFSR affairs).

In the spring of 1959 Ignatov and Aristov suffered sharp reversals at the hands of Khrushchev and Kirichenko: Ignatov was sidetracked from his job as agricultural supervisor, while several of Aristov's associates in the RSFSR Bureau and RSFSR agricultural leadership were demoted. However, the tide began to turn in mid-1959 when serious shortcomings were exposed in cadre work in the non-Russian republics—particularly, nationalistic deviations—and Kirichenko apparently was pinned with the responsibility for these. The cadre chief apparently installed by Kirichenko in March was ousted in August and replaced with Aristov's deputy, V. M. Churayev. Ignatov and other Aristov allies demoted in the spring were quickly restored to prominent positions in late 1959, and Kirichenko was exiled from Moscow in January 1960.

At the 27 January–5 February 1959 21st Party Congress Khrushchev and Kirichenko urged the promotion of younger cadres. Khrushchev complained that "among leading cadres"—including secretaries of oblasts and republics—"there are still too few youthful officials" and "we often think that a man of 35–40 still is insufficiently mature for advancement to leading work." "This is incorrect," he stated.[7] Kirichenko, who concentrated on cadres in his speech, complained that there are still leaders who "fear advancing youthful officials" and "forget that many of them themselves were once advanced by the party to responsible posts at the age of 30–35."[8]

Khrushchev and Kirichenko soon demonstrated that their talk was not just rhetoric: within weeks they promoted their youthful protégés V. Ye. Semichastnyy (only thirty-five) and P. N. Demichev (only forty-one) to the key national posts of Central Committee cadre chief and Moscow first secretary.

The first personnel move against the Aristov–Ignatov group occurred on 2 March 1959, when Kirichenko, accompanied by RSFSR Bureau Deputy Chairman Aristov and Aristov's assistant, V. M. Churayev (head of the Central Committee Section for RSFSR Party Organs and a member of the RSFSR Bureau), supervised removal of Moscow Oblast First Secretary I. V. Kapitonov and his associate Moscow Oblast Executive Committee Chairman N. F. Ignatov (*Pravda*, 3 March 1959). Normally, Aristov or Churayev would have conducted such proceedings themselves. This action was clearly a purge, since Kapitonov and Ignatov did not receive any other prominent posts and soon were accused of wrongdoing by a top Central Committee journal (an editorial in an April 1959 *Partiynaya Zhizn*, no. 8, pp. 10–11, harshly attacking them for "serious mistakes" and "incorrect, unparty relations" which occupied much of their time and diverted them from their work). Kapitonov also lost his membership in the

[7]Stenographic record of the 21st Party Congress, vol. I, p. 115.
[8]Ibid., p. 472.

RSFSR Bureau (see Appendix 3 on the RSFSR Bureau membership). Kapitonov was replaced with Khrushchev's assistant in the Council of Ministers, P. N. Demichev (administrator of affairs of the Council of Ministers).

Shortly afterward, a former subordinate of both Khrushchev and Kirichenko in the Ukraine, V. Ye. Semichastnyy,[9] became the Central Committee cadre chief, and it became obvious that a campaign to promote new cadres was under way. Semichastnyy was released as All-Union Komsomol first secretary on 25 March (*Pravda*, 26 March 1959) and on 22 April (*Pravda*) showed up as head of the Central Committee Section for Union Republics Party Organs. A *Pravda* editorial on 20 March 1959 entitled "More Boldly Promote Young Cadres" recalled Khrushchev's statement at the January 1959 congress on the need to improve cadre work and praised his protégés in Ryazan as examples in promoting young, energetic people to responsible posts. The Central Committee's leading cadre organ, *Partiynaya Zhizn*, soon editorially criticized cadre work[10] and Khrushchev continued his talk about the need for new cadres. In an 11 May speech (*Pravda*, 12 May 1959) Khrushchev declared that "leaders who lag behind life and do not grow must be replaced by more capable and talented ones" and advised that one should not hesitate to replace an old friend if he turns out to be incapable of efficiently handling his job (friendship is fine, he said, but it "must not interfere with business").

Also in early spring Khrushchev precipitated a purge of agricultural officials. In his 11 May speech he revealed that the Presidium had been debating changes in agricultural leadership: "Recently in the Central Committee Presidium we exchanged opinions on the question of improving leadership of agriculture and we ordered the working out of the necessary measures." He attacked the work of the Agriculture Ministry as "not meeting the growing needs of agriculture" and criticized the "poor organizational activity of agricultural organs—from the Agriculture Ministry down to rayon inspection services." In his 29 June 1959 speech at the June Central Committee plenum he again remarked that the Presidium had debated agricultural questions and he raised the "question of reorganization of agricultural leadership" (*Pravda*, 2 July 1959).

Exactly when the Presidium had debated changes in agricultural leadership was not made clear, however shortly after the Kapitonov purge the Central Committee secretary in charge of agriculture and most of the RSFSR agricultural leaders were demoted or transferred. On 16 April Central Committee Secretary N. G. Ignatov was elected RSFSR president—in effect rendering him inactive as Central Committee secretary in charge of agriculture. Aristov, in nominating Ignatov for this post at the April RSFSR Supreme Soviet session on

---

[9]Semichastnyy, as Ukrainian Komsomol first secretary, had worked directly under Ukrainian Central Committee Second Secretary Kirichenko for a short time in 1949 and 1950 (the Ukrainian second secretary is normally in charge of cadre work and supervision of the Komsomol), as well as under Ukrainian First Secretary Khrushchev.

[10]Issues no. 8, 15 April 1959, pp. 9–11; and no. 9, 28 April, p. 26.

behalf of the Central Committee, conspicuously praised Ignatov, calling him a "leading figure" among Politburo members, "a prominent party and state figure," etc. (*Izvestiya*, 17 April 1959). Nevertheless, despite Aristov's praise, the move was clearly a demotion, since Ignatov's new ceremonial duties prevented him from carrying out his more important responsibilities as Central Committee secretary (this was implicitly acknowledged in P. N. Pospelov's statement in the 27 November 1959 *Pravda*—see below).

At about the same time, head of the Central Committee's Agriculture Section for the RSFSR, V. P. Mylarshchikov—who worked under RSFSR Bureau Deputy Chairman Aristov and Central Committee Agriculture Secretary Ignatov—was removed (he was last identified in the 19 March *Izvestiya*, while his successor was first identified in the 28 April *Pravda*). Mylarshchikov also was

Central Committee Bureau for the RSFSR[a]

	March 1959	June 1959	Nov. 1959	1960	Feb. 1961
Chairman	Khrushchev	Khrushchev	Khrushchev	Khrushchev	Khrushchev
Dep. chairman	Aristov	Aristov	Aristov	Aristov	Voronov
					Churayev
Members:					
(CC secretary)	Pospelov	Pospelov	Pospelov	Pospelov	
(RSFSR cadre head)	Churayev	Churayev	M. Yefremov	Yefremov	
(CC cadre head)			Churayev	Churayev	
(RSFSR agri. head)	Mylarshchikov	Vorobyev	Vorobyev	(Vorobyev)[b]	
(RSFSR premier)	Polyanskiy	Polyanskiy	Polyanskiy	Polyanskiy	Polyanskiy
(First dep. prem.)	Yasnov	Yasnov	Yasnov	Yasnov	Yasnov
(RSFSR president)					
(Moscow sec.)	Kapitonov	Demichev	Demichev	Demichev	Demichev
(Leningrad sec.)	Spiridonov	Spiridonov	Spiridonov	Spiridonov	Spiridonov
(Gorkiy sec.)	L. Yefremov	Yefremov	Yefremov	Yefremov	Yefremov
(Others)					Yakovlev

Central Committee Cadre Sections

Union Republics	(none)	Semichastnyy	Churayev	Churayev	Titov
RSFSR	Churayev	Churayev	M. Yefremov	Yefremov	Polekhin

Central Committee Agriculture Sections

Union Republics	Doroshenko	Doroshenko	Denisov	(none)	Karlov
RSFSR	Mylarshchikov	Vorobyev	Vorobyev	(none)	Pankin

[a]See Appendix 3 for more exact details on identifications of RSFSR Bureau members.

[b]Listed as a member 1959–61 in the 1962 *Bolshaya Sovetskaya Entsïklopediya* yearbook, but since he was removed as Agriculture Section head in June 1960 he presumably was also dropped or at least became inactive as a Bureau member in mid-1960.

dropped from the RSFSR Bureau (see Appendix 3)—the second member of Aristov's Bureau demoted and removed in March 1959.

A new team took over RSFSR agricultural leadership in April 1959. Udmurt Obkom First Secretary G. I. Vorobyev, a protégé of Leningrad leader F. R. Kozlov,[11] became head of the Central Committee's RSFSR Agriculture Section and a member of the RSFSR Bureau, while Kirov Oblast Executive Committee Chairman S. V. Kalchenko was appointed RSFSR agriculture minister (*Izvestiya*, 17 April 1959) and Deputy RSFSR Agriculture Minister F. D. Kulakov was promoted to RSFSR grain products minister (*Izvestiya*, 17 April 1959). Vorobyev, Kalchenko, and Kulakov were all suddenly removed and exiled to the provinces in June 1960—at the same time as Kirichenko's final demise and when Aristov's power was again rising in the RSFSR.

The issues apparently in dispute between Khrushchev and the agricultural leaders demoted in the spring of 1959 are not clear, however one issue which clearly involved most of them (especially Kapitonov, Mylarshchikov, and the RSFSR leaders) was Khrushchev's proposal for solving the serious shortages of vegetables and potatoes in Soviet cities, especially in Moscow. In late 1958 and early 1959 Khrushchev became agitated over this question and frequently raised it in his speeches. In a 13 August 1958 Smolensk speech (*Pravda*, 24 August 1958) he revealed that the Presidium had recently examined the question of supplying Moscow with cheap vegetables and potatoes and proposed establishing a trust of specialized sovkhozes in Moscow Oblast to supply the city of Moscow with vegetables and potatoes. At a 16 August 1958 Central Committee conference Khrushchev called the supplying of sufficient vegetables and potatoes "one of the most important tasks" (*Sovetskaya Rossiya*, 17 August 1958). Moscow Oblast First Secretary Kapitonov quickly held oblast meetings at which he promoted Khrushchev's proposal (*Pravda*, 17 September 1958, 23 November 1958, and 12 December 1958). On 2 November 1958 *Pravda* published a Central Committee–Council of Ministers decree creating a specialized sovkhoz trust in Moscow Oblast and later the RSFSR Bureau and RSFSR Council of Ministers adopted a decree to similarly specialize sovkhozes in Leningrad Oblast (*Pravda*, 12 December 1958) and later in some other areas.

Although no one objected to the proposal, the project which was supposed to supply Moscow's needs within one to two years did not turn out as successfully as Khrushchev had hoped, and—whether partly for this reason or not—in the spring of 1959 Kapitonov, who had supervised the project in Moscow Oblast, and RSFSR agriculture chief Mylarshchikov were removed. Mylarshchikov's last appearance as RSFSR Agriculture Section head (*Izvestiya*, 19 March 1959) was at an 18 March Moscow Oblast meeting of workers of the new specialized sovkhozes discussing fulfillment of the November 1958 decree, and

---

[11]Vorobyev served as Leningrad Oblast second secretary and then oblast executive committee chairman under Leningrad Oblast First Secretary F. R. Kozlov, 1953–57.

after his removal he was demoted to director of the new Moscow Oblast specialized trust of vegetable and potato growing sovkhozes (identified in the 26 December 1959 *Pravda*). Mylarshchikov was later criticized by the Moscow City Bureau (*Leninskoye Znamya*, 14 September 1960) and in *Izvestiya* (5 October 1960) for his work in leading the trust, and in October 1962 he was severely censured for his poor leadership of the trust in 1960 and 1961. I. Salnikov, in the 13 October 1962 *Ekonomicheskaya Gazeta*, criticized Mylarshchikov and the Moscow Oblast leaders for incorrectly organizing the Moscow sovkhozes and pointed out that in 1961 Moscow city still had to import half its vegetables and potatoes from elsewhere. *Ekonomicheskaya Gazeta* returned to the attack on 17 November 1962. The sharp October 1962 criticism smacked of a politically motivated attack, since Mylarshchikov no longer headed the trust and had recently been promoted back to a top agricultural post in the RSFSR (as first deputy minister for production and procurement of agricultural products).

In mid-1959, however, a countertrend to the Kirichenko gains developed as nationalistic and localistic deviations began to be exposed. At the 21st Congress, in January, Kirichenko had praised the expansion of the rights of republics and local organs and Khrushchev's economic decentralization; he had bragged of the "remarkable local cadres developed in the union republics" and had urged use of local cadres instead of officials sent from Moscow. In mid-1959 it was revealed that in some republics these "remarkable local cadres" were giving preference to local nationality cadres at the expense of Russians or other outsiders and were favoring their own areas in economic decisions also ("localism").[12]

Apparently the first and most serious such errors were revealed in the Transcaucasian republics. At a 19 June Georgian Central Committee plenum on cadre policy Georgian First Secretary V. P. Mzhavanadze accused the first secretary of the Abkhaz Autonomous Republic, M. Bgazhba, of promoting cadres on a "narrow national basis" (*Zarya Vostoka*, 24 June 1959), and Bgazhba had to confess to this. Most serious was the situation in Azerbaydzhan, where the first secretary himself, I. D. Mustafayev, was removed in early July at an Azerbaydzhan plenum supervised by Central Committee Secretary N. A. Mukhitdinov. The Azerbaydzhani leaders were accused of "serious mistakes" in cadre selection, "localism and violation of state discipline," and introducing "confusion into the language question."[13]

[12] A 25 July 1959 *Pravda Ukrainy* article (by Yu. Shiryayev) defined localism also as a form of nationalism.

[13] The 11 July 1959 *Bakinskiy Rabochiy* announced that "a few days ago" an Azerbaydzhan Central Committee plenum had removed Mustafayev. On 21 June 1959 *Bakinskiy Rabochiy* had published a new Azerbaydzhan decree on the teaching of Russian and Azerbaydzhani in Azerbaydzhani schools, bringing Azerbaydzhan into line with the laws existing in other republics.

On 15 July Latvian Deputy Premier E. K. Berklav was removed and exiled to Vladimir as chief of the local film rental office.[14] Latvian Premier V. Latsis in an August issue of *Partiynaya Zhizn* (no. 16) cited Berklav as one of the leading officials "found among us who attempted to turn the development of the republic from the correct road and lead it toward national exclusiveness and isolation." A 23 July 1959 *Pravda Ukrainy* article assailed Dnepropetrovsk Sovnarkhoz Chairman N. A. Tikhonov (a close Brezhnev associate who became USSR deputy premier in 1965) as "mainly responsible for manifestations of localism" in Dnepropetrovsk. Lithuanian Premier M. Yu. Shumauskas criticized Lithuanian ministries for sometimes following incorrect nationality policies in selecting cadres (*Sovetskaya Litva*, 29 July 1959) and this complaint was repeated in a 30 July *Sovetskaya Litva* editorial.

These exposures were followed by a 14 August *Pravda* article by RSFSR cadre chief Churayev (Aristov's assistant) attacking decentralization, localism, and lack of discipline. Declaring that "the presence of cadres capable of thinking and acting in a government way was one of the important preconditions allowing the party and government in recent years to carry out a number of important measures expanding the rights of union republics and local organs," Churayev wrote that "in a number of republics and oblasts there are serious deviations from the party line" on the intolerability of localism. Kirichenko's "remarkable local cadres" had misused the new rights granted to them.

Union republics cadre chief Semichastnyy was out of the country, visiting Hungary from 9 to 28 July, while the Azerbaydzhan and other exposures were being publicized, and when he returned to Moscow he found himself out of his job. Ironically, he was exiled to Azerbaydzhan as second secretary (*Pravda*, 13 August 1959), and Churayev, after raising doubts about local cadre work and discipline in his 14 August article, took over Semichastnyy's post as head of the Central Committee Section for Union Republics Party Organs. Semichastnyy's fall (after only four months in office—minus three weeks in Hungary) was the first sign of Kirichenko's decline.

Another Kirichenko associate in the Central Committee apparatus was removed about the same time as Semichastnyy. Central Committee Agriculture Section head P. Ye. Doroshenko was removed also apparently in August 1959.[15]

---

[14] So identified in the *Deputaty Soveta Soyuza i Soveta Natsionalnostey* [Deputies of the Council of the Union and the Council of Nationalities], signed to press 30 December 1959. This book contains biographies of Supreme Soviet deputies. New editions appeared in 1962, 1966 and 1970 after the USSR Supreme Soviet elections.

[15] He was last identified as section head in the 19 June 1959 *Sovetskaya Estoniya*; in September he returned to the Ukraine and was elected first secretary of Chernigov Oblast (*Pravda Ukrainy*, 11 September 1959). His successor G. A. Denisov was first identified in the post in the 22 August 1959 *Pravda*. Denisov had last been identified as Saratov Oblast first secretary in the 11 July 1959 *Sovetskaya Rossiya* and was replaced as first secretary by A. I. Shibayev in August 1959 (see Shibayev's biography in the 1962 yearbook of the *Bolshaya Sovetskaya Entsiklopediya*).

Doroshenko had been head of the Ukrainian Central Committee Agriculture Section from at least January 1951 to early 1954, while Kirichenko was Ukrainian second secretary. However, Doroshenko had become CPSU Central Committee Agriculture Section chief in August 1955, under Belyayev (who had become Central Committee agriculture secretary in July 1955), and had worked under agriculture secretaries Belyayev and Ignatov and did not owe his position to Kirichenko.

With Kirichenko's loss of influence over cadre policies RSFSR leaders who had suffered in the spring of 1959 began making comebacks. Kapitonov had already returned from disgrace on 22 September to become first secretary of Ivanovo Oblast (*Pravda*, 23 September 1959), and on 26 November (*Pravda*, 27 November 1959) N. G. Ignatov was relieved as RSFSR president because the "Central Committee considered it necessary," according to RSFSR Bureau member P. N. Pospelov at a RSFSR Supreme Soviet session, that he "concentrate on his main work as secretary of the Central Committee"—thereby regaining the active influence he had been deprived of in April. Thus, Kirichenko's gains in early 1959 were already largely reversed in the fall of 1959.

Kirichenko's final defeat apparently was signaled by the 9 January 1960 Central Committee propaganda decree criticizing "the leaders of some party organizations" for "not properly rebuffing manifestations of nationalism, cosmopolitanism and apolitical attitudes" (*Pravda*, 10 January 1960). Four days later he was exiled to Rostov as first secretary—with Aristov appropriately supervising his installation. The following day purged ex-Moscow leader N. F. Ignatov (who had been reduced to a deputy chief of an administration in the Moscow Sovnarkhoz[16]) reappeared and became first secretary of Orel Oblast.

Aristov Ascendant

With Kirichenko's fall, Central Committee Secretary Aristov wound up with influence over cadre work both in the RSFSR (through his subordinate, RSFSR Party Organs Section head M. T. Yefremov) and in the other union republics (through his former subordinate, Union Republics Party Organs Section head V. M. Churayev), as well as with authority second only to Khrushchev in the RSFSR (as deputy chairman of the RSFSR Bureau). Even after May 1960 when the Secretariat was reorganized and all the RSFSR leaders (Aristov, Ignatov, and Pospelov), as well as their apparent rival, Kirichenko, were dropped, Aristov remained a key influence in cadre work as deputy chairman of the RSFSR Bureau, with Churayev and Yefremov continuing to head the Central Committee cadre sections.

Aristov had also become actively involved in agriculture since succeeding Belyayev as Bureau deputy chairman in 1958. He frequently traveled about the RSFSR, speaking on agriculture in the provinces. For example, he attended an

---

[16] See the 1959 *Deputaty Soveta Soyuza i Soveta Natsionalnostey.*

early 1958 RSFSR agricultural conference (*Sovetskaya Rossiya*, 2 April 1958) and spoke on agriculture at *aktiv* meetings in Novosibirsk, Altay, and Omsk in August 1958 (*Sovetskaya Rossiya*, 26, 29, and 30 August 1958). His first identification as Bureau deputy chairman was in the 28 December 1958 *Sovetskaya Rossiya*, when he and RSFSR Premier Polyanskiy were presented with Orders of Lenin for RSFSR agricultural successes in 1958. At the end of 1959 it was Ignatov, Aristov, and Polyanskiy who were presented awards for RSFSR agricultural successes. Presenting them with their awards at a 31 December 1959 ceremony, Soviet President Voroshilov noted "their big organizational work in mobilizing the workers" to fulfill obligations in agriculture (*Pravda*, 1 January 1960). When an agricultural conference of Soviet bloc leaders was held on 2 February 1960, the Soviet delegation was composed of Khrushchev, Ignatov, Aristov, Kosygin, Matskevich, Central Committee Agriculture Section head G. A. Denisov, and Lysenko (*Pravda*, 3 February 1960).

In early 1960 Aristov appears to have used his position as top RSFSR party official (under Khrushchev) to undermine the top RSFSR government official, Premier Polyanskiy, who was closer to Khrushchev's position on agricultural issues.

In January 1960 G. L. Smirnov, deputy head of the Central Committee Section for RSFSR Agriculture, was appointed RSFSR deputy premier for agriculture. Although he was Polyanskiy's top assistant for agriculture, Smirnov appears to have been closer to Polyanskiy's opponents Aristov and Agriculture Minister V. V. Matskevich (and, after Khrushchev's fall, to Voronov). [17]

In June there were a number of personnel changes which appeared to weaken Polyanskiy. The most pointed one was the removal of D. M. Matyushkin, Polyanskiy's successor as first secretary of Krasnodar Kray, for failings in agricultural leadership. The dismissal was supervised by Aristov himself (*Pravda*, 10 June). Matyushkin was the only provincial first secretary fired for failures in the first half of 1960. Even the final demotions (also in June) of Kirichenko and Belyayev (supervised by Aristov and his deputy Yefremov, respectively) were accompanied by no public criticisms against them.

In June virtually all RSFSR agricultural leaders were replaced and exiled to the provinces: head of the Central Committee's Agriculture Section for the RSFSR G. I. Vorobyev, RSFSR Agriculture Minister S. V. Kalchenko, and RSFSR Grain Products Minister F. D. Kulakov. All three had been appointed during the spring 1959 purge of Aristov allies. Vorobyev now was installed by Aristov as Krasnodar first secretary, replacing Polyanskiy's disgraced associate

---

[17] He was made deputy head of the RSFSR Bureau's section for agriculture under V. P. Mylarshchikov, who was demoted in early 1959 along with other apparent Aristov allies. When Aristov and Matskevich were ousted by Khrushchev and Polyanskiy at the beginning of 1961, Smirnov was replaced as RSFSR agriculture minister and exiled to Penza Oblast as executive committee chairman. After Khrushchev's fall, he returned to prominent jobs in the RSFSR government, where he appeared to reflect RSFSR Premier Voronov's positions.

Matyushkin. Shortly after Polyanskiy's promotion to USSR first deputy premier in charge of agriculture (October 1965), Vorobyev became USSR deputy agriculture minister (*Pravda*, 12 January 1966). Kalchenko now was transferred to chairman of the Altay Kray Executive Committee. By 1966 he had left this post and later was identified as first deputy head of the All-Union Agricultural Achievements Exhibit in Moscow (*Selskaya Zhizn*, 6 January 1967). Kulakov now was installed as Stavropol Kray first secretary by Aristov's deputy, M. Yefremov, replacing Belyayev. Immediately after Khrushchev's fall, Kulakov was named Central Committee Agriculture Section head and later (December 1965), after Polyanskiy's promotion, was elected Central Committee secretary for agriculture as well. As Central Committee agriculture chief, he presumably worked closely with Polyanskiy, the régime's agricultural supervisor.

In the June reshuffle G. L. Smirnov surrendered his post as RSFSR deputy premier to become RSFSR agriculture minister, but since no new deputy premier for agriculture was appointed, he remained the top RSFSR agricultural official under Polyanskiy and now directly supervised agriculture. T. A. Yurkin succeeded Kulakov as grain products minister in September, but does not appear to have been involved in the infighting and retained his post until it was abolished in 1962.

Apparently because of the struggle between Khrushchev, Polyanskiy, and Aristov, no successor for Vorobyev as RSFSR Agriculture Section head could be named. The post remained vacant for almost eight months, until Aristov's ouster and replacement with G. I. Voronov. Then Voronov's associate I. S. Pankin was appointed head (he had been relieved as Stalingrad Oblast Executive Committee chairman on 30 January 1961 and was first identified as section head in the 11 February 1961 *Pravda*). [18]

Belyayev's Fall

Simultaneous with Kirichenko's fall came the fall of Khrushchev's other closest and oldest ally in the leadership, Kazakh First Secretary N. I. Belyayev. As Altay first secretary, Belyayev had acted as advance man for Khrushchev's virgin land campaign in 1953 and 1954. He had broached the ideas of spreading silage corn and mass cultivation of the west Siberian virgin lands in the 11 December 1953 *Pravda*, preparing the way for Khrushchev's January 1954 proposals. He had already organized new virgin land sovkhozes to grow grain by mid–1954 when Khrushchev visited the Altay and, as Belyayev's long-time Altay assistant K. G.

---

[18] The leadership of the Central Committee Agriculture Section for the Union Republics also was vacant in mid-1960. G. A. Denisov, appointed head only months earlier (in the fall of 1959), was removed and sent abroad as ambassador to Bulgaria in May 1960, and his successor, V. A. Karlov, was identified only on 27 January 1961 (although he had been relieved as Kalinin Oblast first secretary in September 1960 and may have taken up his new post about that time).

Pysin noted at the December 1958 plenum,[19] the Altay leaders were censured by Malenkov in 1954 for following Khrushchev's approach in organizing virgin land sovkhozes. Belyayev was one of the first Khrushchev protégés brought into the central leadership, joining the Secretariat in mid-1955, and when Khrushchev set up the RSFSR Bureau in early 1956 he entrusted Belyayev with the leadership of it (as the sole deputy chairman under Chairman Khrushchev).

In December 1957 Belyayev was named first secretary of Kazakhstan, becoming the direct leader of Khrushchev's vital virgin land program. Although he was thus physically removed from Moscow his transfer may not have been intended as a demotion or as a long-term assignment, since he not only retained his Presidium membership but also his post of Central Committee secretary (he was relieved as Central Committee secretary only at the November 1958 Central Committee plenum —*Pravda*, 14 November 1958), and though he was apparently removed as Bureau deputy chairman in December 1957,[20] no new deputy chairman was identified in the press until December 1958.[21] His responsibilities in Moscow were taken over by Ignatov (who became Central Committee secretary in charge of agriculture in December 1957) and Aristov (who succeeded Belyayev as deputy chairman of the RSFSR Bureau).

Belyayev's fall in January 1960 was the direct result of the 1959 Kazakh harvest disaster—although it presumably was determined also by the struggle between Khrushchev and others over agriculture. Since Khrushchev had demoted agricultural leaders in the spring for poor organizational work he could not avoid punishing his ally Belyayev also when Belyayev's leadership failings were exposed in December 1959.

As was pointed out by the December 1959 Central Committee plenum decree (*Pravda*, 27 December), a good crop was grown in Kazakhstan, but due to slowness and poor organization of the harvest hundreds of thousands of hectares of grain crops were still unharvested when bad weather struck and brought enormous destruction. Initially, there appeared to be an attempt to gloss over the poor harvest,[22] but at the December Central Committee plenum Kazakh First Secretary Belyayev and Premier D. A. Kunayev admitted that Kazakhstan

---

[19] Stenographic record of the December 1958 Central Committee plenum, p. 318.

[20] Belyayev's obituary in the 30 October 1966 *Pravda* lists him as Bureau deputy chairman 1956-57.

[21] However, the 1962 and 1966 yearbooks of the *Bolshaya Sovetskaya Entsiklopediya* list Aristov as Bureau deputy chairman starting in 1957.

[22] On the very eve of the 22-25 December Central Committee plenum, the Central Committee and Council of Ministers had warmly congratulated the Kazakh leaders for their 1959 agricultural successes, including the sale of "700 million poods of grain, which is almost five times more than what was procured before the cultivation of the virgin and idle lands" (*Pravda*, 19 December 1959). The message ignored the fact that this was actually well below the average procurements for 1954-58, which amounted to 827 million poods, according to Belyayev at the December 1958 plenum (Stenographic record of the 15-19 December 1958 Central Committee plenum, p. 100).

had fallen 94 million poods short in grain procurements.[23] Khrushchev in his speech at the end of the plenum attacked his ally Belyayev and Premier Kunayev for "lacking the boldness to speak in a party way about shortcomings" in Kazakhstan and declared that on 1 November 1,618,000 hectares of grain had remained uncut there. Declaring that "friendship is friendship, but work is something else," Khrushchev blamed them for sowing the crop late and for the poorly organized harvest.

Shortly after the plenum, in January 1960, the members of the Kazakh Central Committee Bureau and the Kazakh deputy premiers were called to Moscow to a joint Presidium-Secretariat session on Kazakhstan's shortcomings.[24] Then Central Committee Secretary L. I. Brezhnev, who had originally led Khrushchev's virgin land cultivation when it began in Kazakhstan in 1954–55, was dispatched to Kazakhstan to supervise the removal of Belyayev for "serious shortcomings and mistakes."[25] Belyayev was saddled with the blame and demoted to first secretary of Stavropol Kray, while the other leaders were moved up: Premier Kunayev was promoted to first secretary, President Zh. A. Tashenev became premier, and Secretary F. Karibzhanov became president. Two outsiders were brought in: Leningrad City First Secretary N. N. Rodionov became Kazakh second secretary, and Perm Oblast First Secretary T. I. Sokolov became a Kazakh Central Committee secretary.

The new leadership reflected Brezhnev's influence: new First Secretary Kunayev, new Premier Tashenev, and new President Karibzhanov had received their earlier posts in 1954 and 1955 when Brezhnev was second secretary, then first secretary of the Kazakh Central Committee. Both Kunayev and Tashenev specifically pointed out Brezhnev's role in the January 1960 Kazakh Central Committee plenum and his past leadership in Kazakhstan in their January *aktiv* speeches (*Kazakhstanskaya Pravda*, 22 and 24 January), and Tashenev even lavished unusual praise on Brezhnev, calling him "one of the greatest leaders of our party and Soviet state" (*Kazakhstanskaya Pravda*, 24 January). Later, in murky maneuvering involving Khrushchev and F. R. Kozlov, those installed by Brezhnev were ousted in disgrace. In December 1962 and March 1963 First Secretary Kunayev, Second Secretary Rodionov, and Secretary Sokolov were dismissed and the appointment of Premier Tashenev (already replaced in January 1961) was characterized as "certainly a mistake."[26] The 1962–63 purge, in turn,

---

[23] Belyayev apologized for selling "only 700 million poods" to the state (Stenographic record of the 22–25 December 1959 Central Committee plenum, p. 71).

[24] See Z. Golikova, A. Kakimzhanov, S. Kovalskiy, V. Kulikov, N. Lerner, and M. Fazylov, *Kommunisticheskaya Partiya v Borbe za Osvoyeniye Tselinnykh Zemel v Kazakhstane* [The Communist Party in the Struggle for Cultivation of the Virgin Lands in Kazakhstan] (Alma Ata, 1969), pp. 346–47.

[25] Ibid., p. 347, and also the Kunayev and Tashenev speeches at the January Kazakh party *aktiv* meeting in *Kazakhstanskaya Pravda*, 22 and 24 January 1960.

[26] By Semipalatinsk First Secretary M. P. Karpenko in the 20 March 1963 *Kazakhstanskaya Pravda*.

was overturned immediately after Khrushchev's fall. Kunayev (demoted to premier in December 1962) was restored as first secretary within two months after Brezhnev became Central Committee first secretary, and M. B. Beysebayev (who had become first deputy premier in 1955 under Brezhnev) became premier. Kunayev has been Brezhnev's most avid fan, for instance, being the first official to publicly use the controversial formulation "the Politburo headed by Comrade L. I. Brezhnev" (*Kazakhstanskaya Pravda*, 17 April 1969). The two outsiders installed by Brezhnev—Rodionov and Sokolov—had no ties with him, but subsequently benefited from his patronage after Khrushchev's fall.[27]

Brezhnev's role in supervising the important Kazakh shake-up suggested that he was in line to be Kirichenko's replacement as cadre secretary. Previously, he had appeared preoccupied with heavy industry, especially metallurgy,[28] and did not participate in personnel actions. In the 4 May 1960 shake-up he remained in the Secretariat and, with only Suslov and new Secretary Kozlov as serious rivals, could easily have become de facto second secretary. However, three days later, at the 7 May Supreme Soviet session, Brezhnev was elected chairman of the Supreme Soviet Presidium (Soviet president)—apparently being sidetracked from his key duties as Central Committee secretary, just as Central Committee Secretary Ignatov had been sidetracked in April 1959. He appeared to attempt to continue exercising his secretarial functions, however, addressing a conference of secretaries of army party organizations in mid-May (*Pravda*, 15 May 1960). But at the 13-16 July Central Committee plenum, with Khrushchev's power at low ebb,[29] Brezhnev was dropped from the Secretariat altogether, temporarily ending any chance to compete with Kozlov and Suslov.

[27]Rodionov was a protégé of Leningrad leader F. R. Kozlov and was sent to Kazakhstan in January 1960 as "a pupil of the Leningrad party organization" (*Kazakhstanskaya Pravda*, 22 January 1960). After being removed in 1962, he was relegated to a minor industrial job back in Kozlov's bailiwick Leningrad. After Brezhnev had established his primacy in the party apparatus by defeating the challenge by Podgornyy in 1965, Rodionov was one of the first of those disgraced under Khrushchev to become an oblast first secretary (Chelyabinsk). In his speeches he has shown deference to Brezhnev, who, like Rodionov, is a trained ferrous metallurgist. Brezhnev in June 1968 chose a protégé of Rodionov, Chelyabinsk Oblast Ideology Secretary Ye. M. Tyazhelnikov, to become first secretary of the All-Union Komsomol. Sokolov, the closest to Khrushchev on agricultural policy, was placed in charge of the virgin lands, but despite his long connection with Khrushchev, he was disgraced and sacked in 1963. He was one of the first Khrushchev victims rehabilitated in 1965, when he became deputy RSFSR agriculture minister, and later in 1965, at the same time as Rodionov (late October), he was named an oblast first secretary (Orel).

[28]See his 21st Congress speech in January 1959. He clearly had nothing to do with agriculture at this time—for instance, not being included in the long list of officials given awards for agricultural work in the 30 December 1959 *Pravda*.

[29]Although Khrushchev had led the Soviet delegation to the June conference of Communist leaders in Rumania, it was Kozlov who reported to the July plenum on the conference, and Khrushchev, according to the plenum communiqués, said nothing at all at the plenum. Also see Tatu's *Power in the Kremlin* for other signs of Khrushchev's weakness at this time.

Kozlov was later clearly identified as second secretary[30] and in 1962 and 1963 personally conducted the purge of Brezhnev's 1960 Kazakh appointees.

After the purge of Belyayev, Khrushchev's interference in the virgin lands increased as he sought to avoid a repetition of the 1959 mistakes and to achieve big increases in agricultural production. At the same time as Belyayev's fall, Khrushchev proposed establishing a Kazakh Sovkhoz Ministry and a Bureau for the Northern Oblasts, both to be located in Akmolinsk in the virgin lands. [31] The Sovkhoz Ministry was created with A. I. Kozlov[32] as minister (*Pravda*, 26 January 1960), while new Kazakh Central Committee Secretary Sokolov became chairman of the new bureau. Sokolov explained that the new bureau and ministry had been established to improve leadership of virgin land farming and to boost grain production and that they had immediately set to work examining land balance, crop structure, agrotechniques, and possibilities for increasing farming efficiency and soil fertility.[33] On 14 June 1960 he wrote in *Pravda* that 4 million more hectares of virgin land could be cultivated,[34] 1,500,000 hectares in 1960 alone.[35]

The creation of the Northern Oblasts Bureau and the Kazakh Sovkhoz Ministry turned out to be only the first step in Khrushchev's removal of the

[30] Kozlov was chosen to deliver the report on changes in the party statute at the 1961 party congress—an honor ranking him second only to Khrushchev, who delivered the Central Committee report at the congress—and at the conclusion of the congress Kozlov was listed second (out of alphabetical order) in the newly elected Secretariat.

[31] Kunayev in the 22 January 1960 *Kazakhstanskaya Pravda*. Akmolinsk was renamed Tselinograd in 1961.

[32] Kozlov had been Central Committee Agriculture Section head from 1947 to March 1953, then USSR agriculture minister until September 1953, then USSR sovkhoz minister until March 1955. As Malenkov's top agricultural henchman, he was assailed by Khrushchev, and when Malenkov resigned as premier and confessed agricultural errors in early 1955, Kozlov was removed and demoted to director of a sovkhoz in Kazakhstan. However, after his demotion he managed to redeem himself in Khrushchev's eyes. When ordered by Khrushchev to undertake the introduction of corn in his virgin land sovkhoz, Kozlov did so so effectively that Khrushchev at the December 1959 Central Committee plenum cited the results of Kozlov's farm as proof of corn's possibilities in the virgin lands. Khrushchev personally invited Kozlov to the December 1959 plenum, where Kozlov confessed his earlier errors, praised Khrushchev's criticism of him as Central Committee agriculture chief and agriculture minister, and delivered a speech on his successes with corn in the virgin lands (Stenographic record of the December 1959 Central Committee plenum, pp. 357–63). Khrushchev in his closing speech at the plenum lauded Kozlov and even suggested he be given an Order of Lenin (ibid., pp. 406–7). Shortly afterward, Kozlov became head of Khrushchev's new Kazakh Sovkhoz Ministry.

[33] *Partiynaya Zhizn* 16 (August 1960): 27–32.

[34] Also approved by the Kazakh Central Committee Bureau, *Kazakhstanskaya Pravda*, 10 April 1960.

[35] At the same time, Sokolov stressed the need for large areas of fallow, noting that yield after fallow is much higher than after fall plowed land (*zyab*), and also the need for moldboardless plowing and retention of stubble to avoid erosion.

virgin lands from the control of the Kazakh leaders. Soon—either on their own or instigated by Khrushchev—members of Sokolov's bureau urged that the bureau be strengthened, apparently to make it more independent of the Kazakh leadership, and when Kazakh First Secretary Kunayev came to Moscow to report to the Central Committee, he and Khrushchev disagreed over how to improve leadership of the virgin lands.[36] Afterward, in his 29 October 1960 Note to the Presidium, Khrushchev, citing the urgings of "some members" of Sokolov's bureau, proposed creating a separate entity for the Kazakh virgin lands (Tselinnyy Kray),[37] with its own party and government structure subordinate directly to Moscow. The new kray party committee and executive committee and the Kazakh Sovkhoz Ministry were to be led by the CPSU Central Committee and USSR Council of Ministers for the next "5-7 years." This, according to Khrushchev, would improve cadre work since virgin land leaders would be selected from outside Kazakhstan instead of just from within the republic.[38]

The Virgin Land Debate

In his 14 June 1960 *Pravda* article Northern Oblasts Bureau Chairman Sokolov noted the debates between scientists and specialists over cultivation methods but failed to take sides, except on the questions of fallow and stubble retention. However, Sokolov and Kazakh Sovkhoz Minister Kozlov soon appeared to side with Lysenko in this debate.

In June Lysenko made a long trip through the virgin lands, and when Sokolov's bureau and Kozlov's ministry called a virgin land conference in Akmolinsk on 7 July to discuss the first six months of their work, Lysenko was the star speaker at the conference (*Kazakhstanskaya Pravda*, 9 July 1960), and his speech laid down a new program for the virgin lands. Since the 1959 virgin lands disaster resulted largely from the failure to harvest a good crop in time, Lysenko's solution was to plant earlier so the crop would be ready to harvest earlier—giving more time to harvest before the onslaught of frost and bad weather. Most virgin landers sowed crops in mid- or late May, believing, like virgin land scientist A. I. Barayev, that early sown crops would suffer from the May-June droughts, while late sown crops would develop at the right time to take advantage of the moist July-August period. Lysenko did not deny that in practice late sowing did naturally yield better, but he argued that a good crop

---

[36] As Khrushchev related in his 29 October 1960 Note, Kunayev wanted to establish smaller oblasts—see N. S. Khrushchev, *Stroitelstvo Kommunizma v SSSR i Razvitiye Selskogo Khozyaystva* [Construction of Communism in the USSR and the Development of Agriculture], vol. 4, p. 168. (This series is Khrushchev's collected speeches and writings on agriculture from September 1953 to March 1964, published in 8 volumes between 1962 and 1964. Hereinafter referred to as Khrushchev's collected speeches.)

[37] Comprising Kustanay, North Kazakhstan, Kokchetav, Akmolinsk (renamed Tselinograd) and Pavlodar oblasts.

[38] Khrushchev's collected speeches, vol. 4, pp. 169-70.

was useless if it did not ripen until shortly before the fall frosts, so that much was left in the field and lost. To overcome the handicap of the short Siberian growing season, Lysenko announced a program permitting early sowing. He declared that early sown crops yielded less than later sown crops not because of the May–June droughts but because of lack of nutrition in the soil carried over from the previous year. He proposed to plant in the fall of 1960 massive areas (500,000 hectares) with winter rye (winter wheat would not survive the virgin lands' severe winter) on unplowed stubble of the spring crops, in late August and early September. He claimed that lack of plowing would not only fight erosion (by preserving stubble) but would reduce weeds also (the rye would be well developed when the weeds sprouted in May and would choke off the weeds). The rye, ripening early, could be harvested at the end of July and the land could be plowed for fallow in early August. The fallow would accumulate nutrition in late summer and fall. Most of this nutrition would remain through the winter and permit very early sowing of spring wheat (since the spring wheat would not have to wait until nutrition built up after the spring thaw). In other words, the whole crop cycle would be geared to an earlier timetable to beat the weather limitations. Deep plowing up of fallow would kill the weeds and boost spring wheat yield. Weeds would also be eliminated by cleaning the seeds of weed seeds and by eliminating oats—which, according to Lysenko, sometimes change into wild oats (weeds).

Actually, while living in Omsk during World War II, Lysenko, along with the Omsk Agricultural Institute (scientists N. A. Belozerova and G. P. Vysokos), had carried out a similar program of sowing winter rye and wheat on thousands of hectares of Siberian land—with disastrous results (the crops froze).[39] Nevertheless, he and the Omsk Institute revived this program in 1960.

Sokolov afterward expressed his agreement with Lysenko's proposals on early sowing, eliminating wild oats, introducing fallow, using winter rye stubble, and improving corn growing (*Partiynaya Zhizn*, no. 16 [August 1960], p. 30). Kozlov, who had collaborated with Lysenko under Malenkov, apparently supported his program too. However, the program laid down in Lysenko's 7 July speech was apparently so controversial that *Pravda* delayed publishing his speech until 5 August.

In the virgin lands, the opposition to Lysenko's program was led by T. S. Maltsev, director of the Shadrinsk Experimental Station in the west Siberian virgin lands, and A. I. Barayev, director of the Akmolinsk Grain Institute in the Kazakh virgin lands. Barayev and Maltsev warned against the danger of erosion and weeds and insisted on late sowing. Maltsev and his protector Kurgan Oblast First Secretary G. F. Sizov resisted Lysenko's early sowing program and the Altay corn campaign and somehow managed to continue using Maltsev's late sowing, shallow plowing, and clean fallow program—despite severe con-

[39] See M. Popovskiy in *Sovetskaya Rossiya*, 27 November 1964, and L. Ivanov in *Literaturnaya Rossiya*, 19 March 1966.

demnation from Khrushchev and others. Barayev's resistance was encouraged by USSR Agriculture Minister V. V. Matskevich, and at an 8 September conference on seed growing in the virgin lands, called by the Agriculture Ministry and All-Union Agricultural Academy (VASKhNIL), held at Barayev's institute, and attended by Matskevich, Barayev repeated his support for late sowing, despite Lysenko's 7 July Akmolinsk speech.[40]

Meanwhile, various Kazakh press organs and local officials began campaigning for Lysenko's program.[41] In the Siberian virgin lands the leaders of Omsk, Chelyabinsk, Krasnoyarsk, Orenburg, and Altay joined Lysenko's fight for early sowing, along with the agricultural institutes in Omsk (director, I. I. Zezin), Orenburg (director, Sh. Sh. Khayrullin), and Altay (director, G. A. Nalivayko). The Omsk Institute leaders and oblast First Secretary Ye. P. Kolushchinskiy, who welcomed Lysenko as a returning hero (according to Yu. Chernichenko in *Novyy Mir*, no. 11 [1965]) and championed his program in west Siberia (*Selskaya Zhizn*, 30 September 1960), fought Maltsev bitterly, even spreading false rumors to discredit his methods (according to V. Ovechkin in *Selskaya Zhizn*, 23 and 24 November 1960). Maltsev was vindicated when the 1963 drought devastated all virgin land crops, while his antierosion methods permitted Kurgan Oblast to outproduce all the rest of west Siberia (L. Ivanov, *Ekonomicheskaya Gazeta*, 8 August 1964). The debate between the Lysenko supporters and Barayev backers raged in the press in June, July, August, and September 1960.

Matskevich's Opposition

The most formidable opposition to Lysenko's program came from outspoken Agriculture Minister V. V. Matskevich. Already by early 1960 it had become clear that Matskevich was opposing Khrushchev on the issue of creating kolkhoz unions, and later it was indicated that he opposed him on a wide variety of issues: Khrushchev's *agrogorod* plans (to create "agricultural towns" in the countryside) and ideas on internal sovkhoz organization, Lysenko's bull-breeding experiments and early sowing program, Khrushchev's ideas on wages for kolkhozniks and on sovkhoz trusts, his use of corn, beans, peas, etc.

At the December 1959 Central Committee plenum Khrushchev and his allies had promoted the idea of establishing a system of kolkhoz administration outside the control of the Agriculture Ministry. RSFSR Premier Polyanskiy cautiously but approvingly reported proposals for creating kolkhoz unions and declared that if they were created, Matskevich's Agriculture Ministry would have

---

[40]See N. Kosolapov's 30 September 1960 *Selskaya Zhizn* article assailing Barayev for opposing Lysenko.

[41]*Kazakhstanskaya Pravda*, 3 September, 20 November, 25 November, 27 November 1960.

to be reorganized and "significantly reduced"—which he declared was "only for the good."[42] Ukrainian First Secretary N. V. Podgornyy came right out and endorsed the creation of kolkhoz unions at the plenum,[43] and Kazakh First Secretary Belyayev and Sverdlovsk First Secretary A. P. Kirilenko seconded what they called Polyanskiy's and Podgornyy's "proposal" to create kolkhoz unions. Matskevich, however, flatly announced his opposition to kolkhoz unions above the rayon level, declaring that rayon kolkhoz unions should be coordinated by the oblast agricultural administrations (i.e., be subordinate to his ministry's local organs).[44] Khrushchev himself at the plenum revealed that his Note to the Central Committee on the 1958 machine-tractor station reform had advocated the establishment of kolkhoz unions, but admitted that the opposition to national kolkhoz unions made it inadvisable to create them now.[45] The plenum's decree wound up referring the kolkhoz union issue back to the Presidium for further discussion.[46]

Khrushchev criticized Matskevich at the December 1959 plenum and undermined him in April 1960 by transferring the key agricultural newspaper *Selskoye Khozyaystvo* (renamed *Selskaya Zhizn*) from an organ of Matskevich's ministry to an organ of the Central Committee (*Pravda*, 3 April 1960). Khrushchev appointed his protégé, *Pravda*'s agricultural editor V. I. Polyakov, chief editor.

An All-Union Conference of Agricultural Specialists was held in mid-June 1960, and at this conference Matskevich took advantage of Khrushchev's weakened political status to repeat his opposition to kolkhoz unions and also to take other positions later objected to by Khrushchev (*Pravda*, 15 June 1960). Following Matskevich's speech and a May 1960 *Voprosy Ekonomiki* article by A. Pashkov declaring kolkhoz unions unnecessary, the kolkhoz union idea was temporarily laid to rest. Khrushchev, oddly enough, did not even attend the 14–17 June agricultural conference.[47]

Another prime bone of contention was Matskevich's dislike of Lysenko's ideas. At the June All-Union Conference of Agricultural Specialists (*Pravda*, 16 June 1960), Lysenko asked the Agriculture Ministry to pay attention to his research work in raising the fat content of milk by crossing cows with special bulls bred at Lysenko's experimental farm—based on his theory of passing

---

[42]Stenographic record of the December 1959 Central Committee plenum, pp. 32–33.

[43]Ibid., p. 61. *Izvestiya* on 11 December 1959 referred to a note on kolkhoz unions prepared by Podgornyy and shown to Khrushchev while he was visiting Lvov.

[44]Stenographic record of the December 1959 Central Committee plenum, p. 322.

[45]Ibid., p. 408.

[46]Ibid., p. 441.

[47]Khrushchev, reported on vacation in Gagra by the 11 and 13 June *Pravda*s, was apparently still on vacation and not in Moscow. On 18 June he left for Rumania.

acquired characteristics on to succeeding generations. Lysenko directed his statement to Matskevich personally: "I acknowledge that in this case I am talking
about this matter specially for you, Comrade V. V. Matskevich. . . . Without the
appropriate instructions from the USSR Agriculture Ministry the breeding
offices naturally will not buy these hybrid bulls" (*Selskaya Zhizn*, 17 June
1960). Lysenko complained that the Agriculture Ministry collegium was supposed to have met on this subject several months earlier but had failed to do so
and "seemed to have forgotten" about the question. In July or August Lysenko
repeated his appeal in a special letter to the ministry, as he related at the January
1961 plenum.

Matskevich, himself an authority on cattle,[48] opposed Lysenko's plan and
successfully blocked the spread of Lysenko's bulls. When Matskevich was turned
out of office and Lysenko's protégé M. A. Olshanskiy became agriculture minister in January 1961, one of the first things he did was to order a go-ahead on the
bull program (see Lysenko's January 1961 plenum speech, *Pravda*, 16 January
1961).

The Presidium discussed agriculture shortly before Khrushchev left for the
US in early September, and Khrushchev sent his agricultural assistant, A. S.
Shevchenko, to the Altay and Kazakhstan.[49] All the major protagonists in the
virgin land debate also made their own inspection trips and apparently gathered
their own evidence to use in the coming confrontation. Aristov[50] toured west
Siberian agricultural areas in early August (and again in October), Polyanskiy
visited the Lysenkoist center of Omsk in late September, while Matskevich visited Barayev's institute on 8 September, talking with Barayev and, as Lysenko
later complained,[51] admiring his late sown wheat.

After Khrushchev's return from the US on 14 October, his assistant Shevchenko reported to him and later (17, 18, 19 November) wrote a long report for
the press. While praising some Barayev views (such as the need for fallow in some
dry areas), his ambiguous report sided mainly with Lysenko—especially on the
need for early ripening and hence fairly early sowing.

[48] In 1968 he wrote a book on meat-cattle raising, urging adoption of US Santa
Gertruda breeds—see *Ekonomika Selskogo Khozyaystva* 11 (1968): 112.

[49] Khrushchev's 29 October 1960 Note (Khrushchev's collected speeches, vol. 4, pp.
166, 178).

[50] Aristov's attitude toward Lysenko is unclear. Although Aristov fell at the time of
Lysenko's rise in January 1961, and Aristov was singled out for praise by Lysenko's foe
Maltsev at the January 1961 plenum, Aristov's two closest protégés (Omsk First Secretary
Kolushchinskiy and Chelyabinsk First Secretary N. V. Laptev, who both had been promoted
under and had assisted Aristov in Krasnoyarsk and Chelyabinsk) championed Lysenko's
cause. Kolushchinskiy and Laptev were purged in 1961, apparently not because of resistance
to Lysenko but because of their ties with Aristov, poor agricultural results, and slowness in
propagating corn. (B. Gerasenkov, in the 25 November 1961 *Pravda*, criticized the Omsk
Obkom for not backing the Omsk Agricultural Institute's proposals to expand corn.)

[51] In his 14 March 1961 Akmolinsk speech (*Pravda*, 28 April 1961).

Shevchenko was especially in favor of corn, declaring the debate over corn closed and calling it the perfect predecessor for spring crops in north Kazakhstan and west Siberia. To prove corn's value, he cited the Altay intertilled system (replacing fallow and grass with corn, sugar beets, and fodder beans). Khrushchev, who long had been attempting to get farms to grow more corn, was resisted by Matskevich, Maltsev, Barayev, and others, perhaps including Aristov. The Altay Institute's experiments, which supposedly proved that crop fallow (corn) actually increases soil fertility, conserves moisture, combats weeds, and boosts yields of the succeeding crops better than clean fallow or grasses, provided the proof Khrushchev needed to make a breakthrough in his campaign to push corn and overcome the arguments of those who followed the Vilyams grassland system (*travopolnaya sistema*) of crop rotations, which periodically rested the fields by leaving them idle (clean fallow) or by planting them with perennial grasses. Those more or less following this grassland system included Agriculture Minister Matskevich, VASKhNIL[52] President P. P. Lobanov, and the great majority of agricultural scientists and RSFSR oblast leaders. Aristov must have also supported this system—since most of his subordinates in the oblasts (including his protégés Kolushchinskiy and Laptev) did.

Lysenko himself had long backed V. R. Vilyams's grassland system and had even persecuted corn specialists, such as B. P. Sokolov. But showing fine sensitivity for Khrushchev's love of corn, he not only managed to include it in his 1960 recommendations as a good predecessor for early spring wheat which helps clear weeds and build soil nutrition, but even promoted his own method of corn planting (square-cluster sowing). Likewise, with other crops of the intertilled system, his farm proved the advantages of beans, sugar beets, and peas—crops promoted by Khrushchev.

Maltsev was an influential figure in the virgin lands and a favorite of Khrushchev's during the 1950's. However, because of Maltsev's lack of enthusiasm for corn, a rift gradually developed between him and Khrushchev. At the December 1958 plenum Khrushchev complained that Maltsev liked only wheat and related: "I visited his kolkhoz three years ago and asked him to sow corn, and then to sow wheat after the occupied fallow. He spoke here [at the plenum], but said nothing about this, which means that he did not apply this. This criticism is aimed at you, comrade Maltsev."[53] In his plenum speech Maltsev had gone only part way in adopting corn, suggesting a system of clean fallow, followed by corn (occupied fallow), followed by wheat, which he had begun using in 1957. However, he insisted that clean fallow was indispensable, since corn just could not kill weeds as clean fallow could.[54] Under Khrushchev's prodding, Maltsev appeared to back down some in 1959, agreeing that the need for additional fodder was so great that he would rethink his position and try

[52] The All-Union Lenin Academy of Agricultural Sciences.

[53] Stenographic record of the December 1958 Central Committee plenum, p. 322.

[54] Ibid., p. 194.

using occupied fallow instead of clean fallow.[55] However, Khrushchev's pressure on him intensified during the big 1961 drive for intertilled crops.

Orenburg Institute director Khayrullin and Orenburg First Secretary G. I. Voronov also strongly backed the Altay program and were in the forefront of those attacking the grassland system. Vilyam's preference for late fall plowing and not packing the soil conflicted with Khayrullin's basic prescription of early, deep plowing in the fall to destroy weeds, and then leveling the plowed land to hold the moisture through the winter.

Shevchenko's report pleased Khrushchev, Lysenko, and Altay First Secretary K. G. Pysin, all of whom later praised it. Following the report, Khrushchev wrote a Note to the Presidium (29 October 1960)[56] attacking the RSFSR Bureau leaders (Aristov) for giving poor instruction to local leaders, Matskevich for his ideas on sovkhoz organization, and Kunayev for his ideas on virgin land organization. Khrushchev praised early sowing for the virgin lands and suggested creating a virgin land region (Tselinnyy Kray). On the same day as Khrushchev's Note, a Central Committee plenum was announced for 13 December, at which all republics and the Northern Oblasts Bureau (the predecessor of Tselinnyy Kray) would report on their fulfillment of agricultural plans. Khrushchev's Note threatened to give some people a "good shaking" for poor agricultural leadership in the republics and oblasts,[57] and the following day's (30 October) *Pravda* editorial made it clear that leaders of lagging areas were to be called to account for their unfulfilled production pledges. Khrushchev's Note also proposed expansion of the sowing of corn for fodder and said the December plenum would adopt a decision on this question.[58]

Meanwhile, recovering the initiative, Khrushchev began a campaign against Matskevich. During his return from vacation in late August he stopped in his home town of Kalinovka and in a 27 August talk with local kolkhozniks he criticized the June statement by "some agricultural officials" (Matskevich) on concentrating everything at a sovkhoz's central farm (*tsentralnaya usadba*) and eliminating divisions.[59] He assailed Matskevich by name on this score in his 29 October Note. During November and December, articles—especially in papers close to Khrushchev—began attacking Matskevich and his ministry.[60]

However, Khrushchev's drive to get rid of Matskevich encountered resistance in the leadership, and with the Presidium apparently divided the Central Committee plenum set for 13 December could not be held on schedule. *Pravda* on 10 December announced that the plenum would be postponed until January,

---

[55] Stenographic record of the 21st CPSU Congress, vol. 2, pp. 239–40.

[56] Khrushchev's collected speeches, vol. 4, pp. 162–86.

[57] Ibid., p. 166.

[58] Ibid., p. 166.

[59] Ibid., p. 157.

[60] *Selskaya Zhizn*, 23–24 November, 13 December, 20 December; *Izvestiya*, 16 December; *Pravda*, 26 December; and *Partiynaya Zhizn*, no. 23.

but the indecision at the top apparently precluded the announcement of an exact date.

An even clearer sign of the division in the Presidium was Belorussian First Secretary Mazurov's 11 December *Pravda* article defending the Agriculture Ministry. Mazurov urged more precise definition of the duties of the USSR Agriculture Ministry and its local organs and complained that agricultural agencies had been "unjustly deprived" of the "functions of planning agricultural production, planning output and distributing equipment and supplies." In direct contrast, Khrushchev in his 5 January 1961 thesis cited approvingly the transfer of the functions of agricultural planning and distribution of equipment from the USSR Agriculture Ministry to Gosplan and urged further reduction of the ministry's functions.[61]

The issue was finally resolved at a Presidium session shortly before the 20 December Supreme Soviet meeting, which, according to Georgian First Secretary Mzhavanadze at the January 1961 Central Committee plenum, discussed "questions of bringing agricultural science closer to production and also questions of improving the structure and forms of activity of the agriculture ministries."[62] On 25 December *Pravda* was able to announce that the Central Committee plenum would be held on 10 January. On 30 December *Pravda* announced Matskevich's removal as agriculture minister and *Kazakhstanskaya Pravda* reported his appointment as chairman of the executive committee of the newly formed Tselinnyy Kray in Kazakhstan. Thus, after months of resisting Khrushchev's virgin land policies, Matskevich was, ironically, sent to the virgin lands to implement them.

The Ryazan Scandal

Meanwhile, as the virgin land debate hit its climax in September and October, followed by the exile of Matskevich at the end of December, a second crucial struggle was also reaching its climax in September and October—the Ryazan scandal and the discrediting of Khrushchev's frantic meat campaign. This was followed by Aristov's exile in January 1961.

Khrushchev had originally set the goal of overtaking the US in meat, milk, and butter per capita in his 22 May 1957 Leningrad speech.[63] In that speech he recalled asking economists when this goal—which required a 320 percent increase in meat production—could be reached. When economists estimated 1975—almost twenty years—Khrushchev accused some scientific workers of trying "to hold back our forward movement"[64] and turned to leaders of some farms who pledged to double, triple, or quadruple meat production in two, three, or four

[61] Khrushchev's collected speeches, vol. 4, p. 255.

[62] Stenographic record of the January 1961 Central Committee plenum, pp. 149–50.

[63] Khrushchev's collected speeches, vol. 2, pp. 444, 446.

[64] Ibid., pp. 449–50.

years. With this approach, Khrushchev declared it possible to catch the US by 1960, although, he noted, "it will not be any tragedy if, for example, we are not able to catch America in meat production in 1960." "We can permit a certain delay, it won't be bad to resolve this task in 1961 either," he continued, "however, in 1961 we must, as they say, finish it off, while it is necessary to complete the main work in 1960."[65]

Khrushchev's new goal stirred up his foes in the Presidium, and he remarked at the December 1958 plenum that "the Anti-Party Group tried to stifle the patriotic movement begun by advanced kolkhozes and sovkhozes for a quick upsurge of livestock raising and resolution of the task of catching the US in production of livestock products per capita in the shortest period."[66]

At the December 1958 plenum Khrushchev demanded an even faster rate of growth in meat production than the steep rates set in the seven-year plan (1959-65). While the USSR in 1958 was producing 8 million tons of meat and the seven-year plan called for 16 million tons by the end of 1965, Khrushchev declared that 20-21 million tons were necessary to surpass the US in per capita meat production (*Pravda*, 16 December 1958). He flatly asserted that the Soviet Union had the reserves to raise production faster than the seven-year plan provided for, citing results of some farms and oblasts in rapidly boosting production, and he urged making 1959 a "turning point," calling upon every kolkhoz, sovkhoz, rayon, oblast, and republic to reassess its possibilities for boosting its meat production in 1959 in order to overtake the US. Speaking near the end of the plenum, Matskevich noted that many speakers had promised to double meat production, but he declared that this would not be enough to catch the US: "Comrade N. S. Khrushchev has repeatedly pointed out that we can and must increase meat production by two and a half times or even three times; then we will catch America."[67]

Khrushchev's urgent plea was responded to quickly by the Ryazan party organization. At the beginning of January 1959 an oblast party conference announced that Ryazan intended to "set the tone" for the USSR in increasing meat production and planned to boost meat production by 2.4 times in 1959 over 1958 (*Pravda*, 5 January). On 9 January *Pravda* published a long "appeal" by Ryazan agricultural workers challenging their colleagues throughout the Soviet Union to a new competition in doubling and tripling meat production "to carry out as soon as possible the national goal of catching up with the US in per capita meat production." Ryazan raised its pledge of a few days earlier, promis-

---

[65]The paragraphs of Khrushchev's speech containing the embarrassing commitments to catch the US by 1960 or 1961 (contained in the original version of the speech published in the 24 May 1957 *Pravda*) were cut out of the speech when it was republished in Khrushchev's collected speeches in 1962. Only his vaguer references to catching the US in "the next few years" remained.

[66]Stenographic record of the December 1958 Central Committee plenum, pp. 10-11.

[67]Ibid., p. 428.

ing to sell 150,000 tons of meat to the state in 1959, compared with 48,400 tons in 1958.

The following day's *Pravda* editorial lauded the "remarkable initiative" of Ryazan and its "enormous economic significance." *Pravda* declared that Ryazan's initiative "lays the foundation for a national competition for increasing production of livestock products, especially meat" and prodded other areas to follow suit: "if this is possible in Ryazan, obviously it is possible in other regions also."

The 21st Party Congress, which opened on 27 January 1959, heard the Ryazan initiative lauded from its tribune by Khrushchev, RSFSR Premier Polyanskiy, Central Committee Agriculture Secretary Ignatov, Central Committee RSFSR Agriculture Section head Mylarshchikov, and others. By the opening of the congress, according to Polyanskiy, thousands of kolkhozes and sovkhozes had already followed suit by pledging to double or triple meat production in 1959. Polyanskiy and Ignatov indicated that this movement would enable the RSFSR to boost meat production by 1.5 times in 1959 over 1958 and deliver 4,200,000 tons to the state—one million more than planned. According to Ignatov, by 1965 the RSFSR would produce 12,100,000 tons. Ryazan First Secretary A. N. Larionov himself spoke at the congress, telling how his oblast intended to fulfill the seven-year plan for meat production in only two to three years.

Immediately after the congress, on 12-13 February 1959, Khrushchev traveled to Ryazan to present an Order of Lenin to the oblast for its agricultural work, and at the December 1959 plenum he lavished praise on Larionov throughout his speech, declaring that Ryazan was "literally working miracles" and recalling that he himself in early January 1959 had authorized the publication of Ryazan's pledges, rejecting doubts about its ability to fulfill them by declaring that "I know Comrade Larionov as a serious, thoughtful man" who would never "undertake any unrealistic obligation." Khrushchev declared that the "skeptics who did not believe in the creative forces of the Ryazanites" had been proven wrong. He reported that he had even invited Larionov to take over a leadership post in Moscow, but that Larionov had begged off to dedicate himself to developing Ryazan's backward agriculture.

Polyanskiy praised the Ryazan initiative as "a model of a Communist attitude toward a matter of exceptional importance" which deserved the "warmest approval" and proudly reported that the RSFSR as a whole had fulfilled its pledge of selling 4,200,000 tons of meat to the state. Khrushchev interrupted some speakers to point out their areas' unfavorable comparison with Ryazan, badgering Belorussian First Secretary K. T. Mazurov in particular.

Amidst compliments from Khrushchev and other speakers at the December 1959 plenum, Larionov declared that Ryazan had fulfilled its obligation of boosting meat production by 3.8 times and procurement by 4 times (from 30,300 tons to 123,500) and promised even higher achievements in

1960—fulfilling three years' meat plan in one year and finishing the seven-year plan by the end of 1961 instead of 1965. But after the December 1959 plenum, according to Khrushchev's theses for the January 1961 plenum report,[68] some people raised doubts about Ryazan's remarkable achievements and attempts were made to check on them. However, these checks went uncompleted. Those in Ryazan who criticized Larionov's methods of fulfilling plans were expelled from the party (according to his successor as oblast first secretary, K. N. Grishin, in *Oktyabr* 11 [1961] : 132-33).

In the meantime, Ryazan continued to be hailed as an example. In mid-March party agricultural officials led by Central Committee Agriculture Section head G. A. Denisov and his deputy, F. S. Krestyaninov, visited Ryazan to familiarize themselves with its work style, visit livestock farms, and talk with Larionov (*Pravda*, 16-17 March 1960).

However, the picture began to change in mid-summer when raiding parties discovered that neighboring Tula Oblast was failing to live up to its unrealistic obligations. Tula's leaders had followed Ryazan's course, promising to fulfill three years' meat plan in one. After the 21st Congress Khrushchev had traveled to two oblasts—Ryazan and Tula—to present them with Orders of Lenin and praise their initiative in adopting huge meat targets (12-13 February 1959 in Ryazan and 17 February in Tula). Tula and Ryazan became the centers of national attention in the meat-milk campaign, although Tula's build-up did not match Ryazan's and Khrushchev was not so personally committed to the Tula leaders.

A long article in the 8 June 1960 *Selskaya Zhizn* entitled "And Are They Not Resting on Their Oars in Tula?" reported Tula's ambitious meat and milk campaign was failing. *Selskaya Zhizn's* special correspondent in Tula, Yu. Shcheglov noted that Tula was fulfilling its meat procurement obligations by only 57 percent, while its milk production was even falling behind the 1959 rate. He disputed the contention of the Tula Obkom Agriculture Section head, V. S. Baturin, that "the oblast has good prospects for fulfillment of the obligations" and attacked other Tula agricultural leaders for blaming the lag[69] on fodder shortages. Shcheglov attributed the lag to poor organization.

The next day a *Selskaya Zhizn* editorial ["You Gave Your Word—Keep It!"] reported that a nationwide check on fulfillment of obligations had uncovered many shortcomings, including "Tula Oblast, for example," where "present rates of production and procurement are not ensuring fulfillment of their obligations." It complained that "in Tula Oblast certain officials are not against declaring the obligations unrealistic and attributing the lagging to objective reasons." The editorial rejected this and attributed the lag to the fact that in Tula "organizational work has weakened and a feeling of responsibility for fulfillment of the obligations is lacking." On 25 June *Selskaya Zhizn* reported that

---

[68] Khrushchev's collected speeches, vol. 4, pp. 265-66.

[69] The increase in livestock was only slightly exceeding the 1959 rate.

the Tula Obkom Bureau had discussed the 8 and 9 June *Selskaya Zhizn* criticisms and admitted their correctness. First Secretary A. I. Khvorostukhin promised corrective action.

Despite the exposures in Tula, the validity of Ryazan's claims was still
accepted at this point. In fact, the 8 June *Selskaya Zhizn* Shcheglov article
attacked the Tula leaders for wanting to accomplish a jump in meat production
"which only the Ryazanites have been capable of." The mid-June All-Union
Conference of Agricultural Specialists in its official appeal (*Pravda*, 19 June)
praised Ryazan's successes in meat production, specifically citing its 380 percent
increase in 1959.

But by late summer Ryazan was no longer treated as the pacesetter and
may have come under a cloud of suspicion. It was not included in the list of
areas praised in the 8 August, 17 August, and 12 September *Pravda* editorials on
fulfillment of agricultural obligations. The 8 August editorial criticizing "those
leaders who at the beginning of the year made loud speeches and took high
obligations" and then did not follow through may have been aimed at Ryazan as
well as Tula and other oblasts.

By mid-September Larionov probably felt his time was running out. A 21
September *Selskaya Zhizn* editorial entitled "Obligations Must Be Fulfilled!"
expressed "especial alarm" about the failure to fulfill milk procurement plans in
several oblasts, including Ryazan.

At about the same time Tula First Secretary Khvorostukhin received his
punishment for failure and irresponsibility. On 27 September he was removed as
Tula first secretary (*Pravda*, 28 September) and appointed ambassador to Mon-
golia (*Izvestiya*, 27 September), replacing V. M. Molotov, who had been assigned
this post as part of his political disgrace. Khrushchev later[70] accused the Tula
leaders of the same irresponsibility that Larionov was guilty of—promising to
fulfill three years' meat plan in one—and in his 2 November 1961 speech[71] he
specifically linked the "former leaders of Ryazan and Tula oblasts" as guilty of
irresponsibility. Since the decision to exile Khvorostukhin must have been made
at least a few days before the 27 September announcement, this must have
convinced Larionov that his own exposure and disgrace were imminent. On 24
September *Pravda* announced Larionov's death on 22 September "after a serious
illness." Later it was rumored that he had committed suicide.[72]

A month later—in his 29 October 1960 Note to the Presidium—Khrushchev mentioned the rumors about fraud in Ryazan and the earlier uncompleted
attempts to check them and cautiously suggested an investigation.[73] He still
exhibited some doubts by indicating that these assertions might be just
"slander." Even later, after the investigation had revealed that the Ryazan

---

[70] In his 5 January 1961 theses, Khrushchev's collected speeches, vol. 4, p. 264.

[71] Ibid., vol. 6, p. 65.

[72] Michel Tatu, *Power in the Kremlin* (London, 1969), p. 128.

[73] Khrushchev's collected speeches, vol. 4, p. 167.

leaders had used reckless and fraudulent methods in desperately trying to fulfill their politically inspired goals, Khrushchev treated Ryazan rather gently. In his January 1961 theses he praised its raising of meat production, adding that "unfortunately" there were also "distortions," "padding," and "buying livestock on the side" to fulfill the goals. Fulfilling two years' meat plan in one year was fine, he declared, but why did the oblast leaders have to force this up to three years in one?[74]

Khrushchev also treated Tula's irresponsible leaders gently. First Secretary Khvorostukhin was compensated with a respectable ambassadorial post, even though his political career was ended. Tula's agriculture section head, V. S. Baturin, criticized for his optimism and complacency in the 8 June 1960 *Selskaya Zhizn* article, not only did not suffer but soon rose to prominent positions, apparently under Khrushchev's patronage. By early 1961 he was Tula Oblast Executive Committee chairman[75] and in early 1964, after Khrushchev appointed L. I. Maksimov minister of production and procurement of agricultural products for the RSFSR, Baturin appeared as first deputy head of this ministry.[76] He was removed immediately after Khrushchev's fall,[77] and was demoted to chief of the agriculture and procurement department of the RSFSR Gosplan.[78]

Khrushchev's reticence in condemning Ryazan probably reflected the discredit that the scandal had brought on his whole meat campaign, in which the Ryazan initiative had played such an important part.[79] The threat to his entire meat program arising from this scandal he implicitly recognized in his October 1960 Note, in which he strongly defended his assertion that the USSR did indeed have sufficient resources to produce enough meat, attacking doubters as unworthy leaders and "political bankrupts."[80] In an 11 February 1961 speech he declared: "Those people who fear big but realistic plans cannot be considered progressive and cannot successfully lead."[81]

Khrushchev's response to this setback, typically, was to go on the offensive. In his October 1960 Note he demanded exposure of those who irresponsibly accepted obligations and, warning of a crisis in meat supply, he announced a Central Committee plenum for December to discuss livestock and other agricultural matters.[82] He declared that someone needed a "good shaking" for short-

[74] Ibid., pp. 265–66.

[75] *Vedomosti Verkhovnogo Soveta RSFSR*, no. 17 (1961).

[76] First identified in the 26 April 1964 *Izvestiya*.

[77] Last identified in the 12 September 1964 *Pravda*.

[78] See his obituary in the 16 June 1970 *Sovetskaya Rossiya*.

[79] It may also be noted that the exposure of both the Tula and Ryazan leaders occurred while Khrushchev was out of the country.

[80] Khrushchev's collected speeches, vol. 4, p. 163.

[81] Ibid., vol. 5, p. 12.

[82] Ibid., vol. 4, pp. 166–67.

comings in leading agriculture in certain republics and oblasts and that some officials "should be punished and this should be publicized in the press."[83] His words were no idle threat: a campaign exposing padding began immediately. Vologda First Secretary I. S. Latunov and Lipetsk First Secretary K. P. Zhukov were replaced in November and later accused of padding, while Bryansk First Secretary A. U. Petukhov was fired in December for "big shortcomings in agricultural leadership" (*Pravda*, 14 December 1960).

The RSFSR bore the brunt of the campaign. The purge took on a massive scale in 1961 after Aristov's ouster as Khrushchev's deputy for the RSFSR, bringing dismissal of such criticized leaders as Kaluga First Secretary S. O. Postovalov, Kirov First Secretary A. P. Pchelyakov, Novgorod First Secretary V. A. Prokofyev, Pskov First Secretary M. Ya. Kannunikov, Smolensk First Secretary P. I. Doronin, Yaroslavl First Secretary B. A. Barinov, Chita First Secretary A. I. Kozlov, Omsk First Secretary Ye. P. Kolushchinskiy, Tyuman First Secretary V. V. Kosov, and several others. To indicate the purge's thrust against Aristov, all those associated closely with him were among those ousted: Chelyabinsk First Secretary N. V. Laptev, Omsk First Secretary Ye. P. Kolushchinskiy, and Penza First Secretary S. M. Butuzov.

Khrushchev in his October 1960 Note had singled out the RSFSR Bureau as an example of giving poor leadership to oblast authorities.[84] Aristov apparently had to take the blame for the Ryazan scandal, being removed as deputy chairman of the RSFSR Bureau in January 1961 and sent abroad as ambassador to Poland. Although never accused of anything publicly, he presumably was blamed for being negligent in checking on RSFSR oblast authorities, overlooking padding and fraud in Ryazan and other oblasts.[85] Thus, Khrushchev apparently made Aristov the scapegoat for not having prevented the deception of the Central Committee by Ryazan and other oblast leaders. In contrast, Polyanskiy, who as RSFSR premier and as agricultural specialist presumably shared responsibility for any RSFSR agricultural failures and in fact had gone as far as Khrushchev, if not farther, in encouraging the Ryazan initiative, did not suffer at all from the 1960 agricultural scandals. He actually gained from the exposure of padding and other shortcomings, as Khrushchev appears to have

[83] Ibid., p. 166.

[84] Ibid.

[85] Khrushchev in a 31 March 1961 Note declared that only the fact that republic central committees and the RSFSR Bureau had not organized systematic reporting on the work of obkoms "can explain the wide spread of such anti-state phenomena as padding and fraud" (ibid., vol. 5, p. 350). In a 12 March 1963 speech Khrushchev declared that the Ryazan leaders had "cleverly misled the Central Committee. This was an oversight by the Central Committee, RSFSR Bureau, and Council of Ministers RSFSR" (ibid., vol. 7, p. 482). Polyanskiy at the January 1961 plenum declared that the RSFSR Bureau, Council of Ministers, and Agriculture Ministry did not react to the signals about disorders in livestock raising in a number of oblasts, "did little checking locally, often did not see the serious omissions and clear abuses behind the general figures, and in a number of cases permitted liberalism" (Stenographic record of the January 1961 Central Committee plenum, p. 35).

dumped everything on Aristov's doorstep. At the January 1961 plenum Aristov was dismissed and Polyanskiy was given the job of scourging the RSFSR oblast secretaries. Undoubtedly the key reason Polyanskiy escaped blame was that he was on Khrushchev's side, while Aristov apparently was not.

Although few facts regarding the Larionov case were ever made public, after Khrushchev's fall the Ryazan scandal was described in literary works in thinly veiled terms. In 1965 Ryazan writer Sergey Krutilin in his novel *Lipyagi*[86] depicted the exposure of a Ryazan raykom secretary named Paramonov—who clearly was patterned on Larionov. Paramonov pledged that his rayon would fulfill three annual livestock procurement plans in one year and his initiative pleased his patron, obkom First Secretary Chetverikov (apparently patterned on Khrushchev), who offered him the job of obkom agriculture section head, a job which Paramonov declined on the grounds that he preferred to work in his own rayon. (At the December 1959 plenum Khrushchev told how he had offered Larionov a top post in Moscow but Larionov had begged off to devote himself to his beloved Ryazan Oblast—see above). But Paramonov wound up having to resort to cheating in order to fulfill his impossible procurement goal (he counted livestock bought from other rayons and butter bought in stores—just as the real-life Larionov did). Anonymous letters were sent from the rayon to higher authorities exposing this padding of the figures. At first the letters were hidden from Chetverikov, then an obkom bureau meeting had to be held to discuss the problem. "Chetverikov pretended that he knew nothing about the padding. He said: 'Create a commission—let the commission check and report to me!' He said this and then went off for a hunting vacation."[87] In the fall the commission investigated and exposed Paramonov, who was removed at an obkom bureau meeting run by Chetverikov's deputy, Kartsev. Kartsev, according to Paramonov, feared Paramonov as a potential rival for his post as deputy to Chetverikov, because Chetverikov had earlier offered him the post of agricultural leader. Paramonov could not believe that his patron would let this happen to him, but all his efforts to contact Chetverikov were in vain—Chetverikov was off on a hunting trip during the whole affair and could not be reached. (Khrushchev was off in the US during the exposure of Larionov and Larionov's case was presumably handled by the RSFSR Bureau under Khrushchev's deputy, Aristov. It might be recalled that during 1959—apparently when Khrushchev offered Larionov a high post in Moscow—Khrushchev was purging the RSFSR agricultural leaders—Aristov's associates—and seeking new, reliable leaders. In mid-1960, when Khrushchev's fortunes sank, his appointee as RSFSR Agriculture Section

---

[86] Lipyagi is the name of Krutilin's native village in Ryazan. The novel was begun in the February 1963 issue of *Druzhba Narodov* and continued in the April and May 1964 and October and November 1965 issues—however, it was only after Khrushchev's fall that the characters Paramonov–Larionov and Chetverikov–Khrushchev were introduced. The story of the scandal is included in the October 1965 installment.

[87] *Druzhba Narodov* 10 (1965): 21.

head was removed—under the personal supervision of Aristov. In January 1961 Aristov did lose his job—to Orenburg First Secretary Voronov, who like Larionov, won Khrushchev's favor by his successes as a pacesetter in agricultural production.)[88]

Even less thinly veiled is Ryazan writer Nikolay Shundik's 1968–70 novel *V Strane Sineokoy* [In the Country of the Blue Oka River], which portrays Larionov (called in the book Illarion Stepanovich Buyanov), Ryazan Oblast (called Azan Oblast), and Nikita Sergeyevich Khrushchev (called Nikanor Savelyevich Khrumin).[89] A reviewer (Vitaliy Ozerov, chief editor of *Voprosy Literatury*) wrote that "perhaps this is the first work where a writer and his heroes conduct open discussion of the question of the roots and consequences of the subjectivism and hare-brained planning (*prozhekterstvo*) decisively condemned by the October 1964 Central Committee plenum and the 23d Party Congress."[90] In Shundik's version, after the exposure of the "Ryazan miracle," Buyanov died of a heart attack, "forgotten by his high protector" Khrumin.[91]

Shundik, chief editor of *Volga*, explains in his introduction that he "happened to be a participant in these events" and "had the opportunity of closely studying the person who inspired the figure of Buyanov." As for Khrushchev-Khrumin, Shundik writes that "tactfulness and the fear of winding up at variance with the exact facts, which could cast doubt on the author's objectivity, made me change the name of the man who occupied the high responsible post."[92]

Shundik, presumably on the basis of his own personal observations and talks with other Ryazan leaders, reconstructs in detail Khrushchev's 1959 visit to Ryazan.[93] He writes that one could not understand Buyanov's actions unless one understood the role played by Khrumin during this visit—"after which the idea of fulfilling three plans in one year received unconditional support." Before committing himself to the Azan initiative, Khrumin came to personally check on Azan's ability to boost livestock production and brought his own experts from Moscow to analyze the situation. Nevertheless, he was carried away by his desire to make Azan the model for other oblasts and the force of his enthusiasm dissuaded the Azan leaders from voicing doubts. When he gave oblast First Secretary Buyanov the choice of pledging to fulfill two annual plans or three in one year, Buyanov cast aside any lingering doubts: "Three plans, Nikanor Savelyevich, three and only three! We assure you that we'll die fighting but we'll not

[88] In the 22 November 1966 *Pravda*, Krutilin wrote of a 1966 recurrence of some Paramonov methods in Ryazan and recalled that he had written the "story of the fall of our Ryazan leader Paramonov" in hopes it "would never be repeated."

[89] *Volga*, nos. 6, 7, 11 (1968); 6, 10, 11 (1969); and 3 (1970).

[90] *Voprosy Literatury* 3 (1971): 23.

[91] Ibid., p. 23.

[92] *Volga* 6 (1968): 3–4.

[93] *Volga* 6 (1968): 60–68.

let down the Central Committee, the party and you personally." Khrumin carefully covered himself though: "Just remember, dear comrades, that it was not us from Moscow forcing three plans on you, but you, you from below, persuading and assuring us!" Further, he declared that at the coming meeting, publicly "I again will advise you to take not three but two plans. Let people see that I didn't come to press and pressure you."

Shundik portrays Buyanov's subsequent anguish as Azan fulfills two plans but clearly cannot fulfill the pledged third plan without ruining its livestock economy. Eventually, he goes to Moscow to tell Khrumin, who is just back from his trip to the US[94] and is obsessed with the idea of surging ahead and catching up with US production. "Do you understand what it means in present day conditions to tell the whole world: we went overboard, we're retreating? This now, during the merciless war of prestige!" Khrumin reminds Buyanov that he had given him the choice of pledging only two plans instead of three: "But now when we've trumpeted it to the whole world, when all telescopes are trained on us, you begin to lose faith in your bulls?"[95]

Nevertheless, Buyanov's failure is also Khrumin's failure. Khrumin reminds him that when the Azan initiative started he had told Buyanov: "You know, if you lack the strength to back up your word with deeds, I will suffer no less than you, because there will be people who will wag their malicious tongues."[96] Khrumin's reaction to the failing initiative is to cover up and put up a big front. Khrumin tells Buyanov: "Don't panic. . . . The main thing is that people don't get an unhealthy attitude. Lift the feeling of prestige to the highest level. . . . We'll stick up for you. We'll protect [you] with our broad back. . . . I think this is the most proper solution."[97] Shundik describes Khrumin's thinking: "In no case permit failure, especially admission of it if it happens."[98] While henceforth prudently discouraging other oblasts from pledging three plans, Khrumin stubbornly defends Buyanov against accusations that he had gone too far and that he was presenting the hoped-for as reality.

But eventually the cover-up begins to fail and Khrumin abandons Buyanov. Buyanov goes to Moscow to get some more help for Azan's farms but, as he tells his wife: "He just wouldn't receive me. That's all. . . . It's all over with me."[99] Soon he knows he'll be fired as obkom first secretary and perhaps even expelled from the party.[100] "One hour before he was supposed to leave his post of obkom first secretary, he could not bear it, he reached for his heart and collapsed."[101]

---

[94] Here Shundik clearly deviates from the real-life facts, since Larionov was already dead when Khrushchev returned from the US in October 1960.

[95] *Volga* 10 (1969): 68.

[96] Ibid., 70.

[97] Ibid., 69.

[98] Ibid., 70.

[99] Ibid., 11 (1968): 7.

[100] Ibid., 3 (1970): 65.

[101] Ibid., 11 (1968): 5.

CHAPTER II

KHRUSHCHEV'S VICTORY: 1961

The long 1960 struggle between Khrushchev and his opponents was resolved at the beginning of 1961. Matskevich and Aristov were ousted and exiled from Moscow and Khrushchev brought in a new team to take over the Agriculture Ministry and the RSFSR Bureau.

The new team consisted of Lysenko, who had won Khrushchev's total support in late 1958 and now was promoting new techniques for virgin land farming, and a group of virgin land scientists and politicians from the Altay and Orenburg, who won Khrushchev's backing in late 1960 by their agricultural successes and their programs for changing agrotechniques. Khrushchev's most pressing problems were the virgin lands and the livestock lag and this team offered him solutions to these problems. To prevent future virgin land harvest disasters like 1959, Lysenko offered his early sowing program. To increase grain production, the Altay group offered its intertilled program, reducing the need for clean fallow and thereby increasing the amount of land available for production. To provide more fertilizer without the hard-to-get capital investments needed for massively expanding production of chemical fertilizer, Lysenko offered his system of mixing manure with earth. To provide a new breakthrough in meat production the Altay and Orenburg scientists offered new techniques for livestock raising and the intertilled system to boost fodder production and support vastly increased numbers of livestock. To raise milk production Lysenko offered his special breeding bulls to raise the fat content of milk, and Voronov promoted mechanized milking.

During 1961 this new team conducted a thorough purge of agricultural scientists and government and party officials who were unenthusiastic about these new programs. Although working well together in 1960 and early 1961, the team soon split. From this coalition, former Orenburg leader Voronov emerged strongest, even overshadowing Polyanskiy, and in the spring of 1962 the fortunes of Polyanskiy and Lysenko declined while those of Voronov and his Altay allies rose.

Khrushchev's Allies

The leading members of the new Khrushchev team were T. D. Lysenko, who became president of VASKhNIL (the Lenin Agricultural Academy), Altay First Secretary K. G. Pysin, who became first deputy minister of agriculture, and Orenburg First Secretary G. I. Voronov, who became RSFSR Bureau deputy chairman.

Lysenko had won Stalin's support in the 1930's and had virtually ruled Soviet science throughout most of Stalin's reign. After Stalin's death he began a sharp decline, finally losing his post of president of VASKhNIL in April 1956, during the de-Stalinization campaign. His dictatorship in science had been sponsored by Stalin, Premier Molotov, Malenkov, Central Committee Agriculture Secretary Andreyev, Agriculture Minister Benediktov, Central Committee Agriculture Section head Yakovlev, and others in the middle and late 1930's, and Khrushchev had no great personal interest in defending Lysenko when the tide turned against him. As Khrushchev said in an 8 April 1957 speech, "some scientists really excelled in accusing Lysenko of all sins when he was VASKhNIL president. Therefore we agreed with Lysenko when he asked to be relieved as president. They said that Lysenko had the type of character which does not tolerate disagreement, that he does not take the opinions of others into consideration, etc."[1]

Lysenko's vernalization [*yarovizatsiya*][2] program had already won strong government support in the early 1930's, while in February 1935 Stalin himself applauded Lysenko, and in June 1935 Lysenko rival N. I. Vavilov was removed as VASKhNIL president and Lysenko and two supporters (S. S. Perov and I. G. Eikhfeld) were made members of VASKhNIL.[3] When Khrushchev came to the Ukraine as first secretary in 1938, Lysenko was director of the All-Union Selection and Genetics Institute in Odessa and was a favorite adviser to Ukrainian Second Secretary Postyshev.[4] In early 1938 when Stalin proposed making Lysenko president of VASKhNIL, Lysenko sought Khrushchev's counsel.[5] He boasted of Khrushchev's support in a 1944 publication.[6]

---

[1] Khrushchev's collected speeches, vol. 2, pp. 409–10.
[2] Soaking and chilling of winter wheat seed to accelerate its rate of growth. For a fuller explanation see David Joravsky's *The Lysenko Affair* (Cambridge, 1970), pp. 191–92.
[3] Ibid., pp. 84–85, 90, 94.
[4] According to Joravsky (ibid., p. 403), who cites in particular Postyshev's tribute to Lysenko in the 15 March 1935 *Izvestiya*.
[5] Stenographic record of the March 1962 Central Committee plenum, p. 444.
[6] *Nekotoryye Voprosy Agrotekhniki Vesennego Seva* (Moscow, 1944), p. 26–cited in Joravsky, *The Lysenko Affair*, p. 403.

Nevertheless, Khrushchev also had occasional scrapes with Lysenko under Stalin, most obviously in 1947. At the February 1947 Central Committee plenum Maltsev's speech on his high yields of spring wheat in west Siberia persuaded Stalin of the advantages of spring wheat over winter wheat. Khrushchev had long assured Stalin that winter wheat was better for the Ukraine, so Stalin berated Khrushchev for this and the plenum decree condemned the Ukrainian leaders for underrating spring wheat (Khrushchev, in describing the incident in a November 1961 agricultural conference speech, noted: "It is true that my name was not cited. But everyone knowing even the slightest about the essence of the matter understood that this was directed against me personally"[7]). Khrushchev was removed as Ukrainian first secretary and Kaganovich replaced him and began promoting spring wheat. Later Khrushchev managed to partially change Stalin's mind, but Malenkov and the Central Committee Agriculture Section head A. I. Kozlov got Lysenko to write an article against winter wheat. Khrushchev said that only after Stalin's death did he learn that Lysenko had been put up to it by Malenkov and Kozlov.[8] However, Lysenko probably needed little persuading, since spring wheat was an important part of Vilyams's grassland system, which Lysenko was then enforcing on the country. Since this affair almost ended Khrushchev's career, it certainly must have soured his relations with Lysenko, but when he came to Moscow Oblast as first secretary in 1949, he again came into contact with Lysenko, who headed the Institute of Genetics and the Gorki Leninskiye Experimental Farm near Moscow.

After Stalin's death, Khrushchev, while admiring some of Lysenko's practical work (already in his September 1953 plenum report he praised Lysenko's summer potato planting method[9]), did not uphold his scientific dictatorship. He rarely had anything critical to say about Lysenko himself, although he intervened in one case in early 1954 to reverse a decision forced by Lysenko. V. S. Dmitriyev, as chief of Gosplan's agricultural planning administration, had pushed the great Stalin forest belt plan and the grassland system in 1948-49.[10] Khrushchev characterized Dmitriyev as having "brought much harm" to agriculture, fired him, and suggested he go to work in a machine-tractor station or sovkhoz. Instead, "using the patronage of Academician T. D. Lysenko," he applied for a doctorate in biology.[11] Dmitriyev, an economist, wrote a doctoral dissertation defending the Lysenkoist thesis of transformation of species (for example, that sown crops such as oats can turn into weeds). But the dissertation was not accepted after the attestation commission decided that it was methodologically faulty and that Dmitriyev's answers to their questions revealed that he had

[7]Khrushchev's collected speeches, vol. 6, pp. 57-58.
[8]Ibid.
[9]Ibid., vol. 1, p. 37.
[10]Joravsky, The Lysenko Affair, pp. 171, 298.
[11]Khrushchev's 23 February 1954 Central Committee plenum report, Khrushchev's collected speeches, vol. 1, p. 271.

"poor knowledge of elementary biological laws."[12] However, on 20 February 1954 the attestation commission met again, this time with Lysenko (who had supervised Dmitriyev's work) present. Lysenko defended the dissertation and assailed the commission members, forcing them to award Dmitriyev his doctorate.[13] Three days later, in his 23 February 1954 Central Committee plenum report, Khrushchev assailed Dmitriyev and his attempt to gain a doctorate, and, subsequently, the attestation commission met again and having received "additional material characterizing the scientific bankruptcy and incorrect research methods in this dissertation," reversed its position again and rejected Dmitriyev's work and Lysenko's appeal.[14]

At the same time, however, Lysenko scored points with Khrushchev by his aid to Khrushchev's virgin land campaign and his practical recommendations. When Khrushchev sent his 22 January 1954 Note to the Presidium proposing cultivation of the virgin lands, he appended to it a note by Lysenko on yields in the virgin lands.[15] Lysenko also wrote an article on virgin land yields in the 20 February 1954 *Izvestiya* and spoke at conferences on how to get high yields in the virgin lands (*Pravda*, 5 February and 15 April 1954).

In 1954 Khrushchev visited Lysenko's farm and was very impressed by his fertilizer work. He asked Lysenko and Moscow Oblast First Secretary Kapitonov to gather the oblast's agronomists and advise them to test Lysenko's method of fertilizing. But other scientists (especially N. Avdonin, chairman of VASKhNIL's bureau of the section for agrosoil study and agrochemistry) opposed Lysenko's fertilizer method. Khrushchev complained about the interminable theoretical disputes between Lysenko and other scientists and backed Lysenko on the basis of his supposed practical results: "I think that theoretical and scientific arguments should be resolved in the fields."[16] At a 30 March 1957 conference Khrushchev invited Lysenko to speak about his liming method and declared he would back him in the fertilizer dispute.[17] At an 8 April 1957 conference Khrushchev condemned Agriculture Minister Matskevich and Sovkhoz Minister Benediktov for not intervening in the dispute to back Lysenko.[18] In addition to praising his fertilizer mixtures, Khrushchev also cited his bull-breeding experiments.[19]

But it was in 1958 that Khrushchev's support of Lysenko became aggressive. In September 1958 the All-Union Fodder Institute was purged and Lysenko's protégé VASKhNIL Vice President M. A. Olshanskiy was made director (*Pravda*, 7 September 1958). A 14 December 1958 unsigned article in

---

[12] See the 26 March 1954 *Pravda* letter by Moscow State University Professor S. Stankov complaining of Lysenko's interference.

[13] Ibid.

[14] Note by *Pravda's* editors appended to Stankov's letter, *Pravda*, 26 March 1954.

[15] Khrushchev's collected speeches, vol. 1, p. 100.

[16] Ibid., vol. 2, p. 408.

[17] Ibid., p. 375.

[18] Ibid., p. 409.

[19] In his 3 April 1957 speech, ibid., p. 389.

Pravda attacked Lysenko's foes (V. N. Sukachev,[20] chief editor of *Botanicheskiy Zhurnal* and *Byulleten Moskovskogo Obshchestva Ispytateley Prirody*, and also N. K. Koltsov, N. P. Dubinin, and V. Koldanov) and defended his agricultural ideas (on bull breeding, intervarietal crossing, yarovization, fertilizer mixtures, and multiple planting of oak trees) and biological theories (inheritance of acquired characteristics). Lysenko received an Order of Lenin and at the 15–19 December Central Committee plenum Lysenko was given the floor to attack Academy of Sciences President A. N. Nesmeyanov and secretary of the academy's biology department, V. A. Engelgardt, for opposing the theoretical and biological theses which were the bases of his agricultural recommendations. Lysenko accused his foes of not giving farmers any practical recommendations and of preferring theories without practical applications (*Pravda*, 18 December 1958). In his concluding plenum speech Khrushchev praised Lysenko for his "remarkable" speech. By now Khrushchev was defending Lysenko's theories as well as his practical recommendations.

In January 1959 an enlarged session of the Presidium of the Academy of Sciences and its department of biology, chaired by Nesmeyanov, heard Engelgardt report and acknowledge the correctness of the December 1958 criticisms. It was reported that *Botanicheskiy Zhurnal* editor Sukachev had been replaced. Lysenko was among the speakers at the session (*Pravda*, 21 January 1959). *Pravda* on 24 January 1959 carried an attack on Engelgardt's work.

At the June 1959 Central Committee plenum Khrushchev himself directly attacked famous anti-Lysenkoist biologist N. P. Dubinin, whom he called "one of the main organizers of the struggle against the Michurinist views of Lysenko." Khrushchev declared that "if Dubinin is well known for something, it is for his articles and speeches against the theoretical theses and practical recommendations of Academician Lysenko."[21] Khrushchev then forced Dubinin's dismissal as director of the Institute of Cytology and Genetics (which Dubinin had recently founded in Novosibirsk), over the objections of Chairman of the Academy of Sciences' Siberian Department M. A. Lavrentyev.[22]

At the December 1959 Central Committee plenum Lysenko again spoke, promoting his two main projects (his fertilizer mixtures and bull-breeding work) and complaining that his foes were challenging his biological theories which were the basis for his agricultural methods. He thanked the Central Committee and Khrushchev personally for inviting him to the plenum and for support of his

[20] According to Joravsky (*The Lysenko Affair*, pp. 142, 394), Sukachev, who had opposed Lysenko's cluster planting method, had approved the 1948 state forest belt plan involving Lysenko's cluster planting of oak trees and thereby managed to keep his post as chief editor of *Botanicheskiy Zhurnal*. But after Lysenko's cluster-planted trees began failing in 1951, Sukachev was able to use his journal to initiate criticism of him in 1952, and he became the leader of the anti-Lysenkoists (ibid., p. 397).

[21] Stenographic record of the 24–29 June 1959 Central Committee plenum, pp. 466–67.

[22] *Literaturnaya Gazeta*, 24 November 1964, and V. Gubarev in *Komsomolskaya Pravda*, 27 February 1965.

biological science.[23] Khrushchev[24] and Polyanskiy[25] praised his fertilizer composts.

During 1960, as indicated in the previous chapter, Lysenko presented his early sowing program for the virgin lands. This and his bull-breeding and other programs were stubbornly resisted by Agriculture Minister Matskevich and others, further angering Khrushchev, who saw them as keys to great breakthroughs in agriculture.

The Altay group was headed by Altay First Secretary K. G. Pysin, and included Second Secretary A. V. Georgiyev, Altay Agriculture Institute director G. A. Nalivayko and deputy director F. P. Shevchenko. Pysin was a long-time associate of former Khrushchev ally N. I. Belyayev, serving as Altay Kray Executive Committee chairman 1949–55 with kray First Secretary Belyayev, and finally succeeding Belyayev as first secretary in 1955.

Shortly after becoming first secretary, Pysin picked Nalivayko, the director of a selection station in Novosibirsk, to become director of the Altay Agriculture Institute (1956).[26] The ambitious Nalivayko quickly began developing the so-called "*propashnaya sistema*" (intertilled system), using Khrushchev's favorite crop, corn, as its number one basis.[27] With hasty and unscientific experiments the Altay Institute supposedly proved that corn is superior to grass in improving soil fertility—thus making it possible to plant all clean fallow and grassland with intertilled crops. Fodder production would be boosted not only by the planting of formerly idle land but also because corn, peas, and beans would provide a higher yield of fodder units per hectare than grass or oats and would also supposedly be more nutritious. The huge growth of fodder production would make possible a great increase in the number of livestock—solving the meat problem. The higher yield of these fodder crops would mean less grazing land would be needed and a larger percentage of farmland could be used for grain crops. Instead of allowing livestock to wander and graze, they could be kept in barns and fed corn silage year round (the "untethered method"). This also would facilitate mechanization of livestock raising—one of the greatest needs of Soviet agriculture.

This great potential breakthrough for boosting meat production appeared on the scene at precisely the moment Khrushchev's frantic meat campaign was floundering in the Ryazan scandal. Khrushchev's agricultural assistant A. S. Shevchenko in his September 1960 report following his virgin land visit (*Pravda*,

[23] Stenographic record of the 22–25 December 1959 plenum, p. 332.
[24] Ibid., p. 398.
[25] Ibid., p. 12.
[26] See the 1962 yearbook of the *Bolshaya Sovetskaya Entsiklopediya* and the *Deputaty Verkhovnogo Soveta SSSR, 6. Sozyv* [Deputies of the Supreme Soviet USSR, 6th convocation], 1962.
[27] In his speech at the 22d Congress he relates how he began expanding intertilled crops already in 1956.

17, 18, 19 November 1960) praised the Altay leaders for their replacement of clean fallow with corn, and deputy director of the Altay Institute F. P. Shevchenko described the intertilled system in a 26 November 1960 *Sovetskaya Rossiya* article.

A. S. Shevchenko also praised the Altay leaders for their establishment of mechanized links with responsibility for units of land[28] and for Pysin's proposal to build more grain procurement centers. Pysin also busily turned out other proposals which caught Khrushchev's attention, urging better public catering on farms to encourage kolkhozniks and sovkhoz workers to give up private plots (*Pravda*, 30 November 1960), reorganization of crop grading work (*Selskaya Zhizn*, 21 December 1960), and improvements in the labor wage system (at the January 1961 plenum, *Pravda*, 14 January 1961). As a result, even though the Altay was having an unsuccessful harvest,[29] Pysin was able to win an important job in Moscow in the January 1961 reorganization. Pysin's colleague, Altay Kray Executive Committee Chairman S. V. Shevchenko,[30] moved to Moscow with him, becoming chief of the RSFSR Agricultural Equipment Association, when this agency was established in March 1961.

The third element in the new team was the Orenburg group, led by Orenburg First Secretary G. I. Voronov, Orenburg Meat and Dairy Livestock Raising Institute director Sh. Sh. Khayrullin and oblast Second Secretary V. A. Shurygin. Voronov had begun his career in the Siberian oblast of Chita, where he became an oblast secretary in 1939, second secretary by the end of World War II, and first secretary from 1948 to 1955. Here he met his later agricultural partner Sh. Sh. Khayrullin, head of a variety testing operation and director of a selection station. After Voronov became Chita Oblast first secretary, Khayrullin became deputy chief of the oblast agriculture administration.

In October 1954 Khrushchev visited Chita and was greatly impressed by the Chita leaders, who, he said, really "know their business" (see Khrushchev's 29 November 1954 Note to the Presidium on his trip to the Soviet Far East[31]), especially in sheep raising. Shortly afterward, Khrushchev appointed Voronov deputy minister of agriculture in charge of sheep raising,[32] and Voronov led an

[28] Altay's mechanized links with attached land were described in *Pravda* on 14 August 1960. This form of link had been first established in 1958 in Krasnodar by V. Ya. Pervitskiy and soon after in Stalingrad (see Voronov's 11 May 1969 interview in *Komsomolskaya Pravda*).

[29] At least according to a 2 November 1960 *Pravda* article by N. Karasev.

[30] Shevchenko worked as an Altay Kray secretary in the early 1950's, while Pysin was kray executive committee chairman. When Pysin became kray first secretary in 1955, Shevchenko succeeded him as executive committee chairman and worked with him for the next five years.

[31] Khrushchev's collected speeches, vol. 1, pp. 405-7.

[32] In his 18 February 1955 speech at a Ukrainian Central Committee plenum, Khrushchev declared that Voronov was to be a leading member of his new agricultural team: "Take Comrade Voronov, secretary of Chita Obkom. He knows sheep raising well. Although

agricultural delegation to New Zealand for five weeks in October-November 1956 to study that country's sheep raising. He later adopted their methods when he became Orenburg first secretary in 1957 and urged adoption of the New Zealand system for all of the Soviet Union at the January 1961 plenum.

After two years as deputy agriculture minister, Voronov left the ministry to succeed Polyanskiy as Orenburg Oblast first secretary.[33] Khrushchev was stressing the immense possibilities for sheep raising in the spacious Siberian provinces of Orenburg and Altay (in a 24 July 1956 speech at a conference of Siberian agricultural officials [34] and in a 28 July 1956 speech at a conference of Kazakh agricultural officials[35]). Voronov apparently wished to try out his livestock raising ideas by personally supervising agriculture in an important Siberian oblast, and Orenburg certainly posed an exciting challenge. As Voronov declared at the December 1958 Central Committee plenum, Orenburg was in last place in livestock production per land area (*Pravda*, 17 December 1958).

Polyanskiy, as Orenburg first secretary, wrote in October 1956 (*Kommunist*, no. 15) that Orenburg needed a new farming system and urged expansion of corn and sheep raising and specialization of some sovkhozes in meat cattle raising. Voronov came to Orenburg to implement a new system and immediately called his associate Khayrullin from Chita to become director of the Orenburg Institute of Meat and Dairy Livestock Raising. Voronov gave Khayrullin full support. As V. Malygin wrote in the 3 May 1964 *Pravda*, "from the moment of Khayrullin's appearance in Orenburg Oblast in 1957, a special fame began to be created for him as a major specialist both in questions of farming and in questions of livestock raising . . ." and "those who objected to Khayrullin were rebuked and even removed from their posts."

Khayrullin and Voronov then worked out the so-called "Orenburg system" of farming, based on early and deep plowing of fall plowland to destroy weeds and then leveling the land to preserve moisture through the winter. Weeds and lack of moisture were and are the two main scourges of virgin land farming. The system was based on their experience in Chita. Voronov's foe Professor V. Gulyayev charged in 1964 that the Orenburg system had been "imported" from Chita by Khayrullin and that especially the leveling requirement had been developed for dry, snowless Chita instead of the more snowy Orenburg (*Selskaya Zhizn*, 27 February 1964). As early as December 1957 Voronov publicly laid

---

he has no specialized education, he became so interested in sheep raising that he became a specialist in this matter. We proposed that he head the sheep raising administration in the USSR Agriculture Ministry. He gladly agreed" (ibid., vol. 2, p. 17). Voronov soon turned up as deputy agriculture minister (identified in *Izvestiya*, 18 May 1955) and chief inspector for sheep raising (identified in *Izvestiya*, 9 June 1955).

[33]Polyanskiy was elected Krasnodar Kray first secretary in March 1957 (*Pravda*, 2 March 1957), but *Pravda* apparently did not report the Orenburg plenum electing Voronov first secretary. Voronov was still identified as deputy agriculture minister in *Pravda* on 12 March.

[34]Khrushchev's collected speeches, vol. 2, p. 245.

[35]Ibid., p. 255.

out the principles of the Orenburg system (in an article in *Partiynaya Zhizn*, no. 24).

When the debate over virgin land programs developed in 1960, Voronov and Khayrullin wound up on the side of Lysenko and the Altay group. They enthusiastically backed the intertilled system[36] and, in fact, in a 22 December 1961 speech Voronov declared that the Orenburg Institute had switched to it already in 1956[37]—at the time when Nalivayko's institute first began to expand intertilled crops. Although exhibiting no enthusiasm for most of Lysenko's ideas, Voronov and Khayrullin went along with Lysenko's virgin land early sowing program[38] and winter rye campaign.[39]

But Voronov's real path to fame and political power was the successes of the Orenburgers' own system. As press attention for Ryazan faded in the late summer of 1960, Voronov's Orenburg assumed the role of a pacesetter. *Pravda* on 24 July 1960 published obligations adopted by Orenburg Oblast to produce 150 million poods of grain—as against 112 million set in the plan. Orenburg Secretary V. A. Shurygin on 17 August (*Pravda*) described the Orenburg system's advantages in accumulating moisture to fight drought and in combating weeds. A 26 August *Pravda* editorial praised the "remarkable example" of Orenburg in producing 150 million poods of grain and attributed the success to the Orenburg system. On 13 September *Pravda* lauded Orenburg's achievement in producing 160 million poods of grain—even above its pledge of 150—and on the same day carried an article by Orenburg First Secretary Voronov bragging that the Orenburg system had changed Orenburg from a "risk farming" zone to a stable harvest zone. Whereas 40-60 million poods used to be normal, wrote Voronov, the Orenburg system had made possible overfulfillment of the grain plan in each of the three years since its introduction. Voronov declared that the Orenburg system "is finding more and more adherents not only within the oblast, but also outside it."

As with Lysenko's programs and the Altay system, there were doubters who questioned whether these miracle methods had been adequately tested under scientific conditions. Voronov brushed aside such technicalities: "It is true, there are also skeptics who doubt this system of farming, declaring that the Orenburgers have no scientific experiments. In fact, in our oblast we did not organize experiments on plots of land measured in meters but conducted them on millions of hectares." This same rush to put untested ideas into large-scale use characterized Lysenko's virgin land and bull programs and the Altay intertilled system. Voronov again promoted the Orenburg system in a 4 October 1960 *Selskaya Zhizn* article.

[36] For example, Voronov's praise of Nalivayko's system at the 22d Congress (Stenographic Record of the 22d Party Congress, vol. 1, p. 367).

[37] When Polyanskiy was oblast first secretary.

[38] *Pravda*, 13 September 1960.

[39] At the January 1961 plenum Voronov reported sowing 60,000 hectares of winter rye in Orenburg.

Voronov and Khayrullin also developed their own methods of livestock raising. Voronov's proposals on livestock raising were based on borrowing foreign experience and transfering the inefficient, labor-intensive Soviet livestock raising to industrial methods. They also were based on reducing grassland and increasing corn sowing, in accordance with the intertilled system.

In Orenburg the Orenburg Meat and Dairy Cattle Raising Institute put into effect the "untethered" system of handling dairy cattle and a program for creating special meat cattle herds. These were promoted nationally by Voronov.[40] In conjunction with the untethered system, he also pushed the *yelochka* ("Christmas tree") milking machine apparatuses,[41] and later the "carousel" apparatuses.[42] Under the untethered system, cows were kept in an enclosure and foddered with silage, hay, and straw, instead of grazing on pastures.[43] Since less pasturage would be needed, it could be plowed up, reducing grass area (this fit in with the antigrassland campaign). It also required less labor and facilitated mechanization, hence reducing costs. It is the system which predominates in most of the world, especially in the US[44] —but not in the Soviet Union, where it faced great opposition. Shortly after coming to Orenburg, Khayrullin had built a barn for the untethered system (late 1957 or early 1958), but VASKhNIL had censured him for this (as Voronov complained at the January 1961 plenum).

The untethered system was designed for combination with new mechanized milking facilities, usually the "Christmas tree" milking apparatus.[45] V. Melentyev in the 5 August 1969 *Trud* wrote: "In the ideal, the 'Christmas tree' is supposed to be the final stage of the complex known by the title untethered keeping of livestock. In theory and with certain favorable conditions this in fact is an excellent combination of technology and biology." The "Christmas tree" was to be installed in the center of the barn.

Voronov also urged copying the US in creating special meat cattle herds separate from dairy cattle. This had been so successful in Orenburg that Voronov strongly argued for national adoption of it at the January 1961 plenum. In

[40] See his 4 October 1960 *Selskaya Zhizn* article and his speeches in the 14 January 1961 *Pravda* (January 1961 plenum), 13 January 1962 *Sovetskaya Rossiya*, and 7 March 1962 *Pravda* (March 1962 plenum).

[41] See his speeches in the 13 January 1962 *Sovetskaya Rossiya*, 7 March 1962 *Pravda*, and 21 November 1962 *Pravda* (November 1962 plenum).

[42] *Pravda*, 21 November 1962.

[43] The best description is by V. Melentyev in the 5 August 1969 *Trud.*

[44] According to livestock specialist I. A. Danilenko in the 10 October 1970 *Selskaya Zhizn* and V. Melentyev in the 5 August 1969 *Trud.*

[45] The Omsk Institute also developed a "carousel" milker and it was promoted in 1962 and 1963, along with the "Christmas tree," in connection with the untethered system. It had already begun to lose popularity in 1964 and the institute was attacked in 1965 for developing it—see Omsk Institute Prof. A. Malakhovskiy's article in the 22 September 1965 *Sovetskaya Rossiya* and the Party-State Control Committee's attack on the institute in the 20 June 1965 *Selskaya Zhizn.*

contrast to Voronov's other proposals, Khrushchev flatly rejected this idea (see below).

Sheep specialist Voronov had studied Western sheep raising methods during his visit to New Zealand and urged adopting these methods at the January 1961 plenum. At the beginning of 1962 the Altay Institute came up with a new method of sheep raising,[46] and Voronov immediately endorsed it and urged its wide application.[47] In late 1965 Central Committee Agriculture Section deputy head V. Pannikov declared that after only a two-month experiment and "with gross methodological errors at that," the Altay Institute had proposed keeping sheep year-round on corn silage instead of pasturing, arguing that keeping them in stalls increased weight and wool yield.[48]

When Khayrullin and Voronov got in trouble with Khrushchev in 1964, all their livestock raising methods were attacked. *Pravda's* 3 May 1964 attack on the Orenburg leaders declared that "the leadership of the oblast during the course of a number of years[49] had proclaimed about the development of meat livestock raising and sheep raising and about the introduction of new methods in these branches" but meat livestock had wound up in a "neglected" condition. *Pravda* said that their dairy cattle methods had resulted in lower milk yields and their sheep raising methods were a failure: "In Orenburg Oblast they talked much about introducing new methods of sheep raising, held seminars and reported successes in this branch. Yet the facts show that in fact the oblast did not achieve any noticeable increase in sheep raising. In the last five years wool cuttings per sheep have declined from 2.7 kilograms to 2.4 kilograms. This is less than 10 years ago."

As Voronov's and Pysin's stars rose in late 1960, manifestations of opposition to them appeared. A 2 November 1960 *Pravda* article by N. Karasev harshly attacked Altay Kray for not fulfilling its agricultural obligations, assailing kray leaders for not learning from past mistakes, lagging behind 1959, and "superficially" leading livestock raising.

There was a much more pointed attack on Voronov's close associate I. S. Pankin. Although Stalingrad (where Pankin was executive committee chairman) was praised for 1960 successes in grain growing in late 1960,[50] a *Sovetskaya Rossiya* article shortly before Pankin's January 1961 appointment as Voronov's

[46] At the March 1962 plenum Khrushchev cited and praised two recent articles in *Selskaya Zhizn* by Altay farmers telling of their new system of feeding sheep with corn silage year-round in stalls (Stenographic record of the 5–9 March 1962 Central Committee plenum, p. 32).

[47] See his speeches in the 13 January 1962 *Sovetskaya Rossiya* and 7 March 1962 *Pravda*.

[48] *Kommunist* 14 (September 1965): 34.

[49] Apparently meant to include Voronov's period as leader.

[50] For example, a 17 August *Pravda* editorial cited Stalingrad's sale of 100 million poods of grain to the state—30 million above plan—while *Selskaya Zhizn* on 13 August devoted its editorial and a full page to Stalingrad's successes.

assistant (as head of the RSFSR Bureau's Agriculture Section) attacked Pankin personally for nine years of poor agricultural leadership as Stalingrad Executive Committee chairman and expressed the "wish that certain successes at present do not turn the heads of leaders of Stalingrad and other oblasts of the southeast." This would include Voronov's own Orenburg Oblast, which lays mostly in the southeast zone and which was notable also for its successes in 1960. This article appeared on 3 January 1961—while Aristov still was deputy chairman of the RSFSR Bureau and presumably could influence the policies of the Bureau's organ, *Sovetskaya Rossiya*. A further indication that this article was considered a political attack was the firing of the chief editor of *Sovetskaya Rossiya* as soon as Voronov and Pankin took over. Editor I. S. Pustovalov had been appointed in 1958 after Aristov had succeeded Belyayev as Bureau deputy chairman and had fired Belyayev's editor.[51] Now Pustovalov was demoted to deputy editor of the monthly *Voprosy Ekonomiki* (identified in the 6 May 1962 *Moskovskaya Pravda*) and replaced by K. I. Zarodov, deputy head of the Central Committee's Agitprop Section for the RSFSR.[52] Zarodov first appeared as editor on 2 March 1961 (*Pravda*) and the 1966 yearbook of the *Bolshaya Sovetskaya Entsiklopediya* lists him as editor 1961–65.

Voronov's Rise

Voronov's successes came as Khrushchev was desperately searching for new panaceas for virgin land farming and livestock raising, and Voronov, the veteran virgin land farmer (as first secretary of Orenburg and Chita oblasts) and the livestock expert (as deputy agriculture minister in charge of sheep), was selected to replace Aristov as Khrushchev's deputy for party affairs in the whole RSFSR and to conduct Khrushchev's 1961 purge of RSFSR provincial party officials. His qualifications were excellent. In addition to probably having a tie with Polyanskiy, his predecessor as Orenburg first secretary, he was firmly backing the Altay intertilled system and Lysenko's early sowing campaign and vigorously denouncing grasslands and clean fallow. He had his own answers to agricultural problems—the Orenburg system—and a stunning record of success in both grain growing and meat production. Orenburg had overfulfilled even its high grain pledge in 1960 and also was praised by Khrushchev (at the January 1961 plenum) as one of the few areas to meet its livestock production obligations.

---

[51] On 31 May 1958 the RSFSR Bureau attacked the work of *Sovetskaya Rossiya* Chief Editor P. P. Yerofeyev and replaced him with Pustovalov (*Spravochnik Partiynogo Rabotnika* [2nd edition; 1959], pp. 496–97).

[52] Identified as a sector head in the 14 September 1958 *Trud* and as deputy head of the section in the 10 April 1958 *Leningradskaya Pravda*. In the 13 September 1958 and 29 August 1959 *Sovetskaya Rossiyas* he wrote articles on agitprop work. Zarodov's chief was RSFSR Agitprop head V. P. Moskovskiy, who succeeded him as *Sovetskaya Rossiya* editor in late 1965.

Voronov at the December 1958 plenum had noted that Orenburg was in last place in production of livestock per area, but in his 13 September 1960 *Pravda* article he reported raising meat production from earlier years' 30-40,000 tons to 165,000 tons in 1960.

In addition, Voronov had political muscle. In Orenburg he had close protégés, led by Second Secretary V. A. Shurygin, who had served as deputy to both Polyanskiy and Voronov and who succeeded Voronov as oblast first secretary in 1961. Shurygin enthusiastically pushed the Orenburg system.

Relations with the Altay leaders appear to always have been good. Voronov was an adherent of the Altay intertilled system (see his 22d Congress and 22 December 1961 speeches cited above) and Altay First Secretary Pysin talked of changing the Altay to early, deep fall plowing of fall plowland for all spring crops (*Pravda*, 14 August 1960). Even when they wound up on opposite sides of the clean fallow issue in 1964 the Altay and Orenburg scientists had nothing ill to say of each other. Pysin later (December 1964) became RSFSR first deputy premier—the top agricultural assistant to Premier Voronov. He was the only person to publicly defend the Orenburg Institute after Khrushchev's 1964 purge of its leaders (in his March 1965 plenum speech).

Voronov had friends in Stalingrad Oblast also. Long-time (1950-61) Stalingrad Executive Committee chairman I. S. Pankin had worked with Voronov in Chita in the late 1940's as oblast secretary while Voronov was second secretary. As soon as Voronov moved to Moscow in January 1961 to become deputy chairman of the RSFSR Bureau, Pankin became his chief agricultural assistant—head of the Central Committee Section for RSFSR Agriculture. A former associate of Pankin from Stalingrad, V. A. Karlov (secretary 1949-51, second secretary 1951-53), appeared at the same time as head of the Central Committee Union Republics Agriculture Section.

The Stalingrad (after the 22d Congress, renamed Volgograd) party organization had more ties to Voronov than just Pankin's presence. Stalingrad was using Orenburg's early, deep, fall-leveled fall plowland system already in 1960 (according to First Secretary A. M. Shkolnikov at the March 1962 Central Committee plenum). Shkolnikov, who became Stalingrad first secretary in November 1960, became RSFSR first deputy premier in November 1965. Thus, he and Voronov's Altay ally Pysin, who became RSFSR first deputy premier in December 1964, became Voronov's two top assistants. The Stalingrad Oblast agriculture secretary who adopted the Orenburg system in 1959-60, V. A. Belousov, was promoted to chairman of the Kursk Oblast Executive Committee in 1962 (while Voronov was RSFSR Bureau deputy chairman) and in 1964 became first deputy minister of production and procurement of agricultural products RSFSR under RSFSR Premier Voronov. Also, by coincidence, Voronov's close protégé, Shurygin, after being purged by Khrushchev in the 1964 Orenburg affair, surfaced again in 1965—as a Volgograd Oblast secretary under Shkolnikov (*Trud*, 17 September 1965).

However, Voronov by no means agreed with Khrushchev on all issues. While closely collaborating on crop policies (favoring corn, attacking the grassland system) and many livestock techniques (the untethered system and mechanized milking systems), they obviously differed over farm organizational matters (complex brigades, kolkhoz administration) and other livestock techniques (Lysenko's bull-breeding recommendations, specialized meat-cattle farms). On some issues Voronov actually stood closer to his former boss Matskevich.[53]

On organizational matters Voronov and Khrushchev differed. Voronov wrote an entire article in the 4 October 1960 *Selskaya Zhizn* attacking complex brigades as a "backward form of organization of labor" and criticizing various agricultural journals for advocating these as the basic production units for kolkhozes. The consolidation of kolkhozes had resulted in huge kolkhozes which were using complex brigades. Voronov complained that these brigades were really just the old pre-merger kolkhozes. Since kolkhozes had been merged to promote specialization and mechanization, brigades that conducted both field work and livestock raising defeated the whole purpose of kolkhoz amalgamation, according to Voronov. Indicating that complex brigades were especially bad for livestock raising, Voronov wrote that his oblast was separating farming from livestock raising and creating specialized farms (one for dairy cattle, one for meat cattle, one for sheep, one for pigs, one for poultry), each led by a specialist. Yet in his 8 March 1961 Novosibirsk speech,[54] Khrushchev praised "the new form of organization of labor—complex brigades," which, he said, had arisen in the Siberian virgin lands—because they end the separation of farming from livestock raising and carry on production of grain, fodder, milk, and meat.

Voronov carried his ideas on organization to the January 1961 plenum also, attacking the USSR and RSFSR agriculture ministries for opposing the creation of meat-cattle herds separate from dairy cattle herds—which would facilitate US-style large-scale cattle raising. He related that by separating meat cattle from dairy cattle so that meat cattle could be handled on a large scale without milking—which requires much labor—Orenburg Oblast had increased its meat herd from 4,000 in 1959 to 66,000 in 1961. He declared that "it is well known that in the US 23 million of the 44 million cattle are meat cattle" and "therefore" the US produces two and one-half times more beef than the Soviet Union.[55] He even cited Khrushchev's favorite authority, US farmer Roswell Garst, in support of meat-cattle raising.

---

[53] Through the years Voronov has consistently ignored the kolkhoz union proposals and was associated with the establishment of the kolkhoz-sovkhoz production administrations in 1962—virtually the antithesis of kolkhoz unions. He also consistently ignored Lysenko's program for raising fat content of milk by crossing cows with Jersey bulls—even though livestock specialist Voronov has frequently discussed cattle raising. Matskevich was the most outspoken foe of kolkhoz unions in 1959 and 1960 and a bitter foe of the Lysenko program, blocking it in 1960, despite Khrushchev's anger, and playing a big role in discrediting Lysenko's bull-breeding work in 1965, after Khrushchev fell.

[54] Khrushchev's collected speeches, vol. 5, p. 188.

[55] Stenographic record of the January 1961 Central Committee plenum, p. 278.

Khrushchev, in his concluding speech at the plenum, noted Voronov's proposal but disagreed with it, declaring meat herds suitable for the underpopulated US prairies but not for the USSR and declaring that the country needed more milk as well as meat.[56] Although directly opposing Voronov's long-cherished ideas, Khrushchev went out of his way to praise Orenburg's successes with livestock and personally praise Voronov, who, he said, "knows agriculture well," whom "I respect," and with whom "I basically agree." He was willing to ignore or brush aside his serious differences with Voronov, since in late 1960 and early 1961 he was more preoccupied with overthrowing those who were blocking his corn and meat programs—Matskevich and other "grasslanders"—and he saw Voronov as a valuable ally in denouncing the grasslanders and promoting the Altay program. Thus, Khrushchev selected Voronov for his new deputy for the RSFSR and to conduct the 1961 purge of RSFSR provincial party officials.

The January 1961 Plenum

Because the struggle over agricultural issues was still being resolved in December, the scheduled December 1960 Central Committee plenum was postponed until January 1961, by which time Matskevich and Aristov had clearly lost. The victory was evident in the very organization of the plenum as well as the content of the speeches. Matskevich and Aristov had no chance to speak, while Lysenko was given the opportunity of assailing Matskevich and other foes and Voronov and Pysin were given privileged positions on the agenda. Voronov was the first oblast secretary to speak (those preceding him were all republic first secretaries—except for Tselinnyy Kray First Secretary Sokolov), followed by Altay Kray First Secretary Pysin, Krasnodar Kray First Secretary Vorobyev (perhaps reflecting Polyanskiy's influence), and Stalingrad Oblast First Secretary Shkolnikov.

Voronov, who brought Khayrullin with him to the plenum, assailed the RSFSR Agriculture Ministry at length for opposing his livestock raising ideas and offered proposals from Khayrullin's institute on ways to achieve new breakthroughs in meat production. In addition to ardently pushing his controversial meat-cattle proposals, Voronov urged mechanization of livestock raising by changing to the untethered system of keeping cattle in special facilities with corn silage foddering. He told how Khayrullin had already built such a facility in 1958, but VASKhNIL had censured him for it and skeptics were still deriding the silage system. He also called for a restructuring of sheep raising—to follow the New Zealand system copied by Orenburg for the three previous years. Pysin

---

[56] Ibid., p. 586. Voronov finally had his way in 1969 when the RSFSR began a campaign to expand meat cattle. Voronov's old bailiwick of Orenburg—despite the 1964 purge of his protégés—pushed Voronov's meat-cattle program already in 1967 and in 1969 became the RSFSR's model for developing specialized meat livestock farms. Agriculture Minister Matskevich may favor meat herds now also. In 1968 he wrote a book on *Meat Livestock Raising and Raising the Santa Gertruda Breed*, which examines US meat-cattle raising (reviewed in *Ekonomika Selskogo Khozyaystva* 11 [1968]: 112).

was also full of ideas, promoting Altay's mechanized link system, intertilled system, more mechanization of dairying, etc.

Lysenko used his speech to lambast the Agriculture Ministry (Matskevich) for blocking the distribution of his bulls for raising the fat content of milk and also to promote his virgin land early sowing program—although Maltsev also was allowed to speak and cautiously defend late sowing. Lysenko concluded by claiming Khrushchev's endorsement: "I am endlessly glad that my small work has been highly valued by the party and government and Nikita Sergeyevich Khrushchev personally." Lysenko's work was lauded by Khrushchev, Polyanskiy, T. I. Sokolov, and several other speakers. Kolkhoz chairman S. K. Korotkov attacked Agriculture Ministry officials for trying to "run down" Lysenko,[57] and Rostov First Secretary A. V. Basov assailed the Agriculture Ministry for stalling Lysenko's work.[58]

The 1961 Purge

The fall of Matskevich and Aristov set off a purge of the agricultural organs, agricultural scientists, and RSFSR party apparatus and opened the way for forcing the various projects of Khrushchev, Lysenko, and the Altay-Orenburg groups on the whole country. Agriculture Minister Matskevich had been exiled to the virgin lands (as Tselinnyy Kray Executive Committee chairman) at the end of December 1960, and soon his first deputy, Ya. S. Volchenko, and deputy G. A. Borkov retired and two other deputy ministers were transferred out (P. S. Kuchumov and Ye. M. Chekmenev) as the ministry's functions were reduced. A new leadership team took over: Lysenko's close protégé M. A. Olshanskiy became minister, Altay First Secretary Pysin became first deputy minister, and Lysenko defender K. S. Nazarenko became deputy minister.[59]

The new minister, Olshanskiy, immediately ordered a go-ahead on Lysenko's bull-breeding program[60] and later (at the 22d Party Congress in late 1961) announced that Lysenko's "theory on soil nutrition of plants will be the scien-

---

[57]Stenographic record of the January 1961 Central Committee plenum, p. 303.

[58]Ibid., p. 498.

[59]In early 1964 *Komsomolskaya Pravda* writer A. Z. Ivashchenko attempted to promote a seed-treatment method rejected by Lysenko. Nazarenko angrily called a meeting of the Agriculture Ministry's collegium to condemn Ivashchenko and to dissolve *Komsomolskaya Pravda*'s rural department (see A. Strelyanyy in the October 1966 *Sovetskaya Pechat*, p. 56). At this 24 July 1964 meeting Nazarenko assailed *Komsomolskaya Pravda* for "defaming" Lysenko and for suggesting a seed-treatment method contrary to Lysenko's theory of lack of intravarietal struggle. Immediately after Khrushchev's fall, *Komsomolskaya Pravda* (19 November 1964) attacked Nazarenko for his enthusiastic defense of the "Lysenko cult." Nazarenko had been chairman of the State Commission for Testing Varieties prior to becoming deputy minister in 1961.

[60]On 5 January 1961 the ministry issued an order "On the Work Experience of the Gorki Leninskiye Experimental Farm in Raising the Fat Content of Milk of Cows" (*Vestnik Akademii Nauk SSSR*, no. 11 [1965]). This is Lysenko's farm.

tific basis for the new systems of farming."[61] The introduction of Lysenko's programs was facilitated also by the appointment of Lysenkoist P. I. Kralin as chief of the ministry's section for mass production experiments.[62] Khrushchev even proposed moving the Agriculture Ministry to Lysenko's farm near Moscow.[63]

Lysenko became dominant again in agricultural science. By February 1961 VASKhNIL President P. P. Lobanov (who agreed more with Matskevich) was named Gosplan deputy chairman, leaving the VASKhNIL post vacant. Lysenko assumed the post of VASKhNIL president in August. Even the Academy of Sciences President, anti-Lysenkoist A. N. Nesmeyanov, was replaced after Lysenko attacked him at the January 1961 plenum for attributing inheritance to DNA. Lysenko was free to move against scientists who fought his biological and agricultural theories—such as Leningrad Plant Growing Institute director P. M. Zhukovskiy,[64] who was shortly replaced by a Lysenkoist (I. A. Sizov). Only weeks after Lysenko's protégé, Olshanskiy, became agriculture minister, the ministry took action against Lysenko's main virgin land foe Barayev. In March 1961 Barayev's institute was reorganized and subordinated to VASKhNIL, of which Lysenko himself soon became president. Altay agricultural scientist M. Lisavenko even proposed that the new party program[65] itself declare Lysenko's Michurinism dominant in biology (*Pravda*, 14 September 1961).

With Pysin's rise to first deputy minister, the Altay and Orenburg programs also became officially approved. The Agriculture Ministry and scientists were criticized for recommending wrong fodder and tethering of cows. The deputy minister in charge of livestock, Ye. M. Chekmenev, was transferred out of the ministry, and the director of the Institute for Livestock Raising, N. M. Burlakov, was assailed by Khrushchev.[66] In an 11 February 1961 speech Khrushchev declared that "some sort of devil has misled some of our institutes" in designing livestock facilities,[67] and he later blamed the Agriculture Ministry for

[61] Stenographic record of the 22d Party Congress, vol. 2, p. 540.

[62] Kralin was so identified in the 19 November 1964 *Komsomolskaya Pravda*, which quoted from his report on the results of carrying out Lysenko's winter rye program in Siberia. Kralin was a leading promoter of early sowing—see Lysenko in the 28 April 1961 *Pravda* and Khayrullin in the 21 February 1964 *Selskaya Zhizn.*

[63] It was, in fact, moved to a sovkhoz instead (according to Olshanskiy at the 22d Party Congress).

[64] A 16 March 1961 *Trud* article declared that under Zhukovskiy at the institute "leading scientists and passionate advocates of the Michurinist movement in science are being kicked out of leading posts and from the scientific council under all kinds of pretexts." Zhukovskiy had infuriated Lysenko by refuting Lysenko's theory of lack of intravarietal struggle when Lysenko first brought out this theory in 1945 (see Zh. A. Medvedev, "Biological Science and the Cult of Personality," *Grani* 71 [1969] : 94–95).

[65] The party program was to be adopted at the October 1961 22d Party Congress.

[66] Chekmenev was criticized in an 8 March 1961 speech (Khrushchev's collected speeches, vol. 5, p. 179) and Burlakov was attacked in Khrushchev's January 1961 plenum speech (Stenographic record of the January 1961 plenum, p. 536).

[67] Khrushchev's collected speeches, vol. 5, p. 31.

"poorly leading the work of research institutes."[68] Voronov's livestock program (based on the work of the Orenburg and Altay institutes) was enforced to such a degree that Gosstroy (the State Committee for Construction Affairs) even forbad the building of barns where cows were tethered.[69] The switch to intensive livestock raising also brought the promotion of mechanized milking facilities—large "carousel" and "Christmas tree" apparatuses—which later turned out to be a fiasco.

Altay scientist Nalivayko became the nationwide authority on corn and the evils of the grassland system and his recommendations were propagated by Khrushchev. Even Maltsev was forced to study corn, and Barayev, according to the 26 January 1962 *Selskaya Zhizn*, had agreed to begin elimination of clean fallow and to switch eventually to occupied fallow.[70] The Altay Kray Agriculture Administration was moved to Nalivayko's institute and Nalivayko's deputy, F. P. Shevchenko, became its chief. The imposition of Nalivayko's system in the Altay and Khayrullin's in Orenburg were favorably publicized (later both were accused of forcing stereotyped programs on the farmers of their regions). Nalivayko and Khayrullin both were awarded the titles of Heroes of Socialist Labor (as Larionov had been in 1959).

Meanwhile, Voronov and Polyanskiy began purging the RSFSR government and party apparatus. At the January 1961 plenum Polyanskiy berated numerous RSFSR oblast leaders for agricultural deficiencies. At the plenum Voronov was elected a Presidium candidate member and shortly afterward (by late January) received Aristov's job of RSFSR Bureau deputy chairman and proceeded to purge the grasslanders and Aristov supporters in the RSFSR.

Those apparently associated with Aristov and his allies were purged from the RSFSR Agriculture Ministry and sent off to the provinces. Minister G. L. Smirnov[71] was sent to become executive committee chairman in Penza Oblast, where First Secretary S. M. Butuzov, an Aristov associate,[72] was under attack and soon removed. Deputy Minister S. S. Nikulin, who had been chief of the Moscow Oblast Agriculture Administration in March 1959 under oblast First Secretary Kapitonov, became Lipetsk Oblast Executive Committee chairman,

---

[68] His 2 March 1961 speech, ibid., p. 133.

[69] According to Shkolnikov at the March 1965 Central Committee plenum.

[70] According to Kunayev at the March 1965 Central Committee plenum, it was proposed to expel Barayev from the party because of his insistence on large-scale clean fallow.

[71] Smirnov was attacked in the press along with Matskevich—by V. Ovechkin in the 23–24 November 1960 *Selskaya Zhizn*—and was released on 27 January 1961 (*Vedomosti Verkhovnogo Soveta RSFSR* 4 [1961]: 81).

[72] Butuzov was Krasnoyarsk city secretary in the late 1940's under kray First Secretary Aristov and succeeded Aristov as kray first secretary in 1950. He was Penza first secretary in 1953–61. A 10 March 1961 *Pravda* article attacked Butuzov, Oblast Agriculture Secretary A. P. Rubtsov, and Executive Committee Chairman V. I. Pishchulin for not improving agricultural leadership. Butuzov was removed in August (*Sovetskaya Rossiya*, 15 August 1961).

while Deputy Minister A. V. Kardapoltsev, a protégé of Aristov,[73] was sent back to Chelyabinsk as oblast executive committee chairman, replacing another Aristov associate. Nikulin returned to Moscow within a few months, becoming deputy head of the new RSFSR Ministry for Production and Procurement of Agricultural Products when it was established in the spring of 1962. Kardapoltsev returned only after Khrushchev's fall, when he became Matskevich's deputy in the USSR Agriculture Ministry. The new RSFSR minister, V. P. Sotnikov, and his new deputy, I. I. Sinyagin, were both from VASKhNIL's Institute for Fertilizer and Agrosoil Study. Sotnikov had a reputation for being a Lysenkoist (see next chapter).

In the months following the January 1961 plenum, about two dozen new RSFSR regional first secretaries were appointed, about one-third of the total number. As Khrushchev said in his 31 March 1961 Note,[74] many oblast first secretaries "still have not really undertaken to study the economics and techniques of agricultural production" and "in this respect perhaps the greatest weakness of cadres" was in some parts of the RSFSR.

Chelyabinsk, an Aristov stronghold,[75] was one of the first regions to be purged after Aristov's fall: oblast First Secretary N. V. Laptev and Executive Committee Chairman G. A. Bezdomov—both Aristov associates[76]—were replaced by other Aristov associates who were being exiled from Moscow (Kardapoltsev from the RSFSR Agriculture Ministry as new executive committee chairman and M. T. Yefremov, RSFSR cadres chief under Aristov 1959–61, as new first secretary).[77] Voronov's assistant, Pankin, removed Aristov protégé Ye. P. Kolushchinskiy as Omsk first secretary in August 1961.

[73] In 1951 he was promoted to first deputy chief of the Chelyabinsk Agriculture Administration under oblast First Secretary Aristov, later becoming chief and then (1959) obkom secretary under Aristov's successor N. V. Laptev. Since he still was identified as Chelyabinsk secretary in the 30 December 1959 *Izvestiya*, his appointment as deputy agriculture minister occurred during 1960.

[74] Khrushchev's collected speeches, vol. 5, p. 314.

[75] Aristov was first secretary 1950–52.

[76] Laptev became Chelyabinsk city secretary, then oblast secretary in 1951 and succeeded Aristov as oblast first secretary in 1952. Bezdomov served as executive committee chairman under Aristov.

[77] Apparently the occasion for the Chelyabinsk purge was the revelation of housing scandals in Chelyabinsk city. A 1 February 1961 *Izvestiya* article by I. Drozdov exposed this fraud, initiated and led by city First Secretary K. N. Voronin and Executive Committee Chairman M. D. Zakharov. On 3 March 1961 *Izvestiya* reported that the Chelyabinsk Obkom Bureau had discussed the article and criticized oblast Executive Committee Chairman Bezdomov for not checking more carefully and stopping the fraud. *Pravda* on 30 March 1961 indicated that the Central Committee had adopted a decree "On Cases of Padding and Deception of the State in Housing Construction in the City of Chelyabinsk," pointing out these "criminal and antiparty" actions to the obkom bureau. Deputy head of the Central Committee's Party Organs Section for Union Republics P. F. Pigalev was sent to Chelyabinsk to supervise the removal and expulsion from the party of city Secretary Voronin at a plenum addressed by M. T. Yefremov, who had been elected obkom first secretary on 16 March 1961.

Khrushchev, Polyanskiy, and Voronov began campaigning throughout the RSFSR against clean fallow, oats, and grasses, and the RSFSR Bureau (Chairman Khrushchev, Deputy Chairman Voronov) and the RSFSR Council of Ministers (Premier Polyanskiy) adopted decisions to totally liquidate clean fallow in some areas (*Pravda*, 22 December 1961). Khrushchev declared that "he who takes a conservative position in respect to corn can be thrown out of the saddle by life."[78] At the 22d Congress he stated that it is "necessary to replace those officials who . . . do not give corn the opportunity of developing to its full strength."[79]

Voronov also used his new power to strike at his own foes. In a 13 September 1960 *Pravda* article he had attacked the Saratov scientists for disparaging his Orenburg system. After he became deputy chairman of the RSFSR Bureau, the Bureau's organ *Sovetskaya Rossiya* carried articles praising the Orenburg system and attacking the Saratov Institute for Agriculture in the Southeast for sticking to the backward system of cloddy winter fallow, which was labeled part of the grassland system (28 March 1961 and 24 December 1961). At the 22d Congress he plugged his Orenburg system, praised Khayrullin, and assailed the Saratov Institute as separated from life and for making wrong recommendations (late fall plowing and unevened, lumpy fall plowland). Saratov Institute director P. G. Kabanov was forced to declare his institute's views erroneous (*Sovetskaya Rossiya*, 24 December 1961), and in response to the criticisms, Saratov First Secretary A. I. Shibayev had to attack his oblast's institute at the March 1962 Central Committee plenum. Voronov did an effective job of purging the RSFSR and propagandizing Khrushchev's policies: at the conclusion of the October 1961 party congress he was promoted from candidate member to full member of the Presidium and from RSFSR Bureau deputy chairman to first deputy chairman.

[78] His 2 March 1961 speech, Khrushchev's collected speeches, vol. 5, p. 122.
[79] Ibid., vol. 6, p. 26.

CHAPTER III

KHRUSHCHEV GROUP SPLITS: 1961-1962

The alliance between Lysenko and the Altay-Orenburg group broke up in early 1962, with Lysenko going into decline and Voronov and Pysin becoming the dominant forces. The reasons for Lysenko's decline lay in the failure of his virgin land proposals and in the mounting antigrassland campaign.

As Lysenko rose to power again in 1961 and began purging his foes and forcing his ideas on agriculture and science, his opponents fought back, trying to drive a wedge between him and Khrushchev by raising his past responsibility for Stalin-era crimes and suppression of corn and for forcing the grassland system on the country. Although Lysenko now had renounced Vilyams's grassland system and embraced corn, the antigrassland campaign put him and his followers at a disadvantage. Even though Khrushchev excused Lysenko's past and attempted to place responsibility for Stalin-era suppression of corn and of various scientists on Vilyams, many Lysenkoists aroused Khrushchev's anger by their slowness in changing to corn.

The Voronov–Pysin group, which had no enthusiasm for Lysenko in the first place, spearheaded Khrushchev's antigrassland campaign and managed to channel it against Lysenko and some of his allies. Finally, in April 1962, Pysin replaced Olshanskiy as agriculture minister and supervised Lysenko's resignation as VASKhNIL president. At the same time, Voronov was displacing Lysenko-enthusiast Polyanskiy as the most influential agricultural leader. Nevertheless, while Khrushchev apparently found it necessary to rely more on his corn enthusiasts than on Lysenko, Lysenko continued in his good graces, and when his scientific foes attempted to take advantage of his April 1962 decline, Khrushchev sprang to his defense.

Lysenko under Attack

Despite Khrushchev's clear support of Lysenko, Lysenko's foes in 1961 and 1962 attempted to appeal to Khrushchev against him by recalling his leading role in suppressing scientists and blocking Khrushchev's ideas under Stalin. At the very time that Lysenko was becoming president of VASKhNIL (August 1961), *Novyy Mir* (no. 8) carried a long article by anti-Lysenkoist publicist Mark Popovskiy, raising the question of why corn research had been suppressed under Stalin. Popovskiy cited Khrushchev's agricultural adviser, A. S. Shevchenko, who in his 1960 book on corn declared that livestock had made no progress for fifteen to twenty years prior to the September 1953 Central Committee plenum, because of lack of fodder which corn could have provided. Although the article did not name Lysenko, it traced the struggle of his foes to develop corn and their suppression (by Lysenko). It also glorified Khrushchev's role as the stubborn defender of corn (against Lysenko).

The article related how Lysenko's arch-rival and victim, N. I. Vavilov, and his colleagues had carried on hybrid corn research, and by the early 1930's when their corn developments were almost ready to introduce into Soviet agriculture, a "group of biologists" attacked corn hybrid work and managed to get all support for such research stopped. (Vavilov's self-pollination of corn was violently opposed by Lysenko, who insisted that only Darwinian cross-pollination was worth while.)[1] Vavilov was eventually arrested in 1940 and died in a Saratov prison in 1943.

After Vavilov's fall, however, his pupils carried on his work and were also persecuted by Lysenko. Popovskiy related Vavilov pupil B. P. Sokolov's story of how, at a September 1940 Kiev conference on corn raising, one person "not very literate in biology" attacked Sokolov's work on corn hybrids. Sokolov tells how he and other scientists would not have been able to keep up corn hybrid work if corn had not had "one great and sincere friend"—then Ukrainian First Secretary Khrushchev—who defended Sokolov's work. "Even then," says Sokolov, "corn was his favorite crop" and "hybrids also interested Khrushchev." Khrushchev often called Sokolov and others to Kiev for advice on corn.[2] But in September 1948, after Lysenko's crushing triumph at the August 1948 VASKhNIL session,

[1] Joravsky (*The Lysenko Affair* [Cambridge, 1970], pp. 282–87, 434) argues that Lysenko's attack on inbred corn hybrids occurred only after the government had already soured on them and therefore Lysenko was only partly responsible for suppressing corn hybrid work. A big drive to expand corn (even in the north—for half-ripe ears and stalks to use as livestock fodder) began in 1930 and continued through 1933. It failed because of the lack of fertilizer (the hybrids drained the soil of nutrients faster than other corn and expensive mineral fertilizer was a necessity), because of the need to buy seed anew each year (the farmers could not raise their own seed since the inbred hybrids degenerated after the first generation and special seed growing farms were needed to prepare the seed), and because of the backwardness of Soviet farms. As a result, corn hybrid work was sharply cut back in 1934. Lysenko's first attack on inbred hybrids (wheat, later corn) was in the 15 July 1935 *Izvestiya*.

[2] In the midst of another Lysenkoist resurgence at the February 1964 plenum, Sokolov incongruously recalled Khrushchev's support of hybrid corn at the 1940 Kiev conference. He called Khrushchev "the first convinced champion of the introduction of corn hybrids into production" (Stenographic record of the February 1964 Central Committee plenum, p. 354).

Sokolov, then working in Dnepropetrovsk's Sinelnikovo Selection Station, was ordered by the local scientific council to stop work on self-pollinated corn hybrids.

Popovskiy related how Khrushchev himself attempted to convince agricultural authorities of the advantages of hybrid corn in 1952 and how it was rehabilitated at the September 1953 plenum when Khrushchev became first secretary and delivered his condemnation of agricultural neglect under Stalin. A 1 March 1956 government decree expanded the sowing of hybrid corn and an All-Union Scientific Research Institute for Corn (based on the old Sinelnikovo Selection Station) was established in Dnepropetrovsk—the "corn center of the Soviet Union"—at a meeting attended by Agriculture Minister Matskevich and Deputy Premier Lobanov (*Pravda*, 29 March 1956). Only days later (*Pravda*, 10 April 1956) Lysenko was replaced as president of VASKhNIL by Lobanov. Vavilov was posthumously rehabilitated starting in September 1955.[3]

Popovskiy repeated his story after Khrushchev's fall—but then, of course, directly naming Lysenko as the culprit (*Sovetskaya Rossiya*, 27 November 1964 and 4 February 1965). *Literaturnaya Gazeta* on 20 July 1965 reported that Popovskiy was writing a book on Lysenko and Vavilov—but the book has never appeared, probably due to the clamp-down on anti-Lysenko writings later in 1965. Popovskiy did, however, manage to relate his fascinating story of Lysenko's persecution and destruction of Vavilov in the unorthodox Kazakh literary journal *Prostor* ("The 1,000 Days of Academician Vavilov," nos. 7 and 8 [1966]).

Popovskiy's daring 1961 article was followed by a direct attack, which, however, was not published. A devastating and well-documented article by biologist Zhores A. Medvedev entitled "Biological Science and the Cult of Personality," was written and circulated in 1962. Though not published, it eventually found its way abroad and was printed in 1969.[4]

Not only does Medvedev document the viciousness of Lysenko and his philosopher-partner I. I. Prezent (they denounced their foes in VASKhNIL as "enemies of the people" and "Trotskyite bandits"), but, like Popovskiy, he also

---

[3] Zh. A. Medvedev, *The Rise and Fall of T. D. Lysenko* (New York: Columbia University Press, 1969), pp. 72-73.

[4] The émigré journal *Grani* published the 1962 manuscripts in issues no. 70 and 71 (February and May 1969). I. M. Lerner collected these manuscripts, plus additions written in 1963 and 1964 and also in 1966 and 1967, and published them in English in book form as *The Rise and Fall of T. D. Lysenko* (New York: Columbia University Press, 1969). While Lerner's collection is more complete and updated, he unfortunately excluded some important parts included in the *Grani* versions, especially those relating to Vilyams and the grassland system.

Medvedev received help from a large number of top Soviet scientists and cross-checked his own knowledge as an insider in these scientific disputes with that of other participants, producing one of the most remarkable exposés of Soviet politics, as well as science, ever to appear. Medvedev worked at the Timiryazev Agricultural Academy for several years after World War II and observed the purges and disputes at first hand. His anti-Lysenko writings

dwells on Lysenko's past suppression of corn and opposition to Khrushchev. He wrote that Lysenko's foe Vavilov shortly before his arrest was urging expansion of corn sowing, but that this was prevented for fifteen years. While the development of hybrid corn by self-pollination resulted in a 20-30 percent increase in US corn yield, the Soviet Union was denied these advances by Lysenko, Prezent, and Olshanskiy. Hybrid corn was only legalized in 1955—upon Khrushchev's initiative.

Medvedev even suggests that efforts by Khrushchev to defend Vavilov and overthrow Lysenko were the immediate cause for Lysenko engineering Vavilov's arrest in 1940. Medvedev points out that Vavilov's August 1940 arrest—while on a field trip in the west Ukraine—was organized hastily only a few days before Vavilov was scheduled to visit Kiev for a long talk with Khrushchev—a talk requested by Khrushchev. The following month, as Popovskiy's article had pointed out, Khrushchev at a September 1940 Kiev corn conference threatened hybrid corn foes when they attacked Vavilov's pupil, Sokolov. Medvedev writes: "We think that this hasty arrest was caused by the fact that someone was striving to prevent this meeting [with Khrushchev] out of concern that it could facilitate a normalization of the situation in biology and agricultural science."

Vavilov's arrest followed a hostile private talk between Lysenko and Vavilov, during which Vavilov told-off Lysenko: "I told him to his face everything that I think of him" (Medvedev quoting Vavilov's remark to a friend afterward[5]). Medvedev relates later incidents where Lysenko and his partner Prezent (whom Medvedev labels a "gangster in science" for his especially vile role), apparently because of guilty consciences, denied having arranged Vavilov's arrest[6] or his death (at a 1956 VASKhNIL session Prezent, for no apparent reason, shouted during a debate: "We didn't kill Vavilov. Neither I nor Academician Lysenko killed Vavilov"[7]).

Lysenko, Vavilov's superior as VASKhNIL president in the late 1930's, had forced the appointment of Shundenko, a NKVD agent and Lysenkoist, as deputy director of Vavilov's Plant Growing Institute over Vavilov's objections.[8] Shundenko, as Lysenko's agent, attempted to obstruct Vavilov's work and force his resignation as director of the institute. Shundenko failed in this endeavor and in 1940 returned to the NKVD, becoming "leader of the agricultural section of the NKVD" and head of an NKVD investigation of Vavilov.[9] Shortly after

---

resulted in his leaving Timiryazev in 1962 and moving to Kaluga to head a molecular radiology lab in the more favorable atmosphere of the Institute of Medical Radiology at Obninsk. His father had been arrested in 1938 and died in a concentration camp in 1941.

[5] Medvedev, *Rise and Fall of Lysenko*, p. 152.

[6] Ibid., p. 161.

[7] Ibid., p. 159.

[8] Ibid., p. 56.

[9] Ibid., p. 262. Medvedev added this information to his manuscripts in 1967. When the Vavilov family initiated a review of the Vavilov case for rehabilitation in 1954-55 the NKVD files on Vavilov were made available and it was possible to determine who had

Shundenko's return, Vavilov was arrested and a number of agricultural scientists were called upon to back up the charges of "wrecking" against him. These included Lysenkoists such as I. V. Yakushkin, Vodkov, Lysenko's deputy in VASKhNIL V. P. Mosolov, and others, many of whom were also NKVD agents, according to Medvedev.[10] In July 1941 the military collegium of the Supreme Court sentenced Vavilov to death for spying, sabotage, leading a rightist conspiracy, etc. Later the sentence was commuted to ten years, but Vavilov died in prison in January 1943.

Grasslander Vilyams's arch-rival, D. N. Pryanishnikov, was close to Vavilov (who had been a protégé of Pryanishnikov at the Timiryazev Academy[11]) and after Vavilov's arrest daringly went to Beriya and appealed for Vavilov's release, personally guaranteeing Vavilov's innocence. In 1941—while Vavilov was languishing in prison—Pryanishnikov impudently nominated him for a Stalin prize.[12] Medvedev reports that in August–September 1941 Vavilov's prison treatment improved, apparently through Pryanishnikov's indirect influence on Beriya. Beriya's wife was a student of Pryanishnikov and worked in Pryanishnikov's department until 1953.[13]

Medvedev portrays Lysenko not only as an ally of Vilyams during the 1930's but as chiefly responsible for forcing Vilyams's grassland system on the whole country after 1948 and for purging Vilyams's opponents. He asserts that there always was a "close connection between the scientific schools of Lysenko and Vilyams" and that the two schools rose to dominance together. He quotes Lysenko's own statement that "the teachings of Michurin and the teachings of Vilyams are different sides of one materialist biology, which is working out theoretical questions of agroscience and practise."[14] Medvedev declares that Vilyams was one of the few scientists to side with Lysenko in the mid-1930's and tells how Vilyams sent special messages supporting Lysenko to the 1936–37 VASKhNIL sessions debating genetics and Michurinism (Vilyams was apparently too sick to attend in person). Medvedev says that Vilyams "happily contributed his bit to the debate on genetics questions, although he had not the foggiest notions of the essence of the disagreements."[15]

Vilyams died in 1939 and obviously had nothing to do with later imposition of the grassland system. His grassland system, imposed in 1937, was forgotten during World War II, when the country was more interested in immediate

---

participated in the case against Vavilov. Popovskiy was among those who studied the accusations against Vavilov. Among the documents was a letter from Beriya to Molotov asking permission to arrest Vavilov (ibid., pp. 71–73, 262–63). Molotov, then in charge of science in the Politburo and long hostile to Vavilov, undoubtedly was happy to comply.

[10] Ibid., pp. 72 and 262.

[11] Ibid., p. 38.

[12] Medvedev's article in *Grani* 71 (1969): 88.

[13] Medvedev, *Rise and Fall of Lysenko*, p. 73.

[14] Medvedev's article in *Grani*, no. 71, p. 78.

[15] Ibid., pp. 78, 87.

grain production than in long-term improvement of soil structure.[16] His foe Pryanishnikov gained acceptance in the meantime and Vilyams's ideas were imposed only in some places.[17] But his system was revived at the August 1948 VASKhNIL session, at which Lysenko declared Vilyams one of the founders of Michurinist agrobiological science.[18] Shortly afterward, Lysenko attacked Pryanishnikov's orientation toward chemical fertilizer.[19] Medvedev states that the "scientifically bankrupt Vilyamsism preserved its influence in agronomy only as an appendage of Lysenkoism and as such was isolated from criticism."[20]

Shortly after the August VASKhNIL session the Council of Ministers and Central Committee issued a 24 October 1948 decree "On the plan for protective forest belts, introduction of grassland crop rotations, and construction of ponds and reservoirs for ensuring high and stable harvests in the steppe and forest-steppe regions of the European part of the USSR," which, according to the *Bolshaya Sovetskaya Entsiklopediya* (vol. 8, p. 84), was based on the "basic propositions of the grassland system of farming."

Stalin's 1948 "plan for transformation of nature" by planting vast forest belts was part of the grassland system, and the trees were planted using the nest or cluster method developed by Lysenko.[21] According to Lysenko's theory of "self-thining," trees planted in clusters would arrive at the proper spacing themselves. Instead of competing for nutrition, some seeds would voluntarily die out, sacrificing themselves for the sake of the other seeds in the interest of preservation of the species. According to Lysenko, competition took place only between species, not within. In fact, this self-thining did not work and the overcrowded seeds died.[22] This fiasco discredited the forest belt campaign and the massive tree planting—disliked by Khrushchev[23]—lost government support, and was

---

[16] Ibid., p. 92.

[17] Ibid., p. 118. Joravskiy (*The Lysenko Affair*, pp. 131, 391), on the other hand, writes that there was a resurgence of the grassland system immediately after the war and notes that the twenty-one official decrees backing the system in 1945 were the most in any year except 1949.

[18] Medvedev's article in *Grani*, no. 71, pp. 83, 122.

[19] Ibid., p. 128.

[20] Ibid., p. 133. Medvedev is not the only source for the Lysenko-Vilyams tie. The *Bolshaya Sovetskaya Entsiklopediya* (vol. 8, p. 84), issued in 1951, declared that the "agronomical teachings of Vilyams are a composite part of Michurinist agrobiological science successfully developed by Soviet scientists headed by Academician T. D. Lysenko." I. I. Sinyagin, writing on Vilyams in the 2 March 1966 *Leninskoye Znamya*, declared that the grassland system was made the basis of the state plan for development of agriculture in 1948.

[21] Cluster planting also had. the big advantage of being the cheapest method (Joravsky, *The Lysenko Affair*, p. 141).

[22] Medvedev's article in *Grani*, no. 71, p. 149.

[23] See his March 1962 plenum speech, Khrushchev's collected speeches, vol. 6, p. 388.

allowed to dwindle after Stalin's death.[24] This failure also undermined Lysenko's position and opened the door for criticism of him in Sukachev's *Botanicheskiy Zhurnal* in 1952.[25] By 1952 there were rumors circulating that half the trees planted by his cluster method had died, and in an 8 January 1952 *Sotsialisticheskoye Zemledeliye* article Lysenko protégé Olshanskiy cryptically conceded failings, but blamed farmers for sloppiness in planting and attacked Sukachev, who apparently had headed an investigation of the tree plantings.[26] According to a later speech by Sukachev (printed in *Vestnik Akademii Nauk SSSR*, no. 3 [1965][27]), by 1956 only 4.3 percent of the trees planted from 1948 to 1953 had survived. After Lysenko's position had weakened in the mid-1950's, his foes brought these facts out in public. V. Koldanov in the May 1958 *Botanicheskiy Zhurnal* claimed his tree planting method had caused a one billion ruble loss. Koldanov was bitterly attacked for this statement in *Pravda's* 14 December 1958 editorial reviving Lysenkoism. During the anti-Lysenko resurgence in 1963 and 1964, the anti-Lysenkoists "slandered" his nest planting of trees and his forestation work—according to Olshanskiy's 29 August 1964 *Selskaya Zhizn* article, which declared these tree planting methods to be a success.

The nest planting method is another example of Khrushchev's curious attitude toward Lysenko. Although apparently cutting off support for the program after Stalin's death and declaring in a 21 March 1961 speech that "we wasted very much money on forest belts,"[28] Khrushchev nevertheless (in the very same speech) praised the trees planted by his method as "developing well."

Vilyams's system thus was forced on the country in late 1948 by the Lysenkoists. Immediately after the August 1948 VASKhNIL session, according to Medvedev,[29] 3,000 scientists were fired or demoted and the foes of Vilyams were purged, along with the anti-Lysenkoists. Pryanishnikov conveniently died in 1948.

The Presidium of VASKhNIL at the end of 1948 appointed a special commission to investigate the All-Union Fertilizer Institute, which had been founded by Pryanishnikov. The commission was packed with Vilyams adherents, including his son V. V. Vilyams.[30] On the basis of its report, the "Pryanishnikovtsi" were purged from the institute for opposing Vilyams's ideas, as well as

[24] See forester I. Yermolenko's 17 May 1969 *Sovetskaya Rossiya* article.

[25] Issue no. 6 (Joravsky, *The Lysenko Affair*, p. 397).

[26] According to Joravsky (pp. 154, 397). Joravsky also reports that in April 1952 an Agriculture Ministry order recommended alternative planting methods instead of just Lysenko's (*Sotsialisticheskoye Zemledeliye*, 2 April 1952).

[27] As quoted by M. D. Golubovskiy in *Biologiya v Shkole*, no. 4 (1965).

[28] Khrushchev's collected speeches, vol. 5, p. 300.

[29] Medvedev's article in *Grani*, no. 71, p. 93.

[30] Ibid., p. 125.

for opposing Lysenko's fertilizer mixtures and plant nutrition theory.[31] Its director, N. S. Avdonin, was fired. At least one Pryanishnikov adherent, Professor Diskussar—who was fired by later RSFSR Agriculture Minister Sotnikov—was arrested.

The commission's report was kept secret and was only "accidentally extracted from the archive of the president of VASKhNIL" in 1957[32]—i.e., after Lysenko had been replaced as president in 1956. It was read at a December 1961 party committee meeting at the Timiryazev Academy and accused Pryanishnikov of being a German agent during World War II.[33] The publication of this report in the academy's newspaper, the *Timiryazevets*, on 6 January 1962 during the rehabilitation of Pryanishnikov probably was used to oust Vilyams's son from the Timiryazev Academy.

In 1948 the Timiryazev Academy had been purged. V. N. Stoletov from Lysenko's Genetics Institute was named director of the Timiryazev Academy and Lysenko himself became head of its chair for genetics and selection.[34] The dean of the Timiryazev Academy's faculty of agrochemistry and soil studies, B. A. Golubev (a Pryanishnikov pupil), was fired and replaced with Vilyams's son. Golubev's further persecution by Vilyams junior and Stoletov soon led to his death.

In late 1961 Khrushchev opened a bitter attack on the Timiryazev Academy and its rector, G. M. Loza, who had to confess his academy's errors in a letter to *Sovetskaya Rossiya* on 27 January 1962. Vilyams's system had been created at the Timiryazev Academy and the academy had become a "stronghold of grassland agriculture" (Loza in *Sovetskaya Rossiya*, 27 January 1962). During this campaign in 1962 Vilyams junior was fired as dean of the academy's faculty for soil studies and agrochemistry (this is clear from his obituary in *Selskaya Zhizn*, 1 June 1965).

Despite the stereotyped enforcement of Vilyams's ideas in 1948, they received a slight setback as early as 1950. According to Medvedev,[35] many statements by agricultural scientists and a number of conferences condemned defects in his system, and in 1950 the Central Committee sent a special letter to agricultural establishments criticizing these defects. Lysenko then published an article also criticizing his mistakes—but according to Medvedev, Lysenko had been forced to write this article and, even though criticizing some defects, strove to defend Vilyams's main idea—the grassland system.[36] In addition to the Central Committee letter, a Council of Ministers and Central Committee decree in

[31] Ibid., pp. 116–17.
[32] Ibid., p. 127.
[33] Ibid., p. 128.
[34] Ibid., p. 114.
[35] Ibid., p. 124.
[36] Joravsky (*The Lysenko Affair*, pp. 299–300) analyzes the changes in Vilyams's system made by Lysenko's 15 July 1950 *Pravda* article, orienting it more to use of clean fallow before grain in dry areas rather than grasses, which dry out the soil.

1950 also criticized certain errors in his teachings.[37] Nevertheless, the grassland system remained in effect.

In 1954 the stereotyped application of the grassland system in all zones was criticized.[38] Medvedev writes that it was rejected in the south in 1954.[39] Vilyams's ideas had long been opposed in the south. Khrushchev in his 2 November 1961 speech and his March 1962 plenum speech recalled that as Ukrainian first secretary he had been attacked by Stalin in February 1947 for opposing Vilyams's system, specifically for opposing spring wheat, which was favored by Vilyams, Maltsev, and Lysenko.[40] But the grassland system remained dominant in other areas, especially in the non-chernozem zone where it had been developed.

The Attack on Vilyams

Apparently in response to the attacks on Lysenko and also the slowness of agricultural scientists in dumping the grassland system immediately, Khrushchev escalated the campaign against the grasslanders, bringing the Stalinism issue into the agricultural dispute. He had just finished turning the 22d Party Congress into a massive denunciation of Stalin, using this complete discrediting and the public disclosure of his crimes to attempt to smear his own conservative foes and overcome their opposition to his policies. After the at least partial success of this tactic at the October 1961 congress, Khrushchev extended it also into agricultural politics, with the aim of intimidating those who opposed or moved too slowly in adopting the intertilled system and of promoting his demand for more investment in chemical fertilizer and mechanization.

He began portraying Vilyams, the father of the grassland system, as a tyrant, who with Stalin's support suppressed progressive scientists and forced the grassland system on the whole country. Khrushchev rehabilitated Vilyams's main rivals D. N. Pryanishnikov and N. M. Tulaykov and portrayed them as victims of the cult of Stalin's personality. Khrushchev declared at the March 1962 plenum that when "some prominent scientists" challenged Vilyams's grassland system, they "were declared enemies of the people."[41]

It turned out that Pryanishnikov's program for intensive farming (mechanization, fertilizer, and introduction of bean crops) fit perfectly with the programs being promoted by Khrushchev, and Khrushchev insisted that Pryanishnikov's teachings replace Vilyams's grassland system as the scientific basis for training agricultural cadres. Yu. Chernichenko wrote in July 1965 that though Tulaykov

[37] According to Khrushchev at the March 1962 plenum, Khrushchev's collected speeches, vol. 6, p. 391.

[38] Khrushchev at the March 1962 plenum, ibid.

[39] Medvedev's article in *Grani*, no. 71, p. 121.

[40] Khrushchev's collected speeches, vol. 6, pp. 59 and 387.

[41] Stenographic record of the March 1962 Central Committee plenum, p. 376.

was an adherent of the intertilled system "his name is falsely cited by those who wanted to replace the grassland monopoly with intertilled conformity."[42]

On 26 November 1961—less than a month after the anti-Stalin binge at the 22d Congress—in a speech at Novosibirsk, Khrushchev included a whole section on "The Bankruptcy of V. R. Vilyams's Grassland Farming System."[43] Khrushchev contrasted Vilyams's insistence that sowing grasses was the only way to restore or increase soil fertility to the program of Vilyams's rival Pryanishnikov, who urged use of fertilizer and bean crops (the intertilled system relied heavily on bean crops also). Khrushchev told how Vilyams had assailed his scientific foes as "enemies."

About the same time, a drive was begun to rehabilitate Pryanishnikov and later Tulaykov as victims of Stalin and Vilyams. Scientists in *Sovetskaya Rossiya* (16 November 1961) declared that Pryanishnikov had provided the scientific basis for using chemicals in agriculture, while Vilyams regarded mineral fertilizer as useless unless the soil structure already had been improved by perennial grasses. *Sovetskaya Rossiya* on 21 November announced that the RSFSR Agriculture Ministry would reprint Pryanishnikov's works, and *Sovetskaya Rossiya* on 25 November prodded institutes to drive out grassland teachings. *Sovetskaya Rossiya* on 4 January 1962 reported a RSFSR Agriculture Ministry order to all agricultural institutes to remove grassland propaganda from textbooks and have their students study Pryanishnikov.

On 6 January 1962 *Selskaya Zhizn* published an article by K. Tulaykova, apparently a relative of Vilyams's victim N. M. Tulaykov, claiming that Tulaykov had opposed the grassland system and clean fallow and had supported corn and occupied fallow.[44] *Pravda* on 22 August 1962 reported that Tulaykov's works would soon be published also. These works later became the pretext for a curious attack on RSFSR Agriculture Minister Sotnikov and his deputy, Sinyagin, who wrote the preface to the collection and selected the works to include. *Selskaya Zhizn* on 26 September 1962 attacked them for allegedly not including articles critical of the grassland system and accused Sinyagin of claiming credit for having exposed the grassland system when actually it was the

[42]*Novyy Mir*, no. 11, (1965).

[43]Khrushchev's collected speeches, vol. 6, p. 171.

[44]Tulaykov, the founder and first director of Saratov's Southeast Grain Institute, fought Vilyams in 1936–37, advocating corn rather than perennial grasses and winter wheat rather than spring wheat for the southeast zone.

One of Lysenko's graduate students, V. N. Stoletov, attacked Tulaykov in the 11 April 1937 *Pravda* ("Against Hostile Theories in Agronomy"). Stoletov's article was discussed at a meeting in the Saratov Institute, which declared that Tulaykov's "mistaken statement" "was used and is being used now by enemies of the people, wreckers in agriculture, Trotskyites and their rightist accomplices." Saratov was labeled a "hotbed of reactionary theories in agronomy." Among the Saratov scientists condemning Tulaykov was Gulyayev, who later was involved in 1964 attacks on Voronov's protégés. Tulaykov was arrested in 1937 and shot in 1938. He was a close friend of Vavilov and was vice president of VASKhNIL while Vavilov was president (Medvedev's article in *Grani*, no. 71, pp. 89 -91).

Central Committee which had done so. Sotnikov was finally removed as agriculture minister in March 1963 (*Sovetskaya Rossiya*, 30 March) and the ministry was abolished shortly afterward.

Khrushchev's aims became clearer at the March 1962 plenum when he raised the old Vilyams-Pryanishnikov dispute in detail, portraying Pryanishnikov and Tulaykov as having been suppressed by Stalin and Vilyams for promoting the same programs he was now pushing—chemical fertilizer and mechanization. Vilyams's opposition to fertilizer was clear—since he maintained that soil fertility was improved "only by natural means" (grasses) and not by fertilizer. Khrushchev obviously stretched his point when he claimed that Vilyams opposed mechanization also. He lamely stated: "Perhaps not everyone knows ... that Vilyams once even opposed the tractor." It turned out that in 1929 he had briefly objected to use of tractors because their weight supposedly damaged the soil structure—but he soon reversed himself.[45]

Khrushchev explained that the reason Stalin backed Vilyams's grassland system was that it would not require the massive investments for chemical fertilizer production envisaged by Pryanishnikov's program.[46] In 1962 Khrushchev was becoming more and more intent on diverting funds into fertilizer production and in 1963 and 1964 this became a major source of controversy. In his concluding speech at the March 1962 plenum, he indicated the importance he attached to boosting fertilizer production by suggesting that perhaps there should be a special Central Committee plenum on fertilizer.[47] Such a plenum eventually occurred, but only a year and a half later (December 1963).

In raising the repressions of scientists and the disastrous agricultural programs under Stalin, Khrushchev obviously found Lysenko an anachronism and found it necessary to try to deflect blame from him by accusing Vilyams of the sins of which Lysenko was guilty. Khrushchev declared in his March 1962 plenum speech that Soviet agriculture had fallen behind because of Stalin's enforcement of Vilyams's grassland system[48]—not because of Stalin's enforcement of Lysenko's theories. The methods of suppressing debate and even denouncing foes as "wreckers" and "enemies of the people," followed by arrest and even death, were attributed to Vilyams, even though Lysenko was even better known for using these methods.

Indeed, Vilyams, according to Medvedev, had even preceded Lysenko and Prezent in using the device of questioning the loyalty of scientific foes. These methods were already being used before the great purge started in 1937.[49]

---

[45] Khrushchev's March 1962 plenum speech, stenographic record of the March 1962 plenum, p. 45.

[46] Ibid., pp. 43, 378.

[47] Khrushchev's collected speeches, vol. 6, p. 449.

[48] Stenographic record of the March 1962 Central Committee plenum, p. 43.

[49] Medvedev tells of a victim of Prezent as early as 1930, and also drags out a skeleton in Maltsev's closet, claiming that Maltsev and a Lysenkoist NKVD agent Yakushkin

Vilyams, in his seventies in the 1930's, was in such bad physical condition (partially paralyzed for twenty years), that—according to Medvedev—he was not fully responsible for his acts and for that to which he put his signature.[50] Nevertheless, he did participate in 1937 attacks on agricultural officials and scientists and was able to destroy the fertilizer institute created by Pryanishnikov even before the great purge. In 1936 the All-Union Fertilizer Institute was merged with the Soil Studies Institute led by Vilyams and his protégé, Bushinskiy. Director A. K. Zaporozhets of the fertilizer institute was arrested and replaced with Vilyams's protégé, Usachev, who already in March 1937 bragged of the exposure of twelve enemies of the people in the fertilizer institute's leadership, some of whom lost their lives. A November 1937 VASKhNIL session "condemned the speech and conduct . . . of Academician Pryanishnikov as unworthy of a Soviet scientist."[51] Still, Vilyams died in November 1939 and obviously did not participate in later purges.

To erase Lysenko's involvement with Vilyams and the grassland system, Khrushchev began portraying him as a foe of Vilyams. He even went back to assert that Lysenko's mentor I. V. Michurin specifically disagreed with Vilyams and maintained that fertilizer could raise soil fertility.[52] At the 22d Congress, Polyanskiy claimed that Lysenko had in the past sharply criticized the grassland system (Pravda, 24 October 1961).

Lysenko endorsed Khrushchev's attack on the grassland system in Selskaya Zhizn on 15 December 1961, and in Selskaya Zhizn on 23 December Professor V. Kvasnikov cited Lysenko's opposition to Vilyams's system of universal use of perennial grasses, Vilyams's argument that rollers and harrows damaged soil structure, and Vilyams's contention that mineral fertilizer should not be used on nonstructured soil.

Khrushchev, perhaps in response to the stories of his past hostility to Lysenko, took pains to stress his long-time close friendship with him while first secretary in the Ukraine[53] and in Moscow Oblast,[54] and even excused his participation in a 1947 attack on himself.[55]

---

denounced Maltsev's mentor and chief V. K. Krutikhovskiy in the early 1930's. When Krutikhovskiy was arrested, Maltsev took over his job as leader of the Shadrinsk experimental field and appropriated Krutikhovskiy's agricultural ideas, which later became known as "Maltsev's system" (Medvedev's article in Grani, no. 70, p. 161).

[50]Medvedev's article in Grani, no. 71, p. 89.

[51]Ibid., pp. 84–86.

[52]Stenographic record of the March 1962 Central Committee plenum, p. 42.

[53]At the March 1962 plenum he told of Lysenko coming to him in the late 1930's to beg him to intervene with Stalin to dissuade him from appointing Lysenko president of VASKhNIL. Khrushchev cited Lysenko's desire to continue in his research and field work.

[54]At the February 1964 plenum he described his backing of Lysenko's manure composts while obkom first secretary.

[55]Malenkov and Central Committee Agriculture Section head A. I. Kozlov had supposedly forced Lysenko to write an article attacking winter wheat. Khrushchev was then

Lysenko in Decline

Lysenko was not widely popular among politicians; his position rested mainly on the support of Khrushchev and Polyanskiy. When Khrushchev's support wavered and Polyanskiy declined in early 1962, Lysenko became vulnerable and was displaced by the virgin landers. At the December 1959 Central Committee plenum only Khrushchev, Polyanskiy, Moscow First Secretary P. N. Demichev, and plant breeder F. G. Kirichenko (called a "very close pupil" of Lysenko by Khrushchev in a 2 November 1961 agricultural conference speech[56]) praised his work. The only year when Lysenko received support from more than a handful of politicians at Central Committee plenums was in 1961. At the January 1961 plenum his milk-fat work was praised by Lithuanian First Secretary A. Yu. Snechkus, Moldavian First Secretary Z. T. Serdyuk, Estonian First Secretary I. G. Kebin, Moscow Oblast First Secretary G. G. Abramov, Rostov First Secretary A. V. Basov, as well as Khrushchev and Polyanskiy, and his manure composts were praised by Latvian First Secretary A. Ya. Pelshe, Kiev First Secretary P. Ye. Shelest, and Gorkiy First Secretary L. N. Yefremov. Tselinnyy Kray First Secretary T. I. Sokolov called him "remarkable and outstanding." At the 22d Congress, his manure composts were praised by Belorussian First Secretary K. T. Mazurov and G. A. Nalivayko, and his milk-fat work was cited by Krasnodar First Secretary G. I. Vorobyev.

Voronov, although in practice backing Lysenko's early sowing campaign and winter rye program in 1960, never boosted these as Lysenko's programs and his speeches and articles ignored him in all other matters, such as the bull-breeding and manure compost work. Since Voronov was a livestock specialist and frequently wrote or spoke about cattle, his silence on Lysenko's work in his own field could hardly be accidental. The nearest Voronov ever came to expressing support for him was at the height of Lysenko's influence. At the 22d Congress he declared: "We have many remarkable scientists. . . . Everyone knows the names of T. D. Lysenko, K. I. Skryabin, P. P. Lukyanenko, V. S. Pustovoyt, Sh. Sh. Khayrullin and others."[57] While only mentioning Lysenko as one of a number of apparently equally remarkable scientists, Voronov singled out Nalivayko and Khayrullin and their institutes for praise. Later (1964) Voronov's protégé, Khayrullin, publicly repudiated Lysenko's virgin land program—severing even that one line of agreement.

Polyanskiy was a consistent admirer of Lysenko, referring to the "remarkable scientist T. D. Lysenko" in his December 1959 and January 1961 plenum speeches, praising his manure-earth composts (his December 1959 plenum speech and his 12 December 1961 Volga–Vyatka speech) and his milk-fat work

---

under attack for favoring winter wheat instead of spring wheat. Vilyams and the grasslanders favored spring wheat (see Khrushchev's 2 November 1961 speech, Khrushchev's collected speeches, vol. 6, pp. 57–59).

[56] Khrushchev's collected speeches, vol. 6, p. 58.

[57] Stenographic record of the 22d Congress, vol.1, p. 372.

(his January 1961 plenum speech, his Rostov speech in *Sovetskaya Rossiya* on 2 February 1961, and his 4 November 1962 *Izvestiya* article). Lysenko expressed appreciation for Polyanskiy's and Podgornyy's attention to his manure composts at the December 1959 plenum. At the height of the anti-grassland campaign, Polyanskiy attempted to whitewash Lysenko's earlier support of Vilyams's grassland system by claiming that Lysenko had opposed Vilyams under Stalin: "A sharp criticism of the grassland farming system was also given by Academician Lysenko" (in Polyanskiy's 22d Congress speech, *Pravda*, 24 October 1961).

By all odds, Lysenko's loudest supporter was Khrushchev himself, who cited him on a wide variety of subjects: his summer planting of potatoes and raising the winter resistance of wheat,[58] his proving the advantages of sugar beets as fodder,[59] his work with millet,[60] his method of planting oak tree forest belts,[61] his work with seeds,[62] his corn sowing recommendations,[63] and his work with wheat and corn.[64] In addition, he gave constant praise to Lysenko's work on fertilizer composts and raising the fat content of milk. In fact, Khrushchev cites him in fully two dozen of his speeches and notes from late 1959 through early 1964.

Khrushchev had demanded general recognition for Lysenko's work in biology at the December 1958 plenum and vehemently defended him in 1959, as noted above. Under Khrushchev's patronage he again acquired great authority in 1961. But during 1961 and 1962 the Khrushchev–Lysenko relationship became more complicated because of the failure of Lysenko's virgin land program and because of pressures from anti-Lysenkoist forces.

By early 1962 the imposition of Lysenko's early sowing program in the virgin lands had led to such weed infestation that many crops were simply choked off by weeds. Barayev, at the February 1966 VASKhNIL session, stated that Tselinnyy Kray lost 150 million poods of grain because of early sowing in 1961 and that 77 percent of the sown area had become severely weed-infested.[65] By early 1962 Nalivayko had deserted early sowing and sided with Maltsev and Barayev in arguing for late sowing (with late sowing, farmers can wait until the weeds sprout, then plow them under and plant the spring crops on weed-free fields). Since weeds had become the main problem Nalivayko urged that in addition to early fall plowing (as advocated by Lysenko and Khayrullin) farmers

[58] In his 5 January 1961 thesis, Khrushchev's collected speeches, vol. 4, p. 258.

[59] In his 23 February 1961 speech, ibid., vol. 5, p. 83; in his 8 March 1961 speech, ibid., p. 177; in his 31 March 1961 Note to the Presidium, ibid., p. 327; and in his 19 November 1962 plenum speech, ibid., vol. 7, p. 395.

[60] In his 2 March 1961 speech, ibid., vol. 5, p. 118; and in his 21 March 1961 speech, ibid., p. 297.

[61] In his 21 March 1961 speech, ibid., p. 300.

[62] In his 31 March 1961 Note to the Presidium, ibid., p. 325.

[63] In his 12 January 1962 speech, ibid., vol. 6, p. 319.

[64] In his February 1964 plenum speech, ibid., vol. 8, p. 405.

[65] *Vestnik Selskokhozyaystvennoy Nauki*, no. 5 (May 1966).

should plow up the weeds when they sprout in late May and then plant late (early June) crops such as corn, peas, or vetch-oak mixtures.[66]

Khrushchev's enthusiasm for Lysenko's early sowing program cooled and he followed Nalivayko's switch. In his 4 August 1962 Note to the Presidium[67] he declared that those who had sown early had had their crops destroyed by weeds and he defended Nalivayko's late sowing, declaring that "some zealous administrators" had been "criticizing those who, in their opinion, lagged with the spring sowing in the virgin lands in Siberia and Kazakhstan" in trying to follow Nalivayko's late sowing recommendations. Later (in a 28 September 1962 talk in the Turkmen SSR[68]) he attacked Voronov[69] and Polyanskiy by name for forcing farms to sow on weedy fields before the weeds were destroyed in the spring, despite the fact that the Altay Institute opposed haste. However, it is a measure of Khrushchev's continued favoring of Lysenko that he was never blamed for the damage caused by his program. The weediness which developed in the virgin lands, especially during 1961, led "many leaders and specialists to now raise the question of significantly expanding the area of clean fallow" (Khrushchev at the March 1962 plenum[70]), but Khrushchev preferred Nalivayko's method. Nalivayko, of course, still opposed clean fallow.

In addition, Khrushchev came into conflict with many Lysenkoists who allegedly clung to grass and clean fallow. Lysenkoist scientific centers such as the Omsk Institute (and its director, I. I. Zezin[71]), the Krasnoyarsk Institute (and its director, A. T. Belozerov[72]), the Leningrad Plant Growing Institute (and its new director, I. A. Sizov[73]), and the Institute of Agriculture for the Central Non-Chernozem Zone (and its director, Ye. T. Varenitsa[74]) incurred his wrath for

[66]Khrushchev's 26 November 1961 Novosibirsk speech, Khrushchev's collected speeches, vol. 6, pp. 195-96.

[67]Ibid., vol. 7, p. 139.

[68]Ibid., p. 192.

[69]Voronov's ally Khayrullin continued to back early sowing (see Ya. Orishchenko's article in *Ural*, no. 2 [1964]).

[70]Khrushchev's collected speeches, vol. 6, pp. 362–63.

[71]In a 26 November 1961 speech Khrushchev criticized Zezin for having more grass than grain at his institute (ibid., vol. 5, p. 189).

[72]In the same speech Khrushchev urged Belozerov to grow winter rye after vetch-oak mixtures rather than after clean fallow (ibid., p. 196). Belozerov in 1960 had attacked reduction of clean fallow and grasslands (*Pravda*, 11 November 1960). In 1966 Belozerov attacked Nalivayko and his intertilled system and insisted that dry parts of the Altay need 15–20 percent clean fallow (*Vestnik Selskokhozyaystvennoy Nauki*, no. 5 [May 1966]).

[73]In a 14 December 1961 speech Khrushchev reproved Sizov for recommending clover as a predecessor to flax (Khrushchev's collected speeches, vol. 6, pp. 242–43).

[74]Varenitsa was harshly attacked by Khrushchev and Nalivayko at a December 1961 Moscow agricultural conference for writing a May 1961 article defending grassland crop rotations against intertilled crop rotations (*Pravda*, 14, 15, 16 December 1961). V. Mikheyev's 27 January 1962 *Selskaya Zhizn* article assailed RSFSR Agriculture Minister Sotnikov for not cracking down specifically on the "rabid and unyielding grasslander"

being slow in giving up the grasslands system. Khrushchev had conflicts with other Lysenkoists also: P. A. Vlasyuk, S. F. Demidov, I. D. Laptev, and B. P. Bushinskiy—all of whom had been illegally made academicians of VASKhNIL in 1948.[75] At a 22 December 1961 Kiev conference Khrushchev criticized Vlasyuk for defending the grassland system. Vlasyuk boldly responded by stating that the Central Committee had approved the grassland system and he was simply follow- ing Central Committee instructions—thus casting responsibility back on Khrush- chev, which irritated him considerably.[76] Khrushchev attacked Vilyams's protégés, Bushinskiy and M. G. Chizhevskiy, in a 14 December 1961 speech.[77] At the March 1962 plenum he assailed Laptev and Demidov and urged that they be expelled from VASKhNIL. They were expelled at the same April 1962 session at which Lysenko resigned as VASKhNIL president. At that session Pysin com- plained of VASKhNIL's slowness in expelling them.[78]

As the witchhunt for grasslanders progressed, the Altay–Orenburg group appeared to turn it against Lysenko and his allies. After a 24 January 1962 *Pravda* complaint by Nalivayko that agricultural science was being reorganized too slowly, *Selskaya Zhizn* on 27 January carried an article attacking RSFSR Agriculture Minister Sotnikov for not pressing the attack on foes of the Altay intertilled program. The author, V. Mikheyev, characterized the ministry's 20 December 1961 decree written by Sotnikov as "curtsying before the grass- landers." Sotnikov answered in *Selskaya Zhizn* on 24 February, indicating that he was taking measures to crack down. Yet only four days later (28 February) *Selskaya Zhizn* returned to the attack with an article by deputy director of Nalivayko's institute, V. Metelev, assailing Sotnikov and his deputy, Sinyagin, for distorting the Altay Institute's recommendations on bean sowing.[79] *Selskaya*

Varenitsa. On the other hand, Varenitsa apparently cooperated well with Lysenko. At the February 1964 plenum he enthusiastically lauded his plant nutrition theory, his manure- fertilizer composts, his milk-fat work, and Michurinist biology in general.

[75] Most VASKhNIL members opposed Lysenko, so that he could not get his adher- ents elected to VASKhNIL. As a result, there were no elections from 1935 until 1956, when Lysenko was removed as president. By 1948 the number of VASKhNIL academicians had dwindled to seventeen and the need to elect new members was pressing. When his attempts in 1947 and 1948 to get his protégés elected failed, the scheduled elections were canceled. But in mid-1948, immediately after Lysenko's triumph over Zhdanov (see below), he made up a list of thirty-five of his favorites and Stalin appointed them VASKhNIL academicians (see Medvedev, *Rise and Fall of Lysenko*, p. 116). This Council of Ministers decree appoint- ing the thirty-five was issued on 15 July—less than a week after Zhdanov's son was forced to write a letter confessing his errors in attacking Lysenko and protecting the geneticists. The 15 July decree was published in the 28 July *Pravda*—on the eve of the August 1948 VASKhNIL session. Yuriy Zhdanov's 10 July letter was published in the 7 August *Pravda* —during the session.

[76] Khrushchev's collected speeches, vol. 6, pp. 283–84.

[77] Ibid., p. 224.

[78] *Vestnik Selskokhozyaystvennoy Nauki*, no. 6 (1962).

[79] Metelev was the Altay bean expert. As chief of a department of the Altay Institute, he wrote a 11 November 1960 *Selskaya Zhizn* article on beans.

Zhizn on 20 March reported that the RSFSR Bureau itself (Deputy Chairman Voronov) had censured Sotnikov and Sinyagin by name for this, terming it "unsatisfactory leadership" on their part.[80]

Sotnikov had participated in the 1948 purges of foes of Lysenko and Vilyams and was considered a Lysenkoist by Medvedev in 1962.[81] When Khrushchev's campaign to publicize Tulaykov's pro-corn ideas developed in 1962, Sotnikov and his deputy Sinyagin were assigned the task of selecting some of Tulaykov's works for publication and writing the introduction to the collection. After the publication of Tulaykov's works the corn advocates—as they had in January, February, and March 1962—again questioned the sincerity of Sotnikov's change of heart. *Selskaya Zhizn* on 26 September 1962 accused him and Sinyagin of not including Tulaykov's anti-grassland articles. Sotnikov also supposedly changed his anti-Pryanishnikov views to co-author the introduction to the 1962 publication of Pryanishnikov's works. After falling into obscurity in 1963, he returned to prominence after Khrushchev's fall, becoming chief of the Agriculture Ministry's main administration for land use, organization of land use, shelterbelt forestry, and soil conservation—a key post for a "grasslander."

Sinyagin, however, apparently had no ties with Lysenko. In fact, he fought his fertilizer recommendations in early 1964 and replaced a Lysenkoist as vice president of VASKhNIL in February 1965. Both Sotnikov and Sinyagin were closely involved with fertilizer problems. Sinyagin headed the Institute for Fertilizer and Soil Studies in early 1960 and was succeeded in this position by Sotnikov later in 1960. They became the leaders of the RSFSR Agriculture Ministry in early 1961.

The attacks on Sotnikov and Sinyagin were the first move to upset the January 1961 arrangements and the initiative appears to have come from Voronov and the Altay group. Immediately after *Selskaya Zhizn's* strange attacks, *Selskaya Zhizn* chief editor V. I. Polyakov became head of the Central Committee Agriculture Section (first identified as such on 9 March when he spoke at the March 1962 plenum), replacing V. A. Karlov. The removal of Karlov, who was demoted to a Central Committee inspector (identified in *Pravda* on 21 March 1962) and then exiled to Uzbekistan as second secretary (his election was reported in the 3 August 1962 *Pravda Vostoka*), also marked some sort of obscure shift.

Signs of the waning of Lysenko's influence could be seen in the March 1962 Central Committee plenum. Whereas numerous speakers praised him at the January 1961 plenum (where Polyanskiy appeared to be the most prominent figure after Khrushchev) and even at the 22d Congress, the March 1962 plenum (where Voronov appeared to be the most prominent figure after Khrushchev) heard little about Lysenko. Lysenko-admirer Polyanskiy did not even speak.

---

[80] The RSFSR Bureau had criticized Sotnikov already earlier—in May 1961—for slowness in reorganizing his ministry (*Sovetskaya Rossiya*, 16 May 1961).

[81] Medvedev's article in *Grani*, no. 71, pp. 125-26, 131.

Although Khrushchev praised his bull-breeding program in his report[82] and portrayed him as an old friend in his concluding speech,[83] Lysenko was cited by only four other speakers—all of whom were Khrushchev protégés or apparently attempting to curry favor with him: Leningrad First Secretary I. V. Spiridonov, raykom secretary Ya. V. Bichevoy, agricultural scientist M. Ye. Matsepuro, and Lvov First Secretary I. S. Grushetskiy.

Spiridonov's position is complex, since there was a developing rift between Khrushchev and the Leningraders, and shortly after the plenum he was removed from his posts by Khrushchev personally. Perhaps already feeling threatened, he was quite flattering to Khrushchev at the March plenum, crediting him with "a very important further development of the theory of Marxism–Leninism" (by justifying the need to create a material-technical base for communism as the basis for material abundance and justifying the need for using material incentive[84]). He also advocated Lysenko's fertilizer recommendations, as well as his milk-fat program, which his oblast was already widely implementing.[85]

Bichevoy, secretary of a raykom in Stavropol Kray, one of only three speakers at the plenum who spoke of the Central Committee "headed by Comrade N. S. Khrushchev,"[86] told of using Lysenko's bull-breeding method.[87] Director of the Institute for Electrification and Mechanization of Agriculture in the Non-Chernozem Zone Matsepuro praised his fertilizer compost methods and explained that his institute was building machines to carry out Lysenko's method in production. Matsepuro, whom Khrushchev characterized as an old friend[88] and whom he often praised, was the only speaker to use the even more pro-Khrushchev formula, "the Presidium headed by Nikita Sergeyevich Khrushchev."[89] Matsepuro was awarded the Lenin Prize for his agricultural machinery in 1962, but had to rely on Khrushchev's personal protection against attempts by hostile Belorussian leaders to remove him as director of this institute, located in Minsk. This was revealed publicly when the Belorussian authorities ousted him shortly after Khrushchev's fall (*Pravda*, 17 June 1965). Belorussian First Secretary K. T. Mazurov long was at odds with Khrushchev over agricultural policy and had to undergo harsh personal attacks from him at the December 1959 plenum and at a January 1962 Minsk conference (*Pravda*, 16 January 1962). Belorussia opposed at least some of Lysenko's ideas (*Pravda*, 16 January 1962),

[82] Stenographic record of the March 1962 Central Committee plenum, p. 59.

[83] Ibid., p. 444.

[84] Ibid., p. 137.

[85] Ibid., p. 140.

[86] Ibid., p. 368.

[87] Ibid., p. 371.

[88] At the December 1959 plenum, Khrushchev's collected speeches, vol. 4, p. 89; in the 27 August 1960 Kalinovka talk, ibid., p. 158; and in a 12 January 1962 speech, ibid., vol. 6, p. 329.

[89] Stenographic record of the March 1962 Central Committee plenum, p. 257.

although Mazurov occasionally praised his composts (at the 22d Congress). At the March 1965 plenum Mazurov told of some of his disputes with Khrushchev. He was promoted to full Presidium membership soon after Khrushchev's fall.

The fourth and last to praise Lysenko—for his earth-manure composts—was Grushetskiy. While not unusually slavish toward Khrushchev in his plenum speech, Grushetskiy had been associated with him for a long time. He owed his career to Khrushchev, who as Ukrainian first secretary had made him second secretary of Stanislav Oblast (1939-40) and then first secretary of Chernovtsy Oblast (1940-41) in the newly annexed west Ukraine. After the west Ukraine was liberated in 1944 Khrushchev appointed Grushetskiy first secretary of the most important west Ukrainian oblast—Lvov. After Khrushchev left the Ukraine (1950), Grushetskiy's career declined: in early 1951 he was transferred to the less important Volyn Oblast. In February 1961, however, he was again made Lvov first secretary.

Lysenko's decline was confirmed shortly after the plenum. A 5 April 1962 VASKhNIL session released him as president of VASKhNIL "for reasons of health" (*Pravda* 6 April) and his protégé, Olshanskiy, was demoted from agriculture minister to VASKhNIL president. The report (on the results of the March plenum) at this VASKhNIL session was given by a Voronov ally, First Deputy Agriculture Minister Pysin, who soon (*Pravda*, 26 April) became the new agriculture minister. In his report, Pysin attacked "several leaders of the USSR Agriculture Ministry and . . . of VASKhNIL" for ignoring repeated instructions from the Central Committee Presidium to work out proposals for introducing the intertilled system and for continuing to support the grassland system (*Vestnik Selskokhozyaystvennoy Nauki* 6 [1962]: 5-19) and complained of VASKhNIL's slowness in expelling Demidov and Laptev, whom Khrushchev had assailed at the March plenum. Lysenko apparently was reluctant to purge his own protégés.

Lysenko's resignation as president of VASKhNIL and Olshanskiy's demotion apparently encouraged Lysenko's foes in the scientific community to press for a revival of genetics and for an end to his monopoly in general. Western breakthroughs in the genetics field during 1961 and 1962 impressed Soviet scientists and soon made them increasingly impatient at the obstacles to Soviet work in this field.[90] On 11 May 1962 the Academy of Sciences Presidium called a conference on molecular biology, at which Engelgardt (one of the main targets of Lysenko and Khrushchev in December 1958) reported on molecular biology. A scientific council on molecular biology was established and a program adopted to create new institutes and laboratories. The commission's subcommittees began reviewing the research of the Academy of Sciences' biology institutes, including even Lysenko's Genetics Institute. At the end of June 1962—for the first time in twenty years—Lysenko's institute was visited by scientists to investigate its work. At a 10 July 1962 meeting of the commission it was decided

[90] See Medvedev's book *Rise and Fall of Lysenko*, p. 197.

almost unanimously to pass a vote of censure on the institute and its level of research.

But the next day Khrushchev reasserted his support of Lysenko by leading the members of the Central Committee Presidium to visit his farm and see his bull breeding, wheat varieties, and nest planting of trees (*Pravda*, 12 July). Following this visit, the Council of Ministers issued a decree ordering the Agriculture Ministry, VASKhNIL, and other agricultural organizations to promote the use of Lysenko's bulls in cattle breeding (see Lysenko's speech at the February 1964 plenum).

In addition, Lysenko and Olshanskiy quickly came up with another new project to capture Khrushchev's imagination. Seizing upon his growing enthusiasm for peas, they announced that they were developing a winter-resistant pea[91] and Khrushchev asked them to organize a pea-silaging experiment.[92]

With Khrushchev's ostentatious display of approval of the work of Lysenko's farm on 11 July, the Academy of Sciences' commission's scheduled meeting on 12 July, at which it was going to formally censure the farm's work, was suddenly canceled, the commission was dissolved and all its materials were impounded by the Central Committee. In its place, a new Academy of Sciences commission was established—to prepare a decree calling for strengthening biologists' ties with life, using Lysenko's work as a model. The commission was headed by Central Committee Science Section head V. A. Kirillin (a neutral in the Lysenko dispute, according to Medvedev). The commission included anti-Lysenkoists, as well as Lysenko and his friends, and soon it came to a deadlock. A seven-man editorial group was finally appointed and worked out a compromise decree, which was published in *Pravda* on 25 January 1963.[93]

Although the January 1963 decree reaffirmed support for Lysenko, it did not close the door on other schools of biology. Nevertheless, the Lysenkoists quickly seized the initiative and interpreted the decree as an endorsement of their position. Only four days after the publication of the decree, Lysenko published an article reiterating some of his most controversial ideas: the transformation of one species into another, the transformation of nonliving matter into live matter, his denial of DNA's role, and his criticisms of Western geneticists Morgan and Weismann. The fact that both *Pravda* and *Izvestiya* carried this long (two-page) article indicated official support. Medvedev also contends that *Pravda's* publication of a mid-1962 picture of Lysenkoists F. G. Kirichenko and P. F. Garkavyy—for no apparent reason—next to the decree in its 25 January 1963 issue was meant as a symbolic hint that the compromise decree was really to be read in a pro-Lysenko vein.

[91] See Khrushchev's 28 July 1962 Kalinovka speech, Khrushchev's collected speeches, vol. 7, p. 108.

[92] Khrushchev's 12 March 1963 speech, ibid., p. 452.

[93] Medvedev, *Rise and Fall of Lysenko*, pp. 197–200.

A 5-7 March 1963 VASKhNIL session to discuss the January decree heard Olshanskiy assail the gene and Morgan and Mendel and promote Lysenko's compost and milk-fat work. The session was dominated by Lysenkoists (G. P. Vysokos, A. S. Musiyko, V. N. Remeslo, I. A. Sizov, A. S. Vsyakikh, etc.) and adopted a resolution backing Michurinism. The "outstanding Soviet scientist" T. D. Lysenko was in the presidium of the session along with agricultural officials Polyanskiy, Polyakov, and Pankin (*Pravda*, 6 March 1963). While the Lysenkoists used the decree to reinforce their monopoly, the geneticists were unable to reply.[94]

[94] Ibid., pp. 201-3.

CHAPTER IV

KHRUSHCHEV'S REORGANIZATIONS: 1962

In 1962 Khrushchev pushed through two massive reorganizations which brought the party and government into turmoil, alienating many leaders and later becoming one of the prime reasons for his downfall. Like his campaigns for new agrotechniques and crop policies, the reorganizations were in many respects a substitute for resources. In 1961 and 1962 he began pushing hard to shift resources from heavy industry and defense to agriculture and light industry. However, his efforts were not very successful and reorganizations had to suffice instead. The March 1962 Central Committee plenum adopted a system of national, republic, and oblast agricultural committees supervising republic ministries for production and procurement of agricultural products and oblast kolkhoz-sovkhoz production administrations, in place of the republic agriculture ministries and oblast and rayon agriculture administrations.

Voronov clearly was one of the architects of the new system and came out in a very powerful position. As first deputy chairman of the RSFSR Bureau he became head of the new RSFSR Agriculture Committee—while RSFSR Premier Polyanskiy was excluded from the committee. Polyanskiy's eclipse was graphically evident at the May Day 1962 parade when his junior colleague Voronov stood ahead of him in ranking.

The March 1962 reorganization threw agricultural and party officials into confusion due to the vague division of authority between new and old organs and the reshuffle of personnel. Despite the opposition evident at the March plenum, Khrushchev moved ahead to completely eliminate rayons and their party committees and newspapers. This process culminated in the November 1962 plenum's reorganization, changing the party's organizational principle from territorial to production—dividing party organs into agricultural and industrial organs. Thus, following the trail blazed by the March 1962 reorganization, party officials were involved ever more deeply in agricultural production. Rayons were consolidated into larger units corresponding to the kolkhoz-sovkhoz production administrations and party organizations in the area came under the production administration's *partorg* (party organizer) and the rural raykoms were abolished.

These reorganizations kept the party in turmoil from top to bottom throughout 1962. The political frustration and unhappiness they caused undercut Khrushchev's support and became one of the prime reasons for his being removed from power. The opposition by local party officials suffering in the confusion, or even losing their positions, plus the scarcely concealed opposition by even high level leaders, were reflected in the post-Khrushchev reversal of the bifurcation of party organs and the restoration of raykoms and their newspapers and elimination of production administrations' party committees, as well as heavy emphasis on the need for scientific and businesslike leadership—as against harebrained schemes—and for careful objective handling of cadres—as against Khrushchev's hasty and subjective decisions to promote or dismiss individuals.

Voronov's March 1962 victory turned out to be short-lived. Even though the November 1962 reorganization appeared to reflect his thinking (at the March plenum he had spoken even more strongly in favor of powerful production administrations and weakening of raykoms than had Khrushchev), he lost his key position at the end of the November plenum, and was transferred from RSFSR Bureau first deputy chairman to the less powerful position of RSFSR premier. Polyanskiy's authority waned further as he was appointed one of several USSR deputy premiers—a position not normally prominent enough to warrant Presidium membership (while the two *first* deputy premiers, Mikoyan and Kosygin, were Presidium members, none of the other eight deputy premiers held any high party posts).

Meanwhile, Khrushchev began forming a new team of agricultural leaders consisting of close protégés such as L. N. Yefremov and V. I. Polyakov and farmers who caught his attention by condemning the grasslanders and successfully boosting production of corn, peas, and sugar beets (I. P. Volovchenko, R. N. Sidak, and L. I. Maksimov). In November 1962 Polyakov became Central Committee secretary for agriculture and chairman of the new Central Committee Agriculture Bureau, to all appearances supplanting new Deputy Premier Polyanskiy as the top agricultural authority. Also in November 1962, Yefremov became first deputy chairman of the RSFSR Bureau, supplanting Voronov, who now became RSFSR premier, as top authority on agriculture in the RSFSR. Although Polyakov and Yefremov were never able to become full Presidium members, they obviously represented grave threats to Polyanskiy and Voronov, and it is not accidental that upon Khrushchev's fall they were immediately dismissed—suffering more retribution than almost any other Khrushchev agricultural favorites.

The March 1962 Plenum

Searching for new ways to raise agricultural production, Khrushchev found it extremely difficult to pry loose much money or resources for agriculture and instead wound up having to rely on a big reorganization designed to force party officials to give it priority. He had begun urging a shift of resources in his 29 October 1960 Note to the Presidium, which warned that despite the gains since 1953 both livestock raising and grain production were still falling short of needs. He wrote that "obviously we did not act completely correctly when we began to cut capital investments" (i.e., especially in 1958 and 1959) and he complained that the seven-year plan funds for irrigation and agricultural equipment had been cut by 13 billion rubles (1.3 billion new rubles after the 1 January 1961 10-to-1 currency change).[1] Noting that in the first two years of the seven-year plan (1959-60) industry had overfulfilled the plan targets by 120 billion rubles worth of products (12 billion new rubles), growing 23 percent instead of the planned 17 percent, he proposed that some of these above-plan accumulations in industry be diverted to aid agriculture.

Yet only days after Khrushchev's Note had warned alarmingly of the danger of agriculture slipping back to its pre-1953 condition, Kozlov in the 6 November October anniversary address painted a glowing picture of agricultural progress: "We all can now declare with satisfaction that our internal situation never was so solid and promising" (Pravda, 7 November 1960). He even quoted Khrushchev as saying that "we have everything necessary to satisfy the needs of the people." Kozlov singled out only the agricultural successes of the RSFSR and Belorussia—the leaders of which (Aristov and Mazurov) happened to be at odds with Khrushchev in late 1960. While Khrushchev had been championing the slogan of catching the US in meat production, Kozlov stressed the need to catch the US in industrial production, especially in steel.

On 24 December a Council of Ministers session discussed the results of the first two years of the seven-year plan and heavy industry's excellent progress. The outcome was a compromise: noting the proposals by Khrushchev, as well as others at the session, the meeting specified that the above-plan industrial accumulations were to be used for all branches—"industry and agriculture and for satisfaction of the growing demands of the population" (Pravda, 27 December).

In his 5 January 1961 thesis on welfare and agriculture for the delayed 10-18 January Central Committee plenum, Khrushchev again urged diversions of industrial resources to agriculture and complained that some officials still thought that agriculture had "such an abundance of equipment" that the production of agricultural equipment could be further cut. He cited the 1958-59 drop in delivery of tractors from 258,000 in 1957 to 252,000 in 1958 to 236,000 in 1959, of grain combines from 134,000 to 65,000 to 53,000, and of silage combines from 55,000 to 36,000 to 13,000.[2] He announced a new Central Committee-Council of Ministers decree[3] cutting prices of gasoline and spare

---

[1] Khrushchev's collected speeches, vol. 4, p. 181.

[2] Ibid., p. 252.

[3] The decree was officially adopted on 10 January, the opening day of the plenum—see Spravochnik Partiynogo Rabotnika [Party Worker's Handbook] (1961), p. 328.

parts for agricultural equipment and reducing income taxes on the sale of live-stock products, which, he said, would save kolkhozes 539 million rubles a year.[4]

In his 17 January 1961 speech to the plenum Khrushchev stated that "now our country has such powerful industry and such powerful defense that it can allot more funds for developing agriculture, for increasing production of consumer goods and for further raising of the welfare of the Soviet people without detriment to further developing of industry and strengthening of defense."[5] He wrote in his thesis that steel production was 9.7 million tons ahead of plans and at present rates would reach 100–102 million tons in 1965, instead of the planned 86–91 million tons.[6] Noting in his plenum speech that some comrades want to produce more and more steel, he urged instead holding to the original seven-year plan figures and using the funds from overfulfillment of the plans to aid consumer goods and agricultural production.[7]

At the March 1962 Central Committee plenum, Khrushchev's main complaint was that agriculture was being shortchanged in allocation of funds and that even those meager resources which had been allocated to agriculture in the past were often siphoned off for industry. He assailed the "dangerous attitudes" of some Gosplan and Gosekonomsovet (the State Scientific and Economic Council) leaders who wanted to divert funds from agricultural machine building to other branches[8], and again pointed out that output of much agricultural equipment—especially corn combines—had actually dropped since 1957.[9] He also pointed out the virtual stymying of the chemical fertilizer program: in three years (1959–61) output grew from 12 million tons to only 14.9 million—only 44 percent of the plan for new capacity. The goal for 1965 had been set at 35 million tons.[10]

Khrushchev stated flatly in his opening report that neither the proposed reorganization of agricultural administration[11] nor the changeover from the ex-

[4] Khrushchev's collected speeches, vol. 4, pp. 252–53.

[5] Stenographic record of the 10–18 January 1961 Central Committee plenum, p. 527.

[6] Khrushchev's collected speeches, vol. 4, p. 194.

[7] Stenographic record of the 10–18 January 1961 Central Committee plenum, pp. 527–28.

[8] Stenographic record of the 5–9 March 1962 Central Committee plenum, p. 84. Gosplan Chairman V. N. Novikov was removed soon afterward (*Pravda*, 17 July 1962) and transferred to permanent representative to the Council of Mutual Economic Assistance (*Pravda*, 20 July 1962) and in November 1962 was also dropped as deputy premier (*Pravda*, 25 November 1962). Khrushchev in his 31 March 1961 Note had attacked Gosplan for concluding that agriculture already had enough equipment (Khrushchev's collected speeches, vol. 5, p. 319). Novikov, a long-time leader of the defense industry and former head of the sovnarkhoz in Kozlov's Leningrad, clearly shared the Kozlov heavy industrial viewpoint. Novikov was restored to the post of deputy premier shortly after Khrushchev's fall (March 1965).

[9] Stenographic record of the 5–9 March 1962 Central Committee plenum, p. 84.

[10] Ibid., p. 85.

[11] Ibid., p. 82.

tensive (grassland) farming system to intensive farming (the intertilled system)[12] could be successful without supplying agriculture with more machinery and fertilizer. Obviously, the plowing up, sowing, and harvesting of up to 41 million hectares (to be changed from grass and fallow to corn, peas, sugar beets, and beans[13]) would require enormous increases in the output of machinery and fertilizer. But despite his strong plea for expansion of production of agricultural machinery and fertilizer and the backing of most speakers (especially Podgornyy, Spiridonov, Olshanskiy, Latvian First Secretary A. Ya. Pelshe, Bashkir First Secretary Z. N. Nuriyev, A. M. Shkolnikov, G. A. Nalivayko, Kiev First Secretary P. Ye. Shelest, Stavropol First Secretary F. D. Kulakov, and Ukrainian Agriculture Secretary V. G. Komyakhov), he clearly had to backtrack at the end of the plenum. Whereas in his opening report he had spoken of doubling output of agricultural machinery,[14] his concluding speech warned farmers against false hopes for much more aid and equipment and declared the "main and most urgent thing now" is to better use the present equipment and better organize labor.[15] One can send tractors but they may be misused, he declared, so the "main question in agriculture is organizational—selection and training of people"[16] —rather than more equipment. "Aid to kolkhozes and sovkhozes with equipment, mineral fertilizer and herbicides will grow from year to year," but "agricultural workers and especially leaders of republics, krays, oblasts, and rayons must well understand that the planned measures to strengthen aid to agriculture do not mean that now funds will be switched to agriculture to the detriment of the development of industry and strengthening of the country's defense."[17]

His retreat was so obvious that he felt it necessary to deny it: "This does not mean that I to some degree am beating a retreat in comparison with my report regarding allotment of additional material and technical means for agriculture."[18] No one actually voiced opposition to more investments for agriculture, but some speakers ignored the need or just stressed better use of present resources. Khrushchev himself had to eventually accept this latter line.

The hopelessness of getting new resources was recognized by Kostroma First Secretary L. Ya. Florentyev, who declared: "We well understand that we will not be able to receive enough mineral fertilizer for another several years."[19] Lithuanian First Secretary A. Yu. Snechkus's statement that "improving the leadership of agriculture" is now "the main thing" in "further development of farming and livestock raising"[20] shifted the emphasis away from more resource

[12] Ibid., p. 39.
[13] Ibid., pp. 37–38.
[14] Ibid., p. 86.
[15] Ibid., p. 427.
[16] Ibid., p. 437.
[17] Ibid., p. 426.
[18] Ibid., p. 427.
[19] Ibid., p. 345.
[20] Ibid., p. 199.

allocation. On the other hand, Odessa First Secretary M. S. Sinitsa pleaded that the equipment shortage was so great that "along with sharp improvement in the use of the present machines, we must already this year significantly increase output of agricultural equipment."[21]

Voronov was the most prominent speaker not to call for more invest-ments. Speaking right after Khrushchev, he cast some doubt on the hope for new resources by declaring that the RSFSR planned to try to solve its equipment shortage by "some maneuvering of the present equipment" during the year.[22] Polyanskiy reflected the agricultural lobby's pessimism. Reporting on the results of the plenum in a 10 March 1962 speech (broadcast on 12 March), he declared that the plenum had "recognized the necessity in the next few years of sharply increasing the capacity of agricultural machine building," but added that "how-ever, it is impossible to solve such a problem immediately. A number of years will be required and we must consequently first orient ourselves to our available equipment."

The March 1962 plenum was followed by at least some measures to strengthen agriculture and raise incentives. Agricultural equipment production was slightly raised and state purchase prices for livestock products were raised, boosting kolkhoz income by one billion rubles.[23] However, so tight was the money squeeze in 1962 that the price rise was passed on to the consumer by raising retail meat prices (which were below the state's cost of purchase, trans-port, processing, and retailing) by an average of 30 percent. This step was so serious that the 1 June announcement was accompanied by a long explanation from the party and government, appealing to the public to accept the price rises as the only present solution (*Izvestiya*, 1 June 1962). It declared that agricul-tural incentives had to be raised and "all Soviet people understand" that it was impossible to transfer money from defense, industry, or housing construction. However, the 1 June retail price rises produced a violent reaction, including bloody riots in Rostov Oblast.[24]

Despite Khrushchev's efforts the economy continued its lopsided develop-ment. As he pointed out at the November 1962 Central Committee plenum, in 1959–62 industry produced 28 billion rubles of above-plan accumulations—25 billion in group "A" (heavy industry) and only 3 billion in group "B" (light industry).[25] Meanwhile, agriculture developed far below planned rates. Khrush-chev complained that 13 million tons of steel above the plan had been produced, while the plans for the chemical industry (including his chemical fertilizer goals)

---

[21] Ibid., p. 409.
[22] Ibid., p. 107.
[23] V. Khlebnikov in the July 1962 *Voprosy Ekonomiki*. Khlebnikov pointed out that state purchase prices had been below kolkhoz production costs, so kolkhozes had no incentive to produce meat.
[24] See the account in Michel Tatu's *Power in the Kremlin* (London, 1969), pp. 219–20.
[25] Stenographic record of the 19–23 November 1962 Central Committee plenum, pp. 8–9.

were unfulfilled. Attacking Gosplan, he declared that some officials were wearing "steel blinders" and even if material superior to steel appears "they still cry 'steel! steel!' "[26] Economist I. Buzdalov pointed out that in the first nine months of 1962, output of tractors rose only 9 percent over the 1961 period and asserted that the 1962 plan provided 30.5 billion rubles of capital investments for industry, but only 7.6 billion for agriculture, kolkhozes' investments included.[27]

Although failing to achieve any great breakthrough in obtaining new resources, Khrushchev did push through a reorganization to improve agriculture's position in the struggle for priorities and to force industry-oriented party leaders up and down the line to concentrate more attention on agriculture at the expense of industry. In his concluding speech he indicated that he felt industry's successes and agriculture's failures were partly due to party organizations' concentration on industry: "Why does our industry develop so successfully?" he asked. Because "questions of leadership of industry . . . always were at the center of attention of our party."[28] To force party leaders to give more attention to agriculture, he proposed establishing agriculture committees for republics and oblasts to be headed by the area's party first secretary. He made it clear in his opening speech that the purpose of making first secretaries the chairmen of the committees was to give the committees the most authority possible: "If the committee is headed by the kraykom or obkom first secretary, the responsibility of the party organization of the kray or oblast for the state of agricultural production will be raised."[29] He declared that those who favored making the agriculture secretaries chairmen, instead of the first secretaries, are wrong because "just this secretary alone will be powerless; the whole party organization must deal with agriculture."[30]

Less clearly expressed was the intention of forcing industry-oriented party first secretaries to devote more attention to agricultural problems. In his concluding speech, Khrushchev declared: "Agriculture always, every day, must be the first question, the main question."[31] Voronezh First Secretary S. D. Khitrov made the point more directly: the creation of committees headed by first secretaries "will force party and soviet organs to take upon themselves full responsibility for the state of agriculture."[32]

Khrushchev himself had in mind an ambitious role for the USSR Agriculture Committee in the resource struggle. He advocated giving it the right to

[26] Ibid., pp. 50–51.
[27] Voprosy Ekonomiki 1 (1963): 71.
[28] Stenographic record of the March 1962 Central Committee plenum, p. 435.
[29] Ibid., p. 76.
[30] Ibid.
[31] Ibid., p. 437.
[32] Ibid., p. 355.

decide questions such as setting orders for industry, consideration of plans for production of agricultural machinery and agriculture's need for this, and checking on industry's supplying of agriculture's need for parts, fertilizer, etc.[33] Giving the USSR Agriculture Committee the right to check industry's fulfillment of goals for tractor and fertilizer production and possibly even the right to push for raising the plan goals for production of agricultural necessities would institutionalize pressure on Gosplan to counter industrial pressure groups.

The republic and oblast agriculture committees were also intended to be very powerful. They were to have direct control over the new organs established to exercise daily control over kolkhoz and sovkhoz production—the interrayon kolkhoz-sovkhoz production administrations—as well as over the new oblast production and procurement administrations or republic production and procurement ministries.[34] Thus, the government organs for procurement and production were to be organizationally under the party organs.

Khrushchev received support for strong agriculture committees from Podgornyy (who declared they should coordinate the government ministries, decide production questions, and check fulfillment of decisions[35]) and Rostov First Secretary A. V. Basov (who stated that they should "direct the work of all agricultural organs" and issue decrees "obligatory for all agricultural organs"[36]). In his concluding speech, Khrushchev also indicated that one of the reasons for establishing interrayon production administrations instead of rayon administrations was again the intention of giving agriculture a greater voice: rayon agriculture administrations were only one among several rayon administrations and could not pull enough weight, whereas interrayon administrations were special, suprarayon organs which carry the authority of the oblast organs.[37]

But the downgrading of the raykoms brought open controversy in party ranks which extended into the debate at the plenum. While most speakers specifically endorsed the interrayon principle, several (Khrushchev, Voronov, Ukrainian First Secretary Podgornyy, Kiev First Secretary Shelest, Georgian First Secretary Mzhavanadze, Rostov First Secretary Basov, Estonian First Secretary Kebin, and Kostroma First Secretary Florentyev) admitted the existence of opposition to interrayon, rather than rayon, administrations, and Mzhavanadze, Kebin, and Shelest were noticeably cool to the interrayon principle and defended the raykoms. The situation was aggravated by Voronov, Bashkir First Secretary Z. N. Nuriyev, Florentyev, Basov, and Tambov First Secretary G. S. Zolotukhin, who went even further than Khrushchev in pushing interrayon administrations. Voronov, although reassuring the raykoms that they would not lose influence under the new plan (which Khrushchev did not bother to do),

[33] Ibid., p. 77.
[34] Khrushchev's report, ibid., p. 75.
[35] Ibid., p. 120.
[36] Ibid., p. 320.
[37] Ibid., pp. 437–38.

proposed taking the raykoms' newspapers away and transferring them to the interrayon administrations—a considerable blow.[38] Nuriyev[39] and Basov[40] specifically praised Voronov's proposal. Florentyev[41] and, especially, Zolotukhin[42] suggested that production administrations have the right to hire and fire sovkhoz directors and recommend cadres for kolkhozes also, while Basov wanted production administrations' party organizers to virtually replace the raykoms by even running party organizations of kolkhozes and sovkhozes.[43]

In contrast, Kiev First Secretary Shelest hardly even paid lip service to the reorganization and recalled Khrushchev's one-time praise of the role of raykoms and the need to avoid weakening them.[44] Further, Shelest found it "hard to agree with the proposal of comrades Voronov and Nuriyev on liquidation of rayon newspapers."[45] Mzhavanadze also insisted on rayon papers. Khrushchev in his concluding speech noted Kebin's opposition to interrayon administrations and granted him (and others) the right to organize rayon-scale administrations if really necessary. The rural raykoms eventually were abolished in November 1962, but were restored immediately after Khrushchev's fall—at the November 1964 plenum. However, the production administrations were not abolished after his departure.

Voronov Ascendant

The March 1962 plenum showed Voronov's ascendancy over his apparent erstwhile patron Polyanskiy. Next to Khrushchev, Voronov played the most important role at the plenum. Speaking on behalf of the whole RSFSR (which Polyanskiy had done at the January 1961 plenum) his speech immediately followed Khrushchev's report and was the longest speech at the plenum, aside from Khrushchev's report and concluding speech. The contents also marked it as second only to Khrushchev's in importance.

Although differing with Khrushchev in ignoring his calls for more resources for agriculture and his pushing of Lysenko, Voronov strongly backed his proposals on reorganization, and in fact even went further in the direction of strong powers of control for the new production administrations over farms and strong control for his own power base (the RSFSR Bureau and the new RSFSR Agriculture Committee) over the production administrations. He declared that production administrations were to be the "main link" in agriculture and were to "concentrate all functions" of production and procurement[46] and ignored

[38] Ibid., pp. 103–4.
[39] Ibid., p. 266.
[40] Ibid., p. 321.
[41] Ibid., p. 345.
[42] Ibid., p. 419.
[43] Ibid., p. 321.
[44] Ibid., p. 314.
[45] Ibid.
[46] Ibid., p. 101.

Khrushchev's suggestion that farms should have the last word in disputes with production administrations.[47] He also went further in praising *Sovetskaya Rossiya's* proposal for establishing interrayon administration newspapers and eliminating the raykom papers.

The structure described by Voronov clearly would strengthen his own personal position. First, the key party officials under the new plan—the *partorgs* (party organizers) in production administrations who would guide the party organizations of farms and work with raykoms—were to be selected by the RSFSR Bureau, according to Voronov.[48] He declared they would be "our reliable local representatives" and "we will regularly assemble them, consult with them and direct their activities."[49] In contrast, Khrushchev, and others, indicated that the *partorgs* would be controlled either by the Central Committee or obkoms.

Second, the new RSFSR Agriculture Committee was to be under RSFSR Bureau First Deputy Chairman Voronov, with the yet-to-be-selected first deputy premier and minister of production and procurement of agricultural products as deputy chairman. Premier Polyanskiy was excluded—even though he was an agricultural specialist. Polyanskiy's first deputy for agriculture, the RSFSR agriculture minister, the RSFSR Selkhoztekhnika (Agricultural Equipment Association) chief and the RSFSR Gosplan deputy chairman for agriculture were to be members of Voronov's committee—thus Voronov could run agriculture directly through Polyanskiy's subordinates without consulting him at all. Interestingly enough, although excluded from membership, Polyanskiy was permitted to attend the first meeting of the new committee (*Sovetskaya Rossiya*, 25 March 1962). Voronov also excluded sovnarkhoz chairmen from local agricultural committees on the ground that ties between industry and agriculture should be mainly through national, not local, organizations. This probably also would strengthen the RSFSR Bureau's control.

Several speakers showed special deference to Voronov by praising his reorganization plan for the RSFSR (Tatar First Secretary F. A. Tabeyev,[50] and Stavropol First Secretary F. D. Kulakov[51]), or the RSFSR Bureau proposals (Kostroma First Secretary L. Ya. Florentyev[52]), or his position on interrayon newspapers (Bashkir First Secretary Z. N. Nuriyev and Rostov First Secretary A. V. Basov). Basov—the most pro-Voronov speaker—was the only one to repeat his idea of "*partorgs* of the RSFSR Bureau"—in fact, repeating it three times.[53] This would give Voronov's RSFSR Bureau close control over all RSFSR rural party affairs, since, as Basov defined the *partorgs'* role, they would virtually

[47] Khrushchev's report, ibid., p. 71.
[48] Ibid., p. 104.
[49] Ibid.
[50] Ibid., p. 300.
[51] Ibid., p. 334.
[52] Ibid., p. 344.
[53] Ibid., p. 321.

replace other local party organizations and, if under the RSFSR Bureau, would even bypass the obkoms.

Volgograd First Secretary A. M. Shkolnikov, Kuybyshev First Secretary A. S. Murysev, and Stavropol First Secretary F. D. Kulakov also showed deference to Voronov by their praise of the Orenburg system. Shkolnikov told how his oblast's three-year use of early and deep fall plowing with leveling—i.e., Khayrullin's method—had proved its value.[54] Kulakov also praised this system,[55] while Murysev praised Khayrullin by name for "valuable advice."[56] Perhaps it is more than coincidence that many of those showing deference to Voronov prospered after Khrushchev's fall. Kulakov became Central Committee agriculture secretary. Basov became RSFSR agriculture minister in March 1965, and Florentyev succeeded him in November 1965. Shkolnikov became RSFSR first deputy premier in November 1965. The last three, of course, worked directly under RSFSR Premier Voronov in 1965.

Following the plenum, Voronov played a correspondingly bigger role in Soviet politics. As chairman of the RSFSR Agriculture Committee, he carried out a considerable reorganization of RSFSR agricultural organs (he reported on this at a 27 March 1962 RSFSR Bureau session). The RSFSR Procurement Ministry and Sovkhoz Ministry were abolished and replaced by a Ministry for Production and Procurement of Agricultural Products. Oddly, the new ministry was staffed by people apparently in Khrushchev's bad graces: Minister N. I. Smirnov had just three to four months earlier been harshly attacked by Khrushchev for his leadership of agriculture in Leningrad (he was from Kozlov's bailiwick and was, at the time of the attack, Gosplan deputy chairman for agriculture). V. P. Mylarshchikov, who was ousted as head of the Central Committee Section for RSFSR Agriculture in the spring 1959 power struggle, returned to prominence by becoming first deputy minister (he was replaced again in 1963). Among the new deputy ministers was S. S. Nikulin, Moscow Oblast agriculture chief promoted to RSFSR deputy agriculture minister in late 1959 or early 1960 and then exiled to Lipetsk in the 1961 purge of the RSFSR Agriculture Ministry. The RSFSR Agriculture Ministry (Minister Sotnikov)—under attack by Khrushchev as useless—continued its existence until early 1963.

Confusion after March

The creation of the new production administrations in March 1962 caused great local confusion. A 30 May 1962 *Selskaya Zhizn* editorial complained of bad relations between raykoms and production administrations. Some raykom secretaries regarded the production administrations simply as renamed rayon agricultural departments (*Selskaya Zhizn*, 30 May 1962) and "tried to stand above the

54 Ibid., p. 274.
55 Ibid., p. 332.
56 Ibid., p. 294.

production administrations, to command them and to dictate their will to them" (*Sovetskaya Latviya* editorial on 4 July 1962). *Sovetskaya Rossiya* on 17 May 1962 reported the firing of a raykom first secretary for fighting the new interrayon production administrations. Voronov himself admitted that "there are cases of incorrect relations between territorial administrations and rayon organizations in several oblasts" and he cited the "outrageous case" cited by *Sovetskaya Rossiya* of a raykom secretary fighting the new production administrations (*Sovetskaya Rossiya*, 27 June 1962). Other raykom leaders went to the opposite extreme, completely renouncing any responsibility for agriculture and limiting themselves to ideological work (*Selskaya Zhizn*, 30 May 1962). A 19 June 1962 *Pravda* article reported that some raykom officials were offended because they had lost their own newspapers, which were turned into interrayon papers (a 22 March 1962 Central Committee and Council of Ministers decree "On the Reorganization of Agricultural Administration"[57] established interrayon newspapers).

An example of the confusion could be seen in Kazakhstan, where it was necessary to hold a Kazakh conference of obkom *partorgs* of production administrations on 12–13 June and a separate Kazakh conference of rural raykom first secretaries on 20–22 June. Kazakh Second Secretary N. N. Rodionov, who apparently was in charge of organizational questions, addressed both conferences, attempting to explain the new relationships (*Kazakhstanskaya Pravda*, 14 and 23 June). At both conferences he stressed that the establishment of production administrations does not reduce the role of raykoms and he declared that raykoms "were, are and will continue to be organs of political leadership of all aspects of economic and cultural life of rayons" (*Kazakhstanskaya Pravda*, 14 June).

However, in contrast to Rodionov's statements, only days later—at a 27 June Moscow conference of officials of production administrations of the central RSFSR (*Pravda*, 30 June 1962)—Khrushchev revealed that he had intended all along to abolish raykoms, but had temporized at the March 1962 plenum. Calling rayons only "a phenomenon of a transitional period" and raykoms and their methods of leadership outmoded "in new, changing conditions," he stated that in March 1962 the Central Committee could not abolish the raykoms because "the sowing was beginning" and this would have disrupted it. Now, he stated, the Presidium had considered the question of raykoms and production administrations and had decided that "conditions have matured to adopt the decision" to subordinate the raykom secretaries once and for all to the production administrations. This would end the current disputes between raykoms and production administrations over "who is subordinate to whom." He also complained that "certain of our officials have taken a peculiar, insufficiently definite position" on this question of subordination, bowing "respectfully to the produc-

[57]*Spravochnik Partiynogo Rabotnika* [Party Worker's Handbook], edition 4 (1963), p. 326.

tion administration and giving the same bow to the raykom," thereby compounding the confusion.

Continuing opposition to the abolishing of raykoms apparently prompted the Soviet press to go easy on this subject. *Pravda* went as far as any in its 1 July 1962 editorial criticizing "old organizational forms of leadership" for holding back agriculture, criticizing some raykoms for trying to take over production administrations, and declaring that "in the future it will be advisable to consolidate administrative regions approximately to the size of production administrations." Nevertheless, after Khrushchev's speech a Central Committee decision apparently was adopted to subordinate raykom first secretaries to production administration leaders by making them deputies of the production administrations' *partorgs.* Lithuanian First Secretary Snechkus referred to such a recent Central Committee "decree" in his speech at a July Lithuanian Central Committee plenum (*Sovetskaya Litva*, 22 July 1962) and head of the Minsk Obkom Party Organs Section, L. Kletskov, referred to a "recently adopted decision" on this in an August *Kommunist Belorussii* article (no. 8, pp. 17-19). However, such a decree apparently never appeared in the press nor in the *Party Worker's Handbook [Spravochnik Partiynogo Rabotnika]*.

The November 1962 Plenum

The structural reorganization announced at the November 1962 plenum carried further two of the main directions of the March 1962 reorganization: replacing rayon units with interrayon units and forcing local party secretaries to concentrate more on agriculture. The production administrations were declared a success by Khrushchev and Voronov (Voronov declaring that "now even the most inveterate skeptics are forced to acknowledge the enormous value of the reorganization"[58]). The power of the successful production administration units was therefore extended. Khrushchev proposed that party committees of the administrations replace rural raykoms and lead the party organizations of kolkhozes and sovkhozes, declaring that there is no need for rayon organizations any more.[59]

This replacement of raykoms by production administration party committees appears to be a triumph for Voronov's ideas, expressed at the March 1962 plenum. In March, however, widespread sentiment in favor of retaining raykoms apparently prevented giving production administrations as much power as he wished. As noted above, he had gone further than Khrushchev in pushing this idea and had been criticized by other speakers who wished to defend the raykoms.

Even more resentment was caused by Khrushchev's carrying the production principle to its logical conclusion by splitting party organizations into agri-

---

[58]Stenographic record of the November 1962 Central Committee plenum, p. 100.
[59]Ibid., pp. 17 and 19.

cultural and industrial units. Over half the provinces in the RSFSR now had two obkoms—one for industry and one for agriculture (smaller oblasts and autonomous republics did not split). Although this split seemingly restored industry's equality in the organizational system, in fact agriculture still was favored in carrying out this reorganization, since 80 percent of the obkom first secretaries became first secretaries of the new agricultural obkoms rather than of the new industrial obkoms, and thirty-one agricultural obkom first secretaries were Central Committee members or candidate members while only eight industrial obkom first secretaries were.

Opposition to the bifurcation was virtually admitted in some articles defending the new organizational structure. In referring to the November 1962 reorganization, *Sovetskaya Rossiya*, on 5 January 1963, declared that "only hardened dogmatists, persons who are accustomed to thinking in old formulas and are hopelessly isolated from real life, cannot see the vital need and great advantage of organizing party organs according to the production principle." A frequent commentator on party organizational matters, F. Petrenko argued that "there are also no bases for the fears expressed by certain comrades that the division of party organizations and soviets will violate normal relations between town and country" and that division of party organs "does not mean that our entire party will be divided or that now there will be two parties: one for the city and one for the countryside."[60] At the March 1965 plenum Georgian First Secretary Mzhavanadze frankly told of the 1962 opposition to the "totally unjustified" bifurcation: "The Central Committee members with whom I met expressed indignation about this question and told Khrushchev that this would complicate work and that this cannot be done, but he did not want to listen to anyone."[61]

Only a month after Khrushchev's removal, the November 1964 plenum adopted a decree reuniting party organs, abolishing production administrations' party committees (but not the production administrations), and restoring the raykoms (*Pravda*, 17 November 1964). Newspapers were restored to the raykoms in early 1965.[62]

Under the new dual system of party organs there was no longer need for the special agricultural committees established in March 1962. Thus, the RSFSR Agriculture Committee (Chairman Voronov) disappeared and a RSFSR Agriculture Bureau and a RSFSR Industry and Construction Bureau were established. The heads of the RSFSR bureaus were never identified publicly, but presumably were Yefremov (agriculture) and Kirilenko (industry), the two first deputy chairmen of the RSFSR Bureau.[63] Thus, although Voronov played a prominent role

[60] *Partiynaya Zhizn*, 2 (1963): 14–20.
[61] Stenographic record of the March 1965 Central Committee plenum, p. 89.
[62] *Partiynaya Zhizn* 13 (July 1965): 75–76, and *Sovetskaya Rossiya*, 17 March 1965.
[63] Only two members of the RSFSR Agriculture Bureau were identified: RSFSR Agriculture Section head I. S. Pankin (*Leningradskaya Pravda*, 24 August 1963) and RSFSR Agitprop head V. I. Stepakov (*Selskaya Zhizn*, 13 March 1964).

at the plenum and spoke for the RSFSR, the key posts in party leadership of agriculture (first deputy chairman of the RSFSR Bureau and chairman of the RSFSR Agriculture Committee) passed out of his hands.

Voronov and Polyanskiy in Eclipse

Voronov appears to have hit his high point in the spring and summer of 1962, acting as Khrushchev's lieutenant at the March 1962 plenum in promoting the new agricultural reorganization, becoming head of the new RSFSR Agriculture Committee, and having his ally, Pysin, become agriculture minister. But November 1962 saw both Polyanskiy and Voronov being kicked upstairs. Polyanskiy left as RSFSR premier and became a USSR deputy premier in charge of agriculture. Voronov succeeded him as RSFSR premier. Polyanskiy left the RSFSR Bureau and Voronov dropped from first deputy chairman to ordinary member of the Bureau.

The reasons for Voronov's decline in November 1962 are obscure but appear rooted in the decisions and statements at and after the March 1962 plenum. As pointed out above, his speech had somewhat contrasted with Khrushchev's in favoring stronger state control over kolkhozes and in ignoring the urgent issue of more resources for agriculture. He and his allies appear to a considerable extent responsible for weakening Lysenko's position, which Khrushchev was desperately trying to shore-up.

A new source of friction was added immediately after the March plenum when Voronov set up the new RSFSR organs. At a time when Khrushchev's relations with the Leningrad leaders Kozlov and Spiridonov were worsening, Voronov chose as his new top assistant (deputy chairman of the RSFSR Agriculture Committee, RSFSR first deputy premier and minister for production and procurement of agricultural products) former Leningrad Oblast Executive Committee Chairman N. I. Smirnov, a close protégé of Kozlov and Spiridonov. Smirnov had become first deputy chairman of the Leningrad Executive Committee in 1955 and chairman in the spring of 1957, under obkom First Secretary Kozlov. As chairman from 1957 to late 1961, he supervised Leningrad's agriculture under Spiridonov, who was Leningrad Obkom first secretary from December 1957 to April 1962.

At the same time that Spiridonov got a big promotion at the 22d Congress in October 1961 (he became a Central Committee secretary), Smirnov was appointed Gosplan deputy chairman for agriculture (he was released from his Leningrad post in the 3 October 1961 *Leningradskaya Pravda*). He was Leningrad's only representative in the agricultural field. Yet immediately after his appointment, Khrushchev blasted Smirnov, who, he pointed out, had just been put in charge of agriculture in Gosplan, for making a mess of Leningrad's agriculture (*Pravda*, 16 December 1961). At a December 1961 Moscow conference Khrushchev and Polyanskiy assailed the Leningraders harshly for clinging to grass and not switching to corn, peas, beans, and beets (Khrushchev spoke of "criminal utilization of land" in Leningrad—*Pravda*, 16 December 1961). *Sovetskaya Rossiya* on 24 December 1961 described the Leningrad leaders as "shaken" from the criticism, and they dutifully began pressuring their farmers to switch to corn (*Leningradskaya Pravda*, 24 December 1961).

Despite Khrushchev's blast at Smirnov personally, immediately after the March 1962 plenum, where Voronov proposed a reorganization of RSFSR organs, Smirnov was selected to become his top deputy in the new structure—in charge of all RSFSR agriculture. He and Voronov appear to have worked together closely, teaming up to address several conferences during the summer of 1962 (at Rostov, *Pravda*, 26 May; at Leningrad, *Sovetskaya Rossiya*, 13 June; at a 6 July RSFSR livestock conference, *Pravda*, 7 August; and at Kuybyshev, *Sovetskaya Rossiya*, 9 August).

At the same time that Voronov allied himself with Spiridonov's top long-time assistant, Khrushchev began a mysterious campaign against Spiridonov and the Leningrad leaders. An early April Central Committee decree (*Partiynaya Zhizn*, no. 8, 17 April 1962) attacked the Leningrad City Party Committee (First Secretary G. I. Popov) for poor leadership of scientific institutes. Popov responded with an acknowledgement of the shortcomings and a plan to reorganize Leningrad's scientific organizations (*Pravda*, 28 April), and the Leningrad City Party Committee held a special plenum on the question (*Leningradskaya Pravda*, 11 May).

In the meantime, a Central Committee plenum was held and Leningrad Obkom First Secretary Spiridonov was dropped as Central Committee secretary (*Pravda*, 26 April), and on 3 May Khrushchev personally traveled to Leningrad and supervised his removal as Leningrad first secretary, for reasons unspecified (*Pravda*, 4 May). Khrushchev's unusual personal intervention in this regional cadre action was apparently meant to identify him personally with Spiridonov's removal.

The same Central Committee plenum which ousted Spiridonov as Central Committee secretary elected Sverdlovsk First Secretary Kirilenko as a full Presidium member and made him RSFSR Bureau first deputy chairman. This apparently had some connection with Spiridonov's ouster, since both actions were reversals of decisions made at the 22d Congress in October 1961. At that time Spiridonov was dropped from membership in the RSFSR Bureau to assume the higher post of Central Committee secretary, while Kirilenko was dropped as Presidium candidate member to assume the lower post of member of the RSFSR Bureau. Thus, what apparently was a setback for Khrushchev's protégé Kirilenko in October 1961, became a victory in April 1962.

Though there are no overt signs of Voronov's collaboration with Spiridonov, Spiridonov did work with Voronov as a RSFSR Bureau member until October 1961, and Voronov did choose Spiridonov's protégé, Smirnov, as his top assistant, despite Khrushchev's lack of confidence in Smirnov. At the least, Smirnov's appointment must have pleased the Leningraders. Thus, Kirilenko's appointment as a second RSFSR Bureau first deputy chairman in April 1962 may have been aimed partly at Voronov also—although it apparently did not affect Voronov's power over RSFSR agriculture since Kirilenko was an industrial specialist. It may also be more than coincidental that later in 1962 when Voronov declined, sharp attacks were launched against Smirnov and his deputies. I. Salnikov in the 13 October 1962 *Ekonomicheskaya Gazeta* attacked V. P. Mylarshchikov, "now first deputy minister for production and procurement of agricultural products RSFSR," for his leadership of Moscow vegetable and potato growing since 1959. Mylarshchikov had been demoted from Central Committee Agriculture Section head to director of the Moscow trust of vegetable-potato growing sovkhozes in the spring 1959 political struggle. Salnikov also wrote that Smirnov and his ministry had "proved incapable" of effectively using the equipment and fertilizer provided to boost vegetable production. On 17 November the *Ekonomicheskaya Gazeta* editors attacked the response by Smirnov's deputy V. V. Memnonov to the October article and declared they were still awaiting a satisfactory reply from Smirnov and other republic agricultural production ministers. Finally, in January 1964, when Voronov and Khrushchev were apparently quarreling over virgin land policies, Smirnov was removed and replaced by a Khrushchev favorite.

For whatever reason, Voronov definitely declined at the end of the November 1962 plenum and new favorites were raised up by Khrushchev. Gorkiy First Secretary L. N. Yefremov replaced Voronov as first deputy chairman of the RSFSR Bureau and also became a Presidium candidate member. *Selskaya Zhizn* editor Polyakov, also head of the Central Committee Agriculture Section since March 1962, was promoted to Central Committee secretary and chairman of the new Agriculture Bureau as well, at the November 1962 plenum.

The rise of Polyakov and Yefremov brought a gradual influx of other new agricultural leaders, at least some of whom had ties with Yefremov.

In March 1963 Pysin was dropped as agriculture minister and demoted to a Central Committee inspector.[64] He was replaced by a particular favorite of Khrushchev, I. P. Volovchenko, director of the Petrovskiy Sovkhoz in Lipetsk 1951-63. Volovchenko had won high praise from Khrushchev for denouncing the leaders of his oblast for permitting the planting of too much grass and also for his successes in pea raising.

First Deputy Agriculture Minister Levykin was removed in early 1964 after being condemned (in *Izvestiya*, 14 March 1964) for obstructing production of a tractor Khrushchev had urged at the February 1964 plenum. Levykin, an agricultural machinery expert, had been appointed in April 1962, succeeding Pysin, when Voronov and Pysin were at the zenith of their power.

Two new first deputy ministers appeared in mid-1964: P. I. Morozov and R. N. Sidak. Morozov, deputy RSFSR agriculture minister 1955-57 and Amur first secretary 1957-April 1964, was praised by Khrushchev for pushing soy-

---

[64] Identified in *Bakinskiy Rabochiy*, 11 October 1963.

Agricultural Leadership

	1962	1963	1964
Premier and first sec.	Khrushchev	Khrushchev	Khrushchev
Agriculture secretary	none	(Nov 62–) Polyakov	Polyakov
CC Agri. Section head	(Mar 62–) Polyakov	Polyakov	Polyakov
CC Agri. Section deputy head		Pannikov[a]	Pannikov
Deputy premier	Ignatov (–Nov 62)	Polyanskiy	Polyanskiy
Agriculture minister	(Mar 62–) Pysin (–Mar 63)	Volovchenko	Volovchenko
First deputy minister	(Mar 62–) Levykin	Levykin (early 64–) Morozov	(early 64–) Morozov
			(early 64–) Sidak
1st dep. ch. RSFSR Bureau	Voronov (–Nov 62)	Yefremov	Yefremov
CC RSFSR Agri. Section	Pankin	Pankin	Pankin
Premier RSFSR	Polyanskiy (–Nov 62)	Voronov	Voronov
1st dep. prem. and PPAP[b]	(Mar 62–) Smirnov	Smirnov (–Jan 64)	Maksimov
1st dep. min. PPAP	Mylarshchikov	Baturin	Baturin

[a]Identified Feb. 1963.
[b]Ministry for Production and Procurement of Agricultural Products.

beans in 1962 and 1963; he first appeared on 15 May (*Izvestiya*). Sidak was director of the Lgovskaya experimental selection station in Khrushchev's home oblast of Kursk, from 1956 until early 1964. Khrushchev regularly cited his successes in pea-raising and developing of a pea harvester. He was invited to speak at the December 1963 plenum and by 15 June 1964 (*Pravda*) had become first deputy agriculture minister and accompanied Khrushchev as his sole agricultural adviser on a trip to Scandinavia. He had worked under Yefremov, who was Kursk Oblast first secretary from 1954 to late 1958. Khrushchev made frequent visits to Kalinovka (his home town in Kursk) and Yefremov obsequiously praised him, pushed his initiatives, and favored the Kalinovka kolkhoz.

When then Gorkiy First Secretary Yefremov moved to Moscow in December 1962, one of his associates from Gorkiy, V. D. Pannikov, soon showed up in a top agricultural post. Pannikov, director of the Gorkiy Agricultural Institute and later obkom secretary under Yefremov, appeared as deputy head of the Central Committee Agriculture Section in early 1963 (identified in the 1 March 1963 *Sovetskaya Moldaviya*).

L. I. Maksimov, director of a sovkhoz in Krasnodar, won Khrushchev's praise for switching from grass sowing to pea raising and corn sowing in 1962. After becoming a favorite example of Khrushchev's, he was named RSFSR first deputy premier and RSFSR minister for production and procurement of agricultural products in January 1964.

CHAPTER V

KHRUSHCHEV'S
SETBACKS: 1963

The weakening of Khrushchev's position, evident in 1962, was compounded by setbacks in 1963, preparing the way for his 1964 removal. He had stirred wide resentment by forcing through his disruptive 1962 reorganizations. The 1962 Cuban missile misadventure also undermined confidence in his leadership. At the same time, Second Secretary F. R. Kozlov was rising in influence and opposing him, for example, on shifting resources from heavy industry to agriculture and consumer goods.

In late 1962 and early 1963 there were purges of Kazakh leaders, after Khrushchev had accused them of failure in agricultural production and had assailed them for slowness in applying his agricultural policies. However, the Kazakh purges were not simply a Khrushchev action; they reflected the growing power of his rival Kozlov as well. Kozlov traveled to Kazakhstan in December 1962 and February 1963 to conduct the purges, ousting and disgracing the officials installed by Brezhnev in January 1960, including Brezhnev's close protégés. Although the purges represented a setback for Khrushchev's protégé, Brezhnev, Khrushchev had been unhappy with the old leaders anyway and he made only minor changes in the new Kazakh leadership after the removal of Kozlov's influence. The changes were reversed only when Brezhnev succeeded Khrushchev and immediately restored his friends to power in Kazakhstan.

Khrushchev received a big break in early 1963 when his most powerful foe, Kozlov, was incapacitated by a heart attack. This was a setback for the military-heavy industry complex and encouraged Khrushchev to press ahead with plans to transfer funds from defense and heavy industry to fertilizer production. He brought his protégés Brezhnev and Podgornyy into the Secretariat to take over Kozlov's duties.

But Khrushchev soon received his worst agricultural setback when the 1963 virgin land crop failure discredited his agricultural policies and forced the

USSR to buy grain abroad. He had to retreat in his insistence on corn and the intertilled system, and the clean-fallow advocates won recognition in the virgin lands.

Spurred by the grain crisis, he launched an aggressive drive to vastly increase fertilizer production, but the heavy industry-defense complex still predominated and he was forced to retreat on his fertilizer program. At the December 1963 Central Committee plenum Khrushchev wound up on the defensive, admitting virgin land failures and the buying of grain abroad and backing down on his corn and fertilizer programs. But in 1964 he returned to the offensive with new drives against the anti-Lysenkoists and the advocates of clean fallow.

The Kazakh Purge

The Kazakh leaders, frequently criticized by Khrushchev, were purged and disgraced in late 1962 and early 1963. As in late 1959, they were accused of agricultural failures, and an emissary from Moscow was sent to conduct the purge—this time Kozlov instead of Brezhnev. However, there were many other shortcomings besides agricultural failings and this purge was far more thorough. Many facets of it remain unclear, but the main loser was certainly Brezhnev, who was closely associated with the victims. His first achievement after succeeding Khrushchev as first secretary was the reversal of this purge in early December 1964.

Khrushchev had long shown dissatisfaction with the leaders of Kazakhstan and badgered them to adopt Lysenko's early sowing and winter rye programs, Khayrullin's leveled fall plowing, and especially Nalivayko's intertilled system. Kazakh leaders Kunayev and Sokolov had been following Barayev's insistence on clean fallow as a means for fighting weeds.[1] Lysenko also supported clean fallow—but mainly because fallow saves the grain from spring malnutrition and facilitates early sowing and early harvesting (according to Yu. Chernichenko in *Novyy Mir*, no. 11, [1965]). Nalivayko, however, insisted that clean fallow led to erosion and weeds and advocated sown fallow (corn). Khrushchev backed Nalivayko against Barayev[2] and praised a north Kazakhstan sovkhoz director (B. N. Dvoretskiy) for proving that the virgin lands can produce high crops of corn with ears.[3]

At the 22d Congress Khrushchev spoke of "serious shortcomings" in the use of the virgin lands and denounced the Kazakh Central Committee and Council of Ministers for holding "an incorrect position," sowing spring wheat year

[1] See their speeches at the January 1961 plenum, stenographic record of the January 1961 Central Committee plenum, pp. 73 and 93.

[2] See his 22 November 1961 Tselinograd speech, Khrushchev's collected speeches, vol. 6, p. 142.

[3] Ibid., p. 148.

after year and not expanding corn, peas, fodder beans, and sugar beets.[4] A December 1961 Kazakh Central Committee conference discussed "the most rapid execution of the orders and advice given by N. S. Khrushchev" in his recent speeches on changing to the intertilled system and expanding corn, peas, fodder beans, and sugar beets (*Kazakhstanskaya Pravda*, 28 December 1961). *Selskaya Zhizn* on 26 January 1962 even reported that Barayev had announced that he was correcting the shortcomings at his institute, criticized by Khrushchev at Tselinograd, and in "the next few years" would renounce clean fallow and switch to the intertilled system, increasing corn by five times.

At the March 1962 plenum Khrushchev complained that the Kazakh Central Committee and Council of Ministers were still insisting that intensive agriculture could not be carried on in north Kazakhstan and that they were holding back the introduction of intertilled crops and wanted to expand clean fallow. He granted the possibility that some clean fallow might be necessary, but he urged them to look to Nalivayko who was getting along without it.[5] At the March plenum Kunayev recognized the correctness of Khrushchev's criticism[6] and declared that corn would be expanded by 535,000 hectares (to 2,360,000 hectares) above 1961.[7] Sokolov stated that Tselinnyy Kray was reviewing its crop structure and expanding corn, sugar beets, and beans, while reducing clean fallow and grass.[8]

A 4 July 1962 *Pravda* editorial attacked Kazakh First Secretary Kunayev, Premier Daulenov, Tselinnyy Kray First Secretary Sokolov, Tselinnyy Kray Executive Committee Chairman Matskevich, and Tselinnyy Kray Agricultural Production and Procurement Administration chief A. I. Kozlov by name for poor preparations for harvesting. *Pravda* criticized most of them again on 6 and 7 July. During his September 1962 trip through Central Asia Khrushchev criticized the leaders of Kazakhstan and Tselinnyy Kray for sowing wheat after wheat and having weedy fields,[9] and at the November 1962 plenum, recalling his criticisms at the 22d Congress and at the March 1962 plenum, he criticized the Kazakh and Tselinnyy leaders for not listening to "the voice of advanced science and practice."[10]

A 25-26 December 1962 Kazakh Central Committee plenum on the results of the November Central Committee plenum heard Kunayev repeat Khrushchev's criticism of the Kazakh leadership. Kunayev reported that at the Moscow plenum Khrushchev had announced the failure of Kazakhstan to fulfill

[4] Ibid., p. 26.
[5] Ibid., pp. 362–63.
[6] Stenographic record of the March 1962 Central Committee plenum, p. 130.
[7] Ibid., pp. 133–34.
[8] Ibid., p. 208.
[9] Khrushchev's 28 September 1962 speech, Khrushchev's collected speeches, vol. 7, p. 192.
[10] Ibid., p. 388.

its grain delivery plan, selling only 501 million poods of grain to the state instead of the planned 868 million, and that Khrushchev had declared: "For Kazakhstan, such a figure is tantamount to failure in work . . ." (*Kazakhstanskaya Pravda*, 26 December 1962). Kunayev also declared that Tselinnyy Kray had fulfilled the grain delivery plan by only 47 percent, falling short by 362 million poods. He stated that because of "shortcomings in the leadership of virgin lands farming by the Kazakh Central Committee Bureau and the Kazakh Council of Ministers, as well as the Tselinnyy Kray Party Committee and Executive Committee, which are headed by comrades Sokolov and Matskevich," Tselinnyy grain deliveries had fallen from 450 million poods in 1960 to 306 million in 1961 and 318 million in 1962 (*Kazakhstanskaya Pravda*, 26 December 1962).

In addition to the agricultural failings, a major scandal over cadres broke. On 14 September 1962 *Kazakhstanskaya Pravda* announced that Premier S. D. Daulenov had been replaced by Alma-Ata Oblast First Secretary M. Beysebayev. At the December Kazakh Central Committee plenum, under the supervision of Central Committee Secretary F. R. Kozlov, Daulenov was expelled from the Kazakh Central Committee. First Secretary Kunayev was demoted to premier, Premier Beysebayev was demoted to first deputy premier, and Second Secretary Rodionov was transferred out of Kazakhstan, later reappearing in a minor Leningrad post.[11] At the plenum Kunayev confessed that a "mistake" had been made by "the Kazakh Central Committee Bureau and by me personally, as Kazakh Central Committee first secretary, in advancing Daulenov to a high post." Daulenov in "drunken orgies" had made "nationalistic statements."[12]

A new team of leaders was appointed. Kazakh Secretary I. Yu. Yusupov became first secretary, Karaganda First Secretary M. S. Solomentsev became second secretary, and Deputy Premier R. B. Baygaliyev was made Kazakh Central Committee secretary and chairman of the new Kazakh Bureau for Industry. F. S. Kolomiyets, who had been sent to Kazakhstan in May 1962 to become first secretary of West Kazakhstan Oblast, became a Kazakh Central Committee secretary and chairman of the new Kazakh Bureau for Agriculture. Kolomiyets was RSFSR deputy food industry minister when sent to Krasnodar in 1957, where he served as deputy chairman of the Krasnodar Sovnarkhoz while Polyanskiy was Krasnodar Kray first secretary from March 1957 to March 1958. He became kray agriculture secretary in 1958 under Polyanskiy's successor Matyushkin and kray executive committee chairman in 1960.

In February 1963 Frol Kozlov returned to Kazakhstan a second time and supervised a Tselinnyy Kray plenum, at which kray Executive Committee Chairman Matskevich reported on the kray's poor organization of agricultural work.

---

[11] Deputy chairman of the Leningrad Sovnarkhoz—*Leningradskaya Pravda*, 13 June 1963.

[12] Kunayev's speech in the 26 December 1962 *Kazakhstanskaya Pravda*.

Tselinnyy Kray First Secretary Sokolov was attacked for "unsatisfactory and superficial leadership" and removed as first secretary (*Pravda*, 22 February 1963).

Finally, at a March Kazakh Central Committee plenum an orgy of attacks broke loose on almost all Kazakh leaders: former First Secretary Kunayev, former Kazakh Secretary and former Tselinnyy Kray First Secretary Sokolov, former premiers Daulenov and Tashenev, President I. Sh. Sharipov, Ideology Secretary N. D. Dzhandildin, Tselinnyy Kray Executive Committee Chairman Matskevich, Kazakh Trade Union Council Chairman S. Polimbetov, former Kzyl-Orda First Secretary S. T. Toktamysov, former Chimkent First Secretary V. I. Makarov, former Kokchetav First Secretary S. M. Novikov, and Tselinnyy Production and Procurement of Agricultural Products chief A. I. Kozlov.

Kunayev was blamed personally for appointing his protégé, Daulenov, premier and for other cadre errors. New First Secretary Yusupov declared: "Kunayev, knowing well the serious shortcomings and weak organizational abilities of Daulenov, despite the objections of some Bureau members, got Daulenov's promotion to the post of chairman of the Council of Ministers" (*Kazakhstanskaya Pravda*, 19 March 1963). Semipalatinsk First Secretary M. P. Karpenko (Daulenov had been his predecessor in Semipalatinsk September 1960–January 1961) stated: "Former First Secretary D. A. Kunayev of the Kazakh Central Committee expended much effort to advance Daulenov to the post of chairman of the Kazakh Council of Ministers" and did so only out of "considerations of friendship" (*Pravda*, 25 March 1963). Further, Karpenko claimed that "even after Daulenov's downfall, special favor was shown him for some reason or other: an apartment was kept for him in Alma Ata and a special rate established" (*Kazakhstanskaya Pravda*, 20 March 1963).[13] Speakers at the plenum also "noted that D. A. Kunayev bears personal responsibility for the advancement of the immature official Toktamysov to responsible work" (*Pravda*, 25 March 1963). It was pointed out that Kazakh leaders knew about Toktamysov's penchant for gambling even before appointing him obkom first secretary.

Further, Karpenko stated the appointment of Zh. A. Tashenev as premier "was certainly a mistake" (*Kazakhstanskaya Pravda*, 20 March 1963) and Yusupov declared that Tashenev "turned out to be an immature official" (*Kazakhstanskaya Pravda*, 19 March 1963). Tashenev, like Kunayev, was an old colleague of Brezhnev.[14] He was president and Kunayev was premier while

---

[13] After Kunayev was reinstated as first secretary, he did not forget his unfortunate protégé. Despite Daulenov's public disgrace, he got a prominent (if quiet) post as chief of the territorial planning department of the Kazakh Gosplan and member of the Gosplan collegium (first identified in the September 1967 *Narodnoye Khozyaystvo Kazakhstana*, the editorial board of which he had joined in August 1967).

[14] Kunayev apparently provided a sinecure for Tashenev also—a Zh. A. Tashenev was later identified as deputy chairman of the Chimkent Oblast Executive Committee (*Pravda Vostoka*, 7 March 1969, and *Narodnoye Khozyaystvo Kazakhstana* 10 [1970]: 80).

Brezhnev was Kazakh first secretary in 1955. In January 1960 when Central Committee Secretary Brezhnev came to Kazakhstan to install the new leadership, Kunayev was promoted to first secretary and Tashenev was promoted to premier. Tashenev singled out Brezhnev for unusual personal flattery on this occasion (see Chapter I).

Now, in March 1963, it turned out that Brezhnev's installation of Tashenev had been "certainly a mistake" and that Brezhnev's protégé, Kunayev, had committed serious errors and abused his power. Kunayev had allowed disastrous agricultural failures and permitted corruption and immorality among the top leaders of the republic. In addition, the March 1963 Kazakh Central Committee plenum expelled Sokolov from the Bureau and Secretariat (*Kazakhstanskaya Pravda*, 20 March), and Yusupov alleged that Sokolov had "behaved improperly in private life and carried on drinking bouts even in his office" (*Kazakhstanskaya Pravda*, 19 March).

The implications of the December 1962–March 1963 Kazakh purge go beyond agricultural politics. Frol Kozlov, then at the height of his influence, personally conducted this purge, which in effect reversed the January 1960 cadre changes made under Brezhnev's supervision.

Note the rise of Brezhnev's 1955 colleagues Kunayev and Tashenev in 1960:

	1955	1959		1960
First secretary	Brezhnev	Belyayev	(Jan. '60–)	Kunayev
Second secretary	Yakovlev	Karibzhanov	(Jan. '60–)	Rodionov
Secretaries	Karibzhanov	G. A. Kozlov		Kozlov
	Tazhiyev	Yusupov		Yusupov
	Uspanov	Dzhandildin		Dzhandildin
			(Jan. '60–)	Sokolov
President	Tashenev	Tashenev	(Jan. '60–)	Karibzhanov
Premier	Kunayev	Kunayev	(Jan. '60–)	Tashenev
First deputy premier	Beysebayev	Melnik		Melnik
Agriculture minister	Melnik	Roginets		Roginets
Sovkhozes minister	Roginets	Karpenko	(Jan. '60–)	A. I. Kozlov

Note the replacement of the January 1960 team (Kunayev, Rodionov, Sokolov, Tashenev):

	1960	1961		1962	1963
First sec.	Kunayev	Kunayev	(Dec. '62–)	Yusupov	Yusupov
Second sec.	Rodionov	Rodionov	(Dec. '62–)	Solomentsev	Solomentsev
Secretaries	G. Kozlov	Kozlov		Kozlov	Kozlov
	Yusupov	Yusupov	(Dec. '62–)	Baygaliyev	Baygaliyev
	Dzhandildin	Dzhandildin		Dzhandildin	Dzhandildin
	Sokolov	Sokolov		Sokolov (–Mar. '63)	Melnik
			(Dec. '62–)	Kolomiyets	Kolomiyets

(cont.)	1960	1961	1962	1963
President	Karibzhanov[a]	Sharipov	Sharipov	Sharipov
Premier	Tashenev[b]	Daulenov[c]	Beysebayev[d]Kunayev	Kunayev
1st dep. prem.	Melnik	Melnik	Melnik (–Apr. '63)	Dvoretskiy
1st dep. prem.			(Dec. '62–) Beysebayev	Beysebayev
Tselinnyy sec.	Sokolov	Sokolov	Sokolov (–Feb. '63)	Kolomiyets

[a]Died August 1960.
[b]Removed January 1961.
[c]Removed September 1962.
[d]Removed December 1962.

The December 1962 changes, in turn, were upset after Brezhnev became Central Committee first secretary. Brezhnev's associates Kunayev and Beysebayev (first deputy premier under Brezhnev in 1955) were returned to their November 1962 posts of first secretary and premier. Tselinnyy Kray was abolished and control over the virgin lands returned to the Kazakh leaders. Kolomiyets, named Kazakh secretary for agriculture in December 1962 and Tselinnyy Kray first secretary in February 1963, was demoted to a minor job as USSR

	1963–1964		1965–1966
First secretary	Yusupov (–Dec. '64)	(Dec. '64–)	Kunayev
Second secretary	Solomentsev (–Dec. '64)	(Apr. '65–)	Titov
Secretaries	Kozlov (–Jan. '66)		
	Baygaliyev (–Apr. '64)	(Apr. '65–)	Kolebayev
	Dzhandildin (–June '65)	(June '65–)	Imashev
	Melnik		Melnik
	Kolomiyets (–Jan. '66)		
President	Sharipov (–Apr. '65)	(Apr. '65–)	Niyazbekov
Premier	Kunayev (–Dec. '64)	(Dec. '64–)	Beysebayev
First deputy premier	Beysebayev (–Dec. '64)	(Feb. '66–)	Vartanyan
First deputy premier	Dvoretskiy (–June '65)		
Prod.-proc. agri. prod.	Dvoretskiy (–Feb. '65)	(Feb. '65–)	Roginets[a]
Agriculture minister	Yelemanov[b] Subbotin	(Mar. '65–)	Roginets
Tselinnyy first sec.	Kolomiyets (–Oct. '65)[c]		

[a]The Ministry for Production and Procurement of Agricultural Products was abolished in March 1965 and Roginets then became agriculture minister.
[b]Replaced February 1964.
[c]Tselinnyy Kray was abolished in October 1965.

deputy food industry minister in 1966 (identified in *Selskaya Zhizn*, 29 June 1966). First Deputy Premier Dvoretskiy was demoted to head of the newly created Ministry of Grain Products and Mixed Feed Industry in June 1965 (*Kazakhstanskaya Pravda*, 25 June 1965).

Although the 1962–63 changes appear to be a purge of Brezhnev's protégés by Kozlov,[15] the new appointees had no clearly identifiable connections. Khrushchev's attitude toward the new Kazakh leaders is uncertain since he had little to say about them during 1963 and 1964. However, a hint of dissatisfaction with Kozlov's handiwork may be seen in the fact that immediately after his incapacitation, a special favorite of Khrushchev's was made the top Kazakh government agricultural official. Director of the Mamlyutsk Sovkhoz B. N. Dvoretskiy, frequently praised by Khrushchev,[16] became Kazakh first deputy premier and minister for production and procurement of agricultural products on 27 April 1963, succeeding G. A. Melnik, who became Central Committee secretary. At the February 1964 CPSU Central Committee plenum Khrushchev praised the Kazakh Central Committee for appointing Dvoretskiy.[17]

Kozlov's Heart Attack

The power of Second Secretary and heir apparent F. R. Kozlov grew during 1962 and early 1963 as Khrushchev's position weakened. Kozlov represented the so-called "steel-eaters"—those defending priority for heavy industry and defense—and apparently hindered Khrushchev's campaign to shift more resources to agriculture and consumer goods.

At the November 1962 anniversary ceremonies Brezhnev stood second to Khrushchev and Kozlov stood third. However, Brezhnev's favored position was partly due to his protocol ranking as chairman of the Supreme Soviet Presidium and, since losing his Secretariat post in mid-1960, he no longer had any power in the crucial sector of party organizational work. Kozlov acted as organizational secretary and in late 1962 appeared to take over responsibility for Central Asia, supervising the December 1962 Kazakh purge, the December 1962 initial meeting of the new Central Asian Bureau, the February 1963 Tselinnyy Kray purge, and the March 1963 Turkmen purge.

[15] One of the anomalies of the purge was that one of those removed by Kozlov was a former protégé of his from Leningrad–N. N. Rodionov. Rodionov, former Leningrad City first secretary, was transferred back to Kozlov's Leningrad–to the humiliating subordinate post of Leningrad Sovnarkhoz deputy chairman. After Khrushchev's fall and Kozlov's death (30 January 1965), Rodionov staged a comeback under Brezhnev and has appeared to be a Brezhnev client (see Chapter I).

Rodionov and his successor Solomentsev were both heavy industrial specialists. Solomentsev's career also contained apparent contradictions. Installed by Kozlov in December 1962, he was removed in December 1964 when Brezhnev's allies were restored. As Rostov first secretary, he came under fire from the RSFSR Bureau (Chairman Brezhnev, Deputy Chairman Kirilenko) in September 1965, but later (December 1966) was elected Central Committee secretary in charge of heavy industry–a post presumably requiring the confidence of heavy industrial specialists Brezhnev and Kirilenko.

[16] In his 14 March 1961 Akmolinsk speech, Khrushchev's collected speeches, vol. 5, p. 236; his 22 November 1961 Tselinograd speech, ibid., vol. 6, pp. 138 and 148; and his March 1962 plenum speech, ibid., p. 362.

[17] Ibid., vol. 8, pp. 420–21.

At the same time, there were hints that Brezhnev and his colleague Kirilenko were in difficulty. Koziov purged Brezhnev's Kazakh protégés in December 1962, and in early 1963 Kirilenko was subjected to a series of unusual snubs. *Sovetskaya Latviya*, in a 31 January 1963 editorial listing Supreme Soviet election candidates, listed Kirilenko behind Kozlov and also Khrushchev behind Shvernik, violating Russian alphabetical order. On 12 and 13 March 1963 *Pravda* listed Kirilenko behind both Kozlov and Kosygin.

In his February 1963 Supreme Soviet election speech Khrushchev appeared on the defensive, conceding the priority of military spending (he said that while "we would like to invest large sums" in agriculture and consumer goods, the need to spend "huge" sums on the military precluded this).[18]

The military-heavy industrial complex scored a remarkable victory on 13 March 1963, when a joint Presidium–Council of Ministers session created a Supreme National Economic Council with authority over all Soviet industry and construction and placed defense industry leader D. F. Ustinov at its head (*Pravda*, 14 March 1963). Ustinov also became a first deputy premier (joining Mikoyan and Kosygin) and Defense Equipment State Committee Chairman L. V. Smirnov became a deputy premier.

But the erosion of Khrushchev's power was temporarily reversed by an unusual stroke of luck soon afterward. On 11 or 12 April Kozlov was stricken with a heart attack and was incapacitated until his death in January 1965.[19] Khrushchev quickly took advantage of the situation. On 24 April he attacked the defense industry as a bad example of waste and inefficiency and the "undisciplined people working in the defense industry." He declared that Ustinov "who used to answer for the defense industry" and "now has been appointed chairman of the Supreme National Economic Council" should look into the defense industry and improve its efficiency. He also challenged the defense industry's March victory. He declared that the "capitalist press" had made a mistake when it had interpreted Ustinov's appointment as Supreme National Economic Council chairman to mean "militarization of the country" and that the Soviet Union now "will make only rockets." He noted that Smirnov had succeeded Ustinov as head of the defense equipment industry and declared that we will "shake him just as we used to shake Comrade Ustinov, who used to answer for the development of the defense industry" (*Pravda*, 26 April 1963). On 30 April *Pravda* snubbed Ustinov by identifying him as a deputy premier and listing him after deputy premiers Lesechko and Rudnev, even though he was a first deputy premier. In early May, Khrushchev appointed S. M. Tikhomirov, a chemical industry official, deputy chairman of Ustinov's Supreme National Economic Council (*Pravda*, 10 May 1963)—a symbolic assertion of chemistry's priority—and he soon brought his protégés Brezhnev and Podgornyy into the

[18] *Pravda*, 28 February 1963.

[19] He appeared at a 10 April 1963 ceremony, but not at the 12 April cosmonaut day ceremony. After his failure to appear at the May Day parade, *Pravda* (4 May) announced that he was ill.

Central Committee Secretariat to take over Kozlov's duties (they were elected at the June 1963 plenum).

The 1963 Virgin Land Drought

The greatest disaster to befall Khrushchev's agricultural policy was the virgin land crop failure in 1963. Much of the blame was placed on the intertilled system which he had forced on the virgin lands, and he was forced to retreat in his corn campaign and allow the Kazakh leaders to embrace Barayev and his clean-fallow system.

Lysenko's 1960 early sowing program had greatly compounded the already troublesome weed problem. To counter weeds, more frequent plowing was urged by Nalivayko in 1962. The more frequent plowing compounded the damage to the soil already caused by the plowing methods used since the start of the virgin land cultivation. The system of fall plowing with moldboards had been simply transferred from European Russia, with its heavier, long-cultivated soil, to the virgin lands, with their fragile, lighter soil,[20] causing the soil to dry out and be easily blown away by wind storms. Barayev had been warning against this already in 1960[21] but he was not listened to until dust bowl conditions developed disastrously in 1963.

Striving for intensive farming, Khrushchev pushed Nalivayko's intertilled system for the virgin lands and corn sowing was expanded from 241,000 hectares in 1956 to 1,800,000 in 1963. Peas were expanded from 4,100 hectares to 485,200 hectares.[22] In effect, peas and beans were raised for the first time in Kazakhstan in 1961, yet by 1962 they occupied 611,000 hectares (490,000 peas, 116,000 beans):[23]

Thousand Hectares in Kazakhstan						
	1960	1961	1962	1963	1964	1965
Grain beans	3.5	79.2	611	751	388	158
(including, peas)	2.7	56.7	490	687	377	138

Hectares in Tselinnyy Kray					
	1960	1961	1962	1963	1964
Peas	2,500	51,200	434,300	485,200	195,200

[20] See N. Verkhovskiy in *Novyy Mir*, no. 4 (1966), and an article by Kazakh agronomists in the 4 February 1964 *Pravda*.

[21] See L. Laskovaya in *Novyy Mir*, no. 6 (1960), and N. Verkhovskiy in *Kazakhstanskaya Pravda*, 26 August 1960.

[22] V. M. Slobodin, *Vestnik Selskokhozyaystvennoy Nauki*, no. 6 (June 1966).

[23] Z. Golikova *et al.*, *Kommunisticheskaya Partiya v Borbe za Osvoyeniye Tselinnykh Zemel v Kazakhstane*, p. 392. Their figures are taken from the archive of the Kazakh Central Statistical Administration.

Since proper equipment and farming experience with these crops were lacking, they either perished or produced a poor yield.

What was worse, much clean fallow was eliminated and not even planted with corn. The pressure for production prompted farmers to plant grain crops year after year and not to allow the land to rest as clean fallow—which was even worse on the soil than using clean fallow for sown fallow. The 16.2 percent clean fallow in 1961 was reduced to 5.8 percent by 1963.[24] According to a 1968 book by a prominent long-time virgin land leader,[25] the eradication of fallow—which the book's author considers the main cause of the virgin land disaster—actually began on the eve of the 1958 sowing, when he and other virgin land farmers got categorical orders not to put even one hectare of farmland in fallow. Still, as the preceding figures suggest, the most disastrous drive against fallow began in 1961.

According to Barayev,[26] the spring thaw in 1963 came early and the soil dried out. A drought and dust storms followed and wind erosion damaged millions of hectares of cropland. Tselinnyy Kray First Secretary Kolomiyets at the February 1964 plenum declared that "over 3 million hectares of crops perished from drought and wind erosion and the yield on the remaining areas turned out to be extremely low."[27] Khrushchev himself related (in his 31 July 1963 Note[28]) how Kolomiyets called him up in the spring of 1963 to warn of the rampaging wind erosion. By the summer of 1963 the erosion danger was recognized and a commission under Voronov was formed to examine the problem.[29] We have no hint of what the commission's recommendations were, but soon after its creation central and Kazakh officials began paying attention to Barayev again and began campaigning to have virgin landers adopt his anticrosion measures. On 5 June 1963 Barayev addressed a VASKhNIL session on soil erosion (*Selskaya Zhizn*, 6 June 1963). He addressed the November Kazakh Central Committee plenum and wrote a 17 November article in *Izvestiya* urging shallow, moldboardless plowing, late sowing, and clean fallow. November and December saw oblast plenums to promote Barayev's program and such leading Kazakh officials as Tselinnyy Kray First Secretary Kolomiyets, Kazakh Agriculture Secretary Melnik, and Dvoretskiy, Kazakh first deputy premier and minister

[24] V. M. Slobodin, *Vestnik Selskokhozyaystvennoy Nauki*, no. 6 (June 1966).

[25] F. T. Morgun's *Dumy o Tseline* [Thoughts about the Virgin Lands], reviewed by A. Strelyanyy in *Novyy Mir*, no. 5 (1969). Morgun became chief of the Tselinnyy Kray Administration for Production and Procurement of Agricultural Products in March 1964. After the kray was abolished in late 1965 he became a Central Committee official and now is first deputy premier of the Kirgiz SSR.

[26] *Kazakhstanskaya Pravda*, 9 April 1965.

[27] Stenographic record of the February 1964 Central Committee plenum, p. 379. Morgun writes that between 1962 and 1965, 3,900,000 hectares of grain perished from wind erosion and an additional estimated 12,900,000 hectares were damaged (A. Strelyanyy, *Novyy Mir*, no. 5 [1969]).

[28] Khrushchev's collected speeches, vol. 8, p. 86.

[29] Ibid.

for production and procurement of agricultural products, demanded its adoption. In December Barayev was elected a Supreme Soviet deputy in a special by-election. In February 1964 he addressed the Central Committee plenum.

The 1963 drought not only brought Tselinnyy Kray First Secretary Kolomiyets to Maltsev's and Barayev's side but also brought Nalivayko and soon afterward Khayrullin to endorse Maltsev's and Barayev's antierosion measures— shallow plowing with moldboardless plows which leave stubble to hold moisture and protect against wind erosion. Khrushchev, in his 31 July 1963 Note, also conceded the need for shallow plows.

But, though Nalivayko now was supporting both Barayev's moldboardless plowing and late sowing, he resolutely refused to recognize the need for clean fallow as a means to fight both weeds and erosion (drought).[30] Nalivayko's rejection of clean fallow received the bulk of the immediate post-Khrushchev blame for virgin lands erosion problems (for instance, Yu. Chernichenko in *Novyy Mir*, no. 11 [1965], assailed Nalivayko's irresponsible replacement of clean fallow with intertilled crops, writing "that no opportunistic proposal from science ever so disrupted wheat production as this one did"). Even after Khrushchev's fall the Altay leaders (Nalivayko and kray First Secretary Georgiyev) continued to fight clean fallow. Since the basis of their corn program rested on the superiority of crop fallow over clean fallow, they could hardly switch to clean fallow. However, because of the Altay dust storms caused by plowing up of grass and eliminating of fallow, they found it necessary to resort to sowing grass to hold the soil and produce badly needed fodder.

The virgin land disaster appeared to set Voronov against Khrushchev.[31] Although silent on the clean fallow issue, Voronov presumably swung to Barayev's side. As head of the commission to study the virgin land erosion problem, he was placed in the center of the clean fallow–occupied fallow debate, and since Barayev's ideas soon became favored, it seems likely that Voronov's commission must have recognized the correctness of Barayev's views and encouraged their adoption in Kazakhstan. What is more, Voronov's close protégé, Khayrullin, only months later publicly switched sides on the clean fallow issue—as well as on late sowing.

Under the pressure of the new antierosion campaign, Khrushchev made a temporary retreat in late 1963, admitting at the December 1963 Central Committee plenum that some people had expanded corn too much and that clean fallow was needed in dry areas like the virgin lands (but not elsewhere). He even recognized his own deviation by noting that "some people may wonder: What happened? Why does Khrushchev, who fought so hard for the introduction of corn sowing, today seem to be beating a retreat?" Khrushchev answered: "This

[30] See L. Ivanov's article on Maltsev in *Sibirskiye Ogni*, nos. 5 and 6 (1965).

[31] Polyanskiy's position is unknown at this point, since he became silent on agriculture after his November 1962 demotion, except for an unpublished January 1963 talk in Tselinnyy Kray (*Selskaya Zhizn*, 25 January 1963).

is not the matter, comrades. We still stress today that corn is a powerful crop. . . . However, one must stress that we are not sworn forever to any one crop, we do not intend to idolize it."[32] But soon he was back fighting clean fallow again and continued to do so until his overthrow.

The Chemical Fertilizer Program

No sooner had the military-heavy industry complex lost its leading spokesman Kozlov (April 1963) than Khrushchev began a big drive to transfer funds to development of the chemical industry in order to produce vastly increased amounts of fertilizer. He asked Gosplan and the Agriculture Ministry to work out proposals for increasing fertilizer production. The cautious planners reported that agriculture needed "something under 40 million tons"—but that this would cost the "huge" sum of 1.7 billion rubles. Khrushchev was dissatisfied with this and, claiming the sum was too small, ordered them to think in terms of 3-4 billion rubles.[33] In a 12 July 1963 Note to the Presidium on fertilizer, he declared that agriculture needed 86 million tons of fertilizer (100 million, when that for other branches is included), which would require an investment of 5.8 billion rubles for new plants. He revealed the magnitude of the program by noting that the virgin land program had cost 5.3 billion rubles.[34] In a 30 July 1963 talk with US Agriculture Secretary Freeman, he declared that the USSR would raise its 1963 production of 20 million tons of fertilizer to 80-100 million tons by 1970 and "we will cut expenditures on defense and also direct these funds into production of mineral fertilizer."[35] In his 26 September Krasnodar speech he publicly cited the goal of 100 million tons by 1970,[36] and also revealed the purchase of millions of tons of grain abroad and the calling of a Central Committee plenum on the chemical industry.

But Khrushchev's campaign soon ran into trouble. Although a 14 November 1963 *Pravda* editorial quoted him on the goal of 100 million tons by 1970, on 17 November *Pravda* undercut his campaign by publishing a letter to the Central Committee from several chemists claiming that the 1970 grain production goal could be achieved with much less than the 86.4 million tons of fertilizer which, they said, was being proposed by the Agriculture Ministry. The chemists' letter called the ministry's proposal for nitrogen and phosphorus fertilizer inflated, "exceeding the world consumption several times over."[37] The

[32] Stenographic record of the 9-13 December 1963 Central Committee plenum, p. 33.

[33] See his 26 September 1963 Krasnodar speech, Khrushchev's collected speeches, vol. 8, pp. 175-76.

[34] Ibid., pp. 34-35.

[35] Ibid., pp. 44-45, 51.

[36] Ibid., p. 177.

[37] By coincidence, the same issue of *Pravda* carried a cartoon of a bureaucrat delivering a speech and blowing smoke rings in the air which formed the figure "100." The

chemists' letter was also published in the 17 November *Izvestiya* and 19 November *Selskaya Zhizn* and was followed up by *Pravda* with an approving editorial and letter on 18 November stressing more efficient use of present fertilizer.

When the Central Committee plenum on the chemical industry opened on 9 December 1963, Khrushchev noted the chemists' proposal to revise the figure down to 70-80 million tons and stated that "after careful study, it turned out" that 70-80 million tons would be sufficient.[38] This would cost 4.5 billion rubles, said he in his opening plenum speech.[39] Put on the defensive by the strong opposition, in his 13 December concluding plenum speech he promised that defense and other branches would not be harmed by this chemical program. Using the device of attacking Western foes for accusations actually being made by domestic opponents, he declared that "some people in the West think that if we develop chemistry we will forget about defense."[40] Again at the 14 February 1964 plenum, he claimed that "some politicians from capitalist countries are trying to scare us" by asserting that the USSR cannot afford the chemical program.[41] He also complained that foreign foes were claiming the December 1963 plenum's chemical program represented a departure from the heavy industry priority line, but, he said, "only hardened dogmatists" can take this view.[42] He singled out the leaders of Gosplan and the metallurgical industry for opposing chemical development and complained of the difficulties of changing the division of resources to develop any new branches.[43]

Khrushchev did manage to make some small gains. Defense spending was reduced by 600 million rubles in the budget presented in December 1963.

Budget Defense Expenditures (billions)[44]

1962	1963	1964
13.4	13.9	13.3

Planned investments in the chemical industry were to rise to 2,092 million rubles in 1964 and 2,757 million in 1965,[45] as against 1,700 million planned for 1963[46] and 1,450 million actually invested in 1963.[47] Fertilizer production was

---

caption (in verse) read: "The fraud can achieve any indicators in the world—but alas, only with the help of puffed up figures."

[38] Khrushchev's collected speeches, vol. 8, pp. 278 and 302.

[39] Ibid., p. 302.

[40] Ibid., p. 343.

[41] Ibid., p. 390.

[42] Ibid., pp. 449-50.

[43] Ibid., pp. 454-55.

[44] Garbuzov's budget reports in *Izvestiya*, 11 December 1962 and 17 December 1963.

[45] Gosplan Chairman Lomako's plan report in the 17 December 1963 *Izvestiya*.

[46] Sovnarkhoz Chairman Dymshits's plan report in the 11 December 1962 *Izvestiya*.

[47] Lomako, *Izvestiya*, 17 December 1963.

to rise from 20 million tons in 1963 to 25.5 in 1964 and 35 in 1965 (Lomako's plan report, *Izvestiya*, 17 December 1963). However, the 35 million ton goal had been set well before the 1963 campaign[48] —indicating that his efforts had failed to raise short-term goals.

[48] For example, in Dymshits's December 1962 plan report (*Izvestiya*, 11 December 1962). Khrushchev in his 26 September 1963 speech noted that an early 1962 Central Committee–Council of Ministers decree had set 35 million tons for 1965 (Khrushchev's collected speeches, vol. 8, p. 176).

CHAPTER VI

KHRUSHCHEV'S
FALL: 1964

By early 1964 a strong tide was running against Khrushchev on clean fallow and Lysenko. Voronov appeared to oppose Khrushchev on these issues and Voronov's protégé, Khayrullin, propelled both these issues into public debate in his open attack on Lysenko's virgin land early sowing program. The embattled Khrushchev struck down Khayrullin and began a new campaign against the anti-Lysenkoists and clean-fallow advocates. However, before the culmination of his campaign, his colleagues removed him from office.

Even though Khrushchev had already disavowed one of the main elements of Lysenko's program (early sowing) he reacted viciously to Khayrullin's swing to Barayev's and Maltsev's side. This circumstance suggests that while early sowing was the main subject of the dispute, the real cause was something different—probably Khrushchev's continuing hostility to the "unproductive" use of land for clean fallow and his anger at Voronov's probable support of clean fallow. Khrushchev had been forced to retreat on the clean-fallow issue in 1963 as a result of the virgin land disaster—but he came back swinging in 1964. His devoting of so much time to the subject indicated the importance he attached to it and, in fact, he indicated that he intended it to be resolved at an important Central Committee plenum scheduled for November. In late summer and early fall he barnstormed the provinces openly appealing for support for his opposition to clean fallow.

Although Voronov's position in these matters is not certain (he made no public statements at all on agriculture during 1964), his many years of close association with Khayrullin make it likely that he shared his shift of attitude. In any case, as chairman of the commission to study virgin land erosion, he was at the center of the controversy. The presumption that he shared Khayrullin's views is strengthened by the fact that he and his protégés shared Khayrullin's decline after Khrushchev turned on Khayrullin in early 1964. Further, Khayrullin's attack on Lysenko probably also found a sympathetic response with Voronov, who, as shown in Chapter III, contrasted sharply with Khrushchev in his lack of enthusiasm for Lysenko.

Polyanskiy's position is less clear. His role in agriculture had been drastically curtailed by late 1962 (he made his last public statement on agriculture in a 4 November 1962 *Izvestiya* article), suggesting that he disagreed with Khrushchev on important agricultural matters. It is said that it was Polyanskiy who delivered the denunciation of Khrushchev's agricultural policies at the October 1964 plenum which removed the first secretary.[1] If Polyanskiy did disagree with Khrushchev, as seems likely, it presumably was as a result of his changing his position—since earlier he appeared to be a very close supporter of Khrushchev's policies. Thus, as the scheduled November 1964 agricultural plenum approached, Khrushchev was relying on his new agricultural lieutenants Yefremov and Polyakov, while his erstwhile closest lieutenants in agriculture—Voronov and Polyanskiy—appeared opposed to him.

Also in 1964 a remarkable tide of anti-Lysenkoist sentiment built up, and even Khrushchev was unable to hold it back. He endorsed Lysenko's programs at the February 1964 plenum, but recognized the opposition to them and cautiously refused to give Lysenko a carte blanche. But as 1964 wore on Khrushchev's anger rose as the assaults on Lysenko grew. Fertilizer specialists openly resisted Lysenko's manure mixtures. Geneticists increasingly were able to get their views published. The newspaper *Komsomolskaya Pravda* opened an attack on Lysenko's theory of lack of intravarietal struggle. Scientist A. D. Sakharov led an Academy of Sciences revolt against Lysenko in June. Some old Lysenko stalwarts, such as V. N. Stoletov, even began deserting Lysenkoism. Threatened with disaster, the Lysenkoists, with Khrushchev's support, rallied at the end of August and began a series of harsh counterattacks which continued until the eve of Khrushchev's fall. When the Central Committee gathered in October to discuss removing Khrushchev, one of the accusations against him apparently was his intention of reinforcing Lysenko's monopoly in biology and of instituting a new purge of Lysenko's foes.

The February 1964 Plenum

The February 1964 Central Committee plenum, called to discuss "intensification of agricultural production" through use of fertilizer, irrigation, and mechanization, marked a new resurgence of the Lysenkoists. Not only did Lysenko, his assistant F. V. Kallistratov (director of the experimental base of Lysenko's Gorki

[1]Georgian First Secretary Mzhavanadze at the March 1965 Central Committee plenum declared that "serious errors and big shortcomings in the leadership of agriculture during recent years" were revealed at the October 1964 plenum (Stenographic record of the March 1965 Central Committee plenum, p. 88), but there has been no official confirmation of who spoke at the October 1964 plenum.

Leninskiye farm),[2] and his protégé, VASKhNIL President Olshanskiy, speak at the plenum, but other scientists (Ye. T. Varenitsa, director of the Institute for Agriculture of the Central Non-Chernozem Zone, and M. M. Lebedev, director of a Leningrad laboratory for raising agricultural animals) as well as other officials (RSFSR Minister for Production and Procurement of Agricultural Products and First Deputy Premier L. I. Maksimov; Moldavian Minister for Production and Procurement of Agricultural Products and First Deputy Premier M. I. Sidorov;[3] chief of a Belorussian production administration, N. F. Prokopenko; USSR Agriculture Minister I. P. Volovchenko; and, of course, Khrushchev) praised Lysenko and his works.

At the same time, Lysenko opponents also spoke: Barayev (who urged moldboardless plowing, clean fallow, and late sowing), director of the Fertilizer Institute G. A. Cheremisinov (who cautiously challenged Lysenko's manure composts), and B. P. Sokolov (who recalled Khrushchev's 1940 defense of hybrid corn against Lysenkoist attacks). The controversy over Lysenko's various programs was so great by this time that it intruded into the plenum speeches also. Again, the two most discussed issues were Lysenko's composts and milk-fat work.

Even though Agriculture Minister Volovchenko in his report paid obeisance to Lysenko—noting the "substantial contribution" of the "outstanding scientists" Lysenko and K. I. Skryabin[4] and recalling that the January 1963 Central Committee decree on biology had noted that Michurinist biologists "occupied the leading place in the world in the field of genetics, selection and seed raising, especially in questions of guiding inheritance and changeability"[5] —

----

[2] Kallistratov was virtually forced to admit having made fraudulent claims for Lysenko's bull-breeding and manure experiments during the September 1965 investigation of Lysenko—*Vestnik Akademii Nauk SSSR*, no. 11 (1965).

[3] Moldavia was the most receptive to Lysenko's bulls. Kallistratov at the February 1964 plenum praised Moldavia and declared that "if other republics would follow the example of Moldavia it would be possible in the next few years to sharply raise the fat content in milk of sovkhoz and kolkhoz herds" (Stenographic record of the February 1964 Central Committee plenum, p. 324). During the 1965 investigation of Lysenko's bull-breeding experiment it was stated that 64.7 percent of the breeding bulls sold by Lysenko's farm were sold to Moldavia. Member of the investigating commission zoo technician N. A. Kravchenko cited Moldavia as a bad example of the "great harm" caused by using Lysenko's bulls (*Vestnik Akademii Nauk SSSR*, no. 11 [1965]). Moldavian First Secretary Z. P. Serdyuk had endorsed Lysenko's bull-breeding program at the January 1961 plenum. Serdyuk disappeared after Khrushchev's fall, being last identified in the 17 April 1965 *Izvestiya*—as first deputy chairman of the Party Commission (which was reorganized into the Party Control Committee in late 1965). Sidorov was demoted from Moldavian first deputy premier to ordinary deputy premier after Khrushchev's fall and when the investigation of Lysenko's bull experiments began (*Sovetskaya Moldaviya*, 19 February and 9 March 1965).

[4] Stenographic record of the February 1964 Central Committee plenum, p. 33.

[5] Ibid.

Lysenko attacked him for ignoring his mineral-manure, peat-manure, and manure-earth composts and his milk-fat work and criticized the Agriculture Ministry and other organs for not spreading his bulls, despite a 1962 Council of Ministers decree.[6] Khrushchev endorsed Lysenko's attack on Volovchenko for ignoring use of local fertilizer[7] and complained about the continuing debates preventing introduction of Lysenko's bulls into production.[8] Olshanskiy attacked both fertilizer institutes for rejecting Lysenko's fertilizer methods.[9] The director of one of the institutes, G. A. Cheremisinov, who spoke at the plenum, cautiously replied that one should not set mineral fertilizer against manure. Khrushchev noted the "hidden, private dispute" between Olshanskiy and Cheremisinov and declared himself in favor of Lysenko's manure, criticizing some scientists of the fertilizer institutes for rejecting it.[10]

At the same time, Khrushchev tried to avoid Lysenko's misuse of his endorsement, declaring that he, as Central Committee first secretary, did not want to and could not state "that only such-and-such a method must be used." There must be competition of ideas, he declared.[11] He declared further that sometimes one hears speakers say "This was done on the instructions of the Central Committee" or "This was done on the instructions of comrade so-and-so." "One must not misuse references to higher authorities," he warned.[12] He also said: "While citing Academician T. D. Lysenko's school as an example, I do not at all wish to say that we cannot have other opinions in science on the question at issue."[13]

The Orenburg Case

Another controversy arose at the February 1964 plenum, but was not recorded in the stenographic report. After the plenum, in his 28 February 1964 speech, Khrushchev told how Khayrullin "in the presence of all participants in the plenum gave me an article of his about sowing periods and demanded it be printed."[14] Khrushchev, though irritated, ordered *Selskaya Zhizn* to publish it. *Selskaya Zhizn's* editors complained that it was harmful but printed it on 21 February 1964. The article immediately became the subject of attacks by nu-

[6]On 26 June 1963 the Agriculture Ministry had, however, issued an order "On Improving Work in Creating a High-Fat Milk Herd of Cattle at Kolkhozes and Sovkhozes by Using Breeding Animals Produced at the Gorki Leninskiye Farm and Their Descendents," (*Vestnik Akademii Nauk SSSR*, no. 11 [1965]).

[7]Khrushchev's collected speeches, vol. 8, p. 404.

[8]Ibid., p. 416.

[9]Stenographic record of the February 1964 Central Committee plenum, p. 253.

[10]Khrushchev's collected speeches, vol. 8, pp. 403-4.

[11]Ibid., p. 417.

[12]Ibid., pp. 417-18.

[13]Ibid., p. 405.

[14]Ibid., p. 537.

merous letters printed in *Selskaya Zhizn* on 25-27 February, and Khrushchev in his 28 February speech personally assailed Khayrullin for a stereotyped approach. Apparently referring to Voronov's recommendation of Khayrullin, Khrushchev declared: "Some say that he is an experienced and knowledgable person. Others criticize him for a superficial approach. I can't characterize him because I don't know him well" (*Pravda*, 7 March 1964). Nevertheless, he apparently knew Khayrullin well enough to have praised him earlier and urged others to use his system—for example in his 2 March 1961 Sverdlovsk speech[15] and his 21 March 1961 Alma-Ata speech.[16]

In his article, Khayrullin rejected early sowing (Lysenko's program) and backed Barayev's and Maltsev's late sowing for the virgin lands. He blamed the weediness and low harvests on early sowing and assailed Lysenkoist P. I. Kralin (chief of the Agriculture Ministry's mass production experiments section) for pushing Siberian farmers to sow early. He attacked "people who acknowledge the agrobiological Michurinist theses only in words" for opposing late sowing and assailed those who interfered in Siberian farming without knowing anything about it. He also urged moldboardless plowing and more clean fallow (*Selskaya Zhizn*, 21 February 1964).

Although Khayrullin's article meant a change of sides in the virgin land controversy, he held to his Orenburg system for most of his own oblast and the southeast zone. Orenburg lies mainly in the southeast agricultural zone, with only eastern Orenburg in the dry virgin lands region. Khayrullin's program of early, deep plowing in the fall to destroy weeds and then leveling of the plowed land to hold the moisture through the winter applied to southeast zonal conditions. But in 1960-63 he strongly backed Lysenko's early sowing and deep fall plowing program for the virgin lands also, and in March 1961 Khrushchev urged the Kazakh leaders to apply Khayrullin's fall plowing method to areas of Kazakhstan with lumpy soil also, since the leveling would help hold moisture.[17]

As late as October 1963 the Orenburg leaders were attacking farms in the Adamovskiy Rayon (the dry virgin land area of east Orenburg) for late sowing and shallow plowing.[18] But suddenly in early 1964, after observing the advantages of Maltsev's late sowing, moldboardless plowing system in Adamovskiy Rayon during the 1963 drought conditions and after being impressed by seeing Barayev's success with late sowing at the Shortandy Institute, Khayrullin changed sides. He reasserted his Orenburg system for the southeast zone in his speech at the February 1964 plenum, advocating the intertilled system, especially corn, and early sowing for the whole southeast. But his article, presented to Khrushchev at the plenum, takes a contrary line—for the virgin lands.

[15] Ibid., vol. 5, pp. 113 and 115.
[16] Ibid., p. 295.
[17] His 21 March 1961 Alma-Ata speech, Khrushchev's collected speeches, vol. 5, p. 295.
[18] Orishchenko in *Ural*, no. 2 (1964).

Except for the clean-fallow issue, the article seemed to conflict little with Khrushchev's position, since Khrushchev himself had already switched with Nalivayko to flexible sowing periods as advocated then by Maltsev. Khayrullin had no criticism of the Altay intertilled system and repeated his opposition to the grassland system (also opposed by Maltsev). The overreaction to the article suggests that the transparent attack on Lysenko[19] had stung Khrushchev or that some other personal factor or behind-the-scenes issue prompted Khrushchev to make an example of him. No other scientist was subjected to such a concentrated and devastating attack under Khrushchev as Khayrullin. The Lysenkoists and various foes of Khayrullin not only attacked his virgin land ideas but discredited his whole Orenburg system for the southeast zone as well. Khayrullin was fired in disgrace as director of the Orenburg Institute and his patrons in the Orenburg leadership (Voronov's protégés) were assailed and dismissed. Even Maltsev and the Adamovskiy Rayon agronomist cited by Khayrullin disavowed his late sowing proposal as stereotyped (*Selskaya Zhizn*, 28 February 1964, and *Pravda*, 6 April 1964).

Veiled Attacks on Voronov

The overreaction suggests in fact that Khrushchev may have been looking for an excuse to get at Voronov. In addition to having his closest protégés disgraced, Voronov himself was implicated indirectly in some of the attacks, for example, by their stress on the Orenburg leaders' support of Khayrullin in past years— while Voronov was first secretary. Also, Saratov Professor V. Gulyayev declared that the Orenburg system of early, deep, leveled fall plowing had been made a "stereotype" forced first on other oblasts of the southeast zone and then for all zones of the RSFSR. In his attack on the adherents of the Orenburg system, Gulyayev pointedly quoted verbatim from Voronov's 22d Congress speech (without attribution, of course): "Soon they began to even assert that science and advanced experience had proved that supposedly in almost all zones of the RSFSR early, deep, leveled fall plowing has substantial advantages over late fall plowing and especially lumpy fall plowland" (*Selskaya Zhizn*, 27 February

[19] That Khayrullin's article was an attack on Lysenko is obvious from its reference to superficial Michurinists and its attack on Lysenko-supporter Kralin, and from the fact that Lysenkoists like B. A. Malinovskiy, director of the Irkutsk Experimental Station (*Selskaya Zhizn*, 27 February 1964), and G. Vysokos of the Omsk Institute (*Pravda*, 6 April 1964) responded to it. Ye. Raksha of the Krasnoyarsk Agricultural Institute wrote: "To whom are [Khayrullin's] rebukes addressed? To anonymous people. . . . Everyone much connected with farming knows T. D. Lysenko's theses on sowing periods. In speaking of people who acknowledge Michurinist agrobiological theses only in words, Khayrullin apparently was speaking of him and his students. In an honest argument, things are called by the right names and people should all the more be given their proper names. That is, if it is honest. Because Khayrullin is silent about identifying his opponents one wants to exclaim: 'This does not follow the rules of debate!' " (*Selskaya Zhizn*, 27 February 1964).

1964). Voronov at the 22d Congress had said: "Science and advanced experience have proved that in almost all zones of the RSFSR early, deep, leveled fall plowing has substantial advantages over late fall plowing and especially lumpy fall plowland."[20] Voronov, of course, as first deputy chairman of the RSFSR Bureau, was in a position to promote the system throughout the RSFSR. The leaders of two other southeast oblasts (Kuybyshev and Volgograd) endorsed the system at the March 1962 plenum (see below).

Gulyayev also recalled the articles from Orenburg "running down the work of the Saratov scientists." The Saratov Institute for Agriculture of the Southeast was the arch-rival of the Orenburg Institute, and Voronov himself had participated in harsh attacks on the Saratov Institute. Saratov lay in the southeast zone along with most of Orenburg, and the Saratov scientists promoted programs diametrically opposed to the Orenburg programs. Prior to Voronov's arrival, the methods promoted by the Saratov Institute had predominated in Orenburg—but Voronov and Khayrullin immediately threw them out. At the December 1958 Central Committee plenum Voronov declared: "Study of the local farming conditions led us to the need to change the system of soil cultivation spread earlier in the oblast on the recommendations of the Saratov Farming Institute. We rejected the practice of leaving fall plowland in bumpy and cloddy condition for winter, which led to loss of fall moisture and to weediness. . . . There are no longer any backers of this harmful system of soil cultivation left." Voronov noted that those ignoring his new methods were being subjected to "strict measures of administrative action" and "we are striving for unconditional execution of the whole complex of [new] agrotechnical methods."[21]

In a 13 September 1960 *Pravda* article Voronov attacked the Saratov scientists for disparaging the Orenburg system and at the 22d Congress he criticized the Saratov Institute as separated from life and for giving wrong recommendations.[22] An article in the RSFSR Bureau's organ, *Sovetskaya Rossiya*, on 28 March 1961 backed Khayrullin and attacked the Saratov Institute scientists for sticking to the backward system of cloddy soil, which the article labeled part of Vilyam's grassland system. A 24 December 1961 *Sovetskaya Rossiya* article criticized the Saratov Institute for taking a wrong position (supporting clean fallow and grasses and opposing corn) after the January 1961 plenum and only reexamining its position after the sharp attacks on it at the 22d Congress. Institute director P. G. Kabanov was forced to admit his and his institute's mistaken views. The article praised Orenburg's system and attacked Saratov scientists for trying to discredit it and for favoring cloddy, unleveled winter fallow.

At the March 1962 plenum Saratov First Secretary A. I. Shibayev acknowledged the criticisms and criticized his oblast's institute for backing the

[20] Stenographic record of the 22d Party Congress, vol. 1, p. 368.

[21] Stenographic record of the December 1958 Central Committee plenum, pp. 113–14.

[22] Stenographic record of the 22d Party Congress, vol. 1, p. 372.

grassland system.[23] Voronov and Khayrullin had the support of two other oblasts in the southeast zone: Kuybyshev (located between Orenburg and Saratov) and Volgograd (located south of Saratov). At the March 1962 plenum Kuybyshev First Secretary A. S. Murysev praised Khayrullin's system and approved the attacks by Khrushchev, Polyanskiy, and Voronov on the grasslanders at a Saratov conference.[24] Volgograd First Secretary A. M. Shkolnikov also backed the Orenburg system at the March plenum.

In 1964 the Saratov scientists got their chance to strike back. Gulyayev declared that Khayrullin's system had simply been "imported" from Chita by Khayrullin and that while leveled plowland was good for dry, snowless Chita, lumpy soil was better for the snowy Southeast. *Pravda* on 6 April 1964 backed Gulyayev's 27 February *Selskaya Zhizn* article disproving Orenburg's methods. Saratov scientists now were pushing harrowed fall plowland as a substitute for clean fallow[25] and Khrushchev in his 4 August 1964 speech in Saratov Oblast (*Pravda*, 5 August) spoke of the big argument between clean fallow (now pushed by the Orenburgers) and fall plowland.[26] He seized upon figures from Saratov Oblast which showed that wheat sown after fall plowland gave 10 centners more wheat per hectare than wheat sown after clean fallow. He praised Saratov for eliminating grass, and in following speeches on his August tour also set fall plowland against clean fallow (in Rostov, *Pravda*, 8 August; in Tataria, *Pravda*, 11 August).

Already in early March an Orenburg *aktiv* meeting criticized Khayrullin for his stereotyped methods, but "did not hear a direct, precise acknowledgement of his mistakes from comrade Khayrullin" (*Selskaya Zhizn*, 5 March 1964). It was indicated that his system would be improved, rather than abandoned, and he was criticized mainly for being immodest and urging stereotyped approaches. The meeting followed the line of the article by Ya. Orishchenko, chief agronomist of the Adamovskiy Sovkhoz, in *Ural* (No. 2, 1964), treating the Orenburg system as good but enforced in a stereotyped fashion.

But Moscow accelerated the pressure. *Pravda* on 6 April assailed the oblast leaders for enforcing Khayrullin's Orenburg system, and the RSFSR Bureau (now under First Deputy Chairman Yefremov rather than Orenburg patron Voronov) adopted a decree "On the Orenburg Agricultural Obkom's Leadership of Agricultural Production." Yefremov himself went to Orenburg to supervise a 28 April plenum which fired obkom First Secretary Shurygin. On 3 May *Pravda* referred to "former" director Khayrullin and took a slap at Voronov by stressing

---

[23] Stenographic record of the March 1962 Central Committee plenum, p. 325.

[24] Ibid., pp. 292 and 294.

[25] Gulyayev, *Selskaya Zhizn*, 27 February 1964.

[26] In this odd twist of fate, the 1960–62 Saratov–Orenburg positions on clean fallow were partially reversed in 1964. Khayrullin, who opposed clean fallow for the virgin lands in 1960–62, was supporting it in 1964. The Saratov Institute, attacked by Voronov, Khayrullin, and Khrushchev for clinging to clean fallow in 1960–62, now was winning Khrushchev's praise for opposing clean fallow.

that Khayrullin and his discredited methods had had the full support of the oblast party leaders ever since 1957 (when Voronov became first secretary).

Despite Khayrullin's endorsement of clean fallow for the virgin lands, the Altay Institute did not participate in the attack on him and on Voronov's protégés—probably because of the good relations between the Altay and Orenburg groups. It is probably not accidental that the only leader or scientist to express sympathy for the purged Orenburg Institute after Khrushchev's fall was Pysin—the patron of the Altay group (at the March 1965 plenum—when he was Voronov's assistant as first deputy premier of the RSFSR).

Khrushchev and Yefremov apparently used the Orenburg case also as an excuse to get rid of Voronov's protégé, Pankin. After Voronov was transferred from first deputy RSFSR Bureau chairman to RSFSR premier in November 1962, his appointee, Pankin, had remained head of the Central Committee's Agriculture Section for the RSFSR, working under his successor Yefremov. However, Pankin disappeared about the same time that Yefremov purged the Orenburg leaders (Pankin was last identified as Agriculture Section head in the 18 March 1964 *Sovetskaya Rossiya*).

The drastic purge and disgrace of Voronov's closest protégés, Khayrullin, Orenburg First Secretary Shurygin, and other Orenburg leaders was a great setback for him. His standing was apparently well reflected in the photographic lineups in 1964. At the May Day parade, Voronov dropped below junior Presidium member Kirilenko to last place. He was again last at the 10 June RSFSR Supreme Soviet session (even though he was the RSFSR premier) and at the 13 July Supreme Soviet session, while at the 12 June German–Soviet friendship meeting, in a very unusual snub, he was separated entirely from the Presidium and Secretariat and relegated to the end of the third and last row—behind Presidium candidate member Yefremov and all the second and third stringers—in fact, as far back as he could go! The last photo lineup before Khrushchev's fall (in the 29 September 1964 *Pravda*) showed Voronov standing behind all the other Presidium members—in the second row with the candidate members.

The Clean Fallow Debate

At the December 1963 and February 1964 plenums Khrushchev clearly made concessions to those favoring clean fallow and opposing corn, agreeing that clean fallow might be needed in the virgin lands—but not elsewhere. The February 1964 plenum and the 24 March 1964 Central Committee and Council of Ministers decree ("On Crude Violations and Distortions in Planning of Kolkhoz and Sovkhoz Production") appeared to take a hands-off policy, granting farms the right to determine their own crop policies and even to reject recommendations of production administrations. But Khrushchev prevented any cutback in corn or other grain sowings and any expansion of fallow by not altering grain procurement plans for west Siberia and Tselinnyy Kray (fulfillment of which required sowing grain alone on over 70 percent of the land, according to L. Ivanov in

Literaturnaya Gazeta, 6 April 1965) and by laying down a new criterion for local leaders to follow in deciding between clean fallow and occupied fallow or fall plowland. In August 1964 Khrushchev toured the provinces and in his speeches he revealed dissatisfaction with the February 1964 plenum.[27] Since, according to him, the February plenum had only given a general orientation on agricultural issues, he was working out a new program for reorganizing agriculture into specialized administrations which he would present to a November 1964 plenum on agriculture. In his speeches, he declared that the issue of clean fallow versus occupied fallow or fall plowland had been raised again at the February plenum (see his 4 August Saratov speech, *Pravda*, 5 August 1964) and that he had nothing against clean fallow so long as farmers could prove that one crop after clean fallow could outproduce the two crops one would get if one did not leave the land fallow for one year (although he also declared the "resting" of land an outmoded concept in his 12 August Kustanay speech, *Pravda*, 13 August 1964). During his tour Khrushchev directly appealed for facts and support to use in the confrontation to come at the scheduled November 1964 agricultural plenum. He made no secret of disagreements, especially on fallow. Since many Kazakh leaders, as well as Voronov's protégés, had gone on record for Barayev's expansion of clean fallow, the stage was set for conflict. Khrushchev's new favorites, Polyakov and Yefremov, accompanied him on his trip, presumably helping him prepare for the conflict ahead.

Attacks on Lysenko

The controversy over Lysenkoism, like the clean fallow debate, was coming to a head precisely in August and September 1964—the eve of Khrushchev's fall. Despite Khrushchev's constant praise of him, Lysenko's recommendations in science and agriculture were coming under increasing attack. Medvedev had written his monograph on Lysenko's persecution of Vavilov in 1962, but was unable to get it published. Nevertheless, he circulated it, thereby causing considerable uproar, and in the spring of 1963 Medvedev, along with V. Kirpichnikov, was able to get an article on Lysenko published in the sympathetic Leningrad literary journal *Neva* (no. 3),[28] calling the suppression of genetics "a harmful survival of the personality cult." This brought the debate out into the open again.

[27] See his 8 August speech, *Pravda*, 10 August 1964.

[28] Leningrad—Vavilov's long-time home—had a considerable history of receptiveness to anti-Lysenko views. Some Soviets believe that Zhdanov and the Leningrad leaders sympathized with Vavilov and resisted Lysenko as much as they dared—in view of Lysenko's solid backing by Stalin, Molotov, and usually by Central Committee Agriculture Secretary A. A. Andreyev and Agriculture Minister I. A. Benediktov. Vavilov reportedly told friends in 1940 that "even Andreyev fears Lysenko" (Zh. A. Medvedev, *The Rise and Fall of T. D. Lysenko* [New York: Columbia University Press, 1969], p. 151).

Medvedev's 1962 monograph indicated that the Leningrad party organization backed Vavilov in 1940 when Lysenko, as VASKhNIL president, was attempting to interfere in Vavilov's institute and put his own men in control of it (ibid., pp. 149–50). It was also the

Lysenkoists Vsyakikh, Vlasov, and Brigis attacked the *Neva* article in *Zhivotnovodstvo*, no. 6 (1963), asserting again that genes were only imaginary.[29] According to Medvedev, the Lysenkoists hoped to use the June 1963 Central Committee ideological plenum to reinforce their position. Olshanskiy and

Leningrad Obkom which later expelled Lysenko's partner I. I. Prezent from the party for "moral corruption" (as dean of the biology-soil faculty at Leningrad State University, Prezent forced girl students into "cohabitation"–ibid., p. 158).

Popovskiy in his 1966 *Prostor* (no. 8) article describes Vavilov's optimism in early 1940 after a visit with a high "government official." Professor Atabekova, with whom Vavilov spoke after the visit, believes he had talked to Zhdanov and had received some encouragement from him.

More direct evidence of Zhdanov's connection with Lysenko's foes appeared in 1948. According to Medvedev (*Grani*, no. 71, pp. 98-102), at Orgburo sessions in the spring of 1948 Zhdanov sharply attacked Lysenko and proposed that he be removed as president of VASKhNIL. Zhdanov's son Yuriy, who was appointed head of the Central Committee's Science Section right after finishing university, also began attacking Lysenko.

Lysenkoist M. B. Mitin, then deputy chairman of the Znaniye Society, accidentally overheard one of Yuriy Zhdanov's attacks and tipped off Lysenko. Lysenko and Mitin went to Stalin and complained of the intrigues by Zhdanov and his son. Stalin, who had already become cool to Zhdanov because of Malenkov's and Beriya's intrigues against Zhdanov and because of his resentment of Zhdanov's growing popularity, seized upon Lysenko's complaint as a pretext to sharply criticize Zhdanov. As a result, Zhdanov went into retirement and soon died (31 August 1948). Unprecedented glorification of Lysenko began, and during the infamous August 1948 VASKhNIL session, *Pravda* (7 August 1948) carried a letter of confession by Zhdanov's son Yuriy. In this letter (dated 10 July) Yuriy Zhdanov confessed that as an official of the Central Committee's Science Section he had "taken under my protection" programs of "representatives of formal genetics" which "were resisted by supporters of Academician Lysenko," and thus he had wound up defending "Mendelian–Morganist genetics." He wrote: "I underestimated my responsibility and did not imagine that my speech would be regarded as the official point of view of the Central Committee. . . . My sharp and public criticism of Academician Lysenko was a mistake." Only three days later–10 August–*Pravda* published Lysenko's notorious closing speech at the VASKhNIL session.

Another example of Lysenko's strained relations with Leningrad occurred in early 1961 when a big scientific conference on experimental genetics was called by Leningrad State University. Lysenko was not included among the speakers, and when he found this out he forced the cancellation of the conference–only two or three days before its opening (Medvedev's article in *Grani*, no. 71, p. 136).

Joravsky (*The Lysenko Affair*, pp. 109, 240-41) presents Mitin in a somewhat different light. He tells of Mitin attacking Lysenko's partner Prezent at an October 1939 conference and avoiding 100 percent commitment to Lysenko. As late as December 1947, Mitin, while praising Lysenko and condemning his critics, did not condemn genetics (*Literaturnaya Gazeta*, 27 December 1947), and, according to Joravsky, at the August 1948 VASKhNIL session Mitin and fellow philosopher G. F. Aleksandrov blamed each other for previous failure to completely back Lysenko.

After Khrushchev's fall, *Voprosy Filosofii* (under Mitin's editorship until mid-1968) carried numerous attacks on Lysenko, even after the anti-Lysenko campaign died down in late 1965 (such as those in issues no. 1 and 8 for 1967 by I. T. Frolov, who succeeded Mitin as editor). *Voprosy Filosofii* was accused of "running down" Michurinism, and editor Mitin was criticized for abandoning his earlier support of it (see *Oktyabr* 12 [1966]: 167-68).

[29] Medvedev, *Rise and Fall of Lysenko*, p. 205.

Lysenko, through Central Committee Agriculture Secretary Polyakov, tried to get denunciations of Mendelism–Morganism included in ideology Secretary L. F. Ilichev's report at the plenum. But after discussions between Ilichev and the Academy of Sciences leaders, these statements were dropped and only one speaker (Moscow City First Secretary N. G. Yegorychev) raised the issue.

Timiryazev Academy party committee secretary Stepanov, who in July and November 1962 had organized denunciations of Medvedev's manuscript, supplied Yegorychev with the ammunition[30] with which he attacked Medvedev's monograph, citing it by name ["Biological Science and the Cult of Personality"] even though it had not been published.[31] Referring to Medvedev as a "former" senior scientific worker of the chair of agricultural chemistry of the Timiryazev Agricultural Academy, Yegorychev said that after the monograph had been rejected by the academy, Medvedev had moved to Kaluga and prepared a book entitled *The Biosynthesis of Proteins and the Problems of Ontogenesis* which contained similar mistakes, but which was published by the Medical Literature Publishing House.

Medvedev escaped retaliation since the Academy of Medical Sciences was no longer under Lysenkoist control and in fact was reviving the study of medical genetics (on 24 July 1963 the academy adopted a resolution blaming the lag in medical genetics on Michurinist obstruction). The Medical Literature Publishing House also published a book on medical genetics by Lysenko foe Efroimson in 1963. Still, Medvedev's published book was removed from circulation by the Central Committee Ideological Commission. Polyakov, who "always complied with all Lysenkoist requests," according to Medvedev, tried to get the book destroyed, but after a long debate with the Academy of Sciences and the Academy of Medical Sciences, the book was issued with a revised section on Lysenko (it was softened and no names were mentioned).[32]

Then, in *Selskaya Zhizn* on 18 August 1963, Olshanskiy assailed the Medvedev–Kirpichnikov article in *Neva* and also two pro-genetics books by Lysenko foe N. P. Dubinin (who had been fired in 1959 for opposing Lysenko). His article was reprinted three days later in *Pravda*. In a later article (*Selskaya Zhizn*, 29 August 1964) Olshanskiy declared that Medvedev and Kirpichnikov had asserted that the Lysenkoists were guilty of the repressions of scientists under Stalin and Olshanskiy threatened to bring them to trial for slander. In fast reaction to Olshanskiy's attack, the editors of *Neva* were purged and *Neva* reprinted Olshanskiy's article attacking the Medvedev–Kirpichnikov article and printed an apology (*Neva*, no. 9).

Another sign of the increasing boldness of the anti-Lysenkoist forces in 1963 was the refusal of the Lenin Prize Committee to award prizes to Lysenkoists Musiyko and Remeslo in a secret ballot on 11 April 1963. Khrushchev

---

[30]Ibid., p. 206.

[31]See the 20 June 1963 *Moskovskaya Pravda* version of Yegorychev's speech.

[32]Medvedev, *Rise and Fall of Lysenko*, pp. 208–10.

angrily ordered the committee to reconvene and vote again, and at a 15 April meeting, with Lysenko's foes prevented from speaking, the committee reversed itself and voted in favor of Musiyko and Remeslo.[33]

Also in 1963 "insulting attacks" were made on Lysenko for his nest method of tree plantings by Professor F. D. Shchepotyev. Old Lysenko foe V. P. Efroimson[34] also ran down this program ("the sad story of the nest forest plantings") in the *Byulleten Moskovskogo Obshchestva Ispytateley Prirody* [The Bulletin of the Moscow Society of Nature Experimenters], vol. 61.[35] Still, while anti-Lysenkoists were able to criticize Michurinism at conferences, the newspapers were still closed to them.

But the attacks on Lysenko grew rapidly in 1964, despite Khrushchev's endorsement of his programs at the February 1964 plenum and his attack on Khayrullin's anti-Lysenkoist sortie. More anti-Lysenko material came from Leningrad. At the February 1964 plenum, the director of a Leningrad laboratory for raising animals, M. M. Lebedev, attacked Leningrad University Professor M. Ye. Lobashev's new book *Genetika* [Genetics] [36] and his lectures for propagandizing the ideas of Morganism. Lebedev repeated his attack in a 10 March 1964 *Selskaya Zhizn* article, labeling the book a "new attempt to resurrect in biological science the idealistic, metaphysical Weismannist–Mendelist–Morganist ideas of genetics." He criticized RSFSR Minister of Higher and Secondary Specialized Education V. N. Stoletov[37] for recommending publication of the book and Leningrad State University for publishing it.

Another *Selskaya Zhizn* article, on 2 October 1964, assailed old Vavilov pupil,[38] Leningrad Komarov Botanical Institute Professor F. Kh. Bakhteyev for

[33] Ibid., pp. 203–4.

[34] Efroimson had been arrested after the August 1948 VASKhNIL session (see Medvedev's article in *Grani*, no. 71, p. 144).

[35] According to Olshanskiy in the 29 August 1964 *Selskaya Zhizn.*

[36] Lobashev's book was the first genetics textbook since 1938 (David Joravsky, *The Lysenko Affair* [Cambridge, 1970] p. 159).

[37] As head of the Higher Attestation Commission, Stoletov had blocked the advancement of anti-Lysenkoist scientists and their works. For instance, Medvedev notes that in 1962 the commission still had a ban on giving scientific degrees in classical genetics (Medvedev's article in *Grani*, no. 71, p. 113). As RSFSR minister and at the same time head of Moscow State University's genetics department, Stoletov had held back revival of genetics at Moscow State University (Joravsky, *The Lysenko Affair*, p. 159). As a graduate student under Lysenko, Stoletov had begun his career with an 11 April 1937 *Pravda* article assailing Vilyams foe Tulaykov, who soon was arrested and shot. In 1948 Stoletov was sent from Lysenko's Genetics Institute to take over and purge the Timiryazev Academy (Medvedev in *Grani*, no. 71, pp. 90–91, 114). But despite his background as a Lysenko protégé and his prominent role in the suppression of Lysenko's opponents, Stoletov changed his position and attacked him in a 1964 *Filosofskiye Nauki* (no. 6) article (see *Oktyabr*, no. 2 [1966]).

[38] Bakhteyev actually was with Vavilov in the west Ukraine when Vavilov was arrested in 1940 (see Popovskiy's article on Vavilov in *Prostor*, no. 8 [1966], p. 115). Bakhteyev also was one of those attacked as a result of the April 1962 Central Committee decree criticizing the Leningrad Botanical Institute and the Leningrad City Party Committee's

promoting Lobashev's book, which was labeled "open propaganda for idealistic formal genetics and a worthless attempt to silence the achievements of our own native Michurinist biology." According to Medvedev,[39] Olshanskiy asked the Central Committee to ban Lobashev's book and a special commission was established to study this.

After Khrushchev's fall, Leningrad State University awarded a prize to Lobashev's book (*Leningradskaya Pravda*, 30 March 1965) and *Pravda* on 20 August 1965 announced that it would be used at universities starting in the 1965–66 school year. G. Dolmatovskaya described the long years of Lysenkoist persecution of Lobashev in a 7 September 1965 *Literaturnaya Gazeta* article. After working in Vavilov's institute before World War II, Lobashev was labeled a Weismannist, Morganist, and Mendelist and was blocked from joining the party—until 1941, when, as a soldier at the front, he was admitted under the more liberal provisions for soldiers. After the August 1948 VASKhNIL session he was fired from his job as dean of the biology faculty at Leningrad State University and had to live on his wife's salary. His successor as dean was I. I. Prezent, who demanded that Lobashev be expelled from the party.[40] Then Lobashev was "exiled" to the Physiology Institute at Koltushi outside Leningrad, only returning to Leningrad State University in 1957. The controversy over Lobashev continued in 1966, when Lysenkoist biologist N. I. Feyginson attacked him (*Oktyabr*, no. 2 [February 1966]), while Novosibirsk Academician A. Aleksandrov defended him, recalling the 1964 attack (*Pravda*, 12 February 1966).

As revealed at the February 1964 plenum, fertilizer specialists had rejected Lysenko's manure composts and agricultural organs were resisting his bull-breeding work. At a 10 March 1964 VASKhNIL session Olshanskiy argued with anti-Lysenkoists over the relative merits of mineral fertilizer and manure. Among the foes of Lysenko's composts were fertilizer specialists Sinyagin (former RSFSR deputy agriculture minister) and Cheremisinov (director of the Fertilizer Institute).[41]

On 24 July 1964 the Agriculture Ministry collegium argued over a new method of seed cultivation which violated Lysenko's theories on lack of intravarietal struggle. *Komsomolskaya Pravda* and its writer Anatoliy Ivashchenko, who championed the new seed method, were assailed by Deputy Agriculture Minister K. S. Nazarenko for attempting to defame Lysenko.[42] Immediately after Khrushchev's fall, *Komsomolskaya Pravda* got even by publicizing the July

---

leadership of scientific institutes—although apparently it had nothing to do with Lysenko (see A. Zernov, *Leningradskaya Pravda*, 17 April 1962).

[39]Medvedev, *Rise and Fall of Lysenko*, p. 214.

[40]Medvedev's article in *Grani*, no. 71, p. 109.

[41]*Vestnik Selskokhozyaystvennoy Nauki*, no. 6 (1964).

[42]*Sovetskaya Pechat*, no. 10 (1966).

episode and exposing the protection of the Lysenko cult by Nazarenko and Olshanskiy (*Komsomolskaya Pravda*, 19 November 1964).

Apparently the most serious challenge to the Lysenkoists was the June 1964 Academy of Sciences revolt. At Khrushchev's initiative, the government had created an unprecedented number of vacancies in the genetics department of the Academy of Sciences and in June three full and two corresponding members were to be elected. These posts were to go to Lysenkoists P. P. Lukyanenko, V. S. Pustovoyt, N. I. Nuzhdin, and V. N. Remeslo, but a revolt developed against Remeslo and Nuzhdin. Despite the fact that the Academy's Biology Section voted an unprecedented three times on Remeslo's candidacy, he was rejected. Nuzhdin was approved by the section, and in the past whenever a section had approved a candidate the Academy of Sciences' general meeting always had ratified his selection. But this time at the general meeting Engelgardt and A. D. Sakharov challenged Nuzhdin's right to be elected. Famed physicist Sakharov[43] directly appealed for a vote against Nuzhdin and Lysenko: "I call on all those present to vote so that the only 'ayes' will be by those who, together with Nuzhdin, together with Lysenko, bear the responsibility for the infamous pages in the development of Soviet science, which fortunately are now coming to an end." Academy of Sciences President Keldysh criticized Sakharov's speech as "tactless," while Lysenko assailed it as "slanderous." But by a secret vote of 126 to 22 or 24, Nuzhdin was rejected. Khrushchev angrily demanded an explanation from Keldysh and also from Sakharov. But Sakharov's sharp reply only irritated Khrushchev more, and he declared that the Soviet people did not need such an academy and ordered the formation of a commission to study the possibility of reforming the Academy of Sciences into a "Committee on Science."[44]

Last Offensive by Khrushchev and Lysenko

At the end of summer Khrushchev had finished a draft of a report proposing a big new reorganization of agriculture.[45] It was circulated among agricultural

---

[43] Sakharov was author of the long 1968 essay on Stalin's purges, peaceful coexistence, etc. which was widely circulated in the Soviet Union and was published in the *New York Times* on 22 July 1968, causing a sensation. Sakharov coauthored another letter in early 1970 attacking government policy and has become one of the most active and daring dissidents.

[44] Medvedev, *Rise and Fall of Lysenko*, pp. 214–18.

[45] Khrushchev's new program for specialization and intensification of livestock raising and the associated administrative reorganization originated in the spring of 1964. In a long Note to the Presidium on 13 April 1964 he complained that the 8 January 1963 decree on building 150 new poultry factories for egg production and 70 factories for broilers was not being carried out (*Pravda*, 24 April 1964). To produce a big increase in livestock products he proposed creating special national administrations for poultry raising and egg production,

institutions and provincial party organizations and provided for the creation of special committees, boards, and trusts for individual crops to run agriculture. One such trust or board, according to Medvedev, would have dealt with Lysenko's proposals on composts, and the draft report sharply attacked Lysenko's foes.[46] Medvedev also insisted that the Lysenkoists were working to use the reorganization to suppress their foes.[47] Commissions were established to review the work of the Academy of Sciences' biology institutes and these were used to harass anti-Lysenkoists, such as I. A. Rapoport.[48]

The Lysenkoists, under siege from the mounting assaults of their foes but with Khrushchev's renewed support and with the prospect of using the coming organizational changes against their foes, began a series of harsh attacks in August 1964. Olshanskiy asserted that the Mendelists–Morganists were increasing their propaganda and threatened lawsuits for slander against Medvedev and others in his harsh 29 August 1964 *Selskaya Zhizn* article. He also assailed Sakharov's speech at the Academy of Sciences session—but without revealing what had happened at the session. Famous plant breeders F. G. Kirichenko (who described himself as a pupil of Lysenko) and V. N. Remeslo endorsed Olshanskiy's article in *Selskaya Zhizn* on 5 September and 11 September. Lysenkoists D. A. Dolgushin, A. S. Musiyko, F. G. Kirichenko, etc., assailed the chromosome theory in the August 1964 *Vestnik Selskokhozyaystvennoy Nauki.* After

---

pig raising, and beef and milk production. He noted and rejected objections that creation of such administrations would split up livestock raising into narrow "uncoordinated" branches.

On 24 April 1964 *Pravda* published a Central Committee decree approving Khrushchev's Note and establishing a commission to submit within one month proposals on organizing poultry and egg production, big specialized pig sovkhozes and specialized milk sovkhozes. The commission was chaired by Podgornyy and included Brezhnev, Voronov, Kosygin, Mikoyan, Polyanskiy, Yefremov, Polyakov, republic leaders, and others. However, there was never any report on the commission's proposals. Instead, Khrushchev soon announced that there would be a November 1964 Central Committee plenum to debate his new program. In an 8 August speech he demanded: "Why should we keep secret the fact that the Central Committee Presidium has decided to call a plenum and discuss a report on deepening specialization of production and on administration of specialized production?" (*Pravda*, 10 August 1964).

On the eve of Khrushchev's fall, a 3 October 1964 *Ekonomicheskaya Gazeta* editorial stated that "the coming Central Committee plenum will discuss organizational questions of improving the leadership of specialized production. It is proposed to create union-republic administrations for grain, sugar beets, cotton, cattle, pigs, poultry, and other important agricultural products."

Although a union-republic administration for poultry was established in mid-1964, the proposals to create other such administrations were forgotten after Khrushchev's fall. One objection was brought out by Shelest at the March 1965 plenum. He complained that the plans to build poultry factories were too grandiose and required too much investment. He urged reduction of the Ukraine's planned 133 poultry factories to 80 (Stenographic record of the March 1965 Central Committee plenum, p. 42).

[46]Medvedev, *Rise and Fall of Lysenko*, p. 219.

[47]Ibid., p. 220.

[48]Ibid., p. 222.

Khrushchev's fall, Olshanskiy's article immediately became a target for attacks by anti-Lysenkoists (for example, B. M. Kedrov in *Literaturnaya Gazeta*, 24 November 1964, and close Vavilov protégé M. Khadzhinov in *Selskaya Zhizn*, 1 December 1964). Right down to the eve of Khrushchev's removal the Lysenkoists were expanding their attacks on their foes. The last article appeared in *Selskaya Zhizn* on 2 October 1964 (P. Shelest's[49] attack on Lobashev and Bakhteyev)—only days before Khrushchev's removal and only three weeks before the avalanche of attacks on Lysenko began.

Then on 13 October—the day the Presidium summoned Khrushchev back to Moscow to face dismissal—well-known anti-Lysenkoist I. A. Rapoport received a phone call from a leader in the Central Committee Agriculture Section asking him to prepare within twenty-four hours a full-page article on the achievements of genetics for publication in the pro-Lysenko paper *Selskaya Zhizn*, including endorsement of Mendel and Morgan. Rapoport, a past victim of Lysenko[50] who was still being harassed by various review commissions in early October and who was expecting instant dismissal, sent such an article to the Central Committee. However, the leadership was still divided on the Lysenko issue and when the article finally appeared—a week later (*Selskaya Zhizn*, 22 October)—the praise of Mendel and Morgan had been deleted.[51]

Medvedev writes that, "as became known later," the 12–14 October Presidium meeting and 14 October Central Committee plenum which discussed Khrushchev's dismissal, debated Khrushchev's "unconditional support of Lysenko and, in particular, the episode involving the attempt to elect Nuzhdin and Remeslo to the Academy of Sciences, with Khrushchev's subsequent desire to invoke sanctions against the Academy." "Also severely criticized was Khrushchev's unauthorized, personal order to shut down the Timiryazev Agricultural Academy when he found out that it included scientists critical of his agricultural policies." The order was revoked and by 16 October measures were taken to restore the academy.[52]

The Timiryazev Academy episode was mentioned publicly in the local Moscow press in April 1965, when Timiryazev Academy rector I. S. Shatilov at a Moscow *aktiv* meeting revealed that a decision had been adopted to abolish the academy, but had been reversed after the October 1964 plenum.[53]

---

[49]This Shelest is a *Selskaya Zhizn* correspondent, not the Ukrainian first secretary.

[50]After Molotov publicly endorsed Lysenko's biology theories in a November 1948 speech, Rapoport was ordered to publicly renounce the chromosome theory. When he refused, Molotov's statement was cited as proof of Lysenko's correctness. Rapoport replied: "Why do you think that Molotov knows more about genetics than I?" For this he was expelled from the party, fired from his job, and denied any work in the field of biology (see Medvedev's article in *Grani*, no. 71, p. 107).

[51]Medvedev, *Rise and Fall of Lysenko*, pp. 222–23.

[52]Ibid., p. 223.

[53]*Moskovskaya Pravda*, 17 April 1965. The 17 April *Vechernyaya Moskva* version even referred to the decision as a "decree."

Thus, Khrushchev's support of the new campaign to endorse Lysenkoism and apparently even to purge the anti-Lysenkoists which developed in August–October 1964 played a significant role in the final discrediting of his agricultural leadership and in the decision to remove him from office.

CHAPTER VII

REACTION AGAINST
KHRUSHCHEV POLICIES: 1965

Khrushchev's fall in October 1964 naturally brought a sharp reaction against his policies and retribution against his favorites. Lysenko's foes immediately launched an intense attack on Lysenko and his supporters. Officials in the European part of the Soviet Union reacted against Khrushchev's favoritism for the virgin lands. The fiascos caused by the Altay intertilled and livestock raising programs were exposed and, with Khrushchev's opposition removed, the clean fallow advocates carried the day.

The question of who was saddled with the blame for Khrushchev's policies was obviously decided more on the basis of political friendships than of actual responsibility. For example, scientists who no longer had any political patrons— such as Sizov and Matsepuro—were dealt with quickly and harshly. Nalivayko— who still probably had personal connections with Voronov and Pysin—was protected against severe retribution. Although Nalivayko's programs were discredited, his experiments exposed as frauds, and the application of his ideas in production blamed for enormous damage to the country, he did not renounce his ideas and remained director of the Altay Institute for two and a half years— only being quietly removed in 1967.

Lysenko's fate was more complicated. Devastating press attacks discredited him in late 1964 and 1965 and an investigation of his work was launched in early 1965. But despite the revelation of fraud in his work and total discrediting of his programs and of him personally, he never received anything more than a demotion and was permitted to continue his work at his Gorki Leninskiye experimental farm. What is more, press attacks on him were silenced in late 1965—probably signifying both that the régime wished to end the embarrassing exposés of past misdeeds and that he still had friends in the leadership, who, though not willing to defend his discredited ideas, still protected him from the punishment so ardently desired by his foes. Lysenko's protectors were obviously powerful—perhaps including Polyanskiy—since the forces assailing him were formidable. Old Lysenko foe Matskevich, restored to his 1960 post as agriculture minister in February 1965, naturally participated in the attacks on Lysenko. Voronov had an interest in striking back after the 1964 Orenburg affair. Shelepin's Party-State Control Committee initiated attacks on Lysenko allies Matsepuro and Zezin and secured their removal. The end of the press campaign against him was confirmed in December 1965 when the chief editor of the newspaper which had led the campaign—*Komsomolskaya Pravda*—was removed. The newspaper had ceased its attacks shortly before.

In the immediate reaction against Khrushchev's policies, many "grasslanders" persecuted by Khrushchev (and Voronov and Polyanskiy) in 1961 and 1962 returned to positions of authority, and Voronov and Polyanskiy made few public statements. Though they had apparently turned against some of Khrushchev's policies and had probably been saved from eventual demotion by his fall, they still could be reproached for their earlier co-responsibility for repudiated Khrushchev policies. However, most of the blame was apparently directed onto Khrushchev's 1963–64 favorites, who were demoted, rather than onto Voronov and Polyanskiy and their associates. Later in 1965 Voronov and Polyanskiy began reemerging as agricultural leaders.

The Attack on Lysenko

The reaction against Lysenko was swift and devastating. *Komsomolskaya Pravda*, which had tangled with the Lysenkoists already in mid-1964, published writer V. Dudintsev's attack on Lysenkoist I. A. Sizov, director of the Leningrad Plant Growing Institute, as early as 23 October 1964 (according to Medvedev, Dudintsev's article had been written in September–October 1963, but no editor would publish it until October 1964[1]). *Komsomolskaya Pravda*—which also attacked Lysenko more frequently and harder than any other paper—followed this with anti-Lysenko articles on 10 November, 11 November, 17 November, 19 November, and 29 November. By the end of October every Moscow paper had held editorial conferences on biology and dozens of anti-Lysenko articles were ordered.[2] The press attacks on Lysenko slowed down in December, but picked up again in late January.

At the beginning of February the annual session of the Academy of Sciences was held. Academy President M. V. Keldysh criticized Lysenko's monopoly in biology and Lysenko was removed as director of the Academy's Institute of Genetics (to which the Gorki Leninskiye experimental farm belonged). However, his removal was not announced in the press. The question of

[1] Medvedev, *The Rise and Fall of T. D. Lysenko* (New York: Columbia University Press, 1969), p. 224.
[2] Ibid., p. 226.

his dismissal had been raised in the Academy of Sciences Presidium immediately after Khrushchev's fall on 26 October.[3] Lysenko's Genetics Institute was later disbanded, as was his journal *Agrobiologiya*.[4] At a 10 February VASKhNIL session Lysenko foe Lobanov replaced Olshanskiy as VASKhNIL president and attacked the "monopolistic position of certain scientists," demanding the development of genetics in agriculture based on Vavilov's work (*Moskovskaya Pravda*, 11 February 1965). Lysenko foe Sinyagin became vice president of VASKhNIL.

In the 17 November 1964 *Komsomolskaya Pravda* V. Efroimson and R. Medvedev[5] attacked Leningrad Plant Growing Institute director I. A. Sizov "and his protectors in VASKhNIL who appointed Sizov to the post of director of the institute, which had been created by Academician N. I. Vavilov, precisely to drive the Vavilov traditions out of the institute." With the downfall of Olshanskiy and other Lysenkoist VASKhNIL leaders, Sizov lost his "protectors" and on 14 April 1965 *Komsomolskaya Pravda* reported his dismissal.[6]

Lysenko ally Matsepuro was removed as director of the Institute for Mechanization and Electrification of Agriculture of the Non-Chernozem Zone by the Belorussian Party-State Control Committee in June. He and his institute were accused of producing poorly designed machinery causing great losses to the state and of evading responsibility for serious shortcomings by relying on "highly-placed protectors" in Moscow, i.e., Khrushchev. It was even proposed that his Lenin Prize should be taken away (*Pravda*, 17 June 1965).

A 2 March 1965 *Sovetskaya Rossiya* editorial assailed the Lysenkoist Omsk Agricultural Institute for its work on sowing periods and its blaming the spread of wild oats on oat sowing (Lysenko's ideas), as well as for opposing clean fallow. The editorial praised Maltsev and Barayev. Then the Party-State Control Committee attacked the Omsk Institute for its promotion of Lysenko's disastrous Siberian winter crops program (*Selskaya Zhizn*, 20 June 1965), and on 19 August *Selskaya Zhizn* reported that the Party-State Control Committee had fined Omsk Institute leaders. Soon Omsk Institute director I. I. Zezin was replaced with S. S. Sdobnikov, deputy director of Barayev's institute (identified as director in *Sovetskaya Rossiya* on 29 January 1966). Zezin and Maltsev were arch-rivals in the virgin lands, and Sdobnikov himself, while chief of the agricultural division of Barayev's Shortandy institute, had quarreled with Lysenko during Lysenko's eventful July 1960 visit to the virgin lands.[7] Sizov, Matsepuro, and Zezin were the most prominent Lysenkoists among agricultural institute directors.

[3] Ibid.
[4] Ibid., p. 239.
[5] Roy A. Medvedev is Zhores Medvedev's twin brother (*New York Times*, 1 June 1970).
[6] He was demoted to head of the institute's department of technical crops (see his obituary in the 18 July 1968 *Selskaya Zhizn*).
[7] See N. Kosolapov in *Selskaya Zhizn*, 30 September 1960.

But in late summer the anti-Lysenko atmosphere began to change. Whereas Lysenkoists were fair game in mid-summer,[8] the publication of veteran Lysenkoist G. V. Platonov's article in the August issue of the reactionary journal *Oktyabr* (no. 8) signaled the beginning of a counterreaction. While not defending Lysenko's own reprehensible actions, the new Lysenkoist line of defense enunciated by Platonov (and followed by other former Lysenkoists since then) was to accuse the anti-Lysenkoists of trying to establish a new, anti-Lysenko monopoly of ideas. Michurinist ideas, they argued, should be allowed to coexist and compete with anti-Michurinist views. The former Lysenkoists were encouraged by the gradually developing political line of discouraging exposure of abuses under Stalin or Khrushchev—including Lysenko's abuses—which began in early 1966 (most notably in the 30 January 1966 *Pravda* article by conservative historians condemning the use of the term "period of the cult of personality").

After the August Platonov article, anti-Lysenkoist articles dwindled and by the end of the year were rare and limited to journals rather than newspapers. The demise of the anti-Lysenko press campaign was confirmed by the removal of chief editor Yu. P. Voronov of the crusading anti-Lysenko paper *Komsomolskaya Pravda*, announced by TASS on 20 December 1965.[9] Voronov had become deputy editor of *Komsomolskaya Pravda* in 1954 when Shelepin was Komsomol first secretary. His removal as editor in December 1965 followed by only a few days the dissolution of Shelepin's Party-State Control Committee (which had expanded its activities in mid-1965 during Shelepin's challenge to Brezhnev and had secured the removal of Lysenkoists Matsepuro and Zezin) at the 6 December Central Committee plenum. *Komsomolskaya Pravda's* last attack on Lysenko came on 7 September—at the same time that efforts began to reduce the powers of the party-state control system. The September 1965 Central Committee plenum and the October 1965 Supreme Soviet session and the follow-up local plenums and sessions virtually ignored the party-state control system, and a debate developed over the role party-state control organs would play under the new economic system adopted by the September plenum. Editorials on the special party-state control pages in *Izvestiya* (8 October 1965) and *Pravda* (12 October 1965) asserted that the party-state control system's role would grow under the new system. In contrast, an October issue of *Partiynaya Zhizn* (no. 19) carried an editorial completely ignoring party-state control organs

---

[8]The Party-State Control Committee was attacking Lysenkoists Matsepuro and Zezin in June; old Lysenko foe Dubinin was attacking the republication of a Lysenkoist book by V. Yelagin in *Komsomolskaya Pravda* on 28 July; the 20 July *Leningradskaya Pravda* was carrying an attack on Lysenko's 1948 persecution of biologist M. S. Navashin; *Literaturnaya Gazeta* on 20 July was announcing that Popovskiy was writing a book about Lysenko and Vavilov; *Selskaya Zhizn* on 28 July was announcing the establishment of a Vavilov Prize by the Academy of Sciences Presidium; and Lobanov (*Trud*, 5 August) was attacking Sizov's suppression of anti-Lysenkoists at the Leningrad Plant Growing Institute and Lysenko's monopoly in education.

[9]He was transferred to responsible secretary of *Pravda's* editorial board—*Sovetskaya Pechat*, 1 (1966): 45.

and treating party organizations as the checkers on economic organizations. An article by V. Ososkov in the same issue of *Partiynaya Zhizn* downgraded the party-state control organs to only one among many checking organizations and as only an agency of local party organizations rather than part of an independent party-state control chain of command outside the regular party apparatus. A November article in *Sovetskoye Gosudarstvo i Pravo* (no. 11, pp. 19–25) criticized the Party-State Control Committee's statute for being overly broad and called for changes to specify just who the party-state control organs had a right to punish and to avoid their duplicating the work of other checking organizations. Then, in early December they were abolished and a more restricted People's Control Committee replaced the Party-State Control Committee. Shelepin, as chairman of the Party-State Control Committee, had had the privilege of holding leadership posts in both the government and the party. In December he lost his post as deputy premier and, as Central Committee secretary, was given the more innocuous assignment of supervising consumer goods production.

Probably as a result of the changed atmosphere, Lysenko himself escaped being really punished. The investigation of his work begun in late January 1965 dragged on into fall, when relationships in the Presidium (especially between Brezhnev and Shelepin) were changing—apparently in Lysenko's favor.

Following a 23 January *Literaturnaya Gazeta* attack questioning Lysenko's bull-breeding and manure experiments, the Academy of Sciences on 29 January 1965 created a commission to investigate his farm and the authenticity of the results he had claimed for his experiments, especially the claims he and Kallistratov made at the February 1964 Central Committee plenum. The commission visited Lysenko's farm during the period 9 February to 22 March and concluded that he and Kallistratov had deceived the Central Committee and that *Literaturnaya Gazeta's* charges were correct.

The commission, supposedly objective and unbiased, was headed by A. I. Tulupnikov, a close associate of Matskevich,[10] who had fought Lysenko's bull-

---

[10] On the same day that Matskevich was removed as agriculture minister in December 1960, an *Ekonomicheskaya Gazeta* article (29 December 1960) attacked Tulupnikov for using a definition from an August Matskevich article, and a week later an *Ekonomicheskaya Gazeta* article (7 January 1961) attacked Tulupnikov, then director of the Institute of Agricultural Economics, for using his institute to supply Matskevich with data to use in controversies against Khrushchev: the institute "wasted much time on the collection and processing of various 'facts' in justification of the mistaken position of the leadership of the Ministry of Agriculture USSR, which considered inexpedient the organization of divisions in sovkhozes in the virgin lands." An article in *Partiynaya Zhizn* (7 [1961]: 17–24) also attacks him for opposing Khrushchev's position in the controversy over farm wage systems. The same basic charge is made in a *Kommunist* (5 [1961]: 42–51) article. A 12 February 1962 *Ekonomicheskaya Gazeta* editorial criticizing the institute revealed that leadership of the institute had been changed, and shortly afterward K. P. Obolenskiy was identified as director.

breeding program to the last ditch in 1960. Within a week after Matskevich was removed as agriculture minister the new minister, Olshanskiy, (on 5 January 1961) had ordered a go-ahead on the program. The investigation of Lysenko's farm began almost at the same time that Matskevich was reappointed agriculture minister in February 1965 (17 February). Matskevich and Lysenko foe Lobanov (who replaced Olshanskiy as VASKhNIL president on 10 February) even attended the September 1965 Academy of Sciences Presidium session on the results of the investigation of Lysenko's farm, and Matskevich and Tulupnikov interrogated Kallistratov, who had the lack of foresight to show up at the session. Matskevich forced Kallistratov to admit that the result of the bull-breeding experiment had actually been a sharp decline in milk production (*Vestnik Akademii Nauk SSSR*, no. 11 [1965]).

Lysenko himself tried to obstruct the investigation and in a 3 May 1965 letter assailed the commission and the press for trying to "deny the usefulness of all my practical proposals in order to run down the theory of biological science developed by me." Tulupnikov replied with a 31 August 1965 letter in the name of the commission defending its report against Lysenko's attacks. Finally, when the Academy of Sciences Presidium session to discuss the results of the investigation opened on 2 September 1965, Lysenko refused to attend, claiming that the report was full of "distortions" and "malicious slander" against him.

Despite the confirmation of the serious accusations against Lysenko, he escaped any real punishment. The decree of the session only called upon Lysenko and Kallistratov to "eliminate the shortcomings in the work of the farm." Academy of Sciences President Keldysh announced that the decree made it "possible for Academician Lysenko to continue his work" at his farm. Kallistratov remained head of the experimental farm. Lysenko's philosopher-partner I. I. Prezent, sent to the farm after being expelled from the party for "moral corruption" in Leningrad and then reinstated by the Party Control Committee on Lysenko's urgent appeal,[11] was still a senior scientific associate at Gorki Leninskiye when he died in January 1969 (*Selskaya Zhizn*, 9 January 1969).

It is perhaps not accidental that Keldysh took a soft attitude toward Lysenko. He had received his post as Academy of Sciences president in early 1961 when Lysenko, at the height of his power, had attacked the then Academy of Sciences President A. N. Nesmeyanov for opposing Lysenkoist biology and had managed to have him removed. Keldysh at the 1–2 February 1965 Academy of Sciences session took an equivocal position toward Lysenko: "I think that in condemning the monopolistic position held by Academician T. D. Lysenko and in denying his incorrect views on a number of very important questions of biology, we should not sweepingly negate everything that he did. In particular, according to the opinion of some prominent scientists, his theory of stage development of plants has scientific significance and, on the testimony of some of the

---

[11] Medvedev, *Rise and Fall of Lysenko*, p. 158.

plant breeders, they used the methods proposed by him" (*Pravda*, 4 February 1965).[12]

The situation had changed enough so that the journal *Oktyabr* could publish semi-defenses of Lysenko in its February 1966 issue. *Oktyabr's* editors wrote that some people were striking at "even that which is uncontestably valuable" in Lysenko's work, especially the theory of stage development of plants. They wrote: "There were also those who are speaking out against the Michurinist school in biology, which is the glory and pride of our Soviet science," while depicting the "chromosome theory as absolutely infallible." *Oktyabr* quoted some Kazakh scientists who declared that it was wrong to depict Lysenko "as an ignoramus and scoundrel." They cite Professor R. D. Glavinich's interesting claim that Lysenko had opposed Khrushchev's antigrassland campaign: that "Lysenko was not involved in the mistakes committed in agriculture in connection with corn, that he was one of the few who objected to reducing grass sowing, etc."

The former Lysenkoists fiercely singled out some of the present critics for having themselves publicly promoted Lysenko's theories in the past—especially Lobashev and B. M. Kedrov, who had opposed Lysenko before 1948, then were stripped of their jobs and had to write pro-Michurinist articles until his monopoly on biology weakened, whereupon they could revert to their original views. Lysenkoist defender N. I. Feyginson criticized Lobashev for a 1954 book rejecting genes (*Oktyabr*, no. 2 [1966]).

Especially bizarre is the case of Kedrov, who has been one of the most outspoken critics of Lysenko since Khrushchev's fall. According to Ye. Kh. Frauchi (*Oktyabr*, no. 2 [1966]), Kedrov's brother and father were "enemies of the people." Bonifatiy Mikhaylovich Kedrov was the son of Mikhail Sergeyevich Kedrov (1879–October 1941)—one of the first and most celebrated rehabilitees.[13] *Leningradskaya Pravda* on 25 February 1964 told how at the beginning of 1939 Kedrov and his youngest son Igor "spoke out against the hostile activities of Beriya. . . . In February–April 1939, M. S. Kedrov and Igor Kedrov sent Stalin a number of letters revealing cases of Beriya's traitorous activity. As a result of this, Igor Kedrov was arrested and then shot." The elder Kedrov was arrested but later acquitted by the Military Collegium of the Supreme Court. In

[12] Keldysh's deputy, Academy of Sciences Vice President N. N. Semenov soon afterward disagreed with Keldysh publicly. In a devastating attack on Lysenko in *Nauka i Zhizn*, no. 4 (1965), he specifically denied the value of the theory of stage development of plants and of the plant-breeding work. One of Lysenko's main points in his complaint about the investigation was that the commission would turn in its report to Semenov, who as chairman of the academy's section for chemical, technological, and biological sciences, had jurisdiction over the investigation, and that Semenov's article showed him to be completely biased against Lysenko (*Vestnik Akademii Nauk SSSR*, no. 11 [1965]).

[13] Yu. Sharapov and B. Yakovlev in the 11 July 1970 *Izvestiya* praise B. M. Kedrov's memoirs of Lenin, in which Kedrov tells how Lenin visited his father M. S. Kedrov while he was in Swiss exile.

spite of this, he was murdered by Beriya at the end of October 1941. In the indictment against Beriya after Stalin's death, for some reason or other, Kedrov was singled out as virtually Beriya's leading victim. Khrushchev, in his 1956 secret speech at the 20th Congress, devoted much attention to Kedrov and quoted extensively from a letter he wrote from prison in 1940. Khrushchev declared that although Kedrov had been found innocent by a military collegium, he had been shot at Beriya's order.

Oddly, despite the black mark on B. M. Kedrov's record (son and brother of "enemies of the people"), he rose to become editor of the philosophy journal *Voprosy Filosofii*, which was established during Zhdanov's postwar ideological crackdown. Kedrov in August 1947 spearheaded Zhdanov's attack on Central Committee Agitprop head G. F. Aleksandrov, who was ousted. After Stalin's death, Aleksandrov became culture minister under Malenkov, but when Malenkov resigned as premier in early 1955, Aleksandrov was ousted as culture minister. Soon afterward, in a September 1955 *Kommunist* (no. 14) article, Kedrov assailed Aleksandrov for repeating his 1947 mistakes, declaring that Zhdanov's 1947 criticisms of Aleksandrov's writings could be applied to his 1954 writings also.

During the 1949 purge of the Zhdanovites and the Leningrad Case, *Voprosy Filosofii* was criticized for having failed to publicize the August 1948 VASKhNIL session, and Kedrov had to recant in a letter published in *Kultura i Zhizn* on 23 March 1949. He was soon removed as editor (August 1949) and began to write pro-Lysenko articles—apparently under the threat of blackmail because of his father's and brother's record as "enemies of the people." Frauchi tells of the "terrible tragedy of his family" and defends Kedrov's post-1948 Lysenkoist writings: "He had to speak out against his own true convictions."

Reaction against the Virgin Lands

A wave of reaction also set in against Khrushchev's favored treatment of the virgin lands. Particularly those in the non-chernozem zone (mainly the Baltic, Belorussia, and north and west Russia) resented the concentration of money and resources in the virgin lands and the no-investment policy in their own area.[14] They had already caused a fuss over discrimination against their zone in 1964,[15]

[14] See N. Verkhovskiy in *Novyy Mir*, no. 4 (1966).

[15] A controversy over noninvestment in the non-chernozem zone had broken out in early 1964. Professor I. Nazimov had written a 14 December 1963 *Ekonomicheskaya Gazeta* article arguing that investments produced a greater return in the richer agricultural areas (the central black earth zone, the north Caucasus, etc.) than in the non-chernozem zone. Non-chernozem zone first secretaries I. S. Gustov (Pskov) and N. G. Korytkov (Kalinin) reacted with attacks on Nazimov, defending investment in their zone (*Izvestiya*, 19 January and 28 April 1964). Much of the non-chernozem zone had been transferred to specialization in livestock raising in 1963 (as a result of Khrushchev's 31 January 1963 Note to the Presidium "On Several Questions of Agricultural Specialization in Belorussia, the Baltic Republics, and the Northwest Oblasts of the RSFSR") and grain growing had been

and after Khrushchev's fall their resentment became more open and effective. Lobanov, at a late October 1965 meeting in VASKhNIL, declared that some people were saying that the virgin lands had lost their value (*Vestnik Selskokhozyaystvennoy Nauki*, no. 3 [1966]). Belorussian First Secretary Mazurov (Belorussia is in the non-chernozem zone) criticized the concentration on extensive farming (virgin lands) and called for more attention for the non-chernozem zone at the March 1965 plenum. A 26 percent rise in investment in the nonchernozem zone was announced by RSFSR Gosplan Chairman K. M. Gerasimov in *Sovetskaya Rossiya* on 17 December 1965. *Komsomolskaya Pravda* agricultural writer A. Ivashchenko later described this as "that sad period when the very expression 'virgin lands' went out of use and when some people were speaking about this as if it 'was a mistake,' 'we just threw away the money,' and 'we should get rid of this virgin land' " (*Komsomolskaya Pravda*, 25 December 1968). Kazakh historians later complained that "some critics even proposed removing the equipment from the virgin land regions and 'closing down the virgin lands'."[16] As if symbolically, Tselinnyy Kray itself, a creation of Khrushchev, was abolished (*Kazakhstanskaya Pravda*, 20 October 1965).

Matskevich and Lobanov, after being restored to leadership in February 1965, gave preference to the neglected non-chernozem zone and promoted programs popular there (expansion of grass sowing, grass-meal production, crop rotations, oats)—while criticizing the extension of corn and the intertilled system into the north. The March plenum and Brezhnev's report devoted much attention to the neglect of this zone and VASKhNIL devoted its first special zonal session to the non-chernozem zone in November 1965 (*Selskaya Zhizn*, 18 November 1965)—a session on virgin land problems followed in January–February 1966.

Matskevich and Lobanov began again promoting the development of zonal systems of agriculture. This work had almost been completed in 1960, but

---

reduced. But, as Korytkov complained, while prices for grain were high and profitable (exceeding costs by 200 percent), prices for livestock were so low that no profit was possible. Mazurov also complained of this at the March 1965 plenum. The non-chernozem zone was discriminated against by reductions in fertilizer allotments, equipment, and price incentives.

The controversy and attacks on Nazimov continued throughout 1965 (N. Itskov in *Pravda*, 24 July 1965; A. Blinov in *Literaturnaya Gazeta*, 10 August 1965; Gustov at the March 1965 plenum and in *Oktyabr*, no. 12 [1965]). Gustov wrote: "Before the March 1965 Central Committee plenum, the northwest was given undeservedly little attention. The subjective and basically mistaken approach to evaluating the role and significance of the non-chernozem zone in general and the northwest in particular did not permit fully using the huge economic opportunities of this part of the country and led to lagging and neglect" (*Oktyabr*, no. 12 [1965]). At the March 1965 plenum Gustov stated: "At one time, when the virgin lands were cultivated, we understood the line of the Central Committee and government. Now, it seems to us, one can and must invest funds also in the non-chernozem zone" (Stenographic record of the March 1965 Central Committee plenum, p. 145).

[16] Z. Golikova et al., *Kommunisticheskaya Partiya v Borbe za Osvoyeniye Tselinnykh Zemel v Kazakhstane*, p. 564.

because the systems included perennial grass sowing in the crop rotations they were rejected (Lobanov in *Leninskoye Znamya*, 16 February 1965) and Matskevich and Lobanov were soon removed. At the March 1965 plenum Lobanov complained that Khrushchev's American friend Roswell Garst had called crop rotations outdated and Khrushchev had backed this idea. Matskevich stressed the value of Lithuania's grass-meal production[17] and praised Baltic work on meadows and pastures (*Selskaya Zhizn*, 24 June 1965). Grass meal and grazing were stressed by Matskevich and Lobanov instead of corn silage.

Non-chernozem zone people received preference in post-Khrushchev agricultural leadership appointments also. For example, appointments to leading posts in the RSFSR Agriculture Ministry in late 1965 and 1966 were predominantly from the non-chernozem zone: Minister L. Ya. Florentyev from Kostroma, First Deputy Minister V. K. Mesyats and Deputy Minister A. A. Goltsev from Moscow Oblast, Deputy Minister V. G. Agibalov from Murmansk, and Deputy Minister A. A. Abrazyakov from Tataria. Comparatively few virginlanders have gotten agricultural leadership posts since Khrushchev's fall: Pysin, formerly from the Altay, became first deputy premier of the RSFSR in December 1964; T. I. Sokolov became RSFSR first deputy agriculture minister for a short time in early 1965; the exiled Matskevich—not a real virginlander—returned in February 1965 to become agriculture minister; A. V. Kardapoltsev returned from Chelyabinsk to become Matskevich's deputy; P. F. Morozov from Krasnoyarsk became chief of the Agriculture Ministry's Main Administration for Kolkhozes sometime between April 1964 and September 1965; and F. Ye. Savitskiy from Kazakhstan (chief of the Sovkhoz Administration for Tselinnyy Kray March 1961–March 1962, then Kazakh first deputy minister for production and procurement of agricultural products) became chief of the Planning and Economic Administration of the Agriculture Ministry.

There was also a wave of reaction against Khrushchev's favorite crops—corn, peas, sugar beets, and beans (the Altay Institute's favorites), and land

---

[17]Lithuania was especially stubborn in resisting Khrushchev's antigrassland campaign. Lithuanian scientists infuriated him in late 1961 by demanding that 50 percent of Lithuanian farmland be devoted to grass and by criticizing the antigrassland speeches at the October 1961 22d Party Congress. Khrushchev angrily ordered Lithuanian First Secretary Snechkus to investigate this (*Pravda*, 16 January 1962). Lithuanian Agriculture Minister V. Vazalinskas was forced to recant publicly for backing the grasslanders. In *Sovetskaya Litva*, 5 January 1962, he wrote that "I personally, as the minister of agriculture, overrated the part that grasses play in increasing fertility and in agricultural development in general," and that the Lithuanian farming institute and its director, P. Vasinauskas, "also committed serious errors in this regard." He thanked the "convincing" speeches by Khrushchev for helping them to realize their mistakes. Nevertheless, Vazalinskas lost his job. He reappeared in July 1965 when he was appointed Lithuanian deputy premier and since then he has reverted to promoting expansion of grass sowings (*Sovetskaya Litva*, 14 June 1966). At the March 1965 plenum Snechkus praised the scientists of Lithuania's agricultural institutes for their "correct positions" on perennial grass and declared that "with the help of sensible people from the center we withstood this onslaught" against perennial grasses (Stenographic record of the March 1965 Central Committee plenum, pp. 220–21).

allotted to these crops was slashed drastically, while grass and clean fallow were expanded. G. Lisichkin in *Novyy Mir* (no. 2 [1967] : 163) wrote that since 1964, corn sown for grain had been cut by 1,286,000 hectares, while the area allotted to perennial grass had risen by 2.5 million hectares. According to deputy head of the Central Committee Agriculture Section V. Pannikov, already "in 1965 approximately as much grass was sown as in 1961" (*Kommunist*, no. 14 [1965]). Matskevich at the 23d Congress in 1966 declared that there would be 20 million hectares under perennial grass.[18] Matskevich and Lobanov spear-headed a drive to expand production of grass meal—as against corn silage—and an RSFSR Ministry for Grain Products and Mixed Feed and a Main Administration for the Microbiological Industry[19] were established. I. I. Khoroshilov, chief of the Main Administration for Grain Crops of the Agriculture Ministry, wrote in *Sovetskaya Latviya* on 7 October 1966 that there would be 14.6 million hectares of clean fallow in 1966, as against only 6.3 million three years earlier.

Corn was partially rehabilitated in 1967, but only in early 1969—in con-nection with the devastation of winter crops by dust storms in the Ukraine and north Caucasus and with the growing enthusiasm for mechanized links, which are more successful at corn raising—was corn again urged on farmers. An article in a June 1969 issue of *Agitator* (no. 11, p. 20) reported that because of the bad weather (the destruction of winter crops by winterkill and dust storms and the need to replace them with spring crops) corn grain sowing had now been raised from the originally planned 3.6 million hectares to over 5 million.

Barayev and Maltsev Ascendant

The wave of reaction against Khrushchev's virgin land policies put the opponents of clean fallow on the defensive. Barayev and Maltsev became heroes, honored as victims of persecution by Khrushchev, Lysenko, and Nalivayko, and their views were widely promoted in the press. Their supporters became dominant in agri-cultural leadership. Among the first to gain after Khrushchev's fall was Maltsev's protector Kurgan First Secretary G. F. Sizov,[20] who was promoted to full Cen-tral Committee membership at the November 1964 plenum. Kazakh Premier Kunayev was reinstated as first secretary in December.[21] Maltsev–Barayev sup-porters Matskevich and Lobanov returned to their 1960 posts of agriculture minister and VASKhNIL president, and Matskevich's former deputy and Barayev

---

[18] Stenographic record of the 23d Party Congress, vol. 1, p. 297.

[19] This new administration was established to improve the quality of mixed feed—according to Gosplan Deputy Chairman N. Gusev in *Kommunist*, no. 9 (June 1966).

[20] L. Ivanov in *Sibirskiye Ogni*, nos. 5 and 6 (1965), describes Sizov's enforcement of Maltsev's methods on all Kurgan farmers.

[21] Kunayev reiterated his strong support for Barayev at a 10 June 1965 Kazakh Central Committee plenum reported in *Kazakhstanskaya Pravda* on 12 June; the Kazakh Central Committee's agriculture secretaries Melnik and Kolomiyets were on record for Barayev since 1963.

supporter I. I. Khoroshilov returned to get the key post of chief of the Main Administration for Grain Crops in the reorganized Agriculture Ministry. Virgin land clean fallow advocate T. I. Sokolov became deputy head of the newly reestablished RSFSR Agriculture Ministry.

Ironically, after years of being persecuted for stubbornly insisting upon clean fallow and resisting corn,[22] Barayev and his associates, deputy director of his institute V. M. Slobodin and former deputy director Sdobnikov, softened their opposition to moldboard plowing and use of corn and no longer were so insistent upon clean fallow. Barayev in his recommendations to VASKhNIL in early 1966[23] and Sdobnikov in his 1964 book *Questions of Farming in Tselinnyy Kray* advocate alternating moldboard (deep) plowing some years (to kill weeds) with moldboardless (shallow) plowing other years to preserve stubble and hold moisture. Although Barayev still would exclude intertilled crops from regular field crop rotations (which should consist mainly of spring wheat and clean fallow), he proposes special livestock fodder crop rotations which can include 25-75 percent corn—which he rates as the best fodder in the virgin lands—and which can exclude clean fallow. Their estimation of clean fallow declined: they saw its value only in fighting weeds—whereas in the past they valued it for collecting moisture and building soil nutrition. In fact, a *Kazakhstanskaya Pravda* article on 10 March 1965 even criticized Sdobnikov's book for underrating clean fallow!

The Struggle against the Altay Institute

The removal of Khrushchev did not end the debates over policies in the virgin lands. Lysenko's program had long since been discredited, and the 1964 purge of Khayrullin swept the Orenburg system from contention. But despite the ascension of the Barayev–Maltsev supporters and the official promotion of their programs, the struggle against the Altay group and its intertilled system continued until 1967, when Altay First Secretary A. V. Georgiyev finally surrendered and Nalivayko lost his job as director of the Altay Institute.

Khrushchev had protected the Altay Institute in 1963 and 1964 (for example, when L. Ivanov found misuse of data at the institute during a 1963 visit, he was unable to get his exposures published[24]). The Altay leaders managed to escape reprisal for so long after Khrushchev's fall because of the new policy of above all avoiding stereotypes and allowing various systems to coexist[25] and perhaps also because former Altay patron Pysin became RSFSR first deputy premier immediately after Khrushchev's fall.

[22] Barayev was almost expelled from the party for clinging to clean fallow—according to Kunayev at the March 1965 Central Committee plenum.

[23] *Kazakhstanskaya Pravda*, 1 February 1966, and *Vestnik Selskokhozyaystvennoy Nauki*, no. 5 (May 1966).

[24] See *Sibirskiye Ogni*, nos. 5 and 6 (1965).

[25] See Yu. Chernichenko in the 12 October 1966 *Pravda*.

The attack on the Altay Institute was begun by journalists (such as L. Ivanov) in 1963 and 1964 after the failure of the corn program had become obvious, but it only became authoritative after Khrushchev's fall, when important officials like Agriculture Minister Matskevich, VASKhNIL President Lobanov and deputy head of the Central Committee Agriculture Section Pannikov began criticizing the institute. Already in early 1965 Altay First Secretary Georgiyev admitted that the intertilled system had been applied in a stereotyped manner in the kray[26] and the Altay Institute has been on the defensive since then. Meanwhile, Lobanov, Matskevich, and the Kazakh leaders have been pushing the restoration of grass to provide the fodder base instead of corn silage and have encouraged taking eroded virgin land fields out of production for sowing with grass.

VASKhNIL held a session in the virgin lands in January–February 1966 and Lobanov laid out a virgin land program based on Barayev's ideas.[27] At the session, Nalivayko claimed he had recommended intertilled crops only for his zone and others were to blame for overextending corn sowings. He admitted the deficiencies of intertilled crops in many areas, but was badgered for refusing to admit the need for 15–20 percent clean fallow in the dry Kulunda steppe in the Altay (*Vestnik Selskokhozyaystvennoy Nauki*, no. 5 [1966]). *Pravda* on 1 March 1966 carried an attack on Nalivayko and the intertilled system for sowing almost all land (including marginal land, fallow, and grassland) and thereby producing dust storms and erosion unseen previously in the Altay. It also attacked the institute's fodder program for resulting in practically liquidating sheep raising.

Lobanov outlined the new virgin lands program in a 2 March 1966 *Selskaya Zhizn* article, but despite this and the numerous attacks on the Altay Institute, Altay First Secretary Georgiyev continued to resist. In a 22 March 1966 *Sovetskaya Rossiya* article he claimed that Barayev's clean fallow recommendations (33 percent for the dry Kulunda steppe in Altay) were too high.

The Altay Institute tried to avoid attack by lapsing into silence (*Pravda*, 1 March 1966) and probably counting on its protectors; in Altay it had associates in leading posts. Although F. P. Shevchenko (who wrote the key November 1960 article promoting Nalivayko's system) no longer was kray agricultural administration chief (he was now just Nalivayko's deputy again), former institute deputy director Metelev (who made the 1963 attack on Sotnikov) was still chief agronomist for the kray agricultural administration in March 1966, and kray First Secretary Georgiyev was sympathetic. Harder to assess is the attitude of the new kray Executive Committee Chairman I. I. Molchaninov, who was transferred from Orenburg to Altay in early 1966. Molchaninov was a Voronov protégé who had been censured for supporting Khayrullin's Orenburg system in the early

---

[26] At a kray conference reported in *Partiynaya Zhizn* 2 (January 1965): 11.

[27] *Selskaya Zhizn*, 1 February 1966, and *Vestnik Selskokhozyaystvennoy Nauki*, no. 5 (1966).

1964 Orenburg case. He may have supported clean fallow now, following Khayrullin's lead, but presumably would not be harsh with Nalivayko and company. In any case, Chernichenko in a 12 October 1966 *Pravda* article could complain that the Altay Institute had still not admitted the faults of its recommendations and that the intertilled system was still alive. He noted that the Altay's overfulfillment of the 1966 grain plan protected it from criticism at the present time.

On 29 November 1966 (*Selskaya Zhizn*) Georgiyev defended the Altay, while on the same day *Pravda* carried Dronov's attack on the Altay Kray Agriculture Administration for still underrating fallow and for having to switch much land from grain to grass for 1967. On 3 December I. Zaytsev in *Selskaya Zhizn* attacked Chernichenko's fall 1965 book *Strelka Kompasa* [Needle of the Compass] for urging 33–40 percent clean fallow and for comparing the virgin lands with Canada. The argument between the advocates of imitating Canada (Matskevich, Khoroshilov, and Barayev had all visited Canada and advocated borrowing its methods) and their opponents has continued since the late 1950's. Even though *Selskaya Zhizn* refused to print Chernichenko's reply to Zaytsev,[28] Chernichenko was able to publish an article in *Kommunist* (no. 4 [1967]) attacking Nalivayko and the Altay Kray leaders for still clinging to the intertilled system and complaining that articles against clean fallow were still appearing and opponents were representing clean fallow as a borrowing from capitalism.

Barayev had renewed the attack on the Altay and the intertilled system in a 16 February 1967 *Pravda* article assailing resistance to clean fallow. He complained that some people were citing Kuban experience in arguments against clean fallow. The struggle ended abruptly a month later. On 20 March 1967 the Central Committee and Council of Ministers adopted a decree "On Urgent Measures to Protect the Soil From Wind and Water Erosion,"[29] which criticized local party, government and farm leaders and scientists for "underrating the danger" of erosion and which ordered an acceleration of scientific efforts to develop antierosion measures. Altay Institute director Nalivayko—who was being blamed for causing the unprecedented erosion in the Altay and elsewhere— was quietly removed simultaneously with the decree. In an April *Partiynaya Zhizn* article (no. 8, signed to press on 17 April), Altay First Secretary Georgiyev turned around and criticized the Altay Institute and its "*former* director G. A. Nalivayko" for drawing "hasty conclusions from their experiments without sufficient production checking" and for forcing their "advice" on farms. Georgiyev gave no indication of when Nalivayko had been replaced, but Chernichenko had still referred to him as director in his March *Kommunist*

[28] See V. Gurevich's statement in *Zhurnalist* 4 (1967): 14.
[29] The date of the decree was revealed by A. N. Kashtanov in the November 1971 *Selskoye Khozyaystvo Rossii*, p. 11. The decree was published in the 2 April 1967 *Selskaya Zhizn* and commented on in a 4 April 1967 *Selskaya Zhizn* editorial.

article attacking Nalivayko (no. 4, signed to press 9 March). Nalivayko's removal may have been arranged by Polyanskiy, who visited the Altay in early March to make an election speech (*Pravda*, 3 March 1967).

A. N. Kashtanov was appointed director of the institute and initiated a comprehensive program of research into antierosion measures. A new lab was established to study erosion and experiments were begun to test antierosion cultivation techniques and crop rotations.[30] Altay Institute leaders cautiously avoided publicity for the next several years, and only after successfully developing new methods did they make new recommendations to the Altay farms (these were first described by director Kashtanov in a November 1971 *Selskoye Khozyaystvo Rossii* article).

Georgiyev's final surrender was lauded by Barayev's partisans. An 8 August 1967 *Kazakhstanskaya Pravda* article reported that Georgiyev, who "quite recently was against everything" recommended by Barayev's institute, including clean fallow and moldboardless plowing, now was leading a big group of Altay agronomists to visit Barayev and study his methods. It noted that finally even the Altay would join the rest of the virgin lands in using the Barayev system. *Pravda* followed this up with a 13 August attack on the Altay Kray Agriculture Administration for bureaucracy and a 21 August attack on the Saratov Institute for backing Nalivayko's intertilled crop rotations and opposing clean fallow.[31] However, while Nalivayko had been dropped, the same group of politicians continued to run Altay agriculture in 1968 and afterward: Georgiyev as kray first secretary, Molchaninov as executive committee chairman, N. F. Aksenov as kray agriculture secretary, I. S. Protsyuk as chief of the kray agriculture administration, and F. P. Shevchenko as deputy director of the Altay Institute.

Demotion of Recent Khrushchev Favorites

The removal of Khrushchev was immediately followed by reprisals against his most recent favorites (the 1963–64 appointees), virtually all of whom were purged or at least demoted. The first moves were the ouster of Central Commit-

---

[30] In the November 1971 *Selskoye Khozyaystvo Rossii*, Kashtanov describes how this work was begun in 1967, after the 20 March decree.

[31] *Pravda* on 16 November 1967 reported that the RSFSR Agriculture Ministry had discussed the 21 August article on the Saratov Institute and had ordered the institute to eliminate these shortcomings.

Although the Saratov Institute had been accused of backing clean fallow and grass and opposing corn in 1961 and its director, P. G. Kabanov, had been forced to admit the error of his views (*Sovetskaya Rossiya*, 24 December 1961), the Saratov scientists wound up in 1964 supporting fall plowland against their rival Khayrullin, who then was backing clean fallow. Khrushchev praised the Saratov position during his August 1964 speaking tour (see above). Thus, after swinging to the opposite side in the clean fallow debate (its director in 1967 was M. M. Popugayev, instead of Kabanov), the Saratov Institute again came under attack—this time for the opposite sin.

tee Agriculture Secretary and head of the Central Committee Agriculture Section V. I. Polyakov[32] at the November 1964 plenum and the exile of Presidium candidate member and RSFSR Bureau First Deputy Chairman L. N. Yefremov to Stavropol in December 1964. Agriculture Minister Volovchenko was demoted to first deputy minister in February 1965 and first deputy ministers Morozov and Sidak were soon demoted to deputy ministers. RSFSR Production and Procurement of Agricultural Products Minister L. I. Maksimov was dismissed in December and the ministry abolished in March 1965 when the RSFSR Agriculture Ministry was reestablished.

In contrast, the earlier group (those from 1961–62, when Polyanskiy and Voronov played the leading roles) largely escaped blame and some were brought back from obscurity (where Khrushchev had cast them) and given important jobs. Pysin became RSFSR first deputy premier, Karlov became an RSFSR Bureau member apparently with responsibility for agriculture, Sotnikov became chief of the Main Administration for Land Use, Land Organization, Shelterbelt Forestry, and Soil Conservation of the Agriculture Ministry, Sinyagin became vice president of VASKhNIL. Actually, these men, along with Polyanskiy and Voronov, would appear to be the politicians most responsible for the worse agricultural failures in 1961–63, but blame apparently was established according to political rivalries rather than actual responsibility.

Those associated with Matskevich and Aristov were also brought back: G. L. Smirnov became RSFSR deputy agriculture minister and A. V. Kardapoltsev became USSR deputy agriculture minister. Mazurov's man, former Belorussian Agriculture Minister M. N. Lutsenko, who was driven out of office by Khrushchev in December 1961 for implementing Mazurov's pro-grassland policies, was made head of the Main Administration for Livestock Raising of the reorganized Agriculture Ministry.[33]

[32] According to Medvedev (*Rise and Fall of Lysenko*, p. 229), Polyakov became deputy editor of *Ekonomicheskaya Gazeta*. In 1969, along with the other *Ekonomicheskaya Gazeta* editors, Polyakov compiled a volume of articles on the economic reform entitled *Khozyaystvennaya Reforma v SSSR* [Economic Reform in the USSR].

[33] Mazurov's favoring of grass in Belorussia angered Khrushchev, who at a January 1962 Minsk conference demanded of him: "Where were you looking, Comrade Mazurov? Who is leading Belorussia, the Belorussian Central Committee and Council of Ministers or the grasslanders?" (*Pravda*, 16 January 1962). Mazurov was accused of allowing 800,000 hectares of land to be diverted from grain production to grass, and he was forced to attack his own Belorussian Agriculture Ministry officials (*Sovetskaya Belorussiya*, 14 January 1962).

Mazurov got his chance to strike back at the March 1965 plenum, when he told of being attacked for trying to create 500,000 hectares of pasture land (Stenographic record of the March 1965 Central Committee plenum, p. 76). At this plenum Mazurov was promoted to full Presidium membership and named first deputy premier of the USSR. He had been elected a Presidium candidate member in 1957 but his poor relations with Khrushchev apparently doomed him to be a perennial candidate member. He and Khrushchev-critic Mzhavanadze were by far the most senior candidate members. But Mazurov prospered immediately upon Khrushchev's fall. His protégé, Belorussian Second Secretary P. M.

Post-Khrushchev Changes

	1964		1965
First secretary	Khrushchev (–Oct. '64)		Brezhnev
Agriculture secretary	Polyakov (–Nov. '64)	(Sept. '65–)	Kulakov
Agri. section head	Polyakov (–Nov. '64)	(Dec. '64–)	Kulakov
Premier	Khrushchev (–Oct. '64)		Kosygin
Deputy premier for agri.	Polyanskiy		Polyanskiy
Agriculture minister	Volovchenko (–Feb. '65)		Matskevich
First deputy minister	Morozov (–early '65)	(Feb. '65–)	Volovchenko
First deputy minister	Sidak (–early '65)		
Deputy ministers			Morozov
			Sidak
RSFSR Bureau chairman	Khrushchev (–Oct. '64)	(Nov. '64–)	Brezhnev
First deputy chairman	Yefremov (–Dec. '64)		
First deputy chairman	Kirilenko		Kirilenko
Agri. section head		(Mar. '65–)	(Karlov)[a]
Premier	Voronov		Voronov
First deputy premier	Maksimov (–Dec. '64)		Pysin
Prod. and proc. of agri. prod.	Maksimov (–Dec. '64)		(abolished Mar. '65)
Agriculture minister		(established Mar. '65)	Basov
First deputy minister			Sokolov
Deputy minister			G. L. Smirnov

[a]Karlov, as a member of the RSFSR Bureau, presumably acted as head of the section, although he never was actually identified as such.

Immediate Gains for Voronov after Khrushchev's Fall

Khrushchev's fall brought several immediate gains for Voronov—the most important of which was the removal of the threat to his position and the removal of his main rival Yefremov. Voronov was able to bring his old ally Pysin out of disgrace and have him appointed his chief agricultural assistant—RSFSR first deputy premier. Changes in the RSFSR organizational structure—as well as in its leading personnel—strengthened Voronov. The November 1964 plenum reversed the November 1962 changes, ending the bifurcation of party organs into agricultural and industrial, abolishing the RSFSR agriculture and industry bureaus, restoring the rural raykoms (and their newspapers), and eliminating the production administrations' party committees. On the other hand, it endorsed and retained the production administrations themselves, which were created at the March 1962 plenum.[34] Voronov probably encouraged the anti-Lysenko cam-

---

Masherov became a Central Committee member at the November 1964 plenum and Mazurov himself, after playing a big role at the March 1965 plenum—making several proposals—received the two big promotions.

[34] See Kebin's article in *Kommunist*, no. 12 (1966).

paign, perhaps in revenge for the Lysenkoists' hounding of Khayrullin in early 1964. Voronov, who like Khayrullin apparently had switched to backing the clean fallow advocated by Maltsev and Barayev, probably applauded the immediate shift to official approval of clean fallow and the lauding of Maltsev and Barayev as heroes and Khrushchev victims.

Immediately after the 16 November plenum, *Selskaya Zhizn* (22 November) carried a veiled attack on Voronov rival Yefremov. Although nowhere naming Yefremov, the article assailed agricultural leadership in Gorkiy back in 1962—when Yefremov was Gorkiy first secretary. Yefremov, although only a Presidium candidate member, had begun to outrank Voronov in some photo lineups in 1964 (*Pravda*, 13 June). At the beginning of December 1964, Yefremov was exiled to Stavropol and he was badgered in *Izvestiya* on 27 April 1965 and *Pravda* on 20 July 1965. The man he replaced as Stavropol first secretary in December 1964, F. D. Kulakov, moved to Moscow to replace Polyakov as Central Committee Agriculture Section head (first identified in *Pravda* only on 27 May 1965). Kulakov had undoubtedly pleased Voronov at the March 1962 plenum with his praise for his reorganization scheme, for the Orenburg farming system, and for the Altay–Orenburg cattle- and sheep-raising methods. He probably had Polyanskiy's sympathy also since he had backed sharply increased expansion of agricultural machinery production (at the March 1962 plenum) and because he had served under RSFSR Premier Polyanskiy as RSFSR grain products minister from 1959 to June 1960.

The November 1964 plenum's reversal of the November 1962 reorganization also helped Voronov. By ending the separate industrial and agricultural party organs created in November 1962, the RSFSR Agriculture Bureau was eliminated. This, followed by the exile of RSFSR Bureau First Deputy Chairman Yefremov, left Voronov with no competing agricultural authority in the RSFSR. He immediately moved to strengthen his control by getting the replacement of his top agricultural deputy, L. I. Maksimov, as RSFSR first deputy premier and minister for production and procurement of agricultural products in December 1964. Maksimov, a Krasnodar sovkhoz director who became a favorite of Khrushchev's for switching to pea raising and corn sowing in 1962, was appointed to these jobs in January 1964—just before the Khrushchev–Voronov split led to the Orenburg purge. He replaced N. I. Smirnov, who had been appointed in March 1962, when these posts had been set up by Voronov. In Voronov's March 1962 RSFSR reorganization, Smirov had been selected to become Voronov's top deputy for agriculture—deputy chairman of the new RSFSR Agriculture Committee under Chairman Voronov. Smirnov had combined virtually all RSFSR agricultural leadership posts under Voronov: deputy chairman of the RSFSR Agriculture Committee, first deputy premier for agriculture, and minister for production and procurement of agricultural products, while Voronov was chairman of the committee and premier. Khrushchev, in January 1964, thus picked a lowly sovkhoz director who would be totally dependent on his protection and would serve as his loyal agent, and made him

Voronov's top assistant. Voronov now retaliated by returning the hapless Maksimov to obscurity as soon as Khrushchev's agricultural and organizational policies were repudiated at the November 1964 plenum. To replace him as first deputy premier, Voronov chose his old ally Pysin. The post of minister for production and procurement of agricultural products remained vacant until it was abolished and the RSFSR Agriculture Ministry reestablished in March 1965. Voronov's ally, Volgograd Oblast Executive Committee Chairman L. S. Kulichenko proposed the reestablishment of the RSFSR Agriculture Ministry at a December 1964 RSFSR Supreme Soviet session (*Sovetskaya Rossiya*, 18 December 1964), and A. V. Basov, who as Rostov first secretary had enthusiastically backed Voronov at the March 1962 plenum, was appointed RSFSR agriculture minister.[35]

Voronov also may have gained somewhat in the restoration of a strong USSR Agriculture Ministry and the return of Matskevich as minister in early 1965. The Agriculture Ministry had been stripped of most of its power by Khrushchev and Polyanskiy in January 1961. Planning functions had been transferred to Gosplan and the handling of agricultural equipment and repairs had been assigned to the new Agricultural Equipment Association, leaving the USSR Agriculture Ministry to play a role only in agricultural science and propaganda.[36] Further, in 1962 republic ministries for production and procurement of agricultural products were created to supervise farm production and these organs were independent of the weak Agriculture Ministry. A 1 March 1965 Central Committee–Council of Ministers decree "On Raising the Role of the USSR Agriculture Ministry in Leading Kolkhoz and Sovkhoz Production" again made the ministry the supreme organ for agricultural leadership, returning some of its lost functions.[37] The new minister, Matskevich, quickly expanded its structure[38] and began playing a leading role in agriculture.

The strengthening of the Agriculture Ministry was surely favored by Mazurov (who had publicly protested its weakening in his 11 December 1960 *Pravda* article) and was presumably opposed by Polyanskiy (who had urged its weakening in his December 1959 plenum speech). Voronov is not on record directly, but his apparent lack of enthusiasm for kolkhoz unions and his strong support of the March 1962 strengthening of state control over kolkhozes suggest sympathy for a strong ministry. And, as a former deputy agriculture minister, he probably had more sympathy for the ministry than Polyanskiy did. In addition, Voronov's ally, Volgograd province leader Kulichenko, in proposing the restoration of a RSFSR Agriculture Ministry in his December 1964 speech (*Sovetskaya Rossiya*, 18 December 1964), urged that pre-1961 functions be returned to it (especially, by putting the Agricultural Equipment Association back under the

---

[35] He had been removed as Rostov leader after the 1962 riots.
[36] Prof. I. V. Pavlov, *Sovetskoye Gosudarstvo i Pravo*, no. 10 (1965).
[37] Ibid.
[38] See Matskevich's description of its new functions and organizational structure in the 24 June 1965 *Selskaya Zhizn*.

ministry). The Estonian leaders—whose position has frequently paralleled Voronov's—clearly favored a stronger Agriculture Ministry. At the December 1964 USSR Supreme Soviet session, Estonian Premier V. I. Klauson urged restoration of material-technical supply functions to the ministry and declared that one agricultural organ should lead both sovkhozes and kolkhozes (*Pravda*, 11 December 1964).

The strengthening of the ministry must have dampened the hopes of those desiring a kolkhoz union system (including Polyanskiy and Brezhnev). Brezhnev's position is unclear, however, and he may well have supported a stronger ministry. His protégé Kunayev—who worked with Matskevich in Kazakhstan—praised the strengthening of the ministry in his March 1965 plenum speech. Polyanskiy may have won on some points, however, since all pre-1961 functions were not returned to the ministry. Kulichenko, Klauson, and I. V. Pavlov's October 1965 *Sovetskoye Gosudarstvo i Pravo* article favored incorporating the Agricultural Equipment Association into the ministry, but this was not done.

As with the question of a stronger ministry, the choice of Matskevich as minister apparently set Voronov on Mazurov's side against Polyanskiy. Mazurov may have been Matskevich's prime sponsor in early 1965; he had been his defender in December 1960, and, like Matskevich, he was a stubborn foe of Khrushchev's agricultural policies. In the early 1965 reaction against Khrushchev's policies, Mazurov played an especially big role at the March 1965 plenum (for example, initiating the movement to create rural construction ministries) and was promoted to full Presidium member and first deputy premier. After being named agriculture minister, Matskevich appointed Mazurov's protégé M. N. Lutsenko head of the ministry's livestock administration.

Voronov, who once was deputy to Matskevich and who shared his strong opposition to kolkhoz unions and to Lysenko, had even more in common with him since abandoning his opposition to Barayev and clean fallow. Probably less pleasing to Voronov were Matskevich's subsequent criticisms of livestock and farming programs associated with the Altay Institute and formerly with Voronov. Matskevich and new VASKhNIL President Lobanov began pushing livestock raising (grasslands and mixed feed instead of corn silage, sugar beets, etc.) and virgin land farming (clean fallow and grass instead of corn, peas, and wheat) in a different direction than had Khrushchev, Voronov, and Polyanskiy.

On the other hand, Polyanskiy—a direct foe of Matskevich on kolkhoz unions, Lysenko's work, corn sowing, and probably other matters—presumably lost in Matskevich's return. Perhaps it was not accidental that a former subordinate of Polyanskiy,[39] Tselinnyy Kray First Secretary F. S. Kolomiyets, was

[39]Kolomiyets became first deputy chairman of the Krasnodar Sovnarkhoz in 1957 and Krasnodar Kray agriculture secretary in 1958. Polyanskiy was kray first secretary from March 1957 to March 1958. After his 1965 tiff with Matskevich, Kolomiyets's fortunes declined. His job as Tselinnyy Kray first secretary disappeared when the kray was abolished in October 1965, and in January 1966 he was dropped as Kazakh Central Committee secretary and demoted to USSR food industry deputy minister.

involved in a strange last-minute attempt to discredit him on the eve of his appointment as agriculture minister. On 19 January 1965 an *Izvestiya* article by a deputy in the Tselinnyy Kray soviet complained of the way sessions of the kray soviet were being run. Chairman of the kray Soviet Executive Committee Matskevich called in the deputy and rebuked him for making the soviet's leadership look bad. Matskevich attempted to refute the article, but kray First Secretary Kolomiyets defended the deputy and warned those offended by the article not to try to settle accounts with him. These details were revealed in a second *Izvestiya* article on 16 February by the deputy, who contrasted Kolomiyets's "example of a correct, party attitude toward criticism" to Matskevich's attempt to suppress criticism. Matskevich replied in *Izvestiya* two days later, criticizing the deputy for "petty squabbling" and "petty resentment toward members of the executive committee." By coincidence, Matskevich's 17 February appointment as agriculture minister was announced in the press on the same day his reply appeared in *Izvestiya* (18 February). *Izvestiya* delayed reporting his appointment until the following day (19 February). Meanwhile, as Matskevich was being appointed and Mazurov being promoted to first deputy premier, Polyanskiy was passed over, remaining only a deputy premier until later in 1965.

Although Polyanskiy appears to have opposed Matskevich's restoration in 1965, he apparently found him a staunch ally in the later conflicts over investments. Matskevich's ministry has not notably cooperated in Voronov's campaigns for mechanized links and meat-cattle specialization in 1969–70.

The Rise of Voronov and Polyanskiy

Although the decline of Voronov and Polyanskiy had been halted by Khrushchev's fall, both were still vulnerable to criticism for their past support of his policies and they had surely developed many enemies by their past actions, some of whom were restored to power after Khrushchev's fall. *Partiynaya Zhizn's* May editorial (no. 10 [1965]) attacking "Communists, especially leaders, who enthusiastically implemented clearly incorrect, stereotyped recommendations concerning agricultural production" and citing reduction of grasslands as an example could apply to Voronov and Polyanskiy as well as to Khrushchev's most recent favorites Yefremov and Polyakov. First Deputy Agriculture Minister Sidak (a Khrushchev protégé and associate of Yefremov) may have struck close to both Polyanskiy and Voronov when he criticized the Lysenkoist virgin land proposals (sowing winter crops on stubble in the steppe regions of Siberia and Northern Kazakhstan and various "miracle" methods of processing seed), the "so-called Orenburg method of cultivating the soil," and the "premature" (Altay) intertilled crops system (*Radyanska Ukraina*, 1 April 1965). Sidak's criticisms were cut out of *Selskaya Zhizn's* and most other papers' accounts and only carried in the Ukraine, Azerbaydzhan, and Lithuania, and about this same time, first deputy ministers Sidak and Morozov were demoted to plain deputy ministers.

The post-Khrushchev reaction against the emphasis on the virgin lands did not help Voronov, who was so closely associated with virgin land policy. The reaction against Lysenko did not help Polyanskiy, who had associated himself with Lysenko. The reaction against Khrushchev's forced expansion of corn sowing probably reflected against Voronov and Polyanskiy also. Voronov was unable (or possibly for some reason unwilling) to restore the discredited Khayrullin to any prominent position—although Pysin did express sympathy for the purged Orenburg Institute leaders at the March 1965 plenum. Voronov's purged protégé, Shurygin, managed to return to a minor post by late 1965 (becoming a secretary of the Volgograd Obkom). The discrediting of Nalivayko and the Altay intertilled system laid the Altay leaders open to attack and may have hurt Voronov, despite his apparent 1963–64 shift of position.

During 1965 and 1966, in his rare public speeches, Voronov disassociated himself from some of Khrushchev's agricultural policies, criticizing the elimination of crop rotations with grass and fallow in the non-chernozem zone and the imposition of new cultivation methods in unsuitable zones (his 30 October 1965 Kirov speech, *Sovetskaya Rossiya*, 31 October 1965) and advocating clean fallow or sown fallow or grass, depending on local need (his June 1966 election speech, *Pravda*, 4 June 1966). His 1965 speech also criticized overlarge rayons— even though he was closely identified with the 1962 consolidation drive. Ironically, Voronov and his colleagues were especially critical of Khrushchev's livestock policies—even though these were originally the recommendations of the Orenburg and Altay groups. Voronov in his October 1965 speech declared that the "unscientific approach in its most negative form appeared in the development of livestock raising." Pysin at the March 1965 plenum criticized the neglect of hay fields, the confusion over tethered and untethered cattle facilities, and the fiasco with mechanized milking (in the last seven years, he said, 54,000 of the RSFSR's 130,000 milking machines had been written off or remained in warehouses, thousands of others had broken down, and the mechanization of milking had been started without adequate preparation). Also at the March 1965 plenum, Shkolnikov—soon to become Voronov's other top deputy—criticized the fiasco with milking machines (first the "Christmas trees," then the "carousels") and with tethered and untethered facilities, complaining that Gosstroy had gone to the extreme of forbidding construction of tethered-type barns.[40]

[40] These programs for intensified livestock raising (untethered cattle and mechanized milking and sheep foddered year-round with corn silage in barns) had been originated by the Orenburg and Altay leaders themselves. They became fiascos when the intertilled crops failed, causing a corn silage shortage. Since the natural grasslands had been neglected or plowed up, they could not fall back on the traditional fodder and much livestock had to be slaughtered. The corn and sugar beets also proved to be poor quality fodder. The new milking machines ("Christmas trees" and "carousels") were unpopular with farmers and wound up lowering milk yields.

After the initial post-Khrushchev reaction against the untethered system, it began to be cautiously defended. For example, in the 2 June 1967 *Pravda* RSFSR Gosplan Deputy Chairman G. L. Smirnov complained that the reaction against the untethered method had

The status of both Voronov and Polyanskiy in the Presidium rankings continued about the same as before Khrushchev's fall, with Voronov last, behind the other two junior Presidium members Polyanskiy and Kirilenko (see *Pravda's* 7 and 8 November 1964 photos). Polyanskiy's weakness was displayed when the March 1965 plenum did not raise him from deputy premier (which is not a high enough status for a Presidium member) to first deputy premier, passing him by and naming new Presidium member Mazurov a first deputy premier, outranking Polyanskiy. On May Day 1965, Voronov was discriminated against in the lineup, standing next to last and below new Presidium member Mazurov. The junior Presidium members stood in this order:

Polyanskiy	(elected to the Presidium May 1960)
Kirilenko	(elected April 1962)
Mazurov	(elected March 1965)
Voronov	(elected October 1961)
Shelepin	(elected November 1964)

However, later in 1965 both these slights were corrected—Polyanskiy was made first deputy premier by the October 1965 Supreme Soviet session, and Voronov stood ahead of the two new members Mazurov and Shelepin (see *Pravda*, 8 November 1965 and 8 December 1965)—and Voronov and Polyanskiy strengthened their positions.

Voronov's rise was marked by the promotion of several of his protégés and allies. Volgograd First Secretary Shkolnikov moved to Moscow to become Voronov's second first deputy premier (November 1965) and his purged protégé, Shurygin, surfaced as a Volgograd Obkom secretary (September 1965). Voronov protégé I. I. Molchaninov became Altay Executive Committee chairman in early 1966, expanding Voronov's influence there. He was replaced as Orenburg Executive Committee chairman by another who rose under Voronov: A. N. Balandin, who graduated from the Orenburg Agricultural Institute, entered the obkom agriculture section under Voronov, became chief of a rayon agricultural production administration, head of the obkom agriculture section, and then obkom agriculture secretary.[41]

---

been too extreme and that both the tethered and untethered methods could be used, depending on the zone. *Selskaya Zhizn* on 4 June 1967 reported a VASKhNIL session which discussed the relative merits of these methods. Livestock specialist I. A. Danilenko pointed out the advantages of the untethered system (lower costs, healthier animals, etc.), while acknowledging that the system needed improvements. Later (1969 and 1970), after Voronov revived his meat-cattle program, the untethered system and "Christmas tree" milkers began receiving better treatment (see V. Melentyev's 5 August 1969 *Trud* article and Danilenko's speech at an October 1970 livestock conference in *Ekonomika Selskogo Khozyaystva* 12 [1970]: 113), although they are not being officially promoted.

[41] See his biography in *Deputaty Verkhovnogo Soveta SSSR, 7. Syezd* [Deputies of the Supreme Soviet USSR, 7th convocation] (1966).

Less clear but apparently also a gain for Voronov was the naming of Kostroma First Secretary L. Ya. Florentyev—a protégé of First Deputy Premier Pysin—as RSFSR agriculture minister in November 1965. Though A. V. Basov appeared acceptable to Voronov when he was named RSFSR agriculture minister in March 1965, he was removed in November 1965 under mysterious conditions which suggested conflict.[42] His successor Florentyev's relations with Voronov and Pysin were complicated. Florentyev was appointed chief of the Altay Agriculture Administration and then first deputy chairman of the kray executive committee under Altay Executive Committee Chairman Pysin in 1954, and when Pysin became kraykom first secretary in 1955, he brought his trusted deputy Florentyev over to the kraykom and made him his second secretary. In 1956 Florentyev left to become first secretary of his own oblast (Kostroma).

This tie with Pysin may have saved him in 1961, when he was the only non-chernozem zone obkom first secretary criticized at the January 1961 plenum but not subsequently removed. He was attacked by name by Polyanskiy at the plenum and by Khrushchev at the 23 February 1961 non-chernozem zone conference. The RSFSR Bureau rapped the Kostroma leaders in August 1961 as propagandists for the grassland system and for not correcting their errors after Khrushchev's criticism (*Sovetskaya Rossiya*, 27 August 1961). Polyanskiy hit Kostroma again in December 1961 for lagging in expansion of corn sowings (*Pravda*, 13 December 1961). Voronov himself in his 22d Congress speech harshly assailed Florentyev's leadership of Kostroma for not responding to criticism, for not reducing oats, grass, and clean fallow in favor of corn, and for mismanagement—no other oblast leadership was criticized so extensively in his speech. Yet Florentyev in November 1965 became Voronov's agriculture minister and has remained in that post for over five years now. His successor as Kostroma first secretary had ties with Pysin also: I. P. Skulkov was Altay second secretary 1947-51, while Pysin was executive committee chairman 1949-55.

These cadre gains were capped by a remarkable personal gain for Voronov at the 1966 party congress, where the RSFSR Bureau was abolished and he was

---

[42] He was replaced with Florentyev by a 19 November 1965 ukase, but the announcement of this action was delayed a full month. *Pravda* on 14 December announced that a 13 December Kostroma plenum had replaced Florentyev and on 15 December announced Basov's appointment as ambassador to Rumania, and only on 18 December (*Sovetskaya Rossiya*) was the 19 November ukase announced. All those appointed deputy ministers under Basov, when the ministry was reestablished in the spring of 1965, eventually also left the ministry: First Deputy Minister T. I. Sokolov became Orel first secretary in October 1965; Deputy Minister A. S. Mayat had joined the State Committee for Science and Technology as chief of the department for mechanization of agriculture (see the *Vestnik Selskokhozyaystvennoy Nauki* 1 [1966]: 19, for his November identification, and also his obituary in the 26 May 1971 *Selskaya Zhizn*); Deputy Minister G. L. Smirnov became first deputy chairman of the RSFSR Gosplan by early 1967 (identified in *Sovetskaya Rossiya*, 16 March 1967); and Deputy Minister V. I. Poltava (last identified as deputy minister on 6 January 1967 in *Pravda*) left to become head of the RSFSR Inter-Kolkhoz Construction Association in 1967.

promoted to number five ranking in the new Politburo (which succeeded the Presidium). Even after the elimination of his rival Yefremov as first deputy chairman of the RSFSR Bureau in December 1964, he had shared RSFSR leadership with Brezhnev and Kirilenko—the chairman and first deputy chairman of the RSFSR Bureau (of which Voronov was only an ordinary member). In fact, Brezhnev and Kirilenko—as the Bureau's leaders and as the only Presidium members in the Bureau except Voronov—could presumably issue directives in the name of the Bureau and perhaps bypass the Presidium. The Bureau was active in 1965, reviewing the work of local party organizations and exposing shortcomings,[43] issuing instructions to government organizations, holding conferences and promoting the scientific organization of labor initiative of Kirilenko's former bailiwick of Sverdlovsk.[44] It controlled the RSFSR organ *Sovetskaya Rossiya* and the Central Committee sections supervising RSFSR activities. In late 1965 a series of personnel changes began in the RSFSR oblasts, the most important of which appeared to benefit Brezhnev (the appointment of T. I. Sokolov and N. N. Rodionov as oblast first secretaries and, especially, the December 1965 installation of Brezhnev protégé K. F. Katushev as Gorkiy first secretary—which Brezhnev himself supervised).

This advantageous position for Brezhnev and Kirilenko was ended at the 23d Congress in March–April 1966, when the Bureau was abolished. Brezhnev's explanation of the reason for its abolition indirectly recognized the Presidium's distrust of his use of the Bureau: "The opinion is being expressed that at the present time there is no need to retain the Central Committee's RSFSR Bureau. The experience has been such that, even with a Central Committee RSFSR Bureau, all the most important questions of the activity of kray and oblast party organizations of the RSFSR are examined by the Presidium and Secretariat of the Central Committee. Therefore it is inexpedient to have another parallel organ of the Central Committee for the RSFSR. The Central Committee agrees with this opinion" (*Pravda*, 31 March 1966). Only one speaker at the congress praised the change (Perm First Secretary K. I. Galanshin[45]) and he was later removed under a cloud.[46]

---

[43] After June–July visits to Khabarovsk by RSFSR cadre chief Kapitonov and then by Kirilenko, the RSFSR Bureau condemned Khabarovsk's cadre work (*Sovetskaya Rossiya*, 30 July 1965). The Bureau also censured the Voronezh leaders for inadequately spreading advanced experience (*Sovetskaya Rossiya*, 13 May 1965) and the Rostov leaders for neglecting light industry (*Sovetskaya Rossiya*, 14 September 1965).

[44] *Ekonomicheskaya Gazeta*, 12 May 1965, p. 3.

[45] "We presume that the abolition of the Central Committee Bureau for the RSFSR will strengthen the Central Committee sections and that our ties with them will not only not be weakened but on the contrary will become stronger" (Stenographic Record of the 23d Party Congress, vol. 1, p. 544).

[46] A September 1967 Central Committee decree criticized shortcomings in the Perm Obkom's leadership of trade unions (see the 15 November 1967 *Pravda* editorial and Galanshin's 29 June 1968 *Trud* article). *Pravda* on 4 July 1968 reported Galanshin's transfer to minister of the cellulose-paper industry. No sooner had he taken up his new post than a

It seems highly unlikely that Brezhnev would voluntarily give up a potentially important post (chairman of the RSFSR Bureau) and reduce his own authority in running the affairs of the biggest republic. More than likely it was part of a package deal involving the creation of the post of general secretary and the renaming of the Presidium at the congress, and perhaps it was argued as consistent with the principle of separating top posts—such as the posts of first secretary and premier.[47] As a result of the Bureau's liquidation, Bureau First Deputy Chairman Kirilenko became a Central Committee secretary and the Central Committee sections for the RSFSR merged with the regular Central Committee sections. The Bureau's organ *Sovetskaya Rossiya* became a Central Committee newspaper.

The new arrangement did not put the RSFSR party organizations in Voronov's hands, but it clearly did reduce the ability of Brezhnev and Kirilenko to name RSFSR oblast chiefs. After the congress a policy of advancing local men (instead of sending apparatchiks from Moscow) was instituted.[48] The change was also a big boost for Voronov since it made him the sole RSFSR leader, and henceforth RSFSR activities would be supervised by the regular Central Committee sections—presumably less closely than when there were special sections just to observe RSFSR agencies. As Central Committee secretary, long-time RSFSR leader Kirilenko became increasingly involved in foreign affairs, which probably also reduced his direct influence in the RSFSR.

Voronov's ranking in the Politburo rose accordingly. Whereas he was last at the time of Khrushchev's fall (7 November 1964), next to last in May 1965, and only ahead of Mazurov and Shelepin (number 9) on 7 November 1965, he was officially ranked number five at the conclusion of the congress. Brezhnev, reading a hierarchical list, placed Voronov right outside the inner circle (Brezhnev, Kosygin, Podgornyy, Suslov) and ahead of all his peers:

1.	Brezhnev	7.	Shelepin
2.	Kosygin	8.	Mazurov
3.	Podgornyy	9.	Polyanskiy
4.	Suslov	10.	Shelest
5.	Voronov	11.	Pelshe
6.	Kirilenko		

Pravda article criticized the Perm paper combine (7 August 1968) and Galanshin, responsible both as former Perm leader and now as paper industry chief, acknowledged the criticism in the 24 September 1968 *Pravda*.

[47] The original February 1956 decree creating the RSFSR Bureau specified that the post of Bureau chairman was to be combined with that of Central Committee first secretary (*Spravochnik Partiynogo Rabotnika*, 1st edition, p. 127).

[48] From Khrushchev's fall to the 23d Congress, of fourteen new RSFSR oblast and kray first secretaries, seven were local men, while seven were outsiders (three of whom—L. N. Yefremov, T. I. Sokolov and Ye. K. Ligachev—came from the central government or Central Committee). From the 23d Congress through the 24th Congress

The number five position became Voronov's normal ranking. Even though part of his rise is attributable to the dropping of two senior Presidium members (Mikoyan and Shvernik), it still represents a rise above his peers, Polyanskiy and Kirilenko, and is the highest ranking an RSFSR leader ever received.

Polyanskiy's case is less clear. He certainly gained when he finally won his promotion to first deputy premier in October 1965. He probably gained from Kulakov's election as Central Committee secretary for agriculture at the September 1965 Central Committee plenum,[49] and perhaps also from the appointment of I. G. Balyasinskiy[50] and G. I. Vorobyev[51] as deputy agriculture ministers. However, he clearly suffered a defeat at the congress. Whereas he was normally ranked sixth or seventh in 1965, (right after Brezhnev, Kosygin, Mikoyan, Podgornyy, and Suslov, and ahead of his peers Kirilenko and Voronov), Brezhnev listed him ninth at the March 1966 congress (behind his peers Voronov and Kirilenko and his juniors Shelepin and Mazurov). His drop was the most notable change in any Politburo member's standing. Later in 1966 he regained his sixth ranking, but remained below Voronov (see *Pravda*, 3 August, 9 October, 16 October, 7 November 1966, 2 May 1967, 23 May, 11 October, and *Sovetskaya Rossiya* of 12 April 1967), except on one occasion (*Pravda*, 8 November 1966).

(April 1971), of thirty-four new first secretaries, twenty-six were local men, plus one from a neighboring province, while only seven were outsiders (only two of whom—Central Committee cadre section deputy head N. A. Voronovskiy and Central Committee inspector V. P. Lomakin—came from the central apparatus).

[49] Kulakov had worked under Polyanskiy as RSFSR grain products minister 1959–60.

[50] Balyasinskiy was from Polyanskiy's one-time bailiwick of Krasnodar (identified as deputy chairman of the Krasnodar Executive Committee in the 17 June 1960 *Selskaya Zhizn*). He was second secretary of Kuybyshev Oblast by late 1961 (see the Stenographic Record of the 22d Party Congress) and later first secretary of the Kuybyshev Agricultural Obkom (1963–64). Despite being criticized in the 15 December 1964 *Izvestiya* for pressing excessive procurement targets while Kuybyshev agriculture secretary, he was promoted to USSR deputy agriculture minister in late 1965 (identified in *Moskovskaya Pravda*, 18 September 1965). On 13 March 1966 *Izvestiya* announced he had left the ministry to become first deputy chairman of the State Committee for Procurements.

[51] Vorobyev, RSFSR Agriculture Section head 1959–60, was Krasnodar first secretary 1960–66 and became deputy minister in January 1966 (announced in the 13 January 1966 *Pravda*). His tie with Polyanskiy is very tenuous, however.

PART II

THE POST-KHRUSHCHEV ERA

THE POST-KHRUSHCHEV
ERA: 1965-1970

As if learning from Khrushchev's mistakes, his successors have rather successfully avoided interference in disputes over agrotechniques and crop policies. The bitter experiences with government-enforced stereotyped techniques under Khrushchev produced a universal condemnation of *shablon* (stereotype) and an overwhelming sentiment in favor of allowing farmers themselves to decide questions of techniques and crops according to their local circumstances. Debates among farmers have naturally continued, but top leaders have hesitated to speak out and endorse and enforce detailed programs.

The post-Khrushchev disputes have instead been concentrated on questions of resource allocation and organizing agricultural production and, though strenuously fought, have avoided the public acrimony characteristic of the Khrushchev years. Khrushchev frequently exposed policy and personal disputes in his rather frank public statements. Many other hidden facts were also brought out with the breakdown of restraints during the first year after Khrushchev's fall. But after the resolution of the power struggle in Brezhnev's favor in the fall of 1965, controls were firmly reestablished and the régime retreated to a more conservative policy of increased concealment of information[1] —making it much harder to detect and trace policy and personal differences. Nevertheless, disputes have taken place and, despite the usual lack of overt evidence, rather consistent positions in these disputes can be established for a number of Soviet leaders.

Polyanskiy, the first deputy premier in charge of agriculture, clearly established himself publicly as the chief lobbyist for agriculture by repeatedly appeal-

---

[1] For example, Khrushchev's practice of publishing stenographic records of Central Committee plenums ceased after the publication of the record of the March 1965 plenum in August 1965. In fact, after most plenums since late 1965 even the main report has not been printed in the newspapers.

ing for more resources for agriculture. He argues that increased agricultural output can only be achieved by increased inputs of equipment, fertilizer, etc. Supervising rural construction, Polyanskiy has advocated an expensive program for rebuilding villages and improving rural living standards. He has appeared to support organizational measures (establishment of kolkhoz unions, creation of special rural construction ministries) which would strengthen the position of farms in dealing with government agencies and agriculture's position in fighting for resources.

Brezhnev, who as party chief has dominated major agricultural pronouncements (March 1965, May 1966, October 1968, July 1970), has appeared to largely share Polyanskiy's concern for agriculture's interests, although he usually has also defended the heavy industry and military sectors with equal vigor. He has frequently campaigned for more investments for agriculture and has appeared to support establishment of kolkhoz unions and rural construction ministries also.

Sharply in contrast to their position is that of RSFSR Premier Voronov, who has consistently cold-shouldered Polyanskiy's appeals for more resources, has resisted creation of kolkhoz unions and rural construction ministries, and has ignored his rural construction program. Voronov has instead advanced agricultural programs which in effect are alternatives to simply investing more funds in agriculture. He has identified himself with controversial organizational proposals (organizing farm labor in unregulated mechanized links and specialization of livestock raising) which are designed to reduce costs of production and increase agricultural efficiency. One might read a statement in his 21 March 1970 Moscow Oblast speech as reflecting his basic argument: "It turns out that one can have much equipment and mineral fertilizer, but if efficient use of them is not organized we can wind up not achieving good results" (*Leninskoye Znamya*, 24 March 1970). Despite his long involvement in agriculture, Voronov in recent years has associated himself mainly with the interests of the consumer and appears to favor more investments in consumer goods production rather than in agriculture. In this, RSFSR Premier Voronov's position appears similar to that of USSR Premier Kosygin.

Brezhnev and Polyanskiy, who have run national agricultural policy, have in turn cold-shouldered Voronov's ideas on agriculture. But starting in 1969, Voronov began striking off independently on his own, implementing in the RSFSR his long-held ideas on agricultural organization which have not been accepted by USSR agricultural leaders and thus leading RSFSR agriculture in directions somewhat at variance with USSR policy. This unusual situation could not continue for long since the RSFSR is far too big to follow policies shunned or even opposed by USSR authorities, and Voronov and his top agricultural assistant Pysin were removed in 1971.

The other Politburo members have been less involved in agricultural matters and tend to be preoccupied with defending their own favorite sectors as against agriculture (for example, Kosygin and Shelepin with consumer goods, Suslov with defense, Kirilenko with heavy industry, etc.).

Khrushchev's successors began by rejecting his campaign approach and adopted a program for greatly increased investments in agriculture at the March 1965 Central Committee plenum (Chapter VIII). Aided by good weather, the program brought a great boost in agricultural production. The 1966 harvest in fact was so successful that it weakened the argument for continued aid to agriculture, and in 1967, over Polyanskiy's public objections, resources were shifted to other more pressing sectors, especially consumer goods (Chapter IX).

After agricultural progress began slowing down in 1968, there was a partial restoration of resources to agriculture. Brezhnev warned of agricultural stagnation at an October 1968 agricultural plenum but short-changing of agriculture continued. In 1969 Voronov began campaigns promoting his own solutions to the agricultural problems (Chapter X). Extremely bad weather in early 1969 aggravated the agricultural lagging and by the end of 1969 serious meat shortages were developing in Soviet cities. To remedy the livestock lag, Brezhnev and Polyanskiy proposed raising livestock procurement prices and the construction of big specialized livestock complexes. These expensive approaches were opposed by Voronov and the Estonian leaders, who urged better livestock raising techniques instead. Nevertheless, under the pressure of the meat shortages, the Politburo, which had refused to raise most livestock procurement prices in 1968, agreed to pay farmers higher prices in early 1970 and in May 1970 approved an expensive program of constructing new livestock complexes (Chapter XI). At the same time, Polyanskiy and Brezhnev launched a campaign to change the light industry orientation written into the plan by Kosygin and his allies in 1967 to an agricultural orientation. When Gosplan finished its preliminary outline of the 1971-75 five-year plan, Polyanskiy and Brezhnev persuaded the Politburo that the agricultural situation was so serious that agriculture's share of resources had to be sharply raised. Gosplan's outlines were overridden and Brezhnev announced a big new agricultural program at a July 1970 Central Committee plenum—to make up for the badly cut March 1965 program. The adoption of the increased agricultural portion of the new five-year plan left the leaders to wrangle over the shares for light industry, heavy industry, and defense, and, as of January 1971, no agreement on the nonagricultural portion was apparent.

CHAPTER VIII

VICTORY FOR THE AGRICULTURE
LOBBY: 1965-1966

The new leadership got off to an auspicious start by tackling the fundamental problem of providing more resources for agriculture. Starting work on the new five-year plan early in 1965, the leadership first managed to reach agreement on a substantial increase in agriculture's share of state allocations, leaving unresolved the shares of the other sectors. The agricultural portion was worked out and adopted by the March 1965 Central Committee plenum with little sign of serious disagreement. This was followed, however, by a protracted debate to decide the shares of defense, heavy industry, and consumer goods in the remainder of the new plan.

In this debate Kosygin and Podgornyy advocated more for the consumer, while Brezhnev, Suslov, and Shelepin defended the interests of the military and heavy industry. Kosygin appeared to equivocate, however, and Podgornyy wound up in an apparently isolated position as the public defender of consumer goods. The priorities issue also involved the struggle for power between First Secretary Brezhnev and de facto Second Secretary Podgornyy. During 1965 the conservatives became clearly dominant and Podgornyy lost the contest and was kicked upstairs. Named chairman of the Supreme Soviet Presidium in December 1965, he lost his powerful influence over cadres as Central Committee secretary. The priorities debate concluded with heavy industry holding its own and the December 1964 cuts in defense spending being restored.

Two other protracted struggles involving agricultural organization, resources, and state control developed. At the March 1965 plenum Mazurov proposed creation of special rural construction ministries. Apparently with the quiet backing of Brezhnev and Polyanskiy this proposal developed wide public support, but Voronov appeared to resist the campaign and only agreed to create an RSFSR Rural Construction Ministry in late 1966, a year later than other republics. The kolkhoz union issue was revived in late 1965 and early 1966, again with behind-the-scenes encouragement by Brezhnev and Polyanskiy. In this case, however, the opponents (including Voronov) won and discussion of kolkhoz unions lapsed in late 1966.

The March 1965 Plenum

The main feature of the new agricultural program presented by Brezhnev at the March 1965 Central Committee plenum was its provision of more money for agriculture. Brezhnev announced that the new five-year plan (1966-70) would provide 71 billion rubles of investment in agriculture by the state and kolkhozes. The state's share—41 billion—would equal all state investment in agriculture since 1945. The extreme financial squeeze on farms was to be reduced by canceling much kolkhoz indebtedness to the state, by raising prices paid by the state for farm products, and by promising reductions in the prices paid by farms for agricultural equipment and manufactured goods. Complaining that procurement plans under Khrushchev were unrealistically high (they were fulfilled only in 1956, 1958, and 1964) and were frequently altered, Brezhnev proposed a new system of reduced quotas which would not be subject to change during the entire coming five-year period. Thus, the 1965 grain procurement plan was cut from 4 billion to 3.4 billion poods and would remain at that level through 1970. Substantially higher prices would be paid for grain sold to the state above the plan quotas, providing incentives for farms to overfulfill quotas. More tractors, trucks, and other equipment was promised to agriculture and at lower prices. Brezhnev declared that 4 billion rubles must be invested in building new agricultural equipment plants in the next five-year period.

Some speakers at the plenum, while applauding Brezhnev's proposals, urged still more relief. Tambov First Secretary G. S. Zolotukhin declared that while the cancellation of kolkhoz debts described by Brezhnev would amount to 1.8 billion rubles, 65 percent of the debts would still remain. He requested that this question be reconsidered and kolkhoz debts further reduced. RSFSR First Deputy Premier K. G. Pysin requested a further reduction in the RSFSR grain quota—to 2 billion poods instead of the 2.103 billion cited by Brezhnev.

Many of the problems dealt with by the plenum were blamed on decisions made in 1958 and 1959, when the previous plan (the seven-year plan) was worked out. The liquidation of the machine-tractor stations and the sale of equipment to already financially weak farms contributed to the heavy kolkhoz indebtedness. As Kostroma First Secretary L. Ya. Florentyev said, the machine-tractor station reorganization "was carried out in such a way that the economy of many kolkhozes was disrupted." At the same time production of agricultural equipment had been reduced. At the plenum Selkhoztekhnika Chairman A. A. Yezhevskiy explained that equipment production was cut back in 1958 on the assumption that equipment would be more efficiently used after being acquired by the kolkhozes: whereas 948 million rubles worth of agricultural equipment was produced in 1957, only 674 million was produced in 1959, and 758 million in 1960. In 1958 some agricultural equipment plants were transferred to production of other products and in addition sharp increases in prices for equipment and spare parts were adopted. Brezhnev pointed out that while agriculture had received 11.3 percent of all state investments during the 1954–58 period, under the seven-year plan (1959–65) agriculture received only 7.5 percent. Yet while inputs were cut, procurement plans began rising after 1958 (as Florentyev pointed out). Since prices for agricultural products were unjustifiably low and costs were high, many farms were operating at a loss and many products were simply unprofitable to produce. The March plenum's goal was to restore profitability to farming.

The program adopted at the March plenum thus appeared to represent a considerable victory for those advocating more investments for agriculture. Even though Khrushchev had been unable to persuade the Presidium and Central Committee to sharply increase investments in agriculture at previous plenums (for example, the March 1962 plenum), in the reaction against his handling of agriculture, the leadership was able to reach unusual agreement on the need for greater inputs. Agreement was probably spurred by recollection of the 1963 disaster. As Zolotukhin said, "1963 showed the danger of underrating agriculture" and "if it were not for the good year in 1964 one cannot see now how we could have survived the colossal difficulties."

From all appearances, the leaders were in substantial agreement on the need for more aid to agriculture, with even those less enthusiastic than Brezhnev and Polyanskiy voicing approval. Ukrainian First Secretary Shelest, the only Presidium member (besides Brezhnev) who spoke at the plenum, backed the rise in procurement prices, in investments, and in equipment production and the adjustment of equipment prices. Mazurov, who was elected a Presidium member at the plenum, dwelt on improving agricultural profitability and mechanization and altering the proportions between agriculture and other branches in the plan and proposed creating a new rural construction ministry and agricultural machine building ministry to strengthen agriculture's hold on resources. Presidium candidate member Mzhavanadze declared that the price rises were supported "by all our party." RSFSR First Deputy Premier Pysin spoke for the RSFSR instead of Premier Voronov and he also approved Brezhnev's proposals, while Estonian First Secretary Kebin urged more investments, fertilizer, and equipment. Shortly before the plenum, at a 19 March 1965 Gosplan meeting, Premier Kosygin had spoken approvingly of the "significant" increase in investments about to be adopted (*Ekonomicheskaya Gazeta*, 21 April 1965).

However, the March decision to increase aid to agriculture still left the most difficult problems unresolved. While Brezhnev announced that the new agricultural program would require "additional state expenditures" and that these funds must be obtained "by redistributions within the state budget," he nowhere indicated which sectors would suffer cuts. The agricultural portion of the new five-year plan was worked out first and adopted in March 1965; the remaining parts of the plan remained unresolved and were the subject of sharp debate throughout 1965. Although scheduled to go into effect in January 1966, the directives of the new five-year plan were only approved at a 19 February 1966 Central Committee plenum and work on the final draft was still continuing in August 1966 (see Kosygin's statement in the 4 August 1966 *Pravda*).

Even though agriculture's share was already approved, the constant squeeze on resources made it difficult to hold onto funds already allocated. Since projects in other sectors (especially heavy industry and defense) for decades had had top priority, Gosplan and others were accustomed to diverting agricultural and consumer goods funds to other sectors. At the March plenum Zolotukhin complained that no one in Gosplan had "ever really defended the interests of agriculture" and that Gosplan "year in year out has trimmed financial and material-technical aid and has tried to pump as much funds out of agriculture as possible." He insisted that agriculture should rank second only to defense in priority. Also at the plenum, Bashkir First Secretary Z. N. Nuriyev noted proposals to appoint a special Gosplan deputy chairman for agriculture, but declared that there can be "one, two or even three deputies" but this will not help much in defending agriculture's interests "unless the attention of the whole Gosplan is directed to agriculture." These apprehensions proved well founded: within months Brezhnev himself (at the September 1965 plenum) complained of continuing attempts in Gosplan "to 'balance' the figures at the expense of agriculture . . . in spite of the perfectly clear decisions of the March 1965 Central Committee plenum" (*Pravda*, 30 September 1965).

The Resource Debate

After the March plenum the debate over priorities in drawing up the new five-year plan intensified. In 1965 and 1966 the debate appears to have concerned only the shares of defense, heavy industry, and consumer goods, rather than that of agriculture, which supposedly had been fixed by the March plenum. Later, however, after the good 1966 harvest, agriculture's share began to be questioned again.

In 1965 Podgornyy and Kosygin continued Khrushchev's campaign to expand consumer goods production, while Brezhnev and Suslov appealed to the military-heavy industrial complex. In part, these positions reflected personal background: Podgornyy and Kosygin in the food industry and light industry, and Brezhnev in heavy industry and the military. Brezhnev's connection with heavy industry was especially close. A trained metallurgist, he was a long-time leader of the metallurgical centers of Dnepropetrovsk and Zaporozhe and supervised heavy industry while Central Committee secretary in the late 1950's.[1] His

---

[1] Brezhnev's biography in volume 4 of the new *Bolshaya Sovetskaya Entsiklopediya* (signed to press 29 January 1971) gives the first official confirmation of Brezhnev's duties while Central Committee secretary 1956-60: "Upon the orders of the Central Committee, he handled questions of the development of heavy industry and construction, of equipping

associate from Dnepropetrovsk, N. A. Tikhonov,[2] was appointed deputy premier in October 1965 to help supervise metallurgy, and when the new Ferrous Metallurgy Ministry was created in October 1965 most of its leaders were associated with Brezhnev or Kirilenko.[3] Brezhnev's brother, Yakov, became deputy chief of the Metallurgical Industry Administration in the new ministry.[4] Brezhnev's personal assistant as Central Committee first secretary, G. E. Tsukanov, is a metallurgist also and long was an engineer at the Dneprodzerzhinsk metallurgical plant where Brezhnev had begun his career as an engineer.[5]

The debate over priorities also reflected the political rivalry between Brezhnev and Podgornyy. Initially, following his rise to first secretary in October 1964, Brezhnev had appeared weak, especially in cadre matters, which were apparently supervised by Central Committee Secretary Podgornyy and his protégés V. N. Titov (head of the Central Committee Party Organs Section)[6] and P. F. Pigalev (first deputy head)[7]. It was Podgornyy, not Brezhnev, who addressed the November 1964 plenum on reorganizing party organs, and, while

---

the country's armed forces with the newest military equipment, and of the development of the space program."

[2] Tikhonov graduated from the Dnepropetrovsk Metallurgical Institute, worked in Dnepropetrovsk metallurgical plants in the 1930's, and headed the Dnepropetrovsk Sovnarkhoz from 1957 to 1960.

[3] Deputy minister V. Ye. Boyko worked in the Dneprodzerzhinsk metallurgical plant and studied at the Dneprodzerzhinsk Metallurgical Institute along with Brezhnev in the 1930's. Deputy minister L. Ye. Lukich was Dnepropetrovsk Obkom secretary under First Secretary Brezhnev 1948–50 and under Kirilenko 1950–54 and was chairman of the Dnepropetrovsk Sovnarkhoz until his appointment as deputy minister in 1965. Deputy Minister P. Ye. Sokolov was deputy chairman of the sovnarkhoz in Sverdlovsk, while Kirilenko was Sverdlovsk Obkom first secretary. Dnepropetrovsk Sovnarkhoz deputy chairmen A. I. Slivinskiy (1957–61) and V. S. Vinogradov (1960–65) also became deputy ministers.

[4] Identified along with other metallurgical industry personnel in the 27 March 1966 *Moskovskaya Pravda*. Polish leader Gomulka in a 17 October 1964 speech mentioned that Brezhnev's brother had assisted in setting up a Polish metallurgical combine. Yakov Brezhnev received an award from the Polish government for this in September 1964 (*Dziennik Polski*, 4 September 1964).

[5] In 1958 Tsukanov was brought from his chief engineer's job to the Central Committee apparatus after Brezhnev had become a Central Committee secretary. When Brezhnev became chairman of the Presidium of the Supreme Soviet in 1960, Tsukanov joined the Supreme Soviet Presidium apparatus, and when Brezhnev became a Central Committee secretary again in 1963 Tsukanov returned to the Central Committee apparatus (*Deputaty Verkhovnogo Soveta SSSR* [1966]).

[6] Titov was second secretary under Podgornyy in Kharkov and succeeded him as first secretary in 1953. He became party organs head in March 1961.

[7] After Podgornyy lost his Secretariat post and became Supreme Soviet Presidium chairman, Pigalev lost his cadre section post and also moved to the Supreme Soviet Presidium to assist Podgornyy as head of the department of questions of work of soviets (identified in the 7 February 1968 *Izvestiya*).

protégés of Podgornyy[8] were promoted at the plenum, no one closely associated with Brezhnev received a promotion.

One reason why Podgornyy instead of First Secretary Brezhnev was allowed to take the spotlight at the November plenum may have been to balance Brezhnev's designation as chairman of the RSFSR Bureau. According to Brezhnev's biography in volume 4 of the new *Bolshaya Sovetskaya Entsiklopediya* (signed to press 29 January 1971), he was confirmed as Bureau chairman in November 1964. His chairmanship was not revealed, however, until the summer of 1965 when the *Bolshaya Sovetskaya Entsiklopediya* yearbook referred to him as chairman,[9] and the November 1964 appointment date was revealed only in the 1971 encyclopedia. The fact that his appointment as Bureau chairman was delayed (in November 1964 instead of October) and that it was kept secret for many months (until he had bested Podgornyy) surely reduced Brezhnev's advantage and made him appear weaker than he was.

However, in early 1965 there developed a strong conservative trend, which suited Central Committee secretaries Suslov and Shelepin, Belorussian First Secretary Mazurov, Moscow First Secretary Yegorychev, and Georgian First Secretary Mzhavanadze much better than the more liberal Podgornyy or Mikoyan. In a February 1965 *Kommunist* (no. 3) Yegorychev complained of the overly negative Khrushchev-era portrayal of Stalin's war role and his move to partially rehabilitate Stalin was joined by some military leaders.[10] Brezhnev himself apparently pleased the conservatives by mentioning Stalin's wartime role in his V-E Day speech (*Pravda*, 9 May 1965). In reaction to Khrushchev's exposures of Stalin-era repressions, a campaign began to improve the tarnished image of the secret police.[11] Defense industry advocates scored victories with the elevation of six defense industry state committees to ministerial status (*Pravda*, 4 March 1965) and the promotion of two leading defense industry specialists and Khrushchev foes on 26 March. D. F. Ustinov, who had been appointed first deputy premier and head of the new Supreme National Economic Council in March 1963 over Khrushchev's opposition, was elected a Central Committee secretary and candidate member of the Presidium, while V. N. Novikov, ousted

[8]Ukrainian First Secretary Shelest became a Presidium member; Crimean First Secretary I. K. Lutak became a full Central Committee member.

[9]The 1965 yearbook, signed to press 3 June 1965.

[10]Marshal I. Kh. Bagramyan in the 17 April *Literaturnaya Gazeta* and General I. I. Yakubovskiy in his V-E Day speech in the 9 May *Pravda Ukrainy*.

[11]This campaign was promoted by KGB Chairman V. Ye. Semichastnyy in the 7 May *Pravda*, by Belorussian KGB Chairman V. I. Petrov in the 5 May *Sovetskaya Belorussiya*, and by Ukrainian KGB Chairman V. F. Nikitchenko in the 19 June *Radyanska Ukraina*. Articles and films portrayed secret police heroism during the war and glamorized present KGB work (*Izvestiya*, 3 April; *Vechernyaya Moskva*, 4 and 5 May; *Pravda Ukrainy*, 12 May; *Izvestiya*, 10 June; *Sovetskaya Rossiya*, 10 June; *Moskovskaya Pravda*, 18 June; *Sovetskaya Rossiya*, 18 June).

by Khrushchev as Gosplan chairman in 1962, became deputy premier and chairman of the Supreme National Economic Council.

At the same time, Podgornyy's position clearly weakened. Open sniping at Podgornyy's protégés in Kharkov began when the 24 February *Ekonomicheskaya Gazeta* contrasted the allegedly poor economic leadership in Kharkov to the good leadership in Brezhnev's home base of Dnepropetrovsk. On page 2 the magazine editorially attacked the Kharkov Sovnarkhoz, while on page 3 it carried an article by Dnepropetrovsk First Secretary Shcherbitskiy boasting of his oblast's economic successes. Podgornyy's top protégé, Titov, soon came under attack and after the March 1965 plenum was transferred to Kazakhstan as second secretary under Brezhnev's protégé Kunayev. Hints of hostility to Titov appeared as early as 19 March when some papers cut him off of a group photograph,[12] and when his election as Kazakh secretary was announced, the Kazakh paper deleted his title of CPSU Central Committee secretary (*Kazakhstanskaya Pravda*, 6 April), which was used by *Pravda* and all other papers.

Despite the increasingly conservative mood, Podgornyy restated his liberal Khrushchevian views in late May. In a speech in Baku (*Pravda*, 22 May 1965) he declared: "There was a time when the Soviet people consciously accepted some material limitations in the interests of preferential development of heavy industry and strengthening of defense capabilities. . . . Now, however, with each year the public wealth increases and the necessary conditions are created for better satisfying all the growing cultural and everyday demands of the workers." As if in response, only days later in a 2 June Sofia speech Suslov argued that while we would like welfare to grow faster, "objective reality" forces us to "bear significant expenditures for the defense of our country . . ." and our military power "requires from the Soviet people great material sacrifice and expenditure of a significant part of the national income on defense" (*Pravda*, 5 June 1965). As on the Stalin issue, Brezhnev appeared to lean to the prevailing conservative winds, placing welfare well below defense in priority. On 3 July he declared that the new five-year plan would develop industry, strengthen defense "with consideration of the international situation," raise agricultural production, and aid light and food industry and welfare (*Pravda*, 4 July 1965).

By July Podgornyy appeared alone in defending consumer goods. Even Kosygin, who had announced at the December 1964 Supreme Soviet session that the relaxed international situation permitted a half-billion-ruble cut in defense spending for the 1965 budget, began displaying renewed concern for defense. In an 11 July Volgograd speech he noted that maintenance of the armed forces "requires very large funds which we would readily direct to other branches of the economy," but "under present conditions" this cannot be done (*Pravda*, 12 July 1965), and in a 24 July speech he declared that the Central Committee and

---

[12]Mazurov's Belorussian papers (*Sovetskaya Belorussiya* and *Zvyazda*), as well as *Trud* and *Izvestiya* (20 March), carried photos with Titov clipped off the end, while *Pravda* and other papers included him.

government consider "concern for strengthening the defensive might of the country the first duty" (*Pravda*, 25 July 1965). In a 24 July speech Shelepin stated that the new five-year plan will "devote constant attention to further strengthening of the armed forces of our country and development of the defense industry" (*Krasnaya Zvezda*, 25 July 1965). *Pravda's* paraphrasing of Shelepin's speech had him indicating that the Central Committee and government "are taking measures to further strengthen defense preparedness" (*Pravda*, 25 July).

At this critical time Podgornyy apparently fell ill. His meeting with a Turkish delegation on 5 June was canceled at the last minute because of illness[13] and he disappeared for an unusually long period, only reappearing on 24 July to make a speech in Sevastopol and only reappearing in Moscow on 3 August. During his absence from the scene, a major assault was launched against his protégés from Kharkov, who had been supervising cadre work in both Moscow (Central Committee party organs chief Titov) and Kiev (Ukrainian Second Secretary N. A. Sobol[14]). With the physical removal of both Podgornyy (apparently ill) and Titov (in Kazakhstan), the effectiveness of cadre work came under review. Already on 8 June the Central Committee adopted a decree on Turkmen cadre work (*Turkmenskaya Iskra*, 3 July 1965), while the RSFSR Bureau called a 30 June-3 July conference on improving party organizational work (*Pravda*, 4 July 1965) and exposed serious shortcomings in cadre work by the Khabarovsk party organization.[15] Although the shortcomings in cadre work actually began to be publicly revealed only at the beginning of August,[16] the campaign for tightening up on cadre work was publicly foreshadowed by hardliner Georgian First Secretary Mzhavanadze's 25 June speech in Georgia arguing for increased discipline and citing Stalin on the need for an elitist party (*Zarya Vostoka*, 29 June 1965).

It was Podgornyy's home base of Kharkov which was selected to serve as the bad example in cadre work. In July Kharkov First Secretary G. I. Vashchenko was called to Moscow to report on admission of new members to the

---

[13] Michel Tatu, *Power in the Kremlin* (London, 1969), p. 500.

[14] Sobol was director of Kharkov's big Malyshev Machine Building Plant from 1954 to 1958, then becoming Kharkov Sovnarkhoz chairman under oblast First Secretary Titov. In 1960 Ukrainian First Secretary Podgornyy promoted him to sovnarkhoz chairman for the whole Ukraine. When Kharkov First Secretary Titov was called to Moscow in 1961 to become head of the CPSU Central Committee's cadre section, Sobol was selected to succeed him as Kharkov Oblast first secretary. In mid-1963, when Podgornyy was promoted from Ukrainian first secretary to a CPSU Central Committee secretary, he picked Sobol for the key post of Ukrainian second secretary, leaving cadre work in his hands.

[15] See the 5 August 1965 *Pravda* editorial and the unsigned article in the August (no. 15) issue of *Partiynaya Zhizn.*

[16] *Sovetskaya Rossiya*, 30 July; *Pravda*, 5 August, 11 August, 28 August; *Sovetskaya Estoniya*, 13 August; *Zarya Vostoka*, 19 August; *Pravda Vostoka*, 19 August; *Sovetskaya Belorussiya*, 20 August; *Partiynaya Zhizn*, no. 15.

party, and on 20 July[17] the Central Committee adopted a decree assailing Kharkov for being too liberal in admitting new members and initiating a national campaign to tighten up on admissions. The Kharkov decree reflected on Podgornyy and Titov both as former Kharkov leaders and patrons of Vashchenko and also because the laxness revealed there and elsewhere indicated poor leadership of cadre work on their part nationally. Titov, already exiled to Kazakhstan, was finally removed as Central Committee cadre secretary at the September 1965 Central Committee plenum.[18] The post of cadre chief continued vacant until December 1965 when RSFSR Party Organs Section head I. V. Kapitonov was appointed. Kapitonov was RSFSR cadre chief from December 1964 to December 1965 under RSFSR Bureau Chairman Brezhnev and First Deputy Chairman Kirilenko.

In December 1965 Podgornyy's defeat was confirmed when he was elected chairman of the Supreme Soviet Presidium and surrendered his secretariat post. Kharkovites in the Ukraine were demoted also: Kharkov Sovnarkhoz Chairman O. V. Soich, the target of *Ekonomicheskaya Gazeta*'s February attack, was demoted to director of the Kharkov Malyshev Machine Building Plant in late 1965,[19] and Ukrainian Second Secretary Sobol was transferred to the less important post of Ukrainian first deputy premier for industry in early 1966 (*Pravda Ukrainy*, 19 March 1966).

There was another round of statements on priorities at the 23d Party Congress in March–April 1966 and during the June 1966 Supreme Soviet election speeches, after the plan directives had been approved. Most speakers (including Kosygin[20]) carefully balanced their remarks, approving higher rates for consumer goods but with continued heavy industry priority and stronger defense. Brezhnev, Suslov, and Shelepin, however, again put extra emphasis on defense. Brezhnev defended heavy industry more than any other speaker, declaring its priority to be the "unchanging principle of our economic policy" (*Pravda*,

---

[17]The date of the decree is cited by F. Petrenko in *Voprosy Istorii KPSS*, no. 3 (1967). The decree is published in *Partiynaya Zhizn*, no. 15 (August 1965).

[18]Another Kharkovite, A. M. Rumyantsev, who had been appointed *Pravda* editor in mid-November 1964 when Podgornyy was especially influential, was removed as editor in mid-September 1965, after defending liberal positions in culture (Rumyantsev's articles appeared in the 21 February 1965 and 9 September 1965 *Pravda*s). He was replaced by conservative M. V. Zimyanin, an old associate of Mazurov in Belorussia (Mazurov worked under Zimyanin in the Belorussian Komsomol and later in the Belorussian Central Committee during the 1940's and 1950's). Zimyanin became editor shortly after 18 September 1965, when *Pravda* last identified him as deputy foreign minister. Although Rumyantsev was from Kharkov, there is no direct tie between him and Podgornyy, since he left Kharkov in 1949, while Podgornyy first arrived there to become party leader in 1950.

[19]Soich had succeeded Sobol as Kharkov Sovnarkhoz chairman in 1960 when Sobol became Ukrainian Sovnarkhoz chairman.

[20]In his 23d Congress speech, his 8 June election speech, and his 3 August Supreme Soviet speech.

11 June 1966). He also took a hard line on defense: "Under today's conditions, our country is compelled to devote even more forces and attention to strengthening its defense power. . . . Army and weapon expenses are a big burden for our budget" and "we could speed up the advance toward communism if we could throw off this burden . . . but the situation still does not permit us to do this." In a speech to military academy graduates, he declared that "the Soviet people will spare neither strength nor resources to increase the might of the armed forces" (*Pravda*, 2 July 1966).

Stressing the threat from abroad, Suslov declared that "our party and government are . . . adopting all necessary measures to raise still higher the economic and military might of our state and equip the Soviet army with all modern forms of weapons. Naturally this all requires large sums of money. But we do not doubt that all Soviet people fully approve these measures" (*Leningradskaya Pravda*, 9 June 1966). Shelepin, also stressing that the "growing military danger" forces the USSR to strengthen defense, declared that the Soviet people "would give up everything so that our army would not need anything" (*Leningradskaya Pravda*, 3 June 1966). In contrast, Podgornyy continued to stress consumer goods in his 23d Congress speech and in his June election speech. While paying obeisance to heavy industry and defense, he declared the task now is to raise living standards and that just as developing industry was once the national task, now development of agriculture is the task (*Pravda*, 10 June 1966).

The outcome of the priorities debate was a victory for the heavy industry-defense side, reversing the trends set in the 1965 plan adopted in December 1964. The annual plan and budget for 1966, adopted at the December 1965 Supreme Soviet session, restored the previous year's cut in defense spending and increased the gap between heavy industry and light industry:

Budget Defense Spending (billions)[21]

1964	1965	1966	1967
13.3	12.8	13.4	14.5

Planned Growth Rates (percentages)[22]

	1964	1965	1966	1967
Group A (heavy industry)	8.2	8.2	6.9	7.5
Group B (light industry)	6.5	7.7	6.0	6.6
Gap	1.7	.5	.9	.9

[21] Garbuzov's budget report in *Izvestiya*, 10 December 1964, 8 December 1965, and 16 December 1966.

[22] Kosygin's plan report in *Izvestiya*, 10 December 1964 and Baybakov's plan reports in *Izvestiya*, 8 December 1965 and 16 December 1966.

The five-year plan directives adopted at the 19 February 1966 Central Committee plenum set growth rates for group A at 49–52 percent over the five-year period and 43–46 percent for group B (*Izvestiya*, 20 February 1966).

Rural Construction Ministries

Although the March plenum appeared to reflect substantial agreement on a number of key agricultural questions, some matters could not be agreed upon. The first agricultural issue to become a subject of protracted dissension was Mazurov's March 1965 proposal to establish special rural construction ministries. This proposal appeared to pit Polyanskiy against Voronov, although neither mentioned the issue publicly themselves. Despite repeated badgering by *Selskaya Zhizn*, the agricultural lobby's organ and frequent Polyanskiy mouthpiece, Voronov resisted the campaign for over a year, finally setting up an RSFSR Rural Construction Ministry in October 1966. Resistance was overcome after Voronov's submission, and in early 1967 the USSR construction ministries were reorganized, a USSR Rural Construction Ministry established, and the Central Committee construction chief—apparently an ally of Voronov in this dispute—was removed. Sniping and maneuvering over the role of rural construction ministries has continued through 1970, however, with Voronov and Estonian leader Kebin still leading the opposition.

The proposal to create such ministries provoked controversy because the new ministries were designed to strengthen agriculture's ability to compete for resources in the hard-pressed construction field and because the new ministries might represent an expansion of state control over kolkhozes—for example, by threatening the independence of the expanding interkolkhoz construction organizations. As long as rural construction remained in the regular construction ministries under industry oriented leaders it was constantly shortchanged; as an independent ministry it would have its own construction resources which other officials supposedly could not divert into nonrural projects. This factor presumably would please Polyanskiy, who was the leading advocate of more resources for agriculture and who supervised the lagging rural construction program. By the same token, this presumably accounted for the opposition by Voronov and others unenthusiastic about devoting more resources to agriculture.

The second facet—the relation of kolkhozes and their interkolkhoz organizations to the new ministries—caused concern among kolkhoz union advocates in 1965, since it represented a strengthening of the ministerial apparatus, a subordination of interkolkhoz construction organizations to the state, and an additional hindrance to granting interkolkhoz administrative organizations (kolkhoz unions) power to run farm affairs. Mazurov, who initiated the rural construction ministry campaign, was a long-time advocate of a strong agriculture ministry[23]

---

[23] See his 11 December 1960 *Pravda* article.

and no friend of the kolkhoz union movement.[24] This second factor presumably lessened the proposal's appeal to Polyanskiy, who never actually endorsed the proposal.[25] However, Polyanskiy presumably was won over when a formula was worked out to establish rural construction ministries with only limited control over supposedly autonomous interkolkhoz construction organizations.[26] Since the expansion of interkolkhoz construction organizations was seen by some as an essential step toward kolkhoz unions, the preservation of these independent organizations kept kolkhoz union hopes alive.

In presenting his proposal to the March 1965 plenum, Mazurov noted that he had written to the Central Committee three years earlier proposing a rural construction ministry for Belorussia, but had not been permitted to establish one. His proposal won immediate endorsement from several speakers (Kazakh First Secretary Kunayev,[27] Azerbaydzhan First Secretary Akhundov, Latvian First Secretary Pelshe, Kirgiz First Secretary Usubaliyev, Moldavian First Secretary Bodyul, and Lithuanian First Secretary Snechkus). Yet despite the fact that

[24] During his tenure as Belorussian first secretary, Belorussia ignored the campaign for kolkhoz unions waged by the neighboring Ukraine. Strong kolkhoz unions were designed to take over many of the Agriculture Ministry's functions locally.

[25] Perhaps the main reason for the absence of a Polyanskiy endorsement is the fact that he made very few statements on agriculture in 1965 and 1966. He delivered the 7 November 1965 anniversary report for the Presidium—but stuck to generalities. His first detailed post-Khrushchev statement on agriculture was in a 31 May 1966 Krasnodar speech (*Pravda*, 1 June 1966)—after almost all rural construction ministries had been created.

[26] The chairman of the interkolkhoz construction organization council became the first deputy minister of rural construction and his interkolkhoz construction association was made a semi-independent organization within the ministry. As G. Sevlikyants indicated in the 19 March 1966 *Kommunist Tadzhikistana*, this was a compromise between the position of those who wanted the interkolkhoz organizations to remain fully under the kolkhozes and those who wanted to completely subordinate them to the rural construction ministry. Areas favoring strong kolkhoz unions and interkolkhoz organizations—such as Moldavia— stressed that the interkolkhoz construction association would remain independent and its leading bodies would not be subordinate to the rural construction ministry, which would only give technical policy recommendations, coordinate plans, and provide better material supply (Moldavian Rural Construction Minister K. A. Burilkov in the 17 December 1965 *Selskaya Zhizn*). A 14 December 1965 *Selskaya Zhizn* editorial assured its readers that "the organizational and financial independence of the interkolkhoz construction associations will be fully preserved." Others ignored their "independence." Kurgan First Secretary G. F. Sizov wrote that it was "advisable also to subordinate interkolkhoz construction organizations to the rural construction ministry and to create in it a specialized administration for kolkhoz construction" (*Selskaya Zhizn*, 26 December 1965).

[27] Kunayev also noted that Kazakhstan used to have a rural construction ministry but that it had been abolished. Here Brezhnev broke in to ask why it had been dissolved. Kunayev replied: "You well know that we were not asked. This was decided arbitrarily. . . . Now we are speaking softly about this, but everyone knows this was the work of Comrade Khrushchev" (Stenographic record of the March 1965 Central Committee plenum, p. 104).

no one voiced any opposition, only one republic (Kirgizia) established a rural construction ministry after the plenum (*Sovetskaya Kirgiziya*, 18 April 1965), and only when this ministry proved successful did other republics receive the go-ahead in October 1965. Thereupon, twelve republics created them in just one and a half months (20 October to 7 December).

Two republics, however, refused to create rural construction ministries— Estonia and the RSFSR. Estonian Gosstroy Chairman A. Vendelin opposed the separation of rural construction from the regular construction ministry (he told a session of the Estonian Supreme Soviet that "we should not in any case permit the creation of new construction organizations in the Estonian SSR" and "all work must be concentrated in the Ministry of Construction Estonian SSR"— *Sovetskaya Estoniya*, 21 October 1965), and Estonian First Secretary Kebin at the 23d CPSU Congress indirectly backed him up by declaring that "we have experimented and reorganized too much." In December 1969 Estonian Premier V. I. Klauson reaffirmed Estonia's determination not to establish a rural construction ministry and assailed the USSR Rural Construction Ministry for taking "deep offense" at this position and for retaliating against Estonia ("It is hard to explain why specialized organizations directly subordinate to the USSR Rural Construction Ministry build elevators and mills in all republics and oblasts surrounding the Estonian SSR but are not permitted to work in our republic"— *Sovetskaya Estoniya*, 20 December 1969).

The RSFSR leaders also quietly resisted the rural construction ministry campaign. After the other republics created rural construction ministries in October–November–December 1965, *Selskaya Zhizn* began a campaign to establish USSR and RSFSR rural construction ministries.[28] A 22 December 1965 *Selskaya Zhizn* article attacked the RSFSR for not creating a rural construction ministry[29] and criticized those who argued that the present RSFSR construction and agriculture ministries were sufficient to handle rural construction. On 11 May 1966 a *Selskaya Zhizn* editorial attacked the RSFSR for not creating a rural construction ministry and contrasted the RSFSR's poor organization of rural construction to that of "republics where ministries of rural construction have been created," for example, the Ukraine and Belorussia. Yet despite the fact that many RSFSR obkom first secretaries and other local officials were endorsing the

[28] Articles by Voronezh First Secretary S. D. Khitrov on 17 October 1965, Voronezh Interkolkhoz Construction Association Council Chairman I. Dubkov on 22 December 1965, Georgian Rural Construction Minister Sh. Tatarashvili on 24 December 1965, Kurgan First Secretary G. F. Sizov on 26 December 1965, Orenburg First Secretary A. V. Kovalenko on 30 December 1965, Belgorod Interkolkhoz Construction Association Council Chairman I. Anpilov on 23 February 1966, and Amur Oblast Agriculture Administration deputy chief F. Murzov on 16 August 1966.

[29] Voronezh Interkolkhoz Construction Association Council Chairman Dubkov complained that "rural construction ministries are being created everywhere . . . yet in the RSFSR, which is the biggest republic in the country, for some reason or another there is still no single organ which would unite the organizations which are carrying on construction at kolkhozes and sovkhozes."

proposal for an RSFSR rural construction ministry,[30] Premier Voronov, First Deputy Premier Pysin, and Agriculture Minister Florentyev remained silent. Moscow Oblast Construction Secretary A. D. Moshchevitin denied the need for an RSFSR rural construction ministry in *Leninskoye Znamya*, 18 August 1966 ("It seems to us that there is no need to create yet another ministry for construction in the countryside in the RSFSR"), and First Deputy Premier Pysin in his report to the August 1966 RSFSR Supreme Soviet session dwelt on improving the existing rural construction system—under the agriculture and construction ministries (*Sovetskaya Rossiya*, 17 August 1966). The 19 August 1966 *Sovetskaya Rossiya* editorial on the RSFSR Supreme Soviet session also ignored any rural construction ministry and concentrated on the session's instructions to the agriculture and construction ministries to improve rural construction and to aid interkolkhoz construction associations.

Only in October 1966—almost a full year after all the other republics—did the RSFSR suddenly create a rural construction ministry (announced in *Sovetskaya Rossiya*, 21 October 1966). A *Pravda* editorial on 24 October approvingly declared that "rural construction ministries have been created in almost all union republics." The first party leader to applaud the creation of the new ministry was Voronov's old rival L. N. Yefremov (*Sovetskaya Rossiya*, 10 November 1966). Even so, when Voronov and Pysin finally bowed to the pressure and created a separate rural construction ministry, they made sure it would be led by someone responsive to their policies. For the new rural construction minister they picked RSFSR Deputy Construction Minister V. M. Gushchin, who apparently had been supervising the much-criticized rural construction work in the RSFSR Construction Ministry and who was an old associate of Pysin (deputy chairman of the Altay Sovnarkhoz in 1959, while Pysin was Altay first secretary).

Selskaya Zhizn has continued to express its dissatisfaction with the handling of rural construction in the RSFSR. On 10 February 1967 its editorial assailed the RSFSR for delay and bungling in setting up the new ministry. Even after its creation, rural construction work has not improved. *Selskaya Zhizn* on 29 November 1968, 9 March 1969, 14 August 1969, and 17 October 1969 bitterly complained against USSR and RSFSR authorities for assigning RSFSR Rural Construction Ministry units to industrial projects. *Selskaya Zhizn* pointed out that in many places in the RSFSR less rural construction work was being done now than before the creation of a separate ministry to serve rural needs. Voronov himself also acknowledged this problem. In his July 1969 RSFSR

---

[30]Voronezh Interkolkhoz Construction Association Council Chairman Dubkov in the 22 December 1965 *Selskaya Zhizn*, Kurgan First Secretary Sizov in the 26 December 1965 *Selskaya Zhizn*, Belgorod Interkolkhoz Construction Association Council Chairman I. Anpilov in the 23 February 1966 *Selskaya Zhizn*, Kostroma Secretary B. Arkhipov in the 26 March 1966 *Sovetskaya Rossiya*. Others urged a USSR ministry, for instance, Stavropol Komsomol First Secretary V. A. Kaznacheyev in the 21 May 1966 *Komsomolskaya Pravda* and Orel First Secretary T. I. Sokolov in *Partiynaya Zhizn*, no. 14 (July 1966).

Supreme Soviet speech he criticized his minister, Gushchin, and declared that "the Rural Construction Ministry after all still has not developed construction work in the villages . . . and, with the help of the USSR Rural Construction Ministry and USSR Gosplan, has burdened its construction organs with projects unrelated to agriculture" (*Sovetskaya Rossiya*, 31 July 1969).

After the RSFSR Rural Construction Ministry was finally established in October 1966, a considerable struggle apparently occurred over creating a USSR Rural Construction Ministry. Finally on 21 January 1967 a Central Committee–Council of Ministers decree "On Improving the Organization of Administration of Construction" was adopted,[31] and four new USSR construction ministries—including rural construction—were established in a general reorganization.[32] This was almost two years after the initial proposal for rural construction ministries.

Shortly after the USSR reorganization, Central Committee Construction Section head A. Ye. Biryukov was removed. Biryukov, Moscow Oblast and then Moscow City construction secretary 1959-64,[33] presumably shared his successor Moshchevitin's opposition to a separate rural construction ministry. It is probably more than coincidence that Biryukov, after being removed as Central Committee construction chief, became a deputy to Voronov. On 13 April 1967 *Sovetskaya Rossiya* announced Biryukov's appointment as RSFSR deputy premier, and he now supervised RSFSR rural construction (for example, attending a RSFSR rural construction conference, *Selskaya Zhizn*, 23 March 1969). Thus, Deputy Premier Biryukov and Rural Construction Minister Gushchin appear allied to their bosses Premier Voronov and First Deputy Premier Pysin on rural construction. No successor to Biryukov as Central Committee Construction Section head could be agreed on for over two years. Only in mid-1969 (after Kirilenko had displaced Voronov as number five in the rankings) did a new section head appear: Gorkiy Obkom Construction Secretary I. N. Dmitriyev, a protégé of Brezhnev's protégé, Katushev.

Kolkhoz Unions

The other big agricultural issue to arise in 1965 and 1966 was the old idea of creating kolkhoz unions. Though defeated when raised by Khrushchev, Polyanskiy, and Podgornyy in 1959, the idea developed impressive force in 1966. Yet,

---

[31] See USSR Rural Construction Minister S. Khitrov's article in a February 1971 *Partiynaya Zhizn* (no. 4, p. 9).

[32] Announced in *Pravda*, 22 February 1967. In the process, the RSFSR Construction Ministry was abolished and its leaders distributed among the four new USSR construction ministries.

[33] Biryukov was Moscow City Committee Construction Section head, then after November 1959 Moscow Oblast secretary, then from December 1960 to July 1964 Moscow City construction secretary.

despite the apparent support of Brezhnev and several other Presidium members, it again was defeated. As with the rural construction ministry issue, the opposition was led by the Estonian leaders with the quiet support of the RSFSR leaders. This time, however, Mazurov appeared to be on Voronov's side.

The main point at issue was state control over kolkhozes. Though the creation of a semi-independent system of kolkhoz self-management might appear liberal, its backers included many who hardly have been noted as liberals (for example, Brezhnev, Bodyul, and Polyanskiy). Although kolkhoz union proposals varied considerably, the most important involved reducing the Agriculture Ministry's apparatus and transferring some of its functions to councils elected by kolkhozes. Polyanskiy himself declared at the December 1959 plenum that if kolkhoz unions were established the Agriculture Ministry would have to be "significantly reduced" and this would be "only for the good." He also offered an ambitious definition of the role of the new organs: "Such organs will take over the functions of kolkhoz operational administration, strengthening of inter-kolkhoz ties, and organization of joint work, will decide questions of material-technical supply for kolkhozes and will render aid to economically weak farms."[34]

The idea of creating kolkhoz unions was cited by Khrushchev in his Note on reorganizing the machine-tractor stations in January 1958[35] and repeated in his 27 March and 1 April 1958 Supreme Soviet speeches. But, as he said at the December 1959 plenum, "we exchanged opinions on this question" at that time and decided not to create them yet.[36] An extensive public debate over this issue developed during 1958 and 1959, and when the December 1959 plenum opened, kolkhoz unions were more or less endorsed by RSFSR Premier Polyanskiy, Ukrainian First Secretary Podgornyy, Kazakh First Secretary Belyayev, and Sverdlovsk First Secretary Kirilenko—all close Khrushchev allies. Agriculture Minister Matskevich, whose *apparat* was threatened by this proposal, opposed any unions above the rayon level, insisting that they be subordinate to oblast agriculture administrations. Khrushchev's concluding speech indicated that this idea had again not prevailed ("Evidently, a kolkhoz center should not be created, but one must seriously think about interkolkhoz organizations in rayons."[37]) and the plenum decree referred the question back to the Presidium for further study (*Pravda*, 27 December 1959). In late 1959 and early 1960 some rayon kolkhoz unions were created in Lithuania[38] and in Moscow Oblast,[39]

---

[34] Stenographic record of the December 1959 Central Committee plenum, pp. 32-33.

[35] Ibid., p. 408.

[36] Ibid.

[37] Ibid., p. 409.

[38] *Sovetskaya Litva*, 1 December 1959 and 23 March 1960.

[39] *Sovetskaya Rossiya*, 17 March 1960.

and the debate continued in the press after the December 1959 plenum.[40] However, the discussion temporarily ended after Matskevich reiterated his opposition at the June 1960 All-Union Conference of Agricultural Specialists (*Pravda*, 15 June 1960). Advocates revived the proposal in 1961 after Matskevich's removal—although in watered-down form. As in 1959–60, much of the kolkhoz unionists' argument was based on the need for some sort of organ to administer the growing number of interkolkhoz organizations—especially the interkolkhoz construction organizations. Krasnodar First Secretary G. I. Vorobyev proposed an RSFSR interkolkhoz coordinating agency in the 7 September 1961 *Pravda*. Moldavian Premier A. F. Diorditsa suggested revival of something like the old postwar Council for Kolkhoz Affairs in the 24 September 1961 *Izvestiya*. Even Voronov protégé, Orenburg Oblast Executive Committee Chairman I. I. Molchaninov suggested oblast and rayon interkolkhoz councils in the 12 October 1961 *Sovetskaya Rossiya*. The strongest proposal came from a Poltava raykom secretary who backed the establishment of kolkhoz unions from the rayon level through the all-union level (*Selskaya Zhizn*, 13 January 1962).

But with the establishment of kolkhoz-sovkhoz production administrations by the March 1962 plenum, kolkhoz union agitation stopped, according to G. Aksenenok and Z. Belyayeva—who were among the first to revive the kolkhoz union proposals in late 1965 (*Selskaya Zhizn*, 2 December 1965). As kolkhoz union promoter I. Vinnichenko wrote: "The long (and quite bumpy) road of organizational searchings ended with the creation of territorial kolkhoz-sovkhoz administrations, and as a result, the public cooperative farms—by their nature democratic—became subordinate to state administrative organs" (*Literaturnaya Rossiya*, 8 April 1966). The new kolkhoz-sovkhoz production administrations took over leadership of interkolkhoz organizations (according to S. Semin in the January 1967 *Voprosy Ekonomiki*, p. 124)—undoubtedly disappointing kolkhoz union advocates by putting interkolkhoz organizations under state control instead of under kolkhoz unions.

As indicated in Chapter III, Voronov appeared to be the leading champion of the creation of the new kolkhoz-sovkhoz administrations, as well as a principal beneficiary. On the other hand, Polyanskiy, who had advocated kolkhoz unions, fell into eclipse in March 1962. Voronov and Polyanskiy were obviously moving in opposite directions: Voronov for more direct state control over kolkhozes and bringing sovkhozes and kolkhozes under common direction, and Polyanskiy for dismantling at least some of the state agricultural apparatus and establishing an elective administrative system for kolkhozes completely separate from sovkhozes.

Brezhnev started the new campaign by stating at the March 1965 plenum that "the time has come to start working out a new kolkhoz charter" and to

---

[40]V. P. Rozhin in *Nash Sovremennik*, no. 5 (May 1960), against; A. Pashkov in *Voprosy Ekonomiki*, no. 5 (May 1960), against; I. Vinnichenko in *Oktyabr*, no. 6 (June 1960), for.

begin "preparations for the third All-Union Congress of Kolkhozniks so that it can be called already next year." Khrushchev in his 22 December 1961 Kiev speech[41] had promised a new congress, noting that people had requested this earlier, but that it was necessary to work out the new party program (adopted at the 22d Party Congress in October 1961) and a new constitution (still not off the ground in 1971) before holding a new congress of kolkhozniks. Talk of a new congress had ended after the March 1962 plenum.

Talk of kolkhoz unions was revived, after Brezhnev's comment, by N. Karotamm, who advocated a system of unions including a national kolkhoz center (*Sovetskaya Rossiya*, 16 July 1965), and by G. Aksenenok and Z. Belyayeva in the 2 December 1965 *Selskaya Zhizn*. In January 1966 a commission was appointed to write a new draft model kolkhoz charter to submit to a new congress of kolkhozniks (*Pravda*, 26 January 1966). The commission was chaired by Brezhnev and included the Presidium members, Central Committee secretaries, republic first secretaries and agriculture secretaries and agriculture ministers. The 149-man commission included many who later publicly advocated kolkhoz unions—Moldavian First Secretary I. I. Bodyul, Sumy First Secretary B. I. Voltovskiy, Ukrainian kolkhoz chairman A. G. Buznitskiy, Kazakh kolkhoz chairman N. N. Golovatskiy, Vladimir kolkhoz chairman A. V. Gorshkov, Altay kolkhoz chairman F. M. Grinko, Ukrainian Central Committee Agriculture Secretary V. G. Komyakhov, Latvian First Secretary A. Ya. Pelshe, Podgornyy, Ukrainian First Secretary P. Ye. Shelest, Institute of State and Law director V. M. Chkhikvadze, and *Selskaya Zhizn* editor P. F. Alekseyev (whose paper had appeared favorable)—as well as past supporters Polyanskiy and Kirilenko. Two virtually open foes belonged to the commission—Matskevich and Kebin.

As the opening of the 23d Party Congress (29 March) approached, opposition to the kolkhoz union proposals appeared. In the 26 March *Pravda*, P. Bogdashkin rejected kolkhoz unions in favor of ministry control. At the congress Brezhnev cautiously raised the proposal to establish kolkhoz unions,[42] as did Ukrainian First Secretary Shelest, Latvian First Secretary Pelshe, President Podgornyy, and two minor figures: kolkhoz chairman A. G. Buznitskiy, a member of the Brezhnev charter commission who revealed that a congress of kolkhozniks was planned for the end of 1966, and raykom first secretary Yu. D. Filinova, who violated protocol by referring to a Politburo headed by a general secretary, implying that Brezhnev headed the collective body. Kolkhoz union foe Matskevich noted that Brezhnev had raised the question, but he carefully avoided commitment, saying that the proposal would be carefully studied. Kebin—who later became the most outspoken foe of kolkhoz unions—indirectly opposed the proposal by praising the rayon production administrations as the best form for

[41] Khrushchev's collected speeches, vol. 6, p. 286.

[42] "I would like to ask advice: Should we not form elective kolkhoz cooperative organs in rayons, oblasts, krays, republics and the center?" He pointed out their advantages and recalled the kolkhoz unions which existed in the late 1920's (*Pravda*, 31 March 1966).

administering kolkhozes and sovkhozes and by stating "we have experimented and reorganized too much."[43]

Despite the fact that the majority of the eleven-man Politburo was on record as more or less advocating kolkhoz unions (Brezhnev, Shelest, Podgornyy, and Pelshe at the 23d Congress, Polyanskiy and Kirilenko at the December 1959 plenum), the 8 April congress resolution only "instructed the Central Committee to consider the question of forming kolkhoz-cooperative organs in the rayons, oblasts, krays, republics and in the center." Obviously, to stalemate such powerful support, most of the other Politburo members (Voronov, Kosygin, Mazurov, Suslov, and Shelepin) must have opposed kolkhoz unions. Voronov and Mazurov, despite their involvement in agriculture through the years, have always ignored kolkhoz union proposals. The contrast between the total silence on kolkhoz unions in Mazurov's Belorussia and the pro-union clamor in the neighboring Ukraine has always been striking.

Nevertheless, some kolkhoz union advocates considered the 23d Congress a victory, or at least tried to present it as such. Apparently they concluded that with the top-level support registered at the congress, the upcoming congress of kolkhozniks would surely create the kolkhoz union system. I. Vinnichenko, one of the first to broach the kolkhoz union proposal in 1958, immediately after the 23d Congress wrote an exultant article stating "now that the idea of the kolkhoz union has become a reality" and describing the delight that long-time kolkhoz union advocate M. I. Kovalenko must have had in listening to Brezhnev's speech (kolkhoz chairman Kovalenko had sold Vinnichenko on kolkhoz unions in 1957 and has written several articles through the years promoting the idea). One enthusiastic Ukrainian stated flatly that "elective kolkhoz-cooperative organs will be established in rayons, oblasts, krays, republics and at the center, in accordance with the resolutions of the 23d Party Congress."[44] Even *Ekonomicheskaya Gazeta*'s editors wrote that the proposed elective kolkhoz-cooperative organs had been backed by the congress.[45]

Immediately after Brezhnev's mention of the kolkhoz unions, articles endorsing his statement blossomed in the press:

> writer N. Rylenkov in the 30 March *Literaturnaya Gazeta*;
> Vladimir kolkhoz chairman A. Gorshkov in the 3 April *Pravda*;
> Moldavian kolkhoz chairman P. Kozhukhov in the 8 April *Sovetskaya Moldaviya*;
> writer I. Vinnichenko in the 8 April *Literaturnaya Rossiya*;
> I. Minkovich in the 19 April *Pravda Ukrainy*;
> Ukrainian kolkhoz chairman M. Kovalenko in the 20 April *Sovetskaya Rossiya*;

[43] Stenographic record of the 23d Party Congress, vol. I, p. 443.

[44] I. Minkovich, *Pravda Ukrainy*, 19 April 1966.

[45] *Ekonomicheskaya Gazeta*, no. 16 (April 1966), p. 26.

raykom first secretary N. V. Bondarenko in the 21 April *Sovetskaya Moldaviya*;

Gosplan specialist K. Karpov in the 24 April *Pravda*;

Uzbek kolkhoz chairmen A. Odilov and M. Khvan in the 24 April *Selskaya Zhizn*;

Altay kolkhoz chairman F. Grinko in the 5 May *Selskaya Zhizn*;

Kovalenko again in the 8 May *Pravda Ukrainy*;

Ukrainian Secretary V. Komyakhov in the no. 9 *Kommunist* (16 June);

Krasnoyarsk kolkhoz chairman A. Voronkov in the 18 June *Selskaya Zhizn*;

Lvov kolkhoz chairman N. Gavrilenko in the 23 June *Selskaya Zhizn*;

old Bolshevik S. Krutoshinskiy in the 30 June *Izvestiya*;

Kovalenko again in the no. 28 *Ekonomicheskaya Gazeta* (12 July);

and Moldavian I. Piskunenko in the no. 7 *Voprosy Ekonomiki* (22 July).

As in 1958-59, support was concentrated in the Ukraine and Moldavia. Indicative of this is the fact that of the above seventeen articles, ten were by Ukrainians or Moldavians. Most of them included only brief mention of the proposed organs, with no elaboration on what functions they would have. But the more ambitious and enthusiastic articles (by Kovalenko, Odilov and Khvan, Grinko, Voronkov, and Gavrilenko) pictured kolkhoz unions as organs elected by kolkhozes to manage interkolkhoz and/or kolkhoz affairs, protect their interests in dealing with state organizations, run kolkhoz markets and subsidiary organizations, carry on planning and procurement, etc. Gavrilenko wrote that they would prevent administrative interference in kolkhoz affairs, and Kovalenko indicated that some state organizations would have to surrender some of their present functions (for instance, the Agricultural Equipment Association would transfer all its repair units to the unions and retain only a supply function). But unlike Polyanskiy at the December 1959 plenum, kolkhoz unionists were cautious about discussing dismantling of agricultural organs. Kovalenko picked on one of the weakest and most criticized organizations—the Agricultural Equipment Association—instead of the Agriculture Ministry, and even then hastened to assure his readers that he was not advocating the complete abolition of the association (*Ekonomicheskaya Gazeta*, no. 28).

Nevertheless, following Kovalenko's July article, the tide suddenly shifted from unanimous approval to the raising of doubts and restrictive interpretations of kolkhoz unions. *Ekonomicheskaya Gazeta*, which had claimed congress support for them (no. 16, April), opened a special column for discussion of these issues in its no. 28 issue (July). Its new column was inaugurated by Kovalenko's ambitious article, but the following issue (19 July) carried an article by the leader of the Higher Party School's agricultural economics chair, V. A. Abramov, a member of the charter commission, which signaled the beginning of the end of the kolkhoz union campaign. Abramov stressed that the main point in the proposed kolkhoz unions' activities "is not the replacing of existing forms of state organizations" but in improving the kolkhozes' use of reserves. While supposedly supporting the establishment of unions, he defined them as powerless supplements to the agricultural administrations.

After Abramov's article, most kolkhoz union articles expressed doubts, stressed the need for close ties between kolkhozes and sovkhozes (instead of allowing kolkhozes to develop their own independent administrative system), talked of rayon unions instead of republic and national unions (as Matskevich had in December 1959), and stressed that any new kolkhoz unions should not weaken the powers of the present agricultural organs.[46] The new *Ekonomicheskaya Gazeta* column which had opened with Kovalenko's article in issue no. 28, after carrying Abramov's restrictive interpretation in no. 29 and two questioning articles in no. 30, began appearing less frequently and finally ended with issue no. 41 (11 October). The last article in the short-lived column was by the chief of a Latvian rayon agricultural administration, who praised Abramov's limited kolkhoz union version and criticized Kovalenko's comprehensive version. *Selskaya Zhizn* had already dropped its kolkhoz union discussion by the time the Abramov article appeared. The last favorable articles appeared in the 7 September *Sovetskaya Kirgiziya* and the 20 November *Radyanska Ukraina* (the last—by Ukrainian obkom first secretary and charter commission member Voltovskiy). The kolkhoz union proposals were killed without ever being even directly criticized. The two most prominent perpetrators of the deed—Abramov and Kebin—even claimed they were supporting kolkhoz unions, while actually undercutting the idea.

Talk of the congress of kolkhozniks and the new kolkhoz charter disappeared along with that about the kolkhoz unions—even though Polyanskiy in his 31 May 1966 election speech (*Pravda*, 1 June) and Sevlikyants in the 20 July 1966 *Kommunist Tadzhikistana* had spoken of the upcoming congress of kolkhozniks and the new charter it would adopt. The leadership—which had publicly promised to hold a congress in late 1966—had to embarrassingly ignore its own commitment. The fact that the normally noncommittal leaders had committed themselves underscored the fact that Brezhnev and Polyanskiy had suffered unexpected defeat on this subject. Judging by Polyanskiy's 31 May reference to the congress and the pro-union articles still in early July, the congress was still on until Abramov's 19 July article. Quite probably Polyanskiy and other advocates preferred to temporarily drop the kolkhoz union fight rather than agree to a compromise version which would pervert the whole idea. After all, even foes like Kebin and Matskevich were agreeable to kolkhoz unions so long as they were not of the variety Polyanskiy had once urged—namely, with some sort of administrative power which could rival the Agriculture Ministry's functions.

[46] Raykom secretary I. Yudin and economist M. Lapidus in *Ekonomicheskaya Gazeta*, no. 30 (26 July), p. 28; S. Semin in *Ekonomicheskaya Gazeta*, no. 30, p. 29; economist G. Sevlikyants in the 20 July 1966 *Kommunist Tadzhikistana*; Kebin in *Kommunist*, no. 12, 12 August; and Latvian rayon production administration chief I. Viltsin in *Ekonomicheskaya Gazeta*, no. 41, 11 October.

THE CUTBACK:
1967-1968

The gains in resource allocations for agriculture under the program adopted by the March 1965 Central Committee plenum[1] were seriously undermined in 1967 and 1968. The record 1966 harvest eased the country's agricultural crisis but by the same token undermined the arguments of Brezhnev and Polyanskiy on the need for continued aid to agriculture. As a result, despite public warnings by Polyanskiy, resources were quietly shifted from agriculture to heavy industry, defense, and especially consumer goods. A September 1967 Central Committee plenum approved a big welfare program and revised the five-year plan in favor of light industry.

In early 1968 Brezhnev began pushing for a new plenum to stress agriculture, but this was delayed until October 1968. Nevertheless, in mid-1968 agriculture partially recovered its losses through decrees sharply raising fertilizer and agricultural equipment output. At the October 1968 plenum Brezhnev exposed the massive diversion of resources from agriculture and proposed renewed aid. He directed his efforts mainly toward improving agriculture's share in the next five-year plan (1971–75), preparation of which began in 1968. Although the new plan's priorities were supposed to be determined by late 1968, this was delayed by the struggle over resources, and it was not until May 1970 that agriculture's share was determined. As of January 1971—the month the new plan was to go into effect—the other sectors' shares had still not been publicly announced.

The agricultural lobby, and especially its chief spokesman Polyanskiy, also suffered another setback in late 1967 and 1968. In early 1967 a massive long-range program was undertaken to rebuild the countryside—to resettle millions of

---

[1] And, to a lesser extent, by Brezhnev's big irrigation and drainage program adopted at the May 1966 Central Committee plenum.

peasants from tiny, scattered, poorly equipped villages to new, consolidated settlements with urban-type apartment houses. In late 1967 this village reorganization program ran into a barrage of public criticism and in early 1968 Polyanskiy, its supervisor, had to personally intervene, calling both the administrators of the program and their critics into his office. The officials subsequently publicly admitted errors in the program and the ambitious plans were slowed down. In late 1968 the Central Committee intervened to issue a decree criticizing the handling of the program—an implicit rebuke to its supervisor, Polyanskiy.

Agriculture Lobby Overridden

After the record 1966 harvest, pressure developed to transfer resources to other hard-pressed sectors. The major beneficiary of this movement was consumer goods and services—a sector closely identified with Premier Kosygin. In his June 1966 Supreme Soviet election speech Kosygin painted an optimistic picture of the food situation and urged faster development of light industry, even to the extent of using scarce foreign exchange to buy foreign equipment for this branch:

> The necessary reserves have been created for normal food supplies. And if there are still bottlenecks in food deliveries to the population at some point in the country, these are not related to food shortages but to poor organization of deliveries. We have sufficient milk, animal and vegetable fat, sugar, bread, eggs, vegetables and other products. The issue now is to reorganize the food industry. . . .
>
> However, it cannot yet be said that the population's demand for every industrial good is being fully satisfied. . . . Now we can and must develop light industry and the food industry much more rapidly to produce more new goods which will improve daily conditions in the life of the Soviet people. . . . Some equipment, which is not manufactured in the USSR, is being purchased from abroad (*Pravda*, 9 June 1966).

He repeated the same satisfied picture of agriculture in his March 1967 RSFSR Supreme Soviet election speech and added: "In recent years the monetary income of the city and rural population has grown, therefore demand for industrial goods, especially clothes, shoes, refrigerators, furniture and television sets, has risen. Although the output of industrial goods has risen, the demand for a number of them is still not being fully satisfied. Now important measures are being implemented to increase the output of these goods. . . . The production capacity in other branches of light industry is also growing. Large sums have been allocated to this." He also added that "at present the Central Committee and Soviet Government are considering concrete ways and periods" for raising the living standard during the present five-year plan (*Sovetskaya Rossiya*, 7 March 1967).

Kosygin appeared to be supported by Voronov, who devoted "a significant part" of his March 1967 election speech "to questions of expanding production of consumer goods" (*Sovetskaya Rossiya*, 5 March 1967), and Shelepin, who in his March 1967 speech "dwelt in particular on measures being undertaken to raise the living standard of the Soviet people and to increase production of consumer goods" (*Sovetskaya Rossiya*, 4 March 1967). *Sovetskaya Rossiya's* summary of Shelepin's speech reported him saying that the "party and government, firmly following the line of preferential development of heavy industry, at the same time decided to direct more resources into the development of branches producing consumer goods.... This year 21 percent more capital investments are being allotted to development of light industry alone than last year."[2]

Brezhnev also appeared somewhat receptive in his March 1967 election speech, largely ignoring agriculture and discussing the shortage of consumer goods and the growing purchasing power of the population. He said:

> We are reacting to these difficulties. The Central Committee and Government are adopting a number of measures to eliminate the existing shortcomings in supplying the population as fast as possible. Large funds are being allotted to the development of light industry....
>
> At the present time the Central Committee and Council of Ministers are considering a plan to implement measures for raising the living standard of the Soviet people, taking into account the resources and possibilities presently available and those expected in the future (*Pravda*, 11 March 1967).

The movement to cut agricultural investments was alluded to by Polyanskiy and Podgornyy in their March 1967 RSFSR Supreme Soviet speeches. Declaring that the good 1966 harvest had "engendered a complacent attitude in some people," Polyanskiy complained that "some comrades are beginning to think that kolkhozes and sovkhozes can now develop even with less material help and that one can now reduce the volume of land improvement work and reduce deliveries of equipment and mineral fertilizer to agriculture" (*Pravda*, 3 March 1967). "Such thinking is harmful" and "must be stopped," he said. He received some slight support from Podgornyy, who stated that "one cannot in the slightest weaken attention to agriculture" (*Pravda*, 10 March 1967). However, Podgornyy also noted the inflationary rise in savings and the need for more consumer goods.

[2] After being given responsibility for consumer goods production, Shelepin appeared to switch from defense advocate to consumer advocate. His new duties had become evident after the December 1965 abolition of his party-state control committee: he represented the Politburo at a conference of trade workers (*Sovetskaya Rossiya*, 18 June 1966), at a meat and dairy conference (*Pravda*, 23 June 1966), and at a light industry conference (*Pravda*, 6 July 1966), stressed consumer goods production in his June 1966 Supreme Soviet election speech (*Pravda*, 3 June 1966) and in a December speech in Kalinin (*Pravda*, 10 December 1966), traveled to Ivanovo with Central Committee Light Industry Section head P. K. Sizov to study living conditions and consumer goods production in November (*Pravda*, 20 November 1966), attended a fish industry conference in February (*Selskaya Zhizn*, 24 February 1967), etc.

Only a few weeks later Polyanskiy again mentioned the resource debate. Speaking in Blagoveshchensk on 10 June, he declared that "at present agriculture is the subject of the most intense attention" of the party and government. Declaring agriculture the "most complicated sector of communist construction," he demanded it be given "maximal and systematic help in every respect" and that aid in fact be increased. He declared that the time had come to reconstruct villages on a national scale and "regardless of the difficulties of this task, we can and must solve it with the efforts of the whole country."

Nevertheless, despite the warnings by Polyanskiy and Podgornyy, the Politburo soon decided to increase allocations to light industry, heavy industry, and defense. No one said anything publicly about actually diverting funds from agriculture until Brezhnev revealed the diversion at the October 1968 plenum. The increases for consumer goods and services received the greatest fanfare. A 26 September 1967 Central Committee plenum heard Brezhnev report "On Measures To Further Raise the Welfare of the Soviet People" and approved the annual plan proposed for 1968 and also the plans for 1969 and 1970.

The September 1967 plenum's welfare measures raised the minimum wage rate and some other wage rates, granted longer vacations, raised pay for temporary disability, improved pensions, etc.—a package costing over 6 billion rubles in 1968 alone, which almost equaled all expenditures on these during the entire previous five-year plan (according to Gosplan Chairman N. K. Baybakov at the October 1967 Supreme Soviet session, *Izvestiya*, 11 October 1967). Baybakov explained that in 1968 the average worker's wages would rise 6 percent over 1967 and would reach 115.2 rubles in 1970, instead of the 114.7 rubles set in the five-year plan directives approved at the 23d Party Congress in 1966. He also said that "the general sum of monetary income of the population will rise in 1968 by 13 billion rubles, which is considerably higher than the calculations for the directives." Consumption per capita would rise by 6.9 percent in 1968.

To avoid inflation, this decision had to be accompanied by an increase in the production of consumer goods to absorb the increased purchasing power. Baybakov explained: "In connection with the adopted decisions to raise the living standard of the people, which significantly increases the population's purchasing power, the 1968 plan provides for further raising of the rates of growth of consumer goods production and raising them above the rates of growth of production of producer goods: the rate of growth of group 'B' [light industry] comprises 8.6 percent, while group 'A' [heavy industry] is 7.9 percent." In the 1967 plan it had been 7.5 percent for group A and only 6.6 percent for group B (see Baybakov's 1966 Supreme Soviet report, *Izvestiya*, 16 December 1966). Because of the rise in wages, 4 billion rubles more than originally planned had to be invested in retail trade in 1968, according to Baybakov. Spending on everyday services in 1968 had to be raised 3 billion rubles (20 percent) over 1967 (according to Baybakov's deputy, A. Lalayants, in *Ekonomicheskaya Gazeta*, no. 1 [January 1968], pp. 22–23).

Thus, the second half of the five-year plan became light industry oriented instead of agriculture-oriented. As Baybakov put it: "The significant acceleration of the growth of the people's living standard is the main feature of the economic plan for 1968 and the plans for 1969-70. This determined the structure and main tasks of the plans for these years."

The September 1967 decisions meant a considerable revision in the five-year plan adopted in 1966. Industrial growth rates rose: group A (heavy industry) would now grow by 55 percent in the readjusted five-year plan, instead of the previously set 49-52 percent, and group B would grow 49 percent, instead of the previous 43-46 percent. Naturally, the money for the welfare package had to come from somewhere. Part of the resources came from using heavy industry capacity to produce consumer goods. Gosplan Deputy Chairman A. Lalayants wrote: "The measures for raising the standard of living of the people adopted by the September 1967 Central Committee plenum required seeking out additional material resources for meeting the population's ability to purchase. In connection with this it is necessary to stress the role of heavy industry in the production of cultural-everyday and household goods. . . . In 1968 production of these goods at heavy industry enterprises will grow by 1.1 billion rubles, which comprises 50 percent of the general increase in their production."[3] Expanding consumer goods production at heavy industry enterprises had been urged by Moscow City First Secretary N. G. Yegorychev in October 1965 (*Moskovskaya Pravda*, 9 October 1965) and by Yegorychev and Kosygin at the 23d Party Congress. A September 1966 government decision increased consumer goods production in heavy industry and defense plants (*Izvestiya*, 25 September 1966), and Shelepin endorsed the idea at an October 1967 trade union meeting (*Pravda*, 21 October 1967).

In general, however, heavy industry does not appear to have suffered much, since its growth rate was also increased. A steel shortage prevented any cutback in ferrous metallurgy. Investments in ferrous metallurgy rose 20 percent over 1967 in the 1968 plan and more new steel capacity was planned than for 1966 and 1967 combined (according to the Gosplan deputy chairman for ferrous metallurgy, M. A. Pertsev, in the 7 July 1968 *Trud*). Defense spending, instead of being cut, rose steadily, receiving an especially great increase in 1968 budget allocations:

Budget Defense Expeditures (in billions)[4]

1966	1967	1968	1969	1970	1971
13.4	14.5	16.7	17.7	17.9	17.9

[3] *Ekonomicheskaya Gazeta*, no. 1 (January 1968), pp. 22-23.
[4] Garbuzov's budget reports in the 16 December 1966, 11 October 1967, 10 December 1968, 17 December 1969, and 9 December 1970 *Izvestiya*.

In a February 1968 Minsk speech, Kosygin explained that the rise in defense spending was necessitated by the international situation (*Sovetskaya Belorussiya*, 15 February 1968).

The biggest losses were suffered by agriculture. Although some economists complained about this shortchanging,[5] the massive extent was revealed by Brezhnev himself at the October 1968 Central Committee plenum. The original plan[6] provided for 21.2 billion rubles of central state investments in production construction and equipment purchases for agriculture for the first three years of the plan, but "in fact, they have comprised 17.3 billion rubles, or almost 4 billion rubles less" (Brezhnev's report, *Pravda*, 31 October 1968). Investments were reduced in the fertilizer and agricultural equipment industries so that less equipment and fertilizer were delivered than planned. Brezhnev naturally did not blame the leadership decisions to raise funds for other sectors, but rather blamed subordinate organs—especially Gosplan—for quietly draining off funds: "Often planning organs, encountering difficulties in finding capital investments, seek to overcome them with funds designated for agriculture. There are also cases where material-technical resources allotted to agriculture are transferred to other purposes." He cited Azerbaydzhan's use of 3.1 million rubles of agricultural funds to build subways and Moldavia's use of 2.9 million for railroad construction.[7]

The September 1967 shift undoubtedly divided the leadership. It certainly must have been supported by Kosygin, Shelepin, and Voronov, who in recent years have usually stressed consumer goods, particularly as against agriculture. It surely displeased Polyanskiy, who shortly before had protested any weakening of aid to agriculture. Even though Brezhnev presented the plenum report on the welfare program[8] he must have been unenthusiastic about it, both because of the undermining of his agricultural program and also because of the shift of priority from heavy industry to light industry. Brezhnev was more committed to heavy industrial priority than any other Politburo member: only a little more than a year earlier he had flatly asserted that heavy industry priority was an "unchanging principle of our economic policy" (*Pravda*, 11 June 1966).

Though the plenum now set light industry growth ahead of heavy industry, Brezhnev and some others continued to reassert heavy industry's priority— apparently on the grounds that, even though light industry growth was higher in

---

[5]In *Voprosy Ekonomiki*, no. 7 (1968), articles by M. Lemeshev and L. Zlomanov complained that delivery of equipment and fertilizer to farms fell far short of the original five-year-plan goals and that plans for 1968 and 1969 show that this shortfall would continue.

[6]For the whole five-year period 41 billion rubles of state funds were set.

[7]Another way of diverting agricultural resources was described by Agriculture Minister Matskevich in a July 1968 speech (*Selskaya Zhizn*, 6 July 1968). He complained that rural construction units "fully equipped" with resources and funds belonging to agriculture were being assigned to build urban industrial projects.

[8]Brezhnev's report was not published, even in summary, even though one might expect such popular measures to have been widely publicized. Only the short plenum decrees on the specific welfare measures were published.

1968, heavy industry still led for the five-year period taken as a whole. *Pravda's* 28 September 1967 editorial on the 26 September plenum asserted that heavy industry priority "remains the general line of the party" and this formulation was repeated by Finance Minister V. F. Garbuzov in reporting on the 1968 budget to the October 1967 Supreme Soviet session (*Izvestiya*, 11 October 1967). In contrast, Gosplan Chairman Baybakov (who has appeared more closely associated with Kosygin), in reporting on the 1968 plan to the same session, failed to assert heavy industry's continuing priority.

At the big 50th Soviet anniversary ceremony on 3 November Brezhnev declared that "we will continue to devote first rank attention to raising heavy industry" (*Pravda*, 4 November 1967), and a 24 November 1967 *Pravda* editorial repeated his phrase and called heavy industry the "foundation of foundations of our economy." Central Committee Heavy Industry Secretary M. S. Solomentsev wrote in a December 1967 *Kommunist* (no. 18) that now the Soviet state was capable of simultaneously ensuring preferential growth of heavy industry and accelerated development of consumer goods. Brezhnev may have been placated partially by increased aid for metallurgy.[9]

Polyanskiy, however, hinted publicly at his displeasure with the priority shift. Immediately after the 26 September 1967 plenum, Polyanskiy wrote an unusual article in *Kommunist* (no. 15, signed to press 14 October) urging redistributions in favor of agriculture. While paying obeisance to the "huge significance" of the September 1967 plenum decisions and to heavy industry and defense ("The first rank task of the party was and is faster development of heavy industry, the basis of the whole economy. Such a policy was and is dictated also by the tasks of strengthening the country's defense"), he wrote that "high rates of growth of kolkhoz and sovkhoz production are now the same objective necessity as further development of socialist industry." He argued against those taking the view that agriculture's situation had now improved sufficiently to permit diversion of resources elsewhere. Although the five-year plan had increased aid to agriculture, wrote Polyanskiy, "it would be incorrect to suppose that now all questions of raising kolkhozes and sovkhozes have been resolved." He cited Brezhnev's warning against diverting agricultural funds: "In some echelons of our planning and management apparatus, as L. I. Brezhnev has noted more than once, there is still lack of understanding of the importance of faster raising of agriculture and there are still attempts to 'balance' figures in favor of other branches of public production and to correct matters in those at the expense of kolkhozes and sovkhozes. Such tendencies are very dangerous for our general cause, he said." Citing a decision of the 12th Party Congress. Polyanskiy de-

[9] A 2 September 1967 *Pravda* editorial cited a recent Central Committee-Council of Ministers decree on ferrous metallurgy and stated that ferrous metallurgy in 1968-70 must put to use almost twice as much investment in new capacity as in the preceding three years. The 6 August 1967 *Izvestiya* reported a Central Committee-Council of Ministers decree on the rates of ferrous metallurgy development and called for significant intensification of construction rates.

clared that "industry cannot develop by weakening agriculture." "The main question . . . is ensuring high rates of development of kolkhoz and sovkhoz production and establishing sensible proportions between industry and agriculture." "Under present conditions it is especially important to ensure proportional development of all branches of public production and first of all to establish more correct proportions between industry and agriculture."

Polyanskiy wrote that "sharp intensification of rates of growth of kolkhoz and sovkhoz production and its basic funds require some redistribution of national income in favor of agriculture." However, he argued, this would not mean developing agriculture with resources really taken away from other branches. Agriculture generates one-third of the national product yet "significantly less" than this is returned to agriculture. Therefore, simply reinvesting in agriculture the income that it produces itself "would fully satisfy the needs of agriculture." Specifically, Polyanskiy argued for a "fairer exchange between industrial and agricultural production" and a "readjustment of prices of agricultural goods as against industrial goods." "Price formation," he wrote, "is not only a big economic problem but also a political problem." He also argued for "raising of the technical equipping of kolkhoz and sovkhoz production," which "requires significant expansion of the capacity of tractor, vehicle, and agricultural machine building, that is, some change of proportions in developing industry itself, and acceleration of growth rates of those of its branches which are directly connected with agriculture."

Right after the appearance of Polyanskiy's article, he received support from Brezhnev, who declared in his 3 November speech on the 50th anniversary of the revolution that "the country is now in a position to invest more funds in agriculture" (*Pravda*, 4 November 1967). However, the shift in favor of light industry was written into law by the October 1967 Supreme Soviet session.[10] What is more, the plenum and Supreme Soviet session not only adopted the plan for 1968 but inexplicably approved plans for 1969 and 1970 as well, thus making it difficult to reverse the 1968 priority shift in the following year's plan.

In addition, the consumer goods advocates continued to press their advantage. *Izvestiya* on 27 February 1968 reported that the government had recently adopted a decision to produce additional consumer goods and expand services in 1968 by over one billion rubles. Immediately after the adoption of their priority shift, Kosygin and Baybakov began preparations for the next five-year plan, with an eye to retaining light industry's advantage. On 25 December 1967 Kosygin met with participants in an RSFSR agricultural seminar and discussed "correct determining of the basic proportions in the development of the economy for 1971–1975 and the organization of the coming work of compiling the new

[10] Supreme Soviet sessions normally approve the annual plans in December. The timing in 1967—just before the much ballyhooed November 1967 50th anniversary of the October revolution—suggests that the big welfare package was designed as an anniversary present to put the people in a mood to celebrate the jubilee.

five-year plan" (*Sovetskaya Rossiya*, 26 December 1967). Baybakov, in his report to a 14-17 May 1968 national economic conference, declared that "now we have all conditions for making the development of industry, agriculture, construction and transportation in the future five-year plan subordinate to the tasks of further substantial raising of the living standard of the workers. The Central Committee CPSU and Council of Ministers USSR think that precisely this must be the main goal of the USSR economic development plan for 1971-1975" (*Ekonomicheskaya Gazeta*, no. 21, [May 1968]). He specified that the basic directions of the 1971-75 plan should be presented to the directing organs already in August 1968. Kosygin, in his 14 February 1968 Minsk speech, declared that the Politburo and Council of Ministers recently had examined the basic questions of preparing the new five-year plan and had decided that the 1971-75 plan must be ratified in 1969 (*Sovetskaya Belorussiya*, 15 February 1968). Implying no need for further aid to agriculture, Kosygin declared "we have the possibility of fully satisfying the country's need for foodstuffs and for maintaining our grain reserves" and recalled the past resource redistributions in agriculture's favor. In contrast, Brezhnev was attempting to redirect attention to agriculture. In his 16 February 1968 Leningrad speech, he declared that the Politburo had adopted a decision to study the implementation of agricultural decisions at the next plenum, but he did not get his agricultural plenum until October 1968. The next two plenums—in April and July 1968—were devoted to foreign affairs, primarily the Czech situation.

Nevertheless, there was some important readjustment in agriculture's favor in 1968. A May 1968[11] Central Committee-Council of Ministers decree on the fertilizer industry complained that neglect by ministries had led to the nonfulfillment of 1966-67 goals for building new fertilizer capacity. Declaring that the Central Committee and Council of Ministers considered development of the fertilizer industry "one of the very important party and state tasks," the decree ordered a drastic increase in fertilizer output: 48 million tons in the next five years. The highest rates of growth were set for 1969 and 1970: 13 million tons a year of new capacity—according to the decree, almost four times that introduced in 1966 and 1967.[12] The goal for the end of 1972 was set at 95 million tons—as against 43 million tons produced in 1968 (according to Chemical Industry Minister L. A. Kostandov in the 4 January 1969 *Selskaya Zhizn*) and the 1970 goal of 62-65 million tons set in the 1966 five-year plan directives (*Pravda*, 20 February 1966).[13] This marked a considerable restoration of Khrushchev's overambitious

[11] The decree was published in the 6 June 1968 *Pravda*, but Chemical Industry Minister Kostandov identified it as adopted in May—*Selskaya Zhizn*, 4 January 1969.

[12] Brezhnev's October 1968 plenum report stated that capacity had increased only 11-12 million tons in the first three years of the plan (1966-68) combined—*Pravda*, 31 October 1968.

[13] At the October 1967 Supreme Soviet session, Baybakov used the lower variant—62 million tons—as the 1970 goal, declaring fertilizer production capacity would grow by 31

fertilizer program, which had stirred intense opposition among defenders of the military and heavy industry and which was roundly denounced after Khrushchev's fall.

Izvestiya on 7 September 1968 announced a government decree on production of agricultural machinery and spare parts, raising the earlier goals for equipment production to a value of 2,011,000,000 rubles in 1969 and 2,187,000,000 rubles in 1970. Baybakov's figure for 1968 had been 1.8 billion rubles. At the March 1965 plenum Brezhnev had promised 1,790,000 tractors during the coming five-year plan, reaching an annual output of 625,000 by 1970—double the 1965 output. He promised to double truck production—producing 1,100,000 in the five-year period, as against 394,000 in the previous plan.[14] These goals were confirmed in the draft five-year plan directives adopted by the February 1966 plenum (*Pravda*, 20 February 1966). Actual output fell far short of these goals, however, and even the planned goals were reduced in 1968. These targets were given in Baybakov's annual plan reports:[15]

	1966	1967	1968	1969	1970
Tractors (in thousands)	263	287	307	306	312
Trucks (in thousands)	130	150	165	155	156.5

Even these target figures amounted to only 1,475,000 tractors and 756,500 trucks—far less than Brezhnev's March 1965 promise. And actual output continued to lag in 1969. I. Kuznetsov, head of a sector of the Central Committee Agriculture Section, wrote in a September 1969 *Agitator* (no. 18, p. 26) that in the first half of 1969 industry delivered 145,000 tractors and 58,500 trucks—3,000 more tractors and 18,500 more trucks than in the first half of 1968. This rate was considerably short of the 1969 annual goal.

At the October 1968 plenum Brezhnev stated the case for increasing investments in agriculture, based on the need for agricultural production to keep pace with growing consumption. After stressing the projected rise in fertilizer production, Brezhnev addressed himself to the next five-year plan, which, he noted, Gosplan was already working on: "The provision of equipment for agricultural production naturally requires big capital investments from the state and kolkhozes. And we must always consider this and find the opportunities to allocate from our national income funds which would satisfy the growing needs of the countryside and would ensure harmonious development of all branches of the national economy. We must firmly follow this line also in working out the national economic plan for the coming five year period" (*Pravda*, 31 October 1968).

---

million tons during the five-year plan (*Izvestiya*, 11 October 1967). The 1966 directives listed 31.3 million tons as the 1965 production figure.

[14] Stenographic report of the March 1965 plenum, p. 22.

[15] *Izvestiya*, 8 December 1965, 16 December 1966, 11 October 1967, 10 December 1968, 17 December 1969.

Brezhnev reported that the Politburo had decided to retain the procurement plans at about the same level in the 1971-75 plan as in the 1965-70 plan and that the local 1971-75 plans should be worked out and sent to each farm at the beginning of 1970. Meanwhile, the Politburo refused to raise procurement prices (Brezhnev: "The Politburo thinks that for the near future we should basically maintain the existing procurement prices"). He noted with approval the suggestion by many comrades that the 50 percent bonuses for above-plan purchases of grain be extended to other agricultural products. The plenum decree approved Brezhnev's proposals (*Pravda*, 1 November 1968). At the plenum Brezhnev also defended his lagging May 1966 land improvement program, declaring that "now everyone recognizes that we acted correctly in raising the big question of land improvement at the May plenum." He criticized construction ministries for not fulfilling irrigation and drainage construction plans.

The Village Reorganization Program

Another serious setback for Polyanskiy occurred in 1967-68 also. In early 1967 a big rural reconstruction program aimed at consolidating the Soviet Union's 700,000 villages into 110-120,000 was inaugurated. Apparently as part of this decision, a USSR Rural Construction Ministry was finally established about the same time.[16] Although most of the activity was just preparation of plans for the new villages and rural apartment houses, rather than actual construction, even this cost money.[17] And, of course, machinery and materials had to be allotted for the new construction organizations being formed to begin construction of the new villages.[18]

Polyanskiy, as first deputy premier in charge of agriculture, was primarily responsible for running the rural construction program, and he soon appealed for funds. In his 10 June 1967 Blagoveshchensk speech, Polyanskiy declared that the time had come to reconstruct villages on a national scale and "regardless of the difficulties of this task, we can and must solve it with the efforts of the whole country." In his October 1967 *Kommunist* article he again appealed for funds, calling for a speed-up in the preparation of village reorganization plans and stating that the rural construction program would "undoubtedly require large efforts and significant funds." But the ambitious program ran into a flurry of public criticism in late 1967—by coincidence, the same time agriculture was

[16]Polyanskiy in his October 1967 *Kommunist* article wrote that "creation of a special Rural Construction Ministry ... was aimed precisely at ensuring the successful implementation of the party program's instructions on rebuilding the countryside."

[17]Lithuanian First Deputy Premier K. Kayris complained in the 15 June 1968 *Selskaya Zhizn* that progress was being slowed because insufficient funds were being allotted for compiling plans for the new villages.

[18]See Belorussian Deputy Premier V. G. Kamenskiy's speech in the 2 July 1968 *Selskaya Zhizn.*

suffering its big resource cutback. Quite likely, the public attacks were sanctioned by higher authorities. In any case, in 1968 they led to admissions of errors by Polyanskiy's subordinates, a slowdown of the program, and finally a Central Committee decree criticizing the handling of the program—all of which must have been embarrassing to Polyanskiy.

The new village reorganization and rural housing construction program was a less extreme version of Khrushchev's old *agrogorod* or village consolidation plan. Fewer villages were to be eliminated than under Khrushchev. Support shifted from Khrushchev's multi-story rural apartment buildings—which were designed to transform kolkhozniks into workers—to more one- and two-story buildings. Khrushchev's insistence on using urban-type industrial construction methods and materials (for example, prefabricated concrete parts) was condemned in favor of using more practical and cheaper methods and materials (for example, cheaper local building materials, bricks, etc.).

The prototype of the new program was worked out in Belorussia in 1965 and then adopted by the USSR State Committee on Construction Affairs (Gosstroy) in early 1967. Belorussian Gosstroy Deputy Chairman N. Divakov wrote an article in the 28 April 1965 *Ekonomicheskaya Gazeta* (pp. 19–20) reporting Belorussia's decision to reduce its 32,000 villages to 5,000 and attacking the USSR Gosplan and Gosstroy for "in practice" not doing anything to promote planning of new village construction. He assailed the "mechanical" transfer of urban-type housing to villages and advocated two-story apartment buildings with 2, 4, or 8 apartments each with two levels. These, he argued, had some of the advantages of multi-story buildings (being cheaper than building one-story buildings) and also the advantages of one-story buildings (each family has a ground-level entrance with adjoining private plot). He called on the USSR Gosstroy to revise its standard housing designs and work out designs for two-story, two-level apartment buildings.

The USSR Gosstroy adopted Belorussia's two-story, two-level buildings and, in response to Divakov's article, sent a group from Gosstroy's Main Administration for Rural Construction Planning and from various design institutes to Belorussia. This group, together with the Belorussian Gosstroy, worked out recommendations on village planning which were then adopted by the Belorussian Council of Ministers (*Ekonomicheskaya Gazeta*, 11 August 1965, p. 20).

At a February 1967 Belorussian rural construction conference, Belorussian plans for consolidation of villages and building rural housing were endorsed by USSR Gosstroy Chairman I. T. Novikov, who cited Belorussia as an example for other areas. Belorussian leaders began propagating the program in the central press,[19] and in 1967 and early 1968 *Selskaya Zhizn* and *Ekonomicheskaya*

---

[19] Belorussian Central Committee Agriculture Secretary D. F. Filimonov in *Ekonomicheskaya Gazeta*, no. 52 (December 1967); Belorussian Rural Construction Minister N. Kashcheyev in *Pravda*, 13 January 1968; Belorussian Gosstroy Chairman V. Korol in *Selskaya Zhizn*, 28 December 1967.

Gazeta gave much publicity to Belorussia's work. In January 1968 I. Lanshin, head of a sector of the Central Committee Construction Section, wrote that the Central Committee had recently studied Belorussia's village reorganization work (*Partiynaya Zhizn*, no. 1 [1968]), and Moscow Obkom Secretary Moshchevitin reported that the Moscow Oblast Executive Committee had adopted the "Belorussian rural construction experience approved by the Central Committee" and had sent its construction and planning representatives to Belorussia to study its work (*Partiynaya Zhizn*, no. 2 [1969]). New USSR Rural Construction Minister S. Khitrov declared that his ministry was going to study Belorussian rural construction methods in order to determine policy for other republics (*Ekonomicheskaya Gazeta*, no. 1 [1968], p. 18).

Late in 1967 this program ran into serious public criticism—not over the expense involved but over its goals and its bureaucratic management. N. Chetunova in the 30 August 1967 *Literaturnaya Gazeta* attacked the Gosstroy ban on construction in villages designated for later destruction and Gosstroy's unattractive standardized two-story, two-level apartment buildings. Chetunova favored the slowest program possible and insisted on one-story buildings where kolkhozniks could retain their private plots. The editor of the construction department of *Selskaya Zhizn*,[20] P. B. Vaynshteyn, replied to the Chetunova article in the 5 December 1967 *Literaturnaya Gazeta* assailing Chetunova for opposing progress and demanding that Gosstroy move even faster in eliminating villages. Gorkiy Obkom Agriculture Secretary V. I. Semenov sided partially with Chetunova in the 5 December 1967 *Literaturnaya Gazeta*, criticizing Vaynshteyn and Gosstroy and urging provision of one-story buildings for kolkhozniks and two-story buildings for sovkhoz workers and urging better designs. Semenov reported many arguments in Gorkiy over rural housing. His colleague in resolving these problems, Gorkiy Obkom Construction Secretary I. N. Dmitriyev, later became Central Committee Construction Section head.

Literaturnaya Gazeta continued publishing articles critical of Gosstroy[21] and finally, as a direct result of these criticisms, Polyanskiy personally intervened. In March 1968 he invited both the leaders and backers of the village reorganization program (Gosstroy First Deputy Chairman G. N. Fomin, *Selskaya Zhizn* chief editor P. F. Alekseyev and construction editor P. B. Vaynshteyn) and their critics (Mozhayev and Kukhovarenko) to his office for a discussion (*Literaturnaya Gazeta*, 20 March 1968). After the meeting, officials admitted the validity of some of the criticisms and promised modifications (Gosstroy First Deputy Chairman Fomin in the 5 June and 6 August 1968 *Selskaya Zhizn*, Vaynshteyn in the 7 June 1968 *Selskaya Zhizn*, and Deputy Agriculture Minister A. F. Dubrovin in the 17 April 1968 *Literaturnaya Gazeta*).

---

[20]*Selskaya Zhizn*, usually close to Polyanskiy's viewpoint, played a leading role in the village reorganization campaign, as well as the campaign for rural construction ministries.
[21]Agronomist A. Kukhovarenko on 24 January 1968, I. Kopysov on 7 February, and B. Mozhayev on 21 February.

The Central Committee Secretariat stepped in to call an All-Union conference on rural construction for 1–6 July 1968.[22] At this conference, Gosstroy Chairman I. T. Novikov also conceded some shortcomings (that designs were poor, that more than just two-story designs were needed, and that comfort—not economy—must be the main criterion), but he still urged what critic Chetunova termed a "superhasty" program of village reorganization.[23] Novikov demanded completion of national village reorganization plans by 1970 and for all rayons by 1971 (*Selskaya Zhizn*, 2 July 1968). In contrast, Agriculture Minister Matskevich at the same conference warned that haste could compromise the whole program and urged it be completed over the next five years—instead of in Novikov's two to three years.

Chetunova (*Literaturnaya Gazeta*, 21 August 1968) directly criticized Gosstroy's haste and praised those republics which were proceeding especially slowly—for example, Estonia and Latvia. Some other republics were clearly unenthusiastic also. Georgia's Gosstroy chairman warned at the conference against consolidation of mountain villages.[24] Georgian Rural Construction Planning Institute director V. Chkheidze had earlier admitted that Georgia was slow even in beginning its planning work (*Selskaya Zhizn*, 4 April 1968). Armenian First Secretary A. Ye. Kochinyan also urged a go-slow policy in village reorganization, especially for Armenia with its mountain villages, declaring that haste and wilful decisions could discredit a generally good idea (*Selskaya Zhizn*, 11 July 1968). The Turkmen Gosstroy chairman said at the conference that despite a sharp housing shortage in his republic many new two-story apartment buildings were empty because peasants refused to move in, insisting on one-story buildings.[25] The two-story buildings were objected to not only because of lack of adjoining private plots but also because their design failed to take into account hot weather conditions, making them unliveable in Central Asia.[26] Fomin complained of slow progress in rayon planning in Georgia, Armenia, Azerbaydzhan, and Turkmenia (*Ekonomicheskaya Gazeta*, no. 41 [October 1968]).

The surge of opposition stirred up by the program and the revelations of its obvious shortcomings certainly must have embarrassed its supervisor, Polyanskiy, particularly when the leadership intervened to call the July 1968 rural construction conference and then to issue a 12 September 1968[27] Central Committee–Council of Ministers decree criticizing the rural construction program for "serious shortcomings." The program which was intended to save money by building standardized multi-story buildings (the most economical) was

[22] Fomin in the 21 August 1968 *Literaturnaya Gazeta*.

[23] Chetunova in the 21 August 1968 *Literaturnaya Gazeta*.

[24] According to Chetunova in the 21 August 1968 *Literaturnaya Gazeta*.

[25] Ibid.

[26] In addition, large Muslim families in Central Asia often found the apartments too small.

[27] The date of the decree is cited by Belorussian Central Committee Secretary A. A. Smirnov in the 19 December 1969 *Sovetskaya Belorussiya*.

criticized for ineffective use of funds and poor architectural and planning decisions (*Pravda*, 2 October 1968). The decree endorsed the slower schedule for working out plans (five years).

Most of the decree's criticisms and demands had already been recognized by Gosstroy Chairman Novikov at the July Minsk conference and by Gosstroy First Deputy Chairman Fomin in his August article: ordering better architectural work; retention of only the best of the present housing designs and the working out of new designs considering local agricultural conditions, nationality differences, and landscape characteristics; the participation of local representatives in planning; the shifting of more responsibility from the central Gosstroy to local or republic control; more flexibility; aid to cooperative and individual housing construction; and construction of experimental villages in each oblast.

The debate certainly did not end with the braking of Gosstroy's campaign. In 1969 the program's backers expressed resentment about resistance and lagging. *Selskaya Zhizn* editor Alekseyev expressed his amazement that "some writers" were writing articles doubting the need for urban-type villages and raising problems "long ago resolved" and "savoring mistakes and shortcomings long overcome" (*Zhurnalist* [May 1969]). Belorussian Central Committee Secretary A. A. Smirnov attacked those who argued against multi-story apartment buildings (*Pravda*, 9 November 1969). Fomin in the 23 November 1969 *Pravda* again criticized the reluctant Transcaucasian and Central Asian republics for lagging in drawing up rayon plans.

Voronov's Opposition

The village reorganization program and the movement for rural construction ministries both were initiated by Belorussia under Mazurov and were strongly pushed by the agricultural organ *Selskaya Zhizn*. Polyanskiy championed the village reorganization program and appeared to favor creation of rural construction ministries. As with the creation of such ministries and kolkhoz unions, the opposition to village reorganization appeared to center on RSFSR Premier Voronov and his allies. In contrast to Polyanskiy's appeal for more funds and his ambitious state-run village reorganization program, Voronov and his RSFSR colleagues have consistently stressed a less costly self-help approach. His protégé, RSFSR First Deputy Premier Pysin, in reporting to the August 1966 RSFSR Supreme Soviet session on rural amenities, put the stress on what farms themselves could do and largely avoided what the state should do. Pysin stated that "now kolkhozes have become economically stronger and richer and possess big possibilities for increasing basic nonproduction funds" (*Sovetskaya Rossiya*, 17 August 1966). "Cultural and everyday-life construction will take on large scale through the funds of the kolkhozes and also funds of cooperatives, trade union organizations and enterprises." Declaring it "completely incorrect to count only on getting funds from the state," he said that "we must manage matters so that the most important source of financing of cultural and everyday-life construction is internal reserves and local sources," and local soviets must show initiative in seeking out these sources to finance road building. Kolkhozes and sovkhozes should "most actively" participate in building schools, clubs, etc. and in setting up services. He declared that many sovkhozes and kolkhozes have "big possibilities" for construction by their own means and the state should help the farms organize them and help supply materials to encourage this.

Pysin's line was paralleled by Voronov's July 1969 RSFSR Supreme Soviet speech on housing, in which he declared that since 1965 kolkhoz and sovkhoz income had risen sharply "and this means that now the necessary material base has been created in the villages for carrying out measures to basically rebuild the rural way of life on a big scale" (*Sovetskaya Rossiya*, 31 July 1969). He noted that kolkhoz investments in nonproduction projects had risen two and a half times over the 1965 level. Voronov said: "Of course, provision of facilities for cities and villages requires significant financial and material funds. The state is allotting big sums to this. But along with this, additional resources can and must be sought locally." Again in February 1970, on the occasion of the creation of the RSFSR Kolkhoz Council, Pysin repeated his self-help views. After discussing the existing state aid to agriculture, he concluded that "the task is to use this great help from the state more fully and with greater return, and to bring into action all internal resources of kolkhozes to increase production and sale of grain, meat, milk and other agricultural products in 1970 and succeeding years" (*Sovetskaya Rossiya*, 17 February 1970).

During 1966 and 1967 Voronov and Pysin actively promoted nonstate construction methods, looking to housing construction by kolkhozes or inter-kolkhoz units, by cooperatives, and even by contract with private enterprise construction units. Voronov's ally, Volgograd First Secretary L. S. Kulichenko already at the December 1964 RSFSR Supreme Soviet session had urged creation of an RSFSR interkolkhoz construction organization (*Sovetskaya Rossiya*, 18 December 1964), and the RSFSR established such an association in February 1967 (*Selskaya Zhizn*, 12 February 1967). Although the RSFSR showed less enthusiasm for kolkhoz unions than the Ukraine, interkolkhoz construction organizations proliferated in the RSFSR much faster than in the Ukraine[28] and a Ukrainian Interkolkhoz Construction Association was created only in December 1967 (*Radyanska Ukraina*, 8 December 1967). While Pysin ignored the idea of creating a rural construction ministry in his August 1966 speech, he urged expansion of interkolkhoz construction organizations and farms' own construction work.

Pysin and Voronov clearly favored farms and farmers pooling their own savings to form cooperatives to build housing. The Moscow Oblast leaders—who

---

[28]In 1967 the RSFSR had 806 interkolkhoz construction organizations, while the Ukraine had only 352, even though the total number of all types of interkolkhoz organizations in the Ukraine almost equaled that of the RSFSR: 1,386 to 1,664 (See *Narodnoye Khozyaystvo v 1967 g.* [Moscow, 1968]: 478).

were also the most outspoken in opposing creation of a rural construction ministry—took the lead in promoting rural housing cooperatives (Gosbank official V. Chernyshev in the 5 March 1968 *Selskaya Zhizn*). In June 1968 the Moscow Oblast Executive Committee was granted the right to allow housing cooperatives to build one- and two-story apartment buildings in addition to multi-story buildings, and advantages were established for rural housing cooperatives to encourage their proliferation (*Selskaya Zhizn*, 5 June 1968). Moscow Obkom First Secretary Konotop (*Selskaya Zhizn*, 30 June 1968) and obkom Construction Secretary Moshchevitin (*Ekonomicheskaya Gazeta*, no. 24 [1968], and *Partiynaya Zhizn*, no. 2 [1969]) have urged cooperatives. Even *Selskaya Zhizn's* construction editor Vaynshteyn came around to question why kolkhozes or kolkhozniks who used their own savings should not be able to build even one-family houses if they wished (*Selskaya Zhizn*, 7 June 1968). The September 1968 Central Committee–Council of Ministers decree on rural construction instructed government organs to aid cooperative and individual housing construction (*Pravda*, 2 October 1968).

Voronov even endorsed use of the long officially disapproved private construction workers (*shabashniki*). *Pravda* writer Yu. Chernichenko in a 20 November 1966 *Pravda* article urged a new attitude toward these private enterprise construction units, which Khrushchev had attempted to stamp out. Voronov wrote a letter to *Pravda* on 6 January 1967 endorsing Chernichenko's article and ordering the relevant RSFSR officials to study the article and within three months to present proposals to the RSFSR Council of Ministers on how best to put these hundreds of thousands of uncontrolled construction workers to use.[29] Voronov's action in publicly endorsing a press article was unusual for a Politburo member and Chernichenko's article itself—which appeared to be a bold departure from previous official policy—may have been encouraged in advance by Voronov and Pysin, since Chernichenko probably had ties with Pysin.[30]

[29]The *shabashniki* had some of the same advantages as the links which Voronov favored. Since they contracted for jobs and had direct responsibility for completing the work correctly, they had incentive to work faster and better, and even though they were regarded as illegitimate and more costly, farm leaders often had to turn to them for construction work which otherwise simply would not have been done or done properly by state construction organizations (see Georgiy Radov's article in *Literaturnaya Gazeta*, 3 February 1971, pp. 10–11). Links also do better work because of their more direct responsibility for the work and their economic incentive in achieving the highest harvest.

[30]Chernichenko was a correspondent for the Altay paper *Altayskaya Pravda* in the late 1950's, while Pysin was Altay first secretary (see Chernichenko's November 1965 *Novyy Mir* article in which he attacks Khrushchev and Nalivayko but notes that Pysin was "respected for fairness and strict politeness"). Chernichenko later became nationally prominent as a *Sovetskaya Rossiya* feature writer—during the early 1960's when *Sovetskaya Rossiya* was the organ of the RSFSR Bureau, of which Voronov was first deputy chairman. In late 1965, when *Sovetskaya Rossiya* editor K. I. Zarodov transferred to *Pravda* to become first deputy chief editor, Chernichenko transferred to *Pravda* also, as a feature writer.

By coincidence, Chernichenko has been embroiled with those apparently hostile to Voronov. *Selskaya Zhizn* on 3 December 1966 carried I. Zaytsev's article assailing Chernichenko's late 1965 book of agricultural essays. When Chernichenko attempted to reply, *Selskaya Zhizn* refused to print his response. This was revealed in the April 1967 *Zhurnalist* by Chernichenko's publisher, editor of the Political Literature Publishing House, V. Ya. Gurevich, who attacked *Selskaya Zhizn's* editors for their unfair attack on Chernichenko. Voronov's endorsement of Chernichenko's *Pravda* article came only a month after *Selskaya Zhizn's* attack. During 1966 *Selskaya Zhizn* was attacking the RSFSR for resisting the creation of a rural construction ministry. Shortly afterward, in the 5 May 1967 *Pravda*, Chernichenko attacked Stavropol's handling of sheep raising. The leader of Stavropol, Voronov's old rival Yefremov, in a long, defensive letter to *Pravda* (30 September 1967) admitted that Chernichenko's criticisms were "in the main" correct. However, he refused to heed many of them, such as the need to separate sheep raising from wheat growing. In the September 1971 issue of *Zvezda* Chernichenko recalled his September 1967 criticism of this "dangerous Stavropol error" and happily noted that after Yefremov had been removed and transferred to Moscow in early 1970 his successors reversed his policy and followed Chernichenko's advice.

Though Chernichenko has thus appeared on the side of Voronov and Pysin on some issues, he cannot be considered a spokesman for them and sometimes has taken positions apparently differing from their views (in addition, he has also been a severe critic of Altay Institute director Nalivayko, Pysin's erstwhile protégé).

CHAPTER X

VORONOV VS.
POLYANSKIY: 1969

Although debate over the new five-year plan priorities was continuing behind the scenes, there was less public evidence of this in 1969 than in 1968. Instead, the leaders became deeply involved with questions of agricultural organization: Polyanskiy and Brezhnev were preoccupied with organizing the long-awaited congress of kolkhozniks, while Voronov launched campaigns in the RSFSR for the wide adoption of his long-held ideas on agricultural organization. As in 1966, Voronov had nothing to do with the movement to hold a new congress of kolkhozniks and to establish some sort of kolkhoz union system. For his part, Polyanskiy consistently avoided encouraging any of Voronov's campaigns. Though neither Voronov nor Polyanskiy openly opposed each other's ideas, Voronov apparently helped ʒymie the kolkhoz union movement and Polyanskiy apparently vetoed USSR approval of Voronov's RSFSR programs.

Kolkhoz Unions

The proposals for holding a congress of kolkhozniks and rewriting the outdated kolkhoz charter were revived in 1969 and implemented. However, the more controversial kolkhoz union proposal, though revived also, was subverted, and at the November 1969 Congress of Kolkhozniks a powerless "council" of kolkhozes was created with kolkhoz union foe Matskevich as chairman. This was a victory for the anti-union forces led by Estonian First Secretary Kebin, and apparently behind the scenes by Voronov, and a discouraging compromise if not defeat for Polyanskiy and Brezhnev, who directed preparations for the congress and who appeared to be behind the kolkhoz union movement.

    With the cancellation of the promised congress of kolkhozniks in late 1966, talk of kolkhoz unions disappeared from the newspapers. The only significant endorsements[1] during 1967 were by two men associated with Brezhnev. Moldavian First Secretary I. I. Bodyul (who had worked under Brezhnev while he was first secretary in Moldavia) made a strong plea for kolkhoz unions in a June 1967 issue of *Ekonomicheskaya Gazeta* (no. 21), while Brezhnev's personal agricultural assistant, V. A. Golikov, in a July 1967 *Kommunist* (no. 11) served notice that a new kolkhoz charter and a kolkhoz union system still were on the agenda, writing of measures "which are awaiting implementation," such as "the adoption of a new model kolkhoz charter and the formation of kolkhoz-cooperative organs in rayons, oblasts, krays, republics and in the center."

The December 1967 *Sotsialisticheskaya Zakonnost* reported a discussion of kolkhoz unions in Odessa, indicating the subject was still being debated locally. Although there was no word of activity by the Brezhnev charter commission in 1967, Belyayeva and Kozyr in their December 1967 *Sovetskoye Gosudarstvo i Pravo* article mentioned that a new charter was being worked out and that it had been decided to call a congress of kolkhozniks. *Selskaya Zhizn* on 27 June 1968 announced a meeting of the Brezhnev commission at which Brezhnev spoke and "determined the course of further work"—but there were no further signs of progress in 1968.

Opposition surfaced again in January 1968, when V. Yefimov wrote that "no new organizational forms whatever are needed" and that this had been confirmed by the 23d Congress.[2] After that, proposals stopped, except for minor, obscure references.[3] Also contributing to the pessimistic outlook was economist K. Karpov's 11 January 1969 *Izvestiya* proposal of a weak alternative: "an association of state-cooperative agricultural production-sales enterprises" with state leadership clearly dominant.

Then unexpectedly on 26 March 1969 *Pravda* announced that a meeting of the charter commission had been held and that a new draft charter had been approved and would shortly be published. Polyanskiy delivered the report at the meeting and Brezhnev made a speech. Among the thirteen speakers were at least three kolkhoz unionists: Vladimir kolkhoz chairman A. V. Gorshkov, Ukrainian kolkhoz chairman A. G. Buznitskiy, and Kazakh kolkhoz chairman N. N.

---

[1] The economic journal *Voprosy Ekonomiki* also carried A. Frolikov's pro-union article in January 1967, as well as letters proposing substitute organs which would not conflict with agricultural organs in the July issue. Z. S. Belyayeva and M. I. Kozyr in the December 1967 *Sovetskoye Gosudarstvo i Pravo*, recalling that the 23d Party Congress had "instructed" the Central Committee to consider the creation of kolkhoz unions, advocated strong unions but with some kolkhoz leadership functions left to the state organs as well and urged creation of unions in a number of republics, oblasts, and rayons by way of experiment.

[2] *Pravda*, 17 January 1968. At the same time, Yefimov wrote an article in the January 1968 *Kommunist* (no. 1, p. 55) mentioning the need to make changes in the existing kolkhoz charter.

[3] In the no. 9 *Novyy Mir*, G. Lisichkin mentioned the need for rayon-level councils of kolkhozes and in the no. 10 *Neva*, L. Ivanov cited a kolkhoz chairman's proposal for a new charter, new congress of kolkhozniks, and a national kolkhoz union system.

Golovatskiy. Commission member Golovatskiy wrote in the 26 April *Kazakh-stanskaya Pravda* that the kolkhoz union issue had been discussed at this commission session and that kolkhoz unions apparently would be approved. He also asserted that Brezhnev had approved them at the 23d Congress. On 24 April *Pravda* published the draft charter and called for broad public discussion of it, to be concluded with an All-Union Congress of Kolkhozniks scheduled for November 1969. The new draft skirted the kolkhoz union issue—as it did virtually every other controversial issue—by simply granting kolkhozes the right to join "associations and unions."

Despite this breakthrough, however, kolkhoz unionists appeared weaker in 1969 than in 1966. Republic congresses of kolkhozniks in the fall failed to generate strong support, and only Moldavia, Turkmenia, and Kirgizia came out clearly for kolkhoz unions, while the Ukraine and Latvia—which had favored kolkhoz unions in 1966—switched to a less committed stance. On the eve of the Moldavian congress, an article by V. Yakovlev claimed that the 23d Party Congress decisions had envisaged creation of kolkhoz unions (*Sovetskaya Moldaviya*, 20 September 1969), while Moldavian First Secretary I. I. Bodyul declared at the Moldavian congress that "the idea of creating kolkhoz unions has long been promoted by leaders of kolkhozes and party and soviet organs of the republic" and argued vigorously for such unions (*Sovetskaya Moldaviya*, 31 October 1969). Turkmen First Secretary B. Ovezov endorsed unions at the Turkmen congress (*Turkmenskaya Iskra*, 1 November 1969), and Kirgiz Central Committee Agriculture Secretary A. Duysheyev argued at length for their creation in an article published on the day the Kirgiz congress opened (*Sovetskaya Kirgiziya*, 17 October 1969). Some encouragement also was heard from Kazakhstan. A 4 November *Kazakhstanskaya Pravda* article by G. Kurmanov, director of the Kazakh Institute for Economics and Organization of Agriculture, complained that the Agriculture Ministry in essence worked only for sovkhozes (which predominated in Kazakhstan) and urged creation of a system of kolkhoz leadership through the republic level that would be separate from the ministry.

The Ukrainians—previously the main force behind the union movement—now reflected either pessimism or lack of enthusiasm. First Deputy Premier N. T. Kalchenko's keynote report to the Ukrainian congress failed even to mention unions (*Radyanska Ukraina*, 13 November 1969) and First Secretary Shelest's speech only made passing reference to the new draft charter's granting the right of kolkhozes to join associations and unions (*Radyanska Ukraina*, 15 November 1969). Latvian First Secretary A. Voss also simply cited the draft charter provision in his Latvian congress address (*Sovetskaya Latviya*, 4 November 1969).

On the other hand, the Estonian kolkhoz union foes came out vigorously against unions. *Pravda* on 3 November 1969 reported that speakers at the Estonian congress had indicated that "creation of new organs for administering kolkhozes could put kolkhozes in an unequal position in comparison with sovkhozes" and "in addition, the expenses for their upkeep would be an unnecessary burden on the kolkhozes." First Secretary Kebin himself, on 21 November—only four days before the all-union congress opened—wrote in *Pravda* that there was no need for any "additional administrative interkolkhoz organ." "Only united leadership of farms" facilitates agricultural progress, he maintained, and rayon production administrations are "the most efficient forms of leadership." Interkolkhoz associations are fine, but they must not have either administrative or even coordinating functions. "The rayon production administrations and republic Agriculture Ministry can fully handle coordination of the activities of cooperative interkolkhoz associations," wrote Kebin. The Estonian view largely prevailed.

When the All-Union Congress of Kolkhozniks opened on 25 November 1969 even the term "kolkhoz union" was dropped. Brezhnev and Polyanskiy in their opening speeches urged establishment of "councils" and defined their functions as discussion of kolkhoz activities, generalization of the experience of organization of production, and working out of recommendations for fuller use of kolkhoz reserves (*Pravda*, 26 November 1969). Only five congress speakers bothered to endorse the Brezhnev–Polyanskiy proposal: Moscow kolkhoz chairman I. I. Kukhar (*Pravda*, 27 November), Tadzhik kolkhoz chairman M. Makhmudov (in the 28 November *Pravda* but not in the *Selskaya Zhizn* account), Tula kolkhoz chairman I. M. Semenov and Moldavian kolkhoz chairman D. Kh. Rashkulev (in the 27 November *Selskaya Zhizn* but not in the *Pravda* accounts), and Matskevich (*Pravda*, 29 November). Long-time kolkhoz union advocates—such as Kiev kolkhoz chairman A. G. Buznitskiy and Vladimir kolkhoz chairman A. V. Gorshkov—and delegates from most pro-union areas skirted the subject in their speeches.

The powerless elective "council" system established at the end of the congress differed completely from Polyanskiy's own 1959 definition of kolkhoz unions. The new councils not only did not weaken the Agriculture Ministry, but perhaps even strengthened its control over kolkhozes, bringing sovkhozes and kolkhozes under unified leadership as desired by Matskevich, Kebin, Voronov, and others. The leading foe of kolkhoz unions, Agriculture Minister Matskevich, became chairman of the new All-Union Council, and republic councils were headed by republic agriculture ministers, and oblast and rayon councils by oblast and rayon agriculture administration chiefs. The All-Union Council of Kolkhozniks includes the agriculture ministers of all 15 republics as well as the USSR minister and two oblast agriculture administration chiefs—18 of the 125 members. In addition, several other ministerial-level agricultural officials are members.

A "conference of representatives" of the All-Union Council—obviously Matskevich and the core of officials on the council rather than the rank-and-file kolkhoz chairmen members—drew up an official document ("Recommendations for Election of Councils of Kolkhozniks in Rayons, Okrugs, Krays and Republics") setting the norms of representation on the lower-level councils (*Izvestiya*, 6 February 1970). It stipulated that at least 75 percent of the rayon council members must be kolkhozniks. The quota for higher-level councils has not been cited, but 79 percent of the All-Union Council members are kolkhozniks and most republic councils have around 75 percent (Lithuania, Belorussia, and the Ukraine are highest with over 80 percent).

However, Estonia and Georgia, which have been unenthusiastic about kolkhoz unions and which have appeared to strongly defend the rayon echelons,[4] showed marked favoritism for the agricultural bureaucracy in establishing their kolkhoz councils. Only 67 percent of the Estonian council's members appear to be kolkhozniks and only 61 percent of Georgia's. While 54 percent of the Ukrainian council members are kolkhoz chairmen and most republics have over 40 percent kolkhoz chairmen, Estonia has only 36 percent and Georgia only 27 percent. On the other hand, over 20 percent of Georgian and Estonian council members are agriculture ministry officials (compared to only 5 percent of Ukrainian members): Georgia has 12 ministry officials on its 59-member council, Estonia 16 on its 77-member council, while the Ukraine has only 6 on its 115-member council. Georgia has almost as many agriculture ministry officials on it (12) as kolkhoz chairmen (16). Estonia includes the rayon agriculture administration chiefs of all its 15 rayons.

The tendency to pack local councils with agricultural and other government officials became so marked in some places that it provoked an attack in *Izvestiya* on 6 February 1970, in which a letter was published criticizing a Saratov rayon council for violating the official recommendations because only 60 percent of its members were kolkhozniks instead of the stipulated 75 percent. *Izvestiya* also criticized other Saratov rayon councils for including too many nonkolkhozniks. On 18 March *Izvestiya* reported that Saratov authorities had ordered new elections to correct these errors.

Despite the fact that the RSFSR held no congress of kolkhozniks in November 1969 (the only republic not to do so), it did create an RSFSR Council of Kolkhozniks in February 1970 and this occasion was used as a forum to voice the views of the RSFSR leadership on agricultural issues. Pysin, who keynoted the meeting, promoted his and Voronov's views on self-help for agriculture (instead of new investment) and wider application of links, and elaborated on the Brezhnev–Polyanskiy definition of kolkhoz councils' duties—in order to "give a correct orientation to their activities from their very beginning" (*Sovetskaya Rossiya*, 17 February 1970).

The RSFSR and Estonian leaders have shown the most willingness to discuss the new councils—perhaps reflecting their satisfaction at sidetracking the kolkhoz union movement into the creation of powerless councils. While most republics have established councils without discussion (and apparently without enthusiasm), RSFSR First Deputy Premier Pysin and Estonian Agriculture

---

[4] Estonian First Secretary Kebin and Georgian First Secretary Mzhavanadze were the two republic leaders who openly resisted the creation of interrayon organs at the March 1962 plenum.

Minister Myannik made extensive comments on the councils' power. Pysin detailed for them a number of minor duties, and Myannik in the January 1970 *Kommunist Estonii* stressed that the council is not an administrative organ, has no funds or power over investments, but is to assist in implementing policy. However, he said, because of the inclusion of leaders of many state organizations instead of just kolkhoz leaders it could play a big role and would soon make a recommendation on investments.

Even though kolkhoz union supporters surely must have been sorely disappointed there have been few open hints of displeasure,[5] and, in the absence of any encouragement from Brezhnev or Polyanskiy, these hints have been very cautious. In the 10 July 1970 *Literaturnaya Rossiya*, journalist Ivan Vinnichenko, reporting kolkhoz chairman M. I. Kovalenko's views, wrote that in addition to their present duties the new councils should start dealing with "practical questions" such as organizing "production cooperation." In an 18 September 1970 *Literaturnaya Rossiya* article Vinnichenko expressed regret that the new councils have concentrated all their attention on working out recommendations for internal specialization, effective forms of wages, etc., instead of handling "production cooperation of farms." The 23 January 1971 *Izvestiya* reported some kolkhoz chairmen complaining that local kolkhoz councils can only give recommendations and urging that the councils be given the right to adopt practical decisions and coordinate kolkhozes' activities. In a March 1971 *Kommunist* (no. 4, p. 34) kolkhoz union champion M. Kovalenko criticized shortcomings in the work of the new kolkhoz councils and lack of coordination of interkolkhoz organizations, urging that they be combined under one leadership. The first direct proposal for kolkhoz unions since 1969 appeared in an obscure academic journal in early 1971. In the economic series of the *Izvestiya Akademii Nauk SSR* (1 [1971]: 54 and 57), Yu. I. Krasnopoyas wrote that the new kolkhoz councils are only "consultative organs working under corresponding organs of the Ministry of Agriculture" and urged improvement of interkolkhoz administrative functions by creating kolkhoz unions, instead of "concentrating these functions of administration in agricultural or other state organs."

On the other side, however, an RSFSR Agriculture Ministry official (V. Filimonov, deputy chief of the Main Administration for Kolkhoz Affairs) criticized some councils for "trying to take upon themselves functions which do not belong to them" and for "giving orders to kolkhozes" (*Selskoye Khozyaystvo Rossii* [March 1971]: 45). And in March 1971 the Agriculture Ministry further tightened its grip on the USSR Council of Kolkhozes. At a 12 March meeting of

---

[5] At least in the press. Locally, there was grumbling. An 8 January 1972 *Pravda* article by a Belorussian raykom secretary, S. Dikun, recalls that "when rayon councils of kolkhozes were created, various opinions were expressed among us. Some said that this would bring great good. Others skeptically remarked: What good are they? After all, these organs are advisory."

the council which apparently heard ministry complaints that some councils were discussing production questions which were the responsibility of agricultural organs[6] a statute was adopted defining more precisely the councils' functions and relations with agricultural departments. It specified that councils have the right only to give recommendations to kolkhozes, not orders. The meeting also reorganized the leadership of the council, creating an eleven-man ruling presidium, reelecting Matskevich chairman, and electing kolkhoz chairmen I. M. Semenov and A. G. Buznitskiy deputy chairmen, and P. A. Makeyev secretary (*Sovetskaya Rossiya* and *Selskaya Zhizn*, 13 March 1971, and *Ekonomika Selskogo Khozyaystva* 6 [1971] : 27-41). Thus, the daily organizational work of the council now will be run by secretary Makeyev, who is the Agriculture Ministry official in charge of kolkhozes (chief of the ministry's Main Administration for Kolkhoz Affairs) and who had not even been elected to the council at the 1969 congress of kolkhozniks.

Voronov's Initiatives

In 1969 Voronov took the initiative in agricultural policy, moving boldly ahead to adopt and enforce in his republic policies which he had long favored but which USSR authorities either opposed or were unable to act upon. This was in contrast to the 1965-68 period when Voronov made few significant public statements and undertook few official initiatives. In view of the lack of enthusiasm for these policies on the part of Polyanskiy, Voronov's actions must have intensified their conflict.

In March 1969 Voronov's RSFSR government approved the unregulated mechanized link system of farm labor and in June 1969 adopted a big program to create specialized meat-cattle farms. The idea behind both of these was to organize agricultural production more efficiently—cutting production costs rather than simply injecting more funds into agriculture. As such, they appeared in accordance with Voronov's lack of enthusiasm for Polyanskiy's appeals for more money, and Voronov has personally argued strongly for them both in subsequent interviews and speeches. In a third initiative, Voronov reorganized the RSFSR construction ministries, establishing a housing construction ministry in July 1969. Thus, Voronov, who long resisted the establishment of a rural construction ministry in 1965-66, partially reversed that reorganization.

In all three of these initiatives, RSFSR policy is at variance with that of the USSR, whose officials (led by Polyanskiy) have studiously ignored these policies of the largest Soviet republic. Voronov's 1969 initiatives in enunciating and adopting policies may have been aimed at developing the valuable image of an innovative, dynamic leader willing to take a stand on controversial issues,

---

[6] These complaints were made by L. Zaytsev, deputy chief of the Agriculture Ministry's Main Administration for Kolkhoz Affairs, and his subordinate A. Ivanov in their report on the council's March meeting (*Ekonomika Selskogo Khozyaystva* 6 [1971]: 27).

which may appeal to those dissatisfied with the present uninspiring collective of leaders. Interestingly, Voronov's initiatives began shortly after he had suffered a sharp setback in the Politburo, losing his preferred number five status and dropping toward the bottom of the list of Politburo members.

In March 1969 the RSFSR Council of Ministers approved the mechanized link and unregulated work system developed by Pervitskiy in the Kuban and by the Trud Sovkhoz in Volgograd and ordered the RSFSR Agriculture Ministry to work out recommendations to apply them widely (*Sovetskaya Rossiya*, 19 March 1969). On 11 May 1969 *Komsomolskaya Pravda* carried an interview with Voronov on the link decision. In it he strongly endorsed links and repeated arguments against all-purpose kolkhoz brigades which he had used already in his 4 October 1960 *Selskaya Zhizn* article. Voronov has been the only Politburo member to endorse the links—although Politburo candidate member Kunayev later did also.[7]

Voronov's deputy, Pysin, in his speech at the establishment of the RSFSR Council of Kolkhozniks in February 1970, also strongly pushed links, complaining that they "still have not found widespread application" and calling on agricultural organs and farm leaders to discuss them at meetings of the new councils of kolkhozniks and to work out recommendations to apply them more widely starting in 1970 (*Sovetskaya Rossiya*, 17 February 1970). Another sign that RSFSR authorities intended to enforce their link recommendations and crack down on opposition within their borders appeared in a 17 March 1970 *Sovetskaya Rossiya* editorial assailing officials for forbidding links in a Dagestan sovkhoz. This was labeled "ignoring a decision of the RSFSR Council of Ministers."

Voronov's endorsement of links was not fortuitous: his two top deputies, Pysin and Shkolnikov, had long ago approved the creation of links in their regions while first secretaries of the Altay and Volgograd. *Pravda* on 14 August 1960 described Altay's introduction of mechanized units with attached land and Pysin argued at length for this system at the January 1961 plenum.[8] Volgograd had been one of the pioneers in establishing mechanized links in 1958 and 1959.[9] After experimentation with individual links, the Volgograd leaders in 1965 transferred a whole kolkhoz to links[10] and transferred many sovkhozes to links in 1966. The Trud Sovkhoz experiment was organized in February 1966 by oblast Executive Committee Chairman V. P. Borodin and local leaders (*Pravda*,

---

[7]In a December 1969 speech, Kunayev assailed opposition to links and other experimentation (*Kazakhstanskaya Pravda*, 25 December 1969).

[8]Stenographic record of the January 1961 Central Committee plenum, p. 286.

[9]According to Voronov in the 11 May 1969 *Komsomolskaya Pravda* and Volgograd Agriculture Administration chief V. S. Ivanenko in the 28 June 1969 *Komsomolskaya Pravda*.

[10]Volgograd First Secretary Kulichenko in the 15 January 1969 *Selskaya Zhizn*.

30 August 1966). By early 1968 Volgograd had 100 links[11] and Volgograd leaders began to promote them in the central press.[12] Voronov himself presumably was apprised of the Volgograd experiments at an early stage: he visited Volgograd in August 1965 (shortly before First Secretary Shkolnikov became his assistant) inspecting farms and discussing the "condition and prospects for further development of agriculture" in Volgograd (*Sovetskaya Rossiya*, 13 August 1965). When the RSFSR Council of Ministers approved links in March 1969 the experience of a Volgograd sovkhoz was selected for endorsement along with that of link pioneer Pervitskiy. Voronov's own statement on the links in the 11 May 1969 *Komsomolskaya Pravda* devoted much attention to the Volgograders' work, thus praising the initiative of his own close protégés in Volgograd.

In contrast to the RSFSR organs, USSR agricultural leaders and organizations have shown a distinct lack of enthusiasm for links. While *Sovetskaya Rossiya* and *Komsomolskaya Pravda* have vigorously promoted them, the Central Committee agricultural organ *Selskaya Zhizn*, after carrying on a long debate on links during 1968, concluded its discussion in December 1968 by taking a neutral—if not negative—stance (*Selskaya Zhizn*, 27 December 1968). Its editor, P. F. Alekseyev, has stressed the negative aspects of the links (in the May 1969 *Zhurnalist* he cited the objections that links can disrupt brigades' work and hinder correct use of equipment and, further, that it is hard to work out "any one general recommendation for organization of labor and wages for all farms in various zones of the country"). The USSR Agriculture Ministry was already actively studying Volgograd's links in 1968[13] but has still failed to take any position. Polyanskiy himself—who was Krasnodar first secretary (March 1957–March 1958) about the very time that Krasnodar farmer Pervitskiy was developing the first mechanized link—has consistently ignored links. The only boost for links on the all-union level was the April 1969 USSR Agriculture Ministry decision that all corn crops must be assigned to mechanized links (*Selskaya Zhizn*, 17 April 1969). But use of links for specialized crops (corn, sugar beets, etc.) is less controversial than for, say, general grain farming. The new draft Kolkhoz Charter published in April 1969 listed links as only one of several forms of labor organization and gave most attention to brigades. However, it did not, as some link foes requested, specify links as subordinate to brigades. During the November 1969 All-Union Congress of Kolkhozniks and the

[11] According to I. P. Shabunin, chief of the planning and economic department of the Volgograd Oblast Agriculture Administration, in the 19 January 1968 *Selskaya Zhizn*.

[12] Shabunin in the 19 January 1968 *Selskaya Zhizn* and a September 1968 *Kommunist* (no. 14, pp. 105–6), Kulichenko in the 15 January 1969 *Selskaya Zhizn*, and Volgograd Agriculture Administration chief V. Ivanenko in the 28 June 1969 *Komsomolskaya Pravda*.

[13] First Deputy Agriculture Minister Volovchenko told how one of his subordinates had visited a Volgograd kolkhoz and said that the ministry now was "attentively studying the experience of the Volgograders in order to spread it to other farms"—*Krasnaya Zvezda*, 7 April 1968.

preceding republic congresses, the links were totally ignored[14] and when the Kolkhoz Charter was finally adopted by the congress, the link-supporters suffered another slight setback: the final draft dropped a clause on long-term assignment of land and equipment to farm subdivisions (including links)—one of the basic features of the link system.[15]

In June 1969 the RSFSR Council of Ministers decided to specialize a large number of kolkhozes and sovkhozes in meat-cattle raising. This was announced at a June 1969 RSFSR livestock conference by RSFSR Deputy Agriculture Minister for livestock A. A. Abrazyakov (*Selskaya Zhizn,* 24 June 1969). Although the Central Committee organ for the RSFSR, *Sovetskaya Rossiya,*[16] has energetically promoted this meat-cattle program in 1969 and 1970, other papers and republics have largely ignored the campaign and the USSR authorities remain uncommitted.

As indicated earlier, Voronov had created specialized meat-cattle herds while Orenburg first secretary in 1957–61 and had urged the nationwide adoption of these ideas at the January 1961 plenum. Khrushchev blocked the idea at that time, but after his fall Voronov used his position as RSFSR premier to cautiously encourage the program. At the end of 1966 the RSFSR Council of Ministers adopted a special decree on meat livestock, projecting the creation of a meat-cattle herd of 1,500,000 in the next few years[17] and setting aside 162 sovkhozes and 256 sovkhoz divisions for specialization in meat cattle.[18] To facilitate this, the milk procurement plans of a number of RSFSR provinces were reduced in 1968 so that they could concentrate on meat. By 1969, 254 sovkhozes and 28 kolkhozes had been transferred to meat cattle and 1,200 specialized meat farms at kolkhozes and sovkhozes established (*Sovetskaya Rossiya,* 8 July 1969).

But by 1969 the meat-cattle herd still comprised only 400,000 head[19] and a large share of these were in just one oblast—Orenburg.[20] Voronov's old baili-

---

[14] Since the RSFSR did not have a republic congress, Voronov had no forum from which to promote links. However, just before the opening of the congress *Sovetskaya Rossiya* (23 November) announced publication of a seventy-page pamphlet on new wage systems. The pamphlet, issued for the congress, propagandized the links: its first and main chapter was a reprint of Voronov's *Komsomolskaya Pravda* interview on links.

[15] Compare the original draft in the 24 April 1969 *Selskaya Zhizn* and the final version in the 30 November 1969 *Selskaya Zhizn.*

[16] *Sovetskaya Rossiya* is not directly under Voronov and should not be considered his mouthpiece even though it has been vigorously promoting such RSFSR campaigns as the spreading of the links and meat cattle.

[17] RSFSR Gosplan Deputy Chairman G. Smirnov in the 24 March 1970 *Sovetskaya Rossiya.*

[18] G. Smirnov in *Ekonomika Selskogo Khozyaystva* 7 (1969): 58.

[19] Abrazyakov in the 24 June 1969 *Selskaya Zhizn.*

[20] This can be seen from the statement by V. Korchagin, senior zoo technician of the RSFSR Agriculture Ministry's meat livestock raising administration, that Orenburg would have 187,000 meat cattle by the end of 1969—*Sovetskaya Rossiya,* 4 July 1969.

wick of Orenburg led in implementing his 1966 decree, creating already in early 1967 a special meat livestock trust consisting of 19 sovkhozes and later designating another 40 sovkhozes and kolkhozes for specialization in meat production.[21] Orenburg raised its meat-cattle herd from 21,400 in 1966 to 53,200 in 1968.[22]

In view of the increasing meat shortages in 1968 and 1969, the quiet, slow progress was replaced with a major campaign in mid-1969. At a June RSFSR conference on improving the efficiency of livestock raising, Abrazyakov set the goal of raising the RSFSR's meat-cattle herd to 3,000,000 in the next few years and announced the decision to transfer at least 800 sovkhozes to meat livestock and establish over 1,000 specialized meat farms on other kolkhozes and sovkhozes (*Selskaya Zhizn*, 24 June 1969). Orenburg became the model for the RSFSR meat-cattle campaign.[23] In September 1969 the RSFSR Council of Ministers adopted a decree transforming its Main Administration for Livestock Fattening into a Main Administration for Meat Sovkhozes and Procurement of Livestock and ordered it to develop meat livestock and establish specialized farms.[24] In line with the new specialization, Voronov's old Orenburg Milk and Meat Livestock Raising Institute was renamed the Meat Livestock Raising Institute. However, Voronov's drive failed to gain much momentum—probably because of lack of support from Polyanskiy and the Agriculture Ministry. By January 1971 the number of meat cows had risen only to 459,800, increasing only from 3 percent of all RSFSR cows at the beginning of 1969 to 3.4 percent at the beginning of 1971 (according to an April 1972 *Ekonomika Selskogo Khozyaystva* article, which reiterated the goal of 2,100,000 to 2,500,000 RSFSR meat cows by the end of 1975).

A third initiative appeared in July 1969 when the RSFSR Council of Ministers established a special RSFSR Housing Construction Ministry (*Sovetskaya Rossiya*, 29 July 1969). This action appeared to considerably nullify the creation of a rural construction ministry in 1966, since the establishment of a rural construction ministry separated rural housing construction from urban housing construction, which remained with the industrial construction ministries. Creation of a housing construction ministry presumably would remove both rural and urban housing construction from other construction ministries and recombine them. At the RSFSR Supreme Soviet session immediately after the creation

[21] Ibid.

[22] According to Orenburg First Secretary Kovalenko in the December 1969 *Ekonomika Selskogo Khozyaystva*, p. 70.

[23] RSFSR Agriculture Ministry livestock official Korchagin in the 4 July 1969 *Sovetskaya Rossiya*; the 8 July 1969 *Sovetskaya Rossiya* editorial; reports on an RSFSR seminar in Orenburg in the 25 July 1969 *Selskaya Zhizn* and 3 August 1969 *Sovetskaya Rossiya*; a July *Ekonomicheskaya Gazeta* (no. 28, p. 17) article on Orenburg; RSFSR Gosplan Deputy Chairman G. Smirnov in the July *Ekonomika Selskogo Khozyaystva*, p. 57; and RSFSR Agriculture Ministry Livestock Administration chief G. Ogryzkin in the 5 October 1969 *Sovetskaya Rossiya*.

[24] G. Smirnov, *Sovetskaya Rossiya*, 24 March 1970.

of the new ministry, Voronov criticized the RSFSR Rural Construction Ministry for lagging in rural housing construction (*Sovetskaya Rossiya*, 31 July).

Estonia—which like the RSFSR had opposed creation of a separate rural construction ministry—soon hinted it would like to follow the RSFSR's example: Estonian Deputy Premier Kh. Kh. Allik, at the December 1969 USSR Supreme Soviet session, urged that housing construction be taken from all organizations and concentrated in the Estonian Council of Ministers, presumably in a special ministry to be established (*Sovetskaya Estoniya*, 20 December 1969). On the other hand, *Selskaya Zhizn*—which has campaigned hardest for separate rural construction ministries and which has been critical of the RSFSR in this respect—presumably disapproved of Voronov's new ministry. And, in fact, *Selskaya Zhizn's* construction editor, P. B. Vaynshteyn, in the 5 December 1967 *Literaturnaya Gazeta* had accused N. Chetunova of desiring to remove rural housing construction from the new Rural Construction Ministry.

The RSFSR is still unique in having a housing construction ministry. The new minister, A. V. Gladyrevskiy (appointed, *Izvestiya*, 15 August 1969), probably is regarded as reliable by Voronov, since he had first become prominent under Voronov. While Voronov was first deputy chairman of the RSFSR Bureau, a separate Central Committee section for RSFSR construction appeared and Gladyrevskiy headed this section until it was abolished, along with the Bureau, at the 23d Party Congress.

Voronov in Decline

Voronov's 1969 policy initiatives incongruously followed a sharp 1968 decline in his standing among Politburo members. After rather consistently ranking as number five (after Brezhnev, Kosygin, Podgornyy, and Suslov) in pictorial lineups during 1966 and 1967, Voronov slipped behind Kirilenko. The first sign was at cosmonaut Gagarin's funeral in the 30 March 1968 *Pravda*, when Kirilenko stood in fourth position (on the same side of the coffin as Brezhnev, Podgornyy, and Kosygin) in Suslov's absence, while Voronov stood with Shelepin, Mazurov, and Polyanskiy on the opposite side. The May Day 1968 pictures confirmed the shift: Kirilenko stood fifth (after Brezhnev, Kosygin, Podgornyy, and Suslov) and Voronov stood next to last—his lowest standing since the 1966 party congress. Again, at the next lineup which included both Kirilenko and Voronov—the 25 June 1968 Supreme Soviet session—Kirilenko sat next to Suslov, while Voronov sat last on one end. No comparison could be made through most of the second half of 1968, since Kirilenko was absent from mid-1968 photos and Voronov was absent from October–November photos. At the December 1968 Supreme Soviet session Voronov was back in his customary fifth position, with Kirilenko sixth (*Izvestiya*, 11 December). But again in early 1969 Voronov was rivaling Shelepin for last place.[25] *Pravda's* May Day 1969

---

[25] On 22 April, 23 April, May Day, and in most June 1969 photos of the International Communist Conference.

photo showed Voronov clearly in last place—for the first time since 7 November 1964. Later in 1969 and 1970 his status appeared somewhat unclear,[26] but he undoubtedly had suffered a loss of status.

The reasons for Voronov being in disfavor with his Politburo colleagues remain obscure. Surely his disagreements with Polyanskiy and Brezhnev over agricultural issues must have played a role. But perhaps more important in 1968 were his bad relations with Brezhnev and Kirilenko, apparently stemming from the period when they also had a direct hand in running Voronov's republic. His steep decline in the spring of 1968 appears to have been a consequence of a substantial breakthrough for Brezhnev. Not only did Brezhnev's top ally, Kirilenko,[27] displace Voronov as number five, but Brezhnev's close protégé, Gorkiy First Secretary K. F. Katushev, was elevated to Central Committee secretary at the April 1968 Central Committee plenum and was placed in charge of relations with Czechoslovakia and other East European states—under Kirilenko's supervision. Katushev had risen from party secretary of the Gorkiy Auto Plant to Gorkiy City first secretary to Gorkiy Oblast first secretary in only a little over two years, being installed as leader of that major industrial center by Brezhnev

---

[26]Voronov usually sat fifth at Supreme Soviet sessions, but stood last or next to last on other occasions. At the 10 July 1969 USSR Supreme Soviet session he sat after Brezhnev, Kosygin, Podgornyy, and Suslov, and ahead of Pelshe, Shelepin, and Shelest. At the 16 December 1969, 15 July 1970, and 8 December 1970 USSR Supreme Soviet sessions and the 17 December 1970 RSFSR Supreme Soviet session, he was clearly number five. At the 30 June 1970 RSFSR Supreme Soviet session he sat ahead of Polyanskiy, Kirilenko, Mazurov, Shelepin, and Pelshe, i.e., presumably number five.

On the other hand, at the 7 November 1969 anniversary parade he stood ahead of only Shelepin, i.e., number nine or ten (Only ten of the eleven Politburo members are usually present, since Ukrainian First Secretary Shelest attends the Kiev parade). At Voroshilov's 6 December 1969 funeral, Voronov was last. At the 1970 May Day parade he was also last. He was absent from the November 1970 parade.

[27]The ties between Brezhnev and Kirilenko extend back to their days in the Ukraine and are the closest of any Politburo members. Before World War II, Brezhnev had become a secretary of Dnepropetrovsk Oblast, while Kirilenko was second secretary of neighboring Zaporozhe Oblast. During the postwar reconstruction, Brezhnev was first secretary of Zaporozhe Oblast and Kirilenko second secretary. The roles of Brezhnev and Kirilenko in rebuilding Zaporozhe were lauded by Zaporozhe Oblast First Secretary M. N. Vsevolozhskiy in the 13 October 1968 *Radyanska Ukraina* and by USSR Deputy Premier V. E. Dymshits (who worked under Brezhnev in Zaporozhe in 1946–47) in a September 1970 *Ogonek* (no. 36, pp. 15–18). In 1947 Brezhnev became first secretary of Dnepropetrovsk Oblast and Kirilenko became first secretary of neighboring Nikolayev Oblast. In 1950, when Brezhnev left to become Moldavian first secretary, Kirilenko replaced him in Dnepropetrovsk. The roles of Brezhnev, Kirilenko, and Shcherbitskiy (who succeeded Kirilenko as Dnepropetrovsk first secretary in 1955) in rebuilding Dnepropetrovsk were praised by Dnepropetrovsk Oblast Executive Committee Chairman M. V. Pashov in the 25 October 1968 *Izvestiya*. Brezhnev and Kirilenko again worked together as RSFSR Bureau chairman and first deputy chairman in 1964–66. Kirilenko has been the only Politburo member (until the addition of Kunayev to the Politburo in 1971) to personally glorify Brezhnev. In a 1 December 1966 Novorossiysk speech Kirilenko lauded Brezhnev's 1943 war exploits and personal bravery (*Pravda*, 2 December 1966).

personally in December 1965. Soon after, at the March–April 1966 23d Party Congress, Katushev was the only important figure to attempt to set Brezhnev above the collective, declaring that "henceforth the Central Committee would be headed by" the new general secretary.

A series of press attacks on Gorkiy Oblast followed, apparently intended to discredit Katushev's leadership. *Pravda* exposed a case of muzzling press criticism on 26 April 1966, which Katushev answered on 2 July. On 16 July 1966 *Pravda* exposed shortages in consumer goods in Gorkiy. At first, after discussing the article at a 30 August obkom bureau meeting, the Gorkiy leaders sent a letter to *Pravda* denying the charges, but *Pravda* on 26 September published a refutation of the Gorkiy letter. On 30 September the bureau acknowledged that the letter had "distorted" the situation and contained "incorrect facts" and it rebuked obkom Second Secretary V. A. Tikhomirov for carelessness. This was reported by Katushev in the 14 October *Pravda.* Katushev responded to *Pravda* again on 28 October when he finally reported the firing of an official involved in the 26 April press muzzling exposure.

Nevertheless, Brezhnev continued to show signs of favoritism toward Katushev. Katushev accompanied Brezhnev on a trip to Hungary in late November 1966, he was the only oblast secretary added to the reconstituted Constitutional Commission (now headed by Brezhnev instead of Khrushchev) announced in December, and on 13 January 1967 Brezhnev himself journeyed to Gorkiy to present the oblast an Order of Lenin for successes in "economic and cultural construction" and to heap praise on the oblast and its party organization—in effect, vindicating Katushev's leadership.

After the April 1968 promotion, Brezhnev continued to push Katushev forward, stirring up resentment in the Politburo. This became obvious in December 1968. After Brezhnev managed to violate protocol at the 10 December 1968 Supreme Soviet session by having junior Central Committee Secretary Katushev sit among the Politburo members (ahead of all Politburo candidate members and other secretaries), the Politburo administered a public snub to Katushev: *Pravda* on 19 December altered a TASS report to identify Katushev as "secretary under (*pri*) the Central Committee" instead of secretary of the Central Committee. No correction followed and other papers did not follow *Pravda's* example in altering the TASS report. A photo of the Composers Union congress in the 17 December *Izvestiya* showed Katushev back sitting in last place. An unusual spate of articles about collective leadership began immediately after the Katushev affair. These articles, concentrated in a short period in January–February 1969, clearly reflected a top-level decision and stressed the leader's subordination to the collective.[28]

[28] These articles appeared in *Politicheskoye Samoobrazovaniye*, no. 1 (1969), signed to press 25 December 1968; *Kommunist*, no. 1, signed to press 6 January; *Partiynaya Zhizn*, no. 2 (9 January) and no. 3 (28 January); *Komsomolskaya Pravda*, 5 February; *Sovetskaya Rossiya*, 8 February; *Trud*, 9 February; and *Voprosy Istorii KPSS*, no. 3, signed to press 26 February.

After the April 1968 promotion of Katushev, Brezhnev continued to demonstrate strength, moving against the original center of Shelepin's strength—the Komsomol.[29] Shelepin had headed the Komsomol from 1952 to 1958 and was succeeded as first secretary by his protégés V. Ye. Semichastnyy and S. P. Pavlov. After Brezhnev announced a big campaign for ideological orthodoxy and discipline in his 29 March Moscow City party conference speech, Central Committee cadre chief Kapitonov traveled to Krasnoyarsk (*Sovetskaya Rossiya*, 25 April 1968), where he uncovered shortcomings in Komsomol operations, particularly ideological weaknesses in its educational work.[30] In early May the Central Committee adopted a decree criticizing the Krasnoyarsk party committee's weak leadership of Komsomol organs (*Partiynaya Zhizn*, no. 10 [May 1968]) and a nationwide campaign to reassert closer party control over the Komsomol began. Some articles hinted that Pavlov and the Komsomol leaders were too independent of party control (i.e., Brezhnev's control). For example, an 18 October 1968 *Pravda* article by Z. Apresyan and V. Sulemov warned against "opportunists" who "interpret the independence of the union of youth as absolute and unlimited."

Komsomol First Secretary Pavlov's fall was made known on 10 June 1968, when he was elected chairman of the Union of Sports Societies and Organizations (*Komsomolskaya Pravda*, 11 June), a considerable demotion. On 12 June a Komsomol Central Committee plenum was held to discuss the April 1968 Central Committee plenum (which had approved the ideological crackdown announced in Brezhnev's 29 March speech) and the Central Committee decree on Krasnoyarsk's leadership of the Komsomol (*Komsomolskaya Pravda*, 13 June). The plenum, supervised by Central Committee secretaries Suslov and Kapitonov, removed Pavlov as first secretary[31] and elected forty-year-old Chelyabinsk Oblast Party Secretary Ye. M. Tyazhelnikov as first secretary. For the first time in decades, the Komsomol chief was not chosen from the Komsomol ranks but was imposed from without—a good demonstration of the party's new, closer domination over the Komsomol. Tyazhelnikov, a protégé of Brezhnev's apparent client, Chelyabinsk First Secretary N. N. Rodionov, subsequently demonstrated his loyalty to Brezhnev by praising Brezhnev's speeches

[29] Brezhnev had dealt important setbacks to the Shelepin faction already in mid-1967, ousting Shelepin's former Komsomol associate D. P. Goryunov as TASS director in April (he became ambassador to Kenya), Shelepin protégé Semichastnyy from the post of KGB chairman in May (he became a Ukrainian first deputy premier), young Stalinist N. G. Yegorychev as Moscow City first secretary in June (he became deputy minister of tractor and agricultural machine building), and transferring Central Committee Secretary Shelepin himself to trade union chairman in July. Under new KGB Chairman Andropov, Brezhnev associates were moved into key posts in the KGB and Shelepin–Semichastnyy appointees were gradually moved out (for more details, see the Postscript to this volume).

[30] See the 10 June 1968 *Pravda*, 11 June 1968 *Sovetskaya Rossiya*, and 3 July 1968 *Komsomolskaya Pravda*.

[31] It is ironic that the main victim of the 1968 ideological crackdown was the vicious Stalinist youth leader, S. P. Pavlov.

(for example, Tyazhelnikov's speech in the 26 December 1968 *Komsomolskaya Pravda*) and by purging the Shelepin-Semichastnyy-Pavlov appointees from the Komsomol leadership. Brezhnev further demonstrated his new power over the Komsomol by immediately calling the new Komsomol leaders into his office for a talk about future Komsomol work (*Komsomolskaya Pravda*, 19 June 1968).

Brezhnev's takeover of the Komsomol stirred up opposition and later in the year—when Brezhnev appeared slightly less powerful—these complaints were subtly reflected in the press. In a 24 October 1968 *Komsomolskaya Pravda* article Leningrad Oblast First Secretary V. S. Tolstikov hinted displeasure with the party's new crackdown on the Komsomol and warned against "petty supervision of Komsomol organs or replacement of them by party organs." Citing local cases of party interference with Komsomol work, he wrote that "we must not forget Lenin's instruction that without full independence the youth cannot produce from itself good specialists or prepare to lead socialism forward." Tolstikov was no friend of Brezhnev: his Leningrad organization had been criticized for "serious shortcomings" by Brezhnev during his speech at the 16 February 1968 Leningrad party conference and in mid-1970 Tolstikov was removed and packed off to Peking as the new ambassador to China.

In a September 1968 issue of *Kommunist* (no. 14), Voronov's ally L. S. Kulichenko, first secretary of Volgograd, also complained of party organizations' excessive interference in Komsomol work, which he called "a quite widespread error." Perhaps also aimed at Brezhnev was his insistence that Komsomol work be collectively supervised by party leaders instead of making "individual members of party committees or bureaus responsible for the activities of Komsomol organizations."

Voronov's spring 1968 decline and the summer Komsomol purge were followed by moves against his associates in the fall. K. I. Zarodov, appointed editor of *Sovetskaya Rossiya* under Voronov in early 1961 and transferred to *Pravda* first deputy chief editor in October 1965, was removed and transferred to Prague to edit the journal *Problems of Peace and Socialism*, apparently about the time of the August invasion of Czechoslovakia.[32] Volgograd First Secretary Kulichenko came under sharp attack about the same time.[33] A Central Commit-

---

[32] The invasion apparently disrupted the journal's activity, since it failed to publish an October issue. The following issue (a combined October–November issue) mentioned that Zarodov now was chief editor. The appointment of Zarodov's successor at *Pravda* was announced in the October *Zhurnalist* (signed to press 9 September).

[33] Kulichenko may have irritated Brezhnev on Czechoslovakia as well as on the Komsomol issue. Although only secretary of a medium-sized province, he appears to have played some special role in the decisions on Czechoslovakia. On 21 February 1968 he was one of only four leaders visiting Czechoslovakia with Brezhnev (the others were closely involved in Czech events: Katushev, Ukrainian leader Shelest, and Ambassador to Czechoslovakia Chervonenko) and he spoke at both the April and July 1968 Central Committee plenums—which both dealt with Czechoslovakia (few provincial secretaries had the privilege

tee decree in September 1968 censured the Volgograd Obkom's selection, assignment, and training of leaders of industrial production (*Sovetskaya Rossiya*, 29 September 1968) and this was followed by attacks on the obkom's leadership of organizational work and in ideological matters, implicitly casting doubts on First Secretary Kulichenko's leadership. Oblast Executive Committee Chairman V. P. Borodin was attacked for trying to cover up a scandal in the oblast public services administration and had to admit to "serious shortcomings" in his committee's work.[34] Voronov's Orenburg protégé Shurygin (Volgograd secretary since 1965) was especially implicated by the September 1968 Central Committee decree, since it condemned precisely the work he was responsible for. Shurygin had authored an article on Volgograd's industrial leadership cadres in the 3 November 1965 *Izvestiya*, in which he claimed that following the enactment of the September 1965 economic reform Volgograd was devoting the "most intense" attention to selection, assignment, and training of leaders of industrial production. He also had represented the obkom at the September 1965 Volgograd trade union conference (*Trud*, 17 September 1965). The September 1968 decree and a 27 September 1968 *Trud* article assailed shortcomings in Volgograd's handling of labor problems.[35] Eventually, Shurygin was removed.[36]

Another area closely associated with Voronov came under attack on 28 January 1970 when a *Pravda* article assailed the Orenburg leaders for complacency, covering up suppression of local criticism, and ignoring of previous *Pravda* criticisms. This criticism was especially remarkable because Orenburg had been riding the wave of unprecedented agricultural successes in 1968 and 1969 and had been receiving more praise than any other province. Pysin could announce in October 1968 that Orenburg had delivered more grain than any other province ever had (*Sovetskaya Rossiya*, 27 October 1968). Orenburg received an Order of Lenin (*Pravda*, 29 October 1968) and was widely praised. When Voronov began his meat-cattle campaign in mid-1969, Orenburg became the model for the rest

---

of speaking at either of these plenums—let alone both). After the August invasion, he was first to publicly endorse it (see his 11 September 1968 *Komsomolskaya Pravda* article).

[34] *Izvestiya's* criticism in the 17 September 1969 *Izvestiya* and Borodin's acknowledgment in the 18 November 1969 *Izvestiya*. *Pravda* also picked up the charge in a 25 September 1969 editorial, and Kulichenko had to acknowledge the executive committee's shortcomings in the 23 November 1969 *Pravda*.

[35] For other criticisms and acknowledgments of criticism, see L. Morozov's 30 September 1968 *Ekonomicheskaya Gazeta* article, the reports on Volgograd plenums in the 25 October 1968 *Pravda* and 17 December 1968 *Trud*, the 11 January 1969 *Pravda* editorial, a 9 February 1969 *Pravda* article, a 12 March 1969 *Pravda* editorial, obkom Secretary A. Nebenzya's acknowledgment of the 9 February *Pravda* article in the 21 May 1969 *Pravda*, a 12 March 1969 *Sovetskaya Rossiya* article and a follow-up in the 13 May 1969 *Sovetskaya Rossiya*.

[36] The date of Shurygin's removal is unknown, but he was not identified in the press after the 1968 decree and late 1970 identifications of Volgograd leaders indicated that Shurygin no longer was one of Volgograd's secretaries.

of the RSFSR. Its meat-cattle program—so widely praised by RSFSR leaders in 1969—had, of course, been introduced originally by Voronov himself. In October 1969 Orenburg again received favorable publicity as an example for early completion of fall plowing[37]—another practice insisted upon by Voronov when he became obkom first secretary in 1957. As the critical 28 January 1970 *Pravda* article noted, "the drums have been beaten very often lately" about Orenburg's successes.

Other signs of Voronov's disfavor followed in 1970. He stood last at the May Day 1970 parade and in the June 1970 Supreme Soviet elections his close ally and deputy, Pysin, inexplicably was not reelected to the Supreme Soviet. On his 60th birthday on 31 August Voronov suffered an unusual snub: while other Politburo members (most recently Shelest on his sixtieth birthday in February 1968 and Pelshe on his seventieth in February 1969) were addressed as a "prominent leader of the Communist Party and Soviet Government" and were awarded the title Hero of Socialist Labor, a Hammer and Sickle medal, and an Order of Lenin on their birthdays, Voronov received no epithet and only an Order of Lenin (*Pravda*, 1 September 1970)—as he had on his fiftieth birthday.[38] Only a week later *Pravda* (8 September) carried a Volgograd worker's letter attacking Volgograd Oblast First Secretary L. S. Kulichenko and Volgograd City First Secretary V. S. Karpov.

Meanwhile, just before his birthday snub, Voronov disappeared from view. After visiting a Hungarian exhibit on 21 August, he failed to represent the RSFSR at the late August Kazakh fiftieth anniversary or early October Azerbaydzhan fiftieth anniversary or even to attend the 6–7 November October Revolution ceremonies—which are rarely missed by Soviet leaders. For three solid months (21 August to 21 November) Voronov was identified only once in the press: *Komsomolskaya Pravda* on 2 October reported that he had visited a Moscow sovkhoz's cattle-breeding exhibit and the paper carried a long interview with him strongly defending his meat-cattle program. This was by far the longest absence of the normally active Voronov in recent years. Upon his return to public activity, he delivered a speech with implicit attacks on several agricultural policies associated with Brezhnev and Polyanskiy (*Sovetskaya Rossiya*, 25 November 1970—see next chapter).

---

[37] A 3 October 1969 *Sovetskaya Rossiya* editorial, a 6 October 1969 *Pravda* editorial, and a 10 October 1969 *Trud* interview with Orenburg officials.

[38] Pysin also appeared snubbed on his sixtieth birthday when he received an Order of the Red Banner instead of an Order of Lenin—*Pravda*, 24 December 1970.

CHAPTER XI

AGRICULTURE LOBBY'S
SECOND VICTORY: 1970

In 1970 the agriculture lobby won its biggest victory since the March 1965 plenum: the Politburo finally decided to raise prices for livestock products and to greatly increase allocations of money and resources to agriculture. In several respects, the 1970 victory resembled that of 1965. As in early 1965, a new five-year plan was being worked out; agricultural problems appeared serious enough to persuade a majority of the leaders to increase agriculture's share of scarce resources; the agricultural part of the new plan was worked out and formally adopted, leaving the other sectors to fight over the remaining resources; and the ensuing resource struggle delayed completion of the plan for many months, even past the date it was to go into effect.

Although some of 1967's cuts in agriculture were restored during 1968, agricultural problems, primarily in livestock raising, worsened during 1969. Remarkably severe weather in early 1969 aggravated not only the slowdown in agriculture but also the slowdown in industry—intensifying each sector's need for more resources. As the outlines of the 1971–75 five-year plan were being worked out in late 1969 and early 1970, the agriculture lobby launched a campaign to orient the new plan to agriculture. An apparently crucial role in this campaign was played by the crisis in livestock raising, which produced serious meat shortages in Soviet cities. Even the agriculture lobby's foes found it necessary to publicly admit the meat crisis and acknowledge the need for more aid to agriculture. In January and March 1970 the Politburo adopted decisions raising prices for livestock products purchased by the state, but not raising retail prices for consumers—thus leaving the state to absorb the financial losses.

In May the agriculture lobby won Politburo approval of proposals to sharply increase agriculture's share in the new five-year plan and Gosplan's preliminary plan outlines were overridden. As in March 1965, the increased aid for agriculture in the new five-year plan was announced by Brezhnev at a Central

Committee plenum with great fanfare as a huge, unprecedented program. Closer examination, however, suggests that much of the July 1970 program is simply a restoration of the badly cut March 1965 program. Nevertheless, it did mean a large increase in investments for agriculture, and in view of the strained situation of the Soviet economy it probably was a great achievement for Brezhnev and Polyanskiy.

In early 1971 further decisions were taken to initiate a big program to build hundreds of big expensive livestock raising complexes. The complexes, along with the price rises, were Brezhnev's and Polyanskiy's solution to the meat shortage. In contrast, Voronov and the Estonian leaders advocated more efficient livestock raising techniques and opposed both the price rises and complexes—but they were clearly overridden.

After the spring 1970 victory of the agriculture lobby, the new five-year plan outlines had to be redrawn and the shares for heavy industry, consumer goods, and defense worked out. Despite the agricultural victory, Kosygin and his allies eventually managed to retain the consumer orientation of the plan which they had won in 1967. Whether the 1971 shift of resources to consumer goods was sufficient to satisfy Kosygin is impossible to determine; however, it apparently was not great enough to disturb Brezhnev, who publicly embraced and promoted the new consumer orientation. Probably as a compromise solution, a major part of the new expansion of consumer goods production was to be carried out within heavy industry, thus allowing it to retain its traditional overwhelming share of investment money while at the same time increasing output of goods desperately needed to satisfy popular demand and absorb increased purchasing power.

The Meat Crisis

The balance in the resource debate probably was tipped in agriculture's favor by the meat crisis. Brezhnev had warned about the lag in livestock products in his October 1968 plenum report, but the situation continued to deteriorate during 1969, reaching a low point in early 1970—precisely when the decisions over resources in the new five-year plan were being made. The seriousness of the meat shortages persuaded the Politburo to reverse its 1968 decision and raise prices for livestock products—first for privately owned livestock in late January and then for publicly owned livestock in March.

That these decisions to raise prices were bitterly contested is clear from the Estonian leaders' repeated protests and from the RSFSR leaders' studied silence, and later from Voronov's public raising of doubts about the value of the price rises. As on so many previous occasions, the opposition to Brezhnev and Polyanskiy was most obvious on the part of Voronov and the Estonians. Voronov vigorously promoted his own solutions to the meat crisis, centering on more efficient methods rather than increased investment.

After an encouraging rise in 1966 and 1967, livestock raising had begun lagging:

Number of Livestock on 1 January (in millions)[1]

	1966	1967	1968	1969	1970
Cattle	93.4	97.1	97.2	95.7	95
(including cows)	40.1	41.2	41.6	41.2	40.6
Pigs	59.6	58	50.9	49	56.1

Meat production itself stagnated: 10.7 million tons in 1966, 11.5 million tons in 1967, 11.6 million tons in 1968, and again 11.6 million tons in 1969.[2]

The slowdown in livestock growth was pointed to with alarm by Brezhnev at the October 1968 Central Committee plenum. It was especially bad, he noted, because the population was not only growing[3] but also altering its diet to include more meat. He reported that demand for meat per capita in 1967 was 21 percent above 1964, while per capita demand for grain had dropped 6 percent (*Pravda*, 31 October 1968). He declared: "we still are poorly handling questions of livestock raising, especially the economic aspects of its development" and he backed proposals to extend the above-plan incentive system set for grain at the March 1965 plenum[4] to other products, including livestock.[5] This was done. However, as Brezhnev reported, the Politburo opposed any rise for most basic procurement prices.[6] This was especially significant since the key to the livestock decline was profitability.

While the March 1965 plenum had largely turned grain growing into a profitable operation, its measures to aid livestock raising were much less effective.[7] First Deputy Agriculture Minister I. Volovchenko stated in the 14 February 1969 *Selskaya Zhizn* that livestock raising at sovkhozes was still only one-third as profitable as plant-growing. RSFSR Gosplan Deputy Chairman G. L.

[1] *Selskaya Zhizn*, 25 January 1970.
[2] Ibid.
[3] The urban population grew by 12.5 million from 1965 to 1969–P. Yesaulov, *Voprosy Ekonomiki* 12 (1970): 51.
[4] That is, 50 percent higher prices for above-plan procurements.
[5] RSFSR Agriculture Minister L. Ya. Florentyev in the January 1969 *Voprosy Istorii KPSS* specified that the extension primarily was to livestock products (p. 11).
[6] Brezhnev urged adjustments in poultry prices, however, and in April 1969 purchase prices for publicly owned poultry were raised–chickens by 20 percent, broilers by 40 percent, turkeys by 40 percent, ducks by 50 percent, and geese by 60 percent (P. Yesaulov, *Voprosy Ekonomiki* 12 [1970] : 56).
[7] A. M. Yemelyanov explained, for example, that the post-March 1965 plenum deliveries of equipment to agriculture were "primarily intended for mechanizing work in plant growing" and "no noticeable progress occurred in production of a complex of machines for livestock raising" (*Seriya Ekonomicheskaya, Izvestiya Akademii Nauk SSSR* 6 [1970] : 22, signed to press 20 November 1970).

Smirnov wrote in the July 1969 *Ekonomika Selskogo Khozyaystva* that "in 1968 at sovkhozes of the RSFSR Agriculture Ministry the profitability of farming products was 53 percent, that of livestock products 5.4 percent, while milk production was unprofitable" (p. 61). In the 28 March 1970 *Pravda* Kustanay Oblast Secretary V. Galtsov, describing the imbalance between livestock raising and farming in his Kazakh oblast, wrote that production of some grain had become so profitable that some farms "had ceased to bother with livestock raising" and "citing specialization, hurried to get rid of some 'unprofitable' branches," i.e., livestock. A. M. Yemelyanov wrote: "Farms strove to increase grain production to sell it above-plan at the 50 percent bonus prices. And this not only at farms specializing in grain production, but in livestock-raising farms also."[8]

Central Committee Agriculture Section deputy head N. P. Rudenko wrote in the July 1970 *Ekonomika Selskogo Khozyaystva*[9]:

> In recent years the cost of production of livestock products not only did not decline but even rose. This occurred mainly because wages rose, the cost of fodder production rose, expenses for buying equipment and constructing production buildings and facilities rose, and production expenses rose. The cost of fodder during these years rose at sovkhozes by over 50 percent and doubled at kolkhozes. In 1961–1968 man-day wages at kolkhozes rose from 1 ruble, 36 kopeks to 3 rubles, 52 kopeks, and at sovkhozes from 2 rubles, 40 kopeks to 4 rubles, 12 kopeks. The rates of growth of wages significantly outstripped growth of labor productivity.
>
> Despite the significant rise in purchase prices, the level of profitability of production of many types of products remained low. . . . Thus, the profitability of cattle in 1968 was only 3.5 percent at sovkhozes and 16 percent at kolkhozes, while production of milk was unprofitable for both sovkhozes and kolkhozes.

P. Yesaulov explained in the December 1970 *Voprosy Ekonomiki* (pp. 49–50) that the decline in meat and milk production was to a significant degree caused by low profitability, and that while actual profitability of livestock products in 1968 was 7 percent at kolkhozes and 5.2 percent at sovkhozes, expansion of livestock raising required profitability of about 45–50 percent. He attributed the low profitability "primarily" to the rise in costs and explained that "the main elements of cost of livestock products are wages and fodder costs." "In connection with the adjustment of wages in sovkhozes and the introduction of guaranteed wages in kolkhozes, the average pay for one man-day in livestock raising at sovkhozes rose by 34–45 percent since 1962" and at kolkhozes "by 92–93 percent." Because of lack of mechanization, the number of animals serviced by each worker did not rise (he specified that "comprehensive mechaniza-

[8]Ibid., p. 23.
[9]This was written in May, well before the July Central Committee plenum.

tion at the beginning of 1969 encompassed not more than 6-7 percent of the cattle and about 20 percent of the pigs at kolkhozes and sovkhozes"). Insufficient mechanization of fodder production, higher wages, and low yield also boosted fodder costs.

To improve efficiency and profitability, specialization was urged on the kolkhozes and sovkhozes—instead of attempting to raise a large number of varied animals on small, inefficient farms (*fermy*), they were to specialize in one or two types on a larger scale and eliminate the others. But, as a result of bungled planning and implementation, this campaign turned into a disaster, seriously aggravating the existing lag in meat production. The problem was that once planners had determined that a kolkhoz or sovkhoz would henceforth specialize in a particular branch, the kolkhoz's or sovkhoz's livestock farms for other branches were quickly liquidated—long before the specialized farms could be set up and brought up to full production. As Belorussian First Secretary Masherov complained, the small farms were liquidated even though "everyone well knows" that the big specialized farms still "exist only in plans, on paper" (*Sovetskaya Belorussiya*, 15 November 1969). This was recognized in mid-1969 and brought severe censure from the authorities. At the November 1969 Congress of Kolkhozniks Brezhnev pointed out that this practice "often turns farms from producers into consumers" and warned against going to extremes (*Pravda*, 26 November 1969). An 11 February 1970 *Pravda* editorial demanded that "unjustifiably liquidated farms be restored." Pigs and poultry had suffered the biggest cutbacks in this specialization campaign.[10]

Meanwhile, Voronov began pushing his own remedy for inefficiency and unprofitability in livestock raising. After Brezhnev complained of high costs and low profitability at the October 1968 plenum, Voronov organized a June 1969 RSFSR conference on ways to reduce costs of livestock raising.[11] At the conference Voronov's subordinates announced the big RSFSR program to establish 800 specialized meat-cattle sovkhozes and 1,000 specialized meat-cattle farms and raise the number of meat cattle from 400,000 to 3,000,000 (*Sovetskaya Rossiya* and *Selskaya Zhizn*, 24 June 1969). The heavier meat breeds produced much more meat per animal than most dual-purpose cows (milk-meat) and required less labor—hence, reducing cost. Beef is produced at specialized meat-cattle sovkhozes at one-third less cost than at dairy farms.[12] The US example of

[10] Publicly owned pigs dropped from 41.4 million in 1966 to 36.2 million in 1969. Another reason for the drop was the March 1965 rise in grain prices. Pigs were fed mainly on grain and when the 50 percent bonus for above-plan grain was adopted, farms found it more profitable to sell their grain to the state than to use it to raise pigs (A. M. Yemelyanov, *Seriya Ekonomicheskaya, Izvestiya Akademii Nauk SSSR* 6 [1970]: p. 30).

[11] The RSFSR initiative in responding to the October 1968 plenum complaints was praised by an editorial in *Ekonomika Selskogo Khozyaystva* 10 (1969): 4.

[12] P. Yesaulov in *Voprosy Ekonomiki* 12 (1970): 52, and Central Committee Agriculture Section deputy head N. P. Rudenko in *Ekonomika Selskogo Khozyaystva* 7(1970): 4.

reducing dairy cattle in favor of meat cattle was cited at the conference.[13] While three quarters of US cattle are meat cattle, only 3 percent of Soviet cattle are.[14]

The importance of Voronov's program was stressed by RSFSR Gosplan Deputy Chairman G. L. Smirnov in the 24 March 1970 *Sovetskaya Rossiya*. He declared that increasing the number of pigs and poultry[15] could be only a temporary solution to the meat problem and that the full solution lay in sharply expanding beef production, "primarily by fast rates of development of meat livestock raising." G. Ryndin (chief of the Meat Livestock Raising Administration of the RSFSR Agriculture Ministry) wrote that in 1971–75 the RSFSR planned to boost beef production by 1,624,000 tons over 1968's 5,196,000 tons, and 1,207,000 tons of this growth would be from meat livestock.[16] In a 2 October 1970 *Komsomolskaya Pravda* interview, Voronov personally argued strongly for meat cattle as a solution to the meat problem and even cited a quotation from Lenin on the need to develop meat livestock.

The .decline in the number of livestock was especially serious in privately owned animals:

Number of Livestock on 1 January (in millions)[17]

	1966	1967	1968	1969	1970
Cattle (public)	65.6	67.8	68.7	68.4	70.1
(private)	27.8	29.3	28.5	27.3	24.9
(incl. cows) (public)	23.5	24.1	24.5	24.5	24.6
(private)	16.6	17.1	17.1	16.7	16
Pigs (public)	41.4	41.5	37.3	36.2	42
(private)	18.2	16.5	13.6	12.8	14.1

As Voronov explained in a March 1970 speech, after the October 1964 plenum, Khrushchev's limitations on private livestock ownership had been removed and this produced a rise in the number of private livestock in 1965 and 1966. But in 1967–69 the "curve turned sharply downward."[18]

[13] By Professor S. Ya. Dudin, *Ekonomika Selskogo Khozyaystva* 9 (1969): 70.

[14] P. Yesaulov, *Voprosy Ekonomiki* 12 (1970): 52. In a May 1971 *Voprosy Ekonomiki* article V. Desyatov described the vast gap in meat production efficiency between the US and USSR. Although, as he noted, both countries had roughly the same number of cattle (as of 1968, 95.7 million head in the USSR and 108.8 million in the US—only 13.6 percent more), the US produced twice as much beef (10 million tons versus 5 million—as of 1969) and, with a smaller population, this meant two and a half times as much beef per capita (48 kgs as against 19). This was ten years after Khrushchev's original 1960–61 goal of catching up to the US in meat production per capita.

[15] Pigs and poultry can be expanded especially rapidly.

[16] *Selskoye Khozyaystvo Rossii* 4 (1970): 36.

[17] *Selskaya Zhizn*, 25 January 1970.

[18] *Leninskoye Znamya*, 24 March 1970.

Among the reasons for the decline was, ironically, the improvement in rural living standards resulting from the higher earnings, pensions, guaranteed wages, and other progress made since 1965. One of Voronov's subordinates, V. Baturin (deputy head of the Agriculture Department of the RSFSR Council of Ministers), wrote that because of these changes many farmers who used to produce meat and milk now had become consumers.[19] Georgiy Radov in the 15 July 1970 *Literaturnaya Gazeta* described how kolkhozniks no longer are so poor that they have to put up with the long hours of hard work necessary for raising private livestock. As a result, they can afford to get rid of their cows and buy milk in stores. However, he noted, the planners had not expected this and there is not enough milk in the stores to supply the farmers who formerly supplied themselves and even sold surplus milk to the state or in private markets. Young people are especially disinclined toward such long hours and hard work and prefer urban-type living. Yuriy Chernichenko in the June 1970 *Yunost* described how Belgorod farm girls no longer are willing to milk like the old-timers. Having a cow used to be like money in the bank, but now free time is the main value—even if there is nothing to do with the free time. Radov also said that the rural reconstruction campaign, with its emphasis on rural apartment buildings, often with no space for private garden plots, has made it harder for kolkhozniks to raise their own livestock. In addition, of course, many people leave the villages for the cities. *Ekonomika Selskogo Khozyaystva* chief editor N. I. Anisimov recently wrote that in 1959-69 over 16 million persons left agriculture for other branches.[20]

While the elimination of private livestock is a long-term goal of the Soviet leaders, it is possible only when public production can fully supply all needs. Thus, when the decline in private livestock reduced Soviet meat production, leaders began attacking the deliberate or involuntary discouraging of private livestock ownership by local officials. In his 13 November 1969 speech at the Ukrainian Congress of Kolkhozniks Ukrainian First Secretary Shelest complained bitterly that "some shortsighted leaders . . . 'forgot' about providing fodder for kolkhozniks' livestock" with the eventual result that in places where farmers had earlier been selling meat products from their privately owned livestock, they now had to buy meat in the stores (*Radyanska Ukraina*, 15 November 1969). In 1969 the Ukraine acted to encourage private livestock raising, selling 3,200,000 pigs to private farmers and purchasing 1,278,000 calves from private farmers.[21] Pravda's 11 February 1970 editorial noted that "in recent years it has become harder to acquire piglets and fodder for private households and procurement organs have almost stopped buying poultry from the population." It insisted that private livestock raising be assisted actively. On 29 January

[19] *Selskoye Khozyaystvo Rossii*, no. 3 (1970).

[20] *Voprosy Istorii KPSS* 9 (1970): 6.

[21] Ukrainian Premier V. V. Shcherbitskiy's speech at a 31 March 1970 Ukrainian Central Committee plenum on livestock raising (*Radyanska Ukraina*, 1 April 1970).

1970[22] a Central Committee–Council of Ministers decree "On Increasing Production and State Purchases of Pigs and Poultry in 1970" raised prices for pigs and poultry bought from the farmers.[23]

Most branches of livestock raising continued to stagnate or actually decline after 1968, reaching a low point in late 1969 and early 1970.[24] Brezhnev dwelt on livestock raising problems in his November 1969 speech at the Congress of Kolkhozniks (*Pravda*, 26 November 1969) and in his unpublished December 1969 Central Committee plenum report criticized many areas, including the RSFSR as a whole, for the drop in livestock.[25] RSFSR Gosplan Deputy Chairman G. Smirnov wrote in the 24 March 1970 *Sovetskaya Rossiya* that the RSFSR was only satisfying 60 percent of the demand for meat in 1970. Deputy head of the RSFSR Council of Ministers' Agriculture Department V. Baturin wrote that while RSFSR purchases of meat had risen one-third over 1965, they were lagging behind demand. The average monthly wage in the RSFSR had risen 8 percent since 1968, stimulating demand for meat, "while procurements of livestock and poultry during this time increased only by 4 percent."[26]

In early 1970 Soviet leaders began acknowledging meat shortages in public speeches. Voronov was first—his RSFSR had been criticized at the December 1969 plenum for lagging in livestock raising. In a March speech at a Moscow oblast agricultural conference, Voronov declared that "over the course of a number of years now we have had difficulty in supplying the population with meat" (*Leninskoye Znamya*, 24 March 1970). Several other leaders mentioned the meat shortages in election speeches to their constituents during the May–June 1970 Supreme Soviet election campaign.[27] Podgornyy declared that the shortages are "not just a question of an increase in demand" but also of a "weakening of attention" to livestock raising (*Moskovskaya Pravda*, 12 June).

The late 1969–early 1970 meat crisis sparked hot controversy over measures to deal with it. The main proposal apparently was to raise livestock procurement prices. As in so many previous agricultural disputes, especially regarding money, this proposal found the Estonians leading the opposition, with the

[22] The date of the decree is listed as 29 January by G. Rusakov in *Ekonomika Selskogo Khozyaystva*, no. 11 (1970).

[23] This is based on statements in the 11 February 1970 *Pravda* editorial, Pysin's speech in the 17 February 1970 *Sovetskaya Rossiya*, and Kosygin's speech in the 12 June 1970 *Moskovskaya Pravda*. According to P. Yesaulov, this was an extension of the April 1969 price rise for publicly owned poultry to privately owned poultry and went into effect on 1 February 1970. Yesaulov noted that 60 percent of Soviet poultry is privately owned (*Voprosy Ekonomiki* 12 [1970]: 56).

[24] Paul Wohl in the 5 June 1970 *Christian Science Monitor* cited figures on the drop in the number of livestock per 1,000 population: cattle from 415 in 1966 to 394 in 1969, cows from 176 to 168, sheep and goats from 603 to 566, and pigs from 248 to 233.

[25] According to Voronov's March 1970 speech, *Leninskoye Znamya*, 24 March 1970.

[26] *Selskoye Khozyaystvo Rossii* 3 (1970): 6.

[27] Masherov (*Sovetskaya Belorussiya*, 29 May 1970), Mazurov (*Sovetskaya Belorussiya*, 5 June 1970), Kosygin and Podgornyy (*Moskovskaya Pravda*, 12 June 1970).

support of the RSFSR leaders. Speaking to a USSR Supreme Soviet session in Moscow in December 1969, Estonian Premier V. I. Klauson declared that "instead of widely studying, generalizing, and introducing into livestock raising the advanced experience of farms and republics where the level of livestock development is higher, the raising of purchase prices is being proposed as one of the measures to raise the profitability of meat production. This path is hardly correct."[28]

Nevertheless, the agricultural lobby soon won approval for their proposal, apparently because of the seriousness of the meat shortage. First, prices were raised for private livestock products. In late January a Central Committee-Council of Ministers decree "On Increasing Production and State Purchases of Pigs and Poultry in 1970" was adopted. Although the decree was never published nor announced (except in passing in Pysin's speech in the 17 February 1970 *Sovetskaya Rossiya*), it ordered procurement organs to pay higher prices for private livestock products purchased from kolkhozniks and sovkhoz workers—with the aim of encouraging more private livestock ownership. This is clear from the 11 February *Pravda* editorial which revealed that "prices for pigs and poultry procured from the population have been increased and made equal to purchase prices for kolkhozes." The decree presumably was discussed at a 13 February conference of republic procurement ministers on "questions connected with the concluding of contracts for purchase of agricultural products in 1970" (*Pravda*, 14 February). It apparently was also a subject of discussion and explanation at three top-level conferences in the Central Committee. On 4 March Brezhnev met with republic agricultural ministers on questions including the increasing of "state purchases of livestock products." Taking part in the discussion were Polyanskiy, Kulakov, Matskevich, and others (*Pravda*, 5 March). A month later, the leaders of republic party, soviet, planning, agricultural, and procurement organs met with Kirilenko and Kulakov on "fulfillment of party and government decisions on developing livestock raising" (*Pravda*, 5 April). Analogous leaders of oblasts were called to the Central Committee in late April to discuss the same questions with Polyanskiy, Voronov, and Kulakov (*Pravda*, 28 April).

The Estonians may have disliked this price hike also because it encouraged private livestock raising. In a January interview (*Kommunist Estonii*, no. 1 [1970]) Estonian Agriculture Minister Kh. Myannik suggested that Estonians were unsympathetic to the expansion of private livestock ownership. He recalled that during discussion of the draft kolkhoz charter in 1969 many Estonians had complained that too many head of private livestock were permitted by the charter and, while warning against administrative discouragement of private livestock ownership, he declared that "one must prove economically that keeping private livestock is unprofitable and is the livestock raising of yesteryear."

[28]*Sovetskaya Estoniya*, 20 December 1969. His statement was only reported in Estonia's paper.

The January price rise for private livestock was followed by a March price rise for public livestock products to go into effect starting 1 May.[29] The decision to raise livestock prices was alluded to vaguely in Kosygin's 10 June Supreme Soviet election speech (*Moskovskaya Pravda*, 12 June) and in the 16 June *Pravda* editorial,[30] but the Politburo decision was only announced publicly by Brezhnev at the 2 July Central Committee agriculture plenum (*Pravda*, 3 July). The Central Committee–Council of Ministers decree was then published in the 18 July *Pravda*.

Despite approval of the price hikes, the Estonians continued to hint disapproval. Estonian First Deputy Premier E. G. Tynurist wrote in the 10 April 1970 *Izvestiya* that "recently instead of seriously studying zoo-technical problems influencing the growth of production and profitability of livestock raising branches, and generalizing and introducing advanced technology," the USSR Agriculture Ministry "is trying to reduce everything to a review of purchase prices and increasing of capital investments on construction of large [livestock] complexes."[31]

The Estonians' stress on introduction of advanced techniques of livestock raising instead of injecting new funds had much in common with Voronov's theme. Although Voronov and Pysin devoted much attention to livestock problems and meat shortages in their early 1970 speeches, they carefully avoided the question of prices and stressed more efficient methods, cost-cutting and im-

---

[29] This decision involved price rises for milk, cream, sheep, wool, goats, rabbits, and, in some areas, cattle, and above-plan bonuses for livestock, poultry, milk, eggs, and wool. Prices for cattle were not generally raised. In a November 1970 *Ekonomicheskaya Gazeta* (no. 48, p. 19) Moscow Oblast Executive Committee Chairman N. T. Kozlov urged a rise in cattle prices also.

[30] Estonian First Deputy Premier Tynurist referred to "a number" of recent decrees raising prices for milk, beef, and mutton (*Sovetskaya Estoniya*, 16 May 1970).

[31] Tynurist later repeated his attack on the mass construction of expensive livestock complexes—even after this had become a nationwide campaign. In a 16 December 1971 *Pravda* article, he argued again that more efficient techniques, not new complexes, are the key, and this time he cited a computer study to back him up. He complained that farm leaders themselves often "do not see the main cause of a farm's lagging or else consider a less important, secondary matter as the main cause." "Some people, for example, are inclined to overrate the role of building big livestock farms [*fermy*]," he wrote, and "some, not penetrating into the essence of the matter and not seeing the true causes of lagging of production, insistently demand from higher organs the wide development of construction of expensive livestock facilities." Yet, he wrote, modern mechanized barns do not guarantee higher labor productivity, whereas "practise shows that with skilled organization of production and creation of a solid fodder base one can get good results even on the present livestock raising farms." Although Tynurist ostensibly is writing of *local* farm leaders misidentifying the lack of modern facilities as the main cause of lagging, his criticism implicitly includes Brezhnev and Polyanskiy, who have stressed that agriculture can be raised only by greatly improving agriculture's material-technical base. Titling his article "Relying on Electronics," Tynurist argued that an Estonian computer study of livestock farms had made it possible to "reveal the true reasons" for the high cost of livestock products, and two reasons he listed were the high cost of fodder and, in some kolkhozes, excessively high wages.

provement of organization instead.[32] Voronov finally came out more clearly in a 24 November 1970 speech, in which he raised doubts about the value of the early 1970 rises in purchase prices for livestock products. He argued that as long as farms are using inefficient methods resulting in high and even rising costs, "no raising of prices will help such farms turn livestock raising into a highly profitable branch" (*Sovetskaya Rossiya*, 25 November 1970). He declared that "the leaders of many farms correctly think that the only way to increase profitability of livestock raising" is by raising productivity, expanding production, and cutting costs. In a long 2 October *Komsomolskaya Pravda* interview, Voronov pushed his own solution: development of a meat-cattle branch.

Whatever the merits of the price rises were, livestock procurement turned up in early 1970. *Selskaya Zhizn* on 17 June 1970, reporting a meeting of the collegium of the USSR Procurement Ministry, stated that "as a result of implementing the measures adopted by the party and government to increase the production and procurement of livestock products during the past five months the volume of state purchases of meat, milk and eggs somewhat increased in comparison with the same period of last year." In September, Deputy Agriculture Minister P. Morozov reported that in the first half of 1970 the number of cattle had risen by 2.5 million over the first half of 1969, the number of pigs by 8.7 million, sheep and goats 8.8 million, and poultry 74.1 million.[33] RSFSR Agriculture Minister L. Ya. Florentyev in the 10 October 1970 *Sovetskaya Rossiya* reported RSFSR meat procurements in the first three-quarters of 1970 were up 118,000 tons over the first three-quarters of 1969, and milk was up 761,000 tons.

The Resource Debate

Although the outlines for the 1971–75 plan were supposed to have been determined by August 1968[34] and ratified in 1969,[35] preparations dragged on through 1969 and when the preliminary outlines were finally more or less worked out in early 1970 they were overturned by the Politburo, and Gosplan was instructed to rework them to raise agriculture's share. This was the result of a successful campaign by Brezhnev and Polyanskiy to alter the consumer goods

[32] See Voronov's speeches in the 24 March 1970 *Leninskoye Znamya* and 9 June 1970 *Pravda*, and Pysin's speech in the 17 February 1970 *Sovetskaya Rossiya*, and also Pysin's article in the April 1970 *Ekonomika Selskogo Khozyaystva*.

[33] *Agitator* 18 (September 1970): 17. Of course, the 1969 figures may have been especially low because of the severe weather in early 1969.

[34] Baybakov, *Ekonomicheskaya Gazeta*, no. 21 (May 1968).

[35] Kosygin, *Sovetskaya Belorussiya*, 15 February 1968. Gosplan First Deputy Chairman A. A. Goreglyad in the 21 February 1971 *Moskovskaya Pravda* told how in February 1969 Gosplan's "draft of basic directions" had been presented to the Central Committee and Council of Ministers but "after careful, detailed consideration" it was rejected and "it was suggested to us that we seek out additional resources for creation of still more material wealth for the public," especially for boosting housing construction.

orientation of the plan established by Kosygin and his allies since 1967. This movement began with Polyanskiy's late March article appealing for a change in development rates in favor of agriculture. This was followed by Brezhnev's 13 April statement urging more investments in agriculture and by appointment of an agriculture spokesman as first deputy chairman of Gosplan on 10 April.

In May the Politburo raised investments and resources for agriculture in the new plan, and in the June Supreme Soviet election speeches most Politburo members publicly supported increased aid for agriculture. A 2 July Central Committee plenum heard Brezhnev report on the new agricultural program and the agricultural portion of the five-year plan was formally adopted. After the May decision on agriculture, debate over the remaining sectors of the plan intensified, with Brezhnev, Suslov, and Kirilenko supporting the heavy industry-military sector, and Mazurov, Shelepin, Voronov, Kosygin, and Polyanskiy supporting the consumer goods sector. Continued contention delayed announcement of a draft plan until February 1971, disrupting the schedule for the 24th CPSU Congress and local congresses. The draft finally agreed upon included both the big increase in agricultural investments won by Brezhnev and Polyanskiy in 1970 and a continuation of the increase in consumer goods investments won by Kosygin and his allies in 1967.

Despite the 1968 decisions to increase fertilizer production, agricultural equipment output, and land improvement work, these programs continued to lag in 1969. A Council of Ministers decree published in August 1969 (*Izvestiya*, 2 August 1969) demanded that 1969 goals for building new fertilizer plants be fulfilled, but Brezhnev at the November 1969 Congress of Kolkhozniks said fertilizer capacity would rise by only 8 million tons in 1970 (*Pravda*, 26 November 1969)—instead of the 13 million indicated in the May 1968 decree (*Pravda*, 6 June 1968). In the same speech, he admitted that while capital investments in agriculture had significantly increased, "for a number of reasons not everything that we planned has been done in this respect."

Selskaya Zhizn on 30 December 1969 editorially attacked the lag in rural construction, reporting that only 60 percent of construction work for kolkhozes was completed in the first three-quarters of 1969. It stated that while agriculture was supposed to get over 8.5 billion rubles of state aid in 1969, only 4.8 billion had been introduced in the first eleven months.[36] Belorussian Central Committee Secretary A. Smirnov in the 19 December 1969 *Sovetskaya Belorussiya* complained that the USSR Rural Construction Ministry had given the Belorussian Rural Construction Ministry only 14 million rubles instead of the 26 million it needed for 1970, and he asked the USSR Council of Ministers to overrule Gosplan and order more investments and resources for Belorussia's Rural Construction Ministry.

[36] In early 1969 *Selskaya Zhizn* had finally wrung a promise from Gosplan to stop assigning industrial projects to rural construction ministries (*Selskaya Zhizn*, 9 March 1969).

At the December 1969 Supreme Soviet session both Gosplan Chairman Baybakov[37] and Finance Minister Garbuzov[38] openly acknowledged that agriculture was coming out shortchanged. Meanwhile, the preferential development of light industry set in 1967 continued for 1969 and 1970. But there also was a general slowdown of industrial growth:

Planned Growth (percent)[39]				
	1967	1968	1969	1970
Group A (heavy industry)	7.5	7.9	7.2	6.1
Group B (light industry)	6.6	8.6	7.5	6.8

The worsening economic situation became the subject of a 15 December 1969 Central Committee plenum, the details of which are still unknown.[40] According to *Pravda's* 13 January 1970 editorial on the plenum, one of the subjects brought up was the agricultural situation, "especially public livestock raising": there were "difficulties in supplying the population with livestock products—especially in big industrial centers . . . " and "this required serious measures to correct the situation." One measure undoubtedly raised at the plenum was the proposal to raise livestock procurement prices, which was condemned by Estonian Premier Klauson immediately after the plenum (*Sovetskaya Estoniya*, 20 December 1969), but which was soon adopted. Another subject considered by the December plenum was "some important problems arising during the compilation of future plans and especially of the new five-year plan" (*Pravda's* 13 January editorial).

As Gosplan completed its preliminary outlines of the new five-year plan in March and April,[41] Polyanskiy wrote an article in the April *Sovety Deputatov Trudyashchikhsya* (signed to press 20 March) urging that the new plan be "a five-year plan for a significant upsurge in agriculture" and urging an improvement in the development rates of agriculture. Further growth of agriculture

[37]"For the five-year period as a whole state centralized capital investments in the agriculture branch will comprise 32 billion rubles, 1.6 times more than in the preceding five-year period, although targets of the directives of the 23d CPSU Congress on this indicator will be somewhat underfulfilled for a number of reasons" (*Izvestiya*, 17 December 1969).

[38]"However, capital investments in agriculture for a number of reasons will be somewhat lower than the volumes foreseen by the May 1966 Central Committee CPSU plenum for 1970" (*Izvestiya*, 17 December 1969).

[39]Baybakov in the 16 December 1966, 11 October 1967, 10 December 1968, and 17 December 1969 *Izvestiya*.

[40]Brezhnev's report was not published. Later, in January, editorials and speeches reflected the apparent gist of the plenum discussion.

[41]Kirilenko in a 14 April speech in Yerevan stated that Gosplan "at present is completing the working out of the draft of the new five-year plan" (*Kommunist*, 15 April 1970). Polyanskiy's article also referred to the current work on the draft plan.

required "a further significant increase" in equipment deliveries, land improvement, and fertilizer production, he wrote.

In early April the agriculture lobby managed to move sympathizers into two key government posts. On 11 April *Pravda* reported the transfer of Stavropol Kray First Secretary L. N. Yefremov to first deputy chairman of the State Committee for Science and Technology and of Orel Oblast First Secretary T. I. Sokolov to first deputy chairman of Gosplan. Both these men were prominent long-time agricultural specialists[42] and their subsequent duties indicate that they were placed in these government organs to represent agriculture. Previously, the science and technology committee had had no deputy chairman for agriculture and Gosplan had only one deputy chairman—out of about a dozen—for agriculture. In contrast, there long had been a Gosplan *first* deputy chairman for construction—V. Ya. Isayev.

The Sokolov appointment was especially interesting because Gosplan was in the midst of preparing the new five-year plan outlines and also was under attack. It had been criticized at the December 1969 plenum,[43] presumably in Brezhnev's report, and its work was again impugned by Brezhnev at the big 21 April ceremony on the 100th anniversary of Lenin's birth: "It is indisputable, comrades, that many of the complexities which we are encountering in the field of economics have their roots in this or that shortcoming in planning, in poor plans and also in imprecise fulfillment of them" (*Pravda*, 22 April 1970). Gosplan party committee secretary V. I. Balan said at a 10 July Moscow City party *aktiv* meeting that Brezhnev's "serious criticism" of Gosplan "on questions of ensuring proportional development of the economy and raising the efficiency of production and the level of planning" had led to party meetings in Gosplan to discuss shortcomings, improvement of planning, and "measures to create a modern material-technical base for agriculture and raise the level of production of agricultural products" (*Moskovskaya Pravda*, 11 July 1970).

The criticism of Gosplan was followed by the overriding of its preliminary plan outlines in May 1970[44] and then the replacement of A. F. Kolosov, the chief editor of Gosplan's organ *Planovoye Khozyaystvo*. The new chief editor

[42]Yefremov was RSFSR Bureau first deputy chairman for agriculture 1962–64. He now heads the science and technology committee's joint inter-departmental council on problems of agriculture, water and forestry (*Selskaya Zhizn*, 9 October 1970). Sokolov was already a prominent national agricultural figure in October 1946 when he (and Khrushchev) were appointed to the new Council on Kolkhoz Affairs (*Pravda*, 9 October 1946). He was first secretary of the virgin lands kray 1960–63 and in 1965 was briefly RSFSR first deputy agriculture minister (according to the *Deputaty Verkhovnogo Soveta SSSR, 7. Sozyv* [Moscow, 1966]). As Gosplan first deputy chairman he wrote an article on agriculture in *Planovoye Khozyaystvo*, no. 9 (1970).

[43]A. Birman, *Literaturnaya Gazeta*, 11 February 1970, p. 10.

[44]Sokolov wrote in the February 1971 *Ekonomika Selskogo Khozyaystva* (p. 35) that "volumes of capital investments and material-technical means higher than the original outlines were approved" for the five-year plan by the mid-1970 decisions.

was a young, unknown economist from outside Gosplan's apparatus[45] and the first issue under his leadership (no. 9, signed to press 21 August) contained a lead article by new Gosplan First Deputy Chairman Sokolov, warning planners against diverting money from agriculture ("Attempts to resolve particular economic problems at the expense of agricultural development must be decisively suppressed"). Sokolov's warning was similar to Brezhnev's past warnings and Sokolov obviously was placed in Gosplan to prevent new diversions from agriculture. In a later article (*Ekonomika Selskogo Khozyaystva* 2 [1971]: 35), Sokolov indicated that he intended to use Gosplan to improve aid to agriculture, for example, by setting quotas on ministries, starting January 1971, to ensure their fulfillment of orders for agricultural machinery, parts, and fertilizer production. Also, starting in 1971, changes were introduced in Gosplan's planning procedures regarding agriculture. P. Poletayev writes in the July 1971 *Voprosy Ekonomiki* (pp. 52-53) that before 1971 planning of rural construction was hampered by lack of coordination between agricultural production construction and nonproduction construction in Gosplan, but that now construction of sovkhoz schools, housing, etc., is being planned as part of the agricultural category. He notes that in the past nonproduction projects were often built only if there was money left over. These planning changes were probably part of Polyanskiy's efforts to increase investments for rural construction and improvements in rural living conditions. In the 1971-75 five-year plan, for the first time the state began making large-scale investments in rural housing and cultural construction (according to S. I. Polovenko in the *Vestnik Moskovskogo Universiteta*, Economic Series, 4 [1971]: 10-11). At the December 1971 RSFSR Supreme Soviet session RSFSR Gosplan chief K. M. Gerasimov said that state investments in rural housing construction would rise 40 percent in the new five-year plan (*Sovetskaya Rossiya*, 9 December 1971).

Voronov may have opposed Sokolov's appointment. Shortly before the appointment, a 20 March Sc *'etskaya Rossiya* editorial reported that the RSFSR Council of Ministers recently had noted serious shortcomings in livestock raising in Sokolov's Orel Oblast. The editorial used a full paragraph to attack Orel's work, including the charge that "the low rates of growth of production and procurement of livestock products here are the result of a lowered level of organizational work in sovkhozes and kolkhozes in the oblast." In view of the apparent Voronov-Yefremov rivalry in 1963-64 and Yefremov's role in purging Voronov's protégés in 1964, it seems likely that Voronov also opposed Yefremov's appointment.[46]

---

[45] V. S. Glagolev, thirty-three years of age, had held only two previous jobs, according to the November 1970 *Zhurnalist*: science editor of the Soviet Encyclopedia Publishing House (1960-66) and consultant to the political economy department of *Kommunist* (1966-70).

[46] However, in Yefremov's case, the transfer was not necessarily an advancement. Although now a senior bureaucrat in Moscow, his new post does not carry some of the

Polyanskiy's appeal was quickly supported by Brezhnev. In a 13 April Kharkov speech Brezhnev declared "our country now is in a condition to invest in the development of agriculture significantly more funds than we could earlier." He noted the meat shortages and argued that the rise in wages had caused not only increased demand for consumer goods but also for meat, milk, butter, and eggs: "once we took the course of raising the welfare of the workers" we must make a "corresponding expansion of production of consumer goods, including livestock products" (*Pravda*, 14 April 1970). *Pravda* appeared to take issue with Brezhnev's argument in a 30 May editorial on agricultural reserves. Quoting his April statement on the country's ability to now invest more in agriculture, the editorial stated: "However, scientific-technical progress in agriculture cannot be reduced only to growth in the delivery of new machines, chemical fertilizer and other means of production. An inseparable, active part of this process is the ability to effectively use land and fertilizer, each machine, and each ruble invested in production. Analysis shows that with the present level of material-technical supply kolkhozes and sovkhozes can produce more products than now. The thing is that not all farms are applying modern production technology; many of them ineffectively use equipment and poorly introduce achievements of science and advanced practice." It concluded that "no matter how solid a material base there is, the success of the matter is decided by skillful organization of labor and selfless work by people in the fields and in the [livestock] farms."

Nevertheless, Brezhnev and Polyanskiy prevailed. As Brezhnev related in his 2 July Central Committee plenum report, in May 1970 "the Politburo considered the document 'On the Situation in Agriculture,' which is well known to you," "approved the conclusions and proposals" in it, "adopted a decree to increase the volumes of capital investments and to strengthen the material-technical equipping of agriculture," and decided to call the July Central Committee plenum (*Pravda*, 3 July). At a late May USSR Council of Ministers session Premier Kosygin reported on the basic directions of the new plan and Brezhnev took the unusual step of addressing the Council also (*Pravda*, 2 June). On 1 June Brezhnev spoke to the RSFSR Council of Ministers on the directions of the new plan (RSFSR Premier Voronov—who appeared least enthusiastic about the new directions—did not speak at his own cabinet's session).

When the June Supreme Soviet election campaign speeches began, the usual divergences over resources appeared, but this time with agriculture's defenders having the clear advantage. Brezhnev, Polyanskiy, and Central Committee Agriculture Secretary Kulakov pressed the need for more resources for agriculture and simultaneously promised that the new five-year plan would provide that aid. Brezhnev argued that "further sharp increase" of agricultural produc-

---

advantages he had as a regional party chief: in June 1970 he was not reelected to the Supreme Soviet and in April 1971 he was elected only to the Central Auditing Commission instead of to the Central Committee.

tion rested squarely on the creation of the necessary material-technical base for agriculture and that this was "the essence of the matter." This means, he explained, "sharply" raising the production of agricultural equipment, "seriously" increasing the production of fertilizer, "consistently and firmly" carrying out the land improvement program, and "drastically" improving rural construction. Implicitly refuting the opponents of increased investments for agriculture, he stated that these tasks would certainly be accomplished, but it is "all a question of time periods": it can be dragged out for twenty-five years or it can be "significantly accelerated." "We favor the second course," he declared; in the new five-year plan "the volume of capital investments in agriculture will be increased still more" (*Moskovskaya Pravda*, 13 June 1970). Polyanskiy declared that "the tasks of creating an abundance of agricultural products" and of bringing rural living standards up to urban standards require "improving the proportions in the development of the two leading branches of public production—industry and agriculture—and overcoming the lagging of light industry, and the food and meat-dairy industries behind the growing needs of the country." The new five-year plan would provide an unprecedented increase in agricultural investments, he said (*Pravda*, 4 June). Kulakov said that the Central Committee attributed the "unsatisfactory level" of agricultural production to failure to provide a more powerful material-technical base and "the creation of such a base will be one of the central tasks of the new five-year plan" (*Pravda*, 5 June).

Podgornyy, Kirilenko, and Pelshe also promised more equipment for agriculture. Podgornyy declared that "we intend to considerably increase capital investments in agriculture and to strengthen even more its material-technical base" (*Moskovskaya Pravda*, 12 June). Kirilenko promised a "sharp strengthening" of agriculture's material-technical base and unprecedented deliveries of equipment and fertilizer (*Pravda*, 6 June).[47] Pelshe stated that in the new plan "measures will be taken to significantly raise the level of agricultural production and seriously strengthen its material-technical base" (*Sovetskaya Latviya*, 4 June). Even most of those normally unreceptive to agriculture's needs expressed vague support. Kosygin recognized the serious agricultural problems—the meat shortages and the recent price rise necessitated by them—and stated that "measures will be taken to ensure further growth of agricultural production" (*Moskovskaya Pravda*, 12 June). Suslov declared that "the CPSU Central Committee and Soviet Government are taking the necessary measures so that agriculture will develop at an even faster rate in years to come" (*Pravda*, 10 June). The furthest Shelest would go was to acknowledge that "raising agriculture is a matter for the whole party and all the Soviet people" (*Radyanska Ukraina*, 2 June).

[47]Later in the month, in a speech in the Tatar Republic, Kirilenko stated that in connection with the growth of the population and welfare and the lag in agriculture, especially meat, it is necessary "to adopt new important measures to further raise agriculture" and "the main condition for resolving this task is the strengthening of the material-technical base of agricultural production" (*Pravda*, 26 June).

Mazurov and Shelepin backed more aid for agriculture—but linked it to more aid for light industry. Mazurov noted that "one must intensify the rates of agricultural development" and the new plan would include "appropriate measures to raise agriculture," but, he said, "the same approach is needed for resolving the tasks of supplying the population with enough consumer goods" (*Sovetskaya Belorussiya*, 5 June). Shelepin spoke of narrowing the differences between rural and urban living standards, but, like Mazurov, linked agriculture and consumer goods: "In the coming five-year plan more energetic measures will be taken to significantly increase production of agricultural products and consumer goods" (*Pravda*, 5 June). Only Voronov totally ignored new inputs for agriculture, stressing instead reducing of costs (*Pravda*, 9 June).[48] Meanwhile, Voronov, like Shelepin and Mazurov, backed raising of consumer goods production, labeling it "one of the central tasks" of the new five-year plan. Consumer goods advocate Kosygin applauded the "closing of the gap between the pace of producing the means of production and that of consumer goods" but cautiously did not promise anything for the future.

As usual, Suslov was strongest on defense, warning that because of US aggressiveness, "we must not weaken vigilance for a moment, we must constantly improve the country's defenses and arm the Soviet army and navy with the most up-to-date weapons" (TASS, 9 June). Brezhnev and Kirilenko also made statements in spring and summer supporting defense. At the 21 April Lenin anni-

---

[48]In a 24 November 1970 speech at an RSFSR conference of heads of soviets, Voronov almost openly challenged the agriculture lobby, raising doubts about the 1970 price rises, the decision to produce more equipment for agriculture, and the handling of rural construction. He argued that "no raising of prices" will make farms really profitable as long as they are using inefficient methods. He downplayed the 1970 shift of priorities by declaring that "as before, industry will develop at high rates" in the new plan, mentioning only that "a big program has been outlined for further raising of agricultural production." Although he noted the July plenum decision to deliver more equipment to agriculture, Voronov pointed out the "enormous unused reserves," i.e., many tractors being used only one shift and only on weekdays.

While Polyanskiy has pushed village reorganization and rural construction programs to make rural life attractive enough to stem the huge outflow of youths from farms (most recently, in his April 1970 article and June 1970 speech), Voronov in his November speech said: "often the reason for the outflow of youths from some rural districts is attributed only to shortcomings in housing, cultural and living conditions. . . . However, reducing the whole matter to just these things hardly is correct." He cited a study by the RSFSR State Committee for Use of Labor Resources which found that "a large part of the youth" cite shortcomings in labor and production organization, dissatisfaction with their jobs, and lack of opportunity as reasons for leaving the farm. The link system promoted by Voronov is often advanced as a means to hold youths on the farm by providing more incentives and opportunities—more individual initiative and better pay. Voronov also took a swipe at Polyanskiy's leadership of the rural construction program. He noted the "many errors in rural construction" and recalled the September 1968 Central Committee–Council of Ministers decree on shortcomings in the handling of rural construction. While conceding that some improvement had been made since the decree, Voronov stated that "far from all has been done and not always done well" (*Sovetskaya Rossiya*, 25 November).

versary Brezhnev said "we will continue to strengthen the defense of the mother-land and equip the army with the most modern weapons" (*Pravda*, 22 April). Kirilenko in a 25 June speech stated that "the present-day international situation obliges us to maintain high vigilance in respect to the aggressive actions of imperialism" and "to strengthen the might of our state and its defensive capacity. Our party, its Central Committee, the Central Committee's Politburo and the Soviet Government are constantly concerned about this" (*Pravda*, 26 June).

As before, Brezhnev was foremost in defending heavy industry, telling his constituents "I can assure the electors" that the new five-year plan "provides for further significant growth of industry, primarily those branches which produce the means of production, ensure the power base of the economy, and determine scientific-technical progress" (*Moskovskaya Pravda*, 13 June). The heavy industry interests appeared to be defended also by Masherov and Shelest.[49] Brezhnev's ally Kirilenko, in a 25 June speech in Tataria, picked up Brezhnev's statement: "In characterizing the main directions of the new five-year plan, comrade L. I. Brezhnev in his pre-election speech said that the plan provides for further serious growth of industry, especially those branches which produce the means of production, ensure the power base of the economy, and determine scientific-technical progress" (*Pravda*, 26 June). *Pravda* featured this same Brezhnev formulation in its 2 July editorial.

During June Gosplan worked out the revised agricultural portion of the plan,[50] and by early July the figures for the new agricultural program were ready for Brezhnev to present at a 2 July Central Committee plenum. In his July 1970 plenum report he argued that even though grain production had reached new high levels, "we must direct our main attention to how the growing demands of the population and the economy as a whole are being satisfied" and from this position grain production is still insufficient. The situation with livestock was worse, he indicated: "As is known, the population's demand for livestock products, especially meat, is far from being satisfied."[51] He repeated his June election speech argument that further progress depends mainly on increasing input: "the decisive factor determining rates of development of agricultural production

[49]*Pravda*'s version of Masherov's statement was: "As before, the branches ensuring technical progress in the economy will develop at preferential rates" (*Pravda*, 29 May). Shelest said: "The main economic task of the new five-year plan is to comprehensively utilize the achievements of science and technology, improve methods of administering the economy, raise effectiveness, and strengthen the intensification of social production. Carrying out the tasks of the new five-year plan will make it possible to further strengthen the economic and military power of our fatherland" (*Radyanska Ukraina*, 2 June).

[50]In his 12 June election speech Brezhnev indicated that work on the plan was still continuing and "it would be premature to speak about concrete figures and assignments" (*Moskovskaya Pravda*, 13 June).

[51]He explained the March decree raising livestock procurement prices—without raising retail meat prices—and indicated that this involved additional state expenditures.

and growth of productivity of labor" is the further strengthening of the material-technical base of agriculture. He warned that if agriculture is not aided "we will accumulate new shortcomings and create still more difficulties." He also warned of the futility of following Khrushchev-type approaches: "As is well known, in the past we undertook attempts by various other paths to solve problems of agriculture. But they did not bring the desired results." There is no more virgin land to develop, he stated, so the only path now is to raise production on the present territory, and this means providing fertilizer and equipment to maintain and raise productivity. Yet, as he indicated, the aid to agriculture provided for in his big March 1965 program had been partially diverted: "For a number of reasons during the current five-year plan agriculture has not received all the capital investments provided in the plan nor the set amount of equipment. The quotas for introducing capacity, for production of fertilizer and for deliveries of it to agriculture were not fulfilled" (*Pravda*, 3 July). Then he announced that "the Politburo has recognized that for the next few years our central task should be the comprehensive strengthening of the material-technical base of agriculture, equipping kolkhozes and sovkhozes with advanced modern machinery, supplying them with mineral fertilizers and the wide development of land improvement. . . . The Politburo has determined that in the new five-year plan 77.6 billion rubles of state capital investments should be allocated to agriculture for production construction, acquiring equipment, and housing and cultural construction, including 45.9 billion for construction-installation work." This, he stated, exceeds the 1966–70 five-year plan investments by 70 percent. Judging from Brezhnev's statement, actual investments during 1966-70 must have been about 45.6 billion rubles. The goal he set in March 1965 was 41 billion—but this did not include the housing and cultural (schools, theaters, hospitals, etc.) construction.

Although the 77.6 billion goal sounds impressive, specific goals listed by Brezhnev for the main sectors—fertilizer production, agricultural equipment, and land improvement—suggest that the July 1970 program was in many respects primarily a restoration of cuts in previous programs. The fertilizer goal actually represented a significant cutback. The 1971–75 plan provides for 40 million tons of new fertilizer production capacity, to reach an annual level of 90 million tons in 1975. The May 1968 Central Committee–Council of Ministers decree[52] provided for increasing capacity by 48 million tons in the next five years and set a late 1972 goal of 95 million tons.[53] Thus, the new goal for 1975 is 5 million tons less than the old goal for 1972. Khrushchev had advocated 100 million tons by 1970. The new goal may simply be more realistic in view of continuing nonfulfillment of plans. Brezhnev bragged that while fertilizer production had grown by only 3.3 million tons in 1966 and 1967 and by 5.2 in

[52] Brezhnev refers to it as a Politburo decree in his speech.
[53] According to Chemical Industry Minister L. A. Kostandov in the 4 January 1969 *Selskaya Zhizn.* Brezhnev, of course, did not cite these embarrassing figures.

1968, in 1969 it grew by over 11 million tons. Yet, the 1968 decree had called for 13 million tons in 1969. In his June election speech Kosygin said that fertilizer production would rise to 57.5 million tons in 1970. This is well below the 62–65 million ton goal in the original 1966 directives.

The equipment and land improvement goals appeared to represent some reduction also. Brezhnev stated that the new five-year plan would deliver 1,700,000 tractors, 1,100,000 trucks, and 541,000 grain combines. In 1965, he had promised 1,790,000 tractors, 1,100,000 trucks, and 625,000 grain combines during the 1966–70 five-year plan. In July 1970 he promised 3 million hectares of newly irrigated land and drainage of 5 million hectares during the 1971–75 five-year plan. At the March 1965 plenum he had promised irrigation of 3 million hectares and drainage of 6 million hectares during the 1966–70 five-year plan.

There was a significant rise in state investments in construction: 45.9 billion rubles for 1971–75 as against 21 billion rubles for 1966–70 (however, Brezhnev did not mention housing and cultural construction in his March 1965 statement). The increase included a new program for construction of big suburban complexes for raising pigs, cattle fattening, milk production, poultry factories, and mechanized sheep-raising farms. Deputy chief of Gosplan's agricultural department, P. A. Yesaulov, set a 5 billion ruble cost on this program (*Voprosy Ekonomiki* [December 1970] : 59). The high cost of these complexes had been objected to by the Estonians[54] and won no applause from Voronov either. This program was extended in early 1971 and became the most distinctive feature of the new agricultural program. According to Komsomol First Secretary Ye. M. Tyazhelnikov,[55] at the first Politburo meeting after the 24th congress Brezhnev proposed additional measures to aid livestock raising, and on 16 April 1971[56] a Central Committee–Council of Ministers decree on livestock raising was adopted, ordering construction of 1,170 big livestock complexes and 585 poultry factories in the next three years.[57] Naturally, the cost of the program for complexes rose also. Poletayev in the July 1971 *Voprosy Ekonomiki* (pp. 54–55) set a 9 billion ruble cost on the program to build "highly-mechanized livestock raising facilities."

The new stress on big livestock complexes soon turned into a campaign, causing the usual excesses. P. Chervenko, director of the Central Institute of Mechanization and Electrification of Livestock Raising, complained in the 19 May 1971 *Selskaya Zhizn* that people had gotten the opinion that now big complexes were to be virtually the only form of livestock raising. He criticized a January *Ekonomika Selskogo Khozyaystva* editorial for writing that "industrial

[54] See Estonian First Deputy Premier Tynurist's 10 April 1970 *Izvestiya* complaint about the USSR Agriculture Ministry's efforts to increase capital investments on construction of big livestock complexes.

[55] In a speech in Kirgizia (*Sovetskaya Kirgiziya*, 7 July 1971).

[56] The date is given by Poletayev in the July 1971 *Voprosy Ekonomiki*, p. 55.

[57] The decree was published in the 27 April 1971 *Selskaya Zhizn*.

complexes" in meat production are now the "main direction in which we must conduct organizational work on all levels, in all echelons, in every kolkhoz and sovkhoz." "Reading such recommendations," wrote Chervenko, "everyone is striving to create 'complexes,' " and farm leaders are turning to our institute for designs for complexes and when "we ask why precisely complexes and not comprehensively mechanized farms (*fermy*)," farm leaders explain that "that is the assignment given by local organizations: 'Just a complex and nothing else!' "

In his July 1970 plenum speech, Brezhnev employed the device used to boost consumer goods production since 1966: using heavy industry's facilities to produce goods for agriculture. Declaring that building new plants for agricultural equipment would take too long, Brezhnev stated that the Politburo wanted all branches to participate in equipping farms: "We must organize things so that not one plant, regardless of its departmental subordination, stands aside from this big and noble cause." He came to the plenum armed with promises from Aviation Industry Minister P. V. Dementyev to produce equipment for poultry factories in his plants, from Defense Industry Minister S. A. Zverev to produce tractors and fertilizer spreaders at his plants, from Shipbuilding Minister B. Ye. Butoma to produce sprinkler systems, from Machine Building Industry Minister V. V. Bakhirev to produce seeders, etc.

The New Five-Year Plan

While the 2 July plenum basically determined agriculture's share, the shares for the other sectors were still up for debate, and this debate caused a year's delay in adopting the five-year plan and apparently also in holding the 24th Party Congress. After adopting the new agricultural program, the Politburo apparently recognized the impossibility of quick completion of the five-year plan and did an about-face on the question of holding the party congress (which was to adopt the plan). Although Brezhnev had announced at the 2 July agricultural plenum that the coming 24th Congress would be held in 1970,[58] a second Central Committee plenum was called less than two weeks later (13 July) to hear him announce the postponement of the congress until March 1971. The leaders had presumably agreed in early 1970 that it was to be held sometime that year, since almost half of them had publicly stated in their election speeches that it would be in 1970.[59]

On 16 July the Council of Ministers met to discuss the July plenum and preparation of the new five-year plan. Gosplan was instructed to go back to

---

[58] By party statute the congress was to be held every four years and was already overdue, the previous congress having been held in March–April 1966.

[59] Brezhnev (*Moskovskaya Pravda*, 13 June), Polyanskiy (*Pravda*, 4 June), Pelshe (*Pravda*, 4 June), Shelest (*Radyanska Ukraina*, 2 June), Kunayev (*Kazakhstanskaya Pravda*, 28 May), Mzhavanadze (*Pravda*, 6 June), Shcherbitskiy (*Radyanska Ukraina*, 28 May), Katushev (*Pravda*, 4 June), Solomentsev (*Pravda*, 4 June). Voronov had also announced this in his March 1970 Moscow speech (*Leninskoye Znamya*, 24 March).

work on the draft (*Pravda*, 17 July). With the Politburo badly split over priorities, the date the plan was to go into effect (January 1971) came and went with no sign of agreement. Republic party congresses (which were to discuss the five-year plan draft) scheduled for January and early February 1971 had to be postponed, and as February wore on without publication of a draft plan some congresses had to be postponed a second time.[60] The first announcement that the draft plan had been completed was made by Gosplan's party committee secretary V. I. Balan at a 5 February local conference in Moscow (*Moskovskaya Pravda*, 9 February 1971) and the draft was finally published only on 14 February 1971. Even then it was published without formal Central Committee approval: instead of calling a Central Committee plenum to approve it (as was done in February 1966), only the Politburo[61] approved it and it appeared over Brezhnev's signature as general secretary. The draft was approved at the 24th Congress (the resolution on the plan was published in the 11 April 1971 *Pravda*). This draft still failed to specify the actual investments for light industry and heavy industry, although it did specify agriculture's share of investments, and this figure indicated that the agriculture lobby had scored further gains. Whereas the July 1970 plenum had approved 77.6 billion rubles of state investment in agriculture (including production, housing and cultural construction, and purchase of equipment),[62] the 1971 draft specified 82.2 billion (*Izvestiya*, 14 February 1971).

However, while Brezhnev and Polyanskiy even increased their 1970 gains for agriculture, the most notable feature of the new plan was its historic shift to consumer goods priority. This priority, established in 1967 for the 1968, 1969, and 1970 annual plans, now was extended for the first time to a whole five-year plan,[63] providing a 44-48 percent growth rate for consumer goods and only 41-45 percent for heavy industry. In addition, heavy industry was ordered to greatly expand its production of consumer goods.

While Brezhnev in his 24th Congress Central Committee report presented a strong argument for the change to a consumer goods orientation (even threatening officials who tried to resist the change or who neglected consumer goods production), his past record of defending heavy industrial priority made it unlikely that he was willing to go as far as Premier Kosygin, Gosplan Chairman

---

[60]The first congress—Georgia's—scheduled for 27 January was postponed to 17 February at the end of December. However, on 14 February it was postponed again (until 27 February). During late January and early February nine other congresses were also postponed and reports on the five-year plan were added to their agendas. The first congress opened on 17 February (Estonia's).

[61]See Estonian Premier Klauson's remark that the draft was "approved in the Politburo" (*Sovetskaya Estoniya*, 20 February 1971).

[62]Brezhnev's report, *Pravda*, 3 July 1970.

[63]Actual average annual growth for heavy industry (group A) was slightly larger (8.5 percent) than that for light industry (8.3 percent) during the 1966–70 five-year plan, despite the change to higher consumer goods rates in 1968, 1969, and 1970 (V. Mayer, *Politicheskoye Samoobrazovaniye* [December 1970] : 13–14).

Baybakov, and other consumer advocates. Indeed, his report contained echoes of his past commitment to heavy industry:

> "This measure, of course, does not change our general line of accelerated development of production of means of production."

> "This change of economic ratios in no way means that we are lowering attention to heavy industry."

> "High rates of development of heavy industry fully retain their importance in the present day conditions also" (*Pravda*, 31 March 1971).

Brezhnev stressed again the use of more heavy industrial facilities to produce for the agricultural and consumer sectors and again indicated that heavy industry's expansion of consumer goods production would enable it to continue its preferential role: "Consequently, at the present stage the role of heavy industry not only does not diminish but even grows, since the circle of direct practical problems which it decides is widening."

The priorities question was avoided by almost all other speakers at the congress. Only Krasnodar First Secretary Zolotukhin and Gosplan Chairman Baybakov strongly pushed their favorite sectors.[64] Zolotukhin, a long-time supporter of the agriculture lobby, declared that while forced heavy industrial growth had been necessary for survival in the past, the government could now allot funds to agriculture, light industry, food industry, and welfare without weakening industry or defense, and he called on everyone to "rebuff and correct those officials who still do not fully understand the role and needs of agriculture" (*Pravda*, 2 April 1971). Baybakov stressed that from the very beginning all work on the new five-year plan had followed the main goal of "fuller and fuller subordination of economic development to the interests of raising the living standard of the Soviet people," and he stated that consumer goods production will be increased both by increasing development of light industry, the food industry, and agriculture, and by increasing output of consumer goods in heavy industry. He noted that while the general growth of output of consumer goods will be 44–48 percent, "their production in heavy industrial branches will increase over 80 percent." He went further, however, declaring this to be only the minimum and clearly desiring more: "However, this planned volume of production of consumer goods in heavy industrial branches must be considered minimal. It is the task of ministries and planning organs to more fully use possibilities in these branches for more significant growth of production and expansion of the assortment of consumer goods" (*Pravda*, 9 April 1971).

With the adoption of a higher growth rate for consumer goods than for heavy industry it became necessary to explain that this did not contradict

[64]In addition, Ferrous Metallurgy Minister I. P. Kazanets noted Brezhnev's call for more consumer goods production in heavy industry and promised to comply by expanding such output in his ferrous metallurgy industry (*Pravda*, 3 April).

Lenin's law of preferential development of means of production. The 1968–70 argument that heavy industrial priority was preserved by taking the five-year plan as a whole naturally no longer could be used. Economists reverted to two main explanations: that heavy industrial priority continued because in terms of volume group A is still growing faster than group B, and that with agricultural means of production added in, means of production is still growing faster than consumption items.

L. Logvinov (*Voprosy Ekonomiki* 9 [1971]: 107) presented the clearest figures for the first argument. The total volume of industrial production reached 373 billion rubles in 1970, of which the share of group A was 74 percent and of group B only 26 percent. Even with a slightly higher planned growth rate for B (3 percent higher than A), this vast disparity would hardly change by the end of the new five-year plan in 1975.

	1970 industrial production	Annual planned growth 1971–75 (in billions)	1975 planned industrial production	1975 percentages
Group A	276	22.6–24.8	389–400	73.66
Group B	97	8.5– 9.3	139–143	26.33
	373 billion rubles		528–543 billion	

The second argument was best explained in a May 1971 *Ekonomicheskaya Gazeta* (no. 20) article by Yu. Belik, who noted that the new priority of group B (consumer goods) over group A (heavy industry) does not really mean consumer goods priority because groups A and B (which apply only to industry) do not correspond to economic subdivisions I (means of production) and II (consumption items). Subdivision I is growing faster than subdivision II because subdivision I includes not only heavy industrial production (group A) but also major portions of agricultural production (agricultural products used for industry or for further agricultural production—seeds, fodder, etc.), construction (construction of production facilities) and transportation (transport of means of production), leaving in subdivision II light industry (group B), agricultural products intended directly for consumption (meat, milk, vegetables, etc.), nonproduction construction (schools, hospitals, theaters, housing), and transportation of consumer goods. Since, as some economists pointed out,[65] output of agriculture and construction for subdivision I will be growing at faster rates now (probably as a result of the 1970 increases in agricultural investment), means of production may even increase its growth rate in relationship to subdivision II. G. M. Sorokin in the July 1971 *Voprosy Istorii KPSS* wrote that "if one takes not only industry but all social production the share of subdivision I even in the 9th five-year plan is planned to increase somewhat."

[65] L. Ya. Berri and A. M. Zagorodneva in the *Seriya Ekonomicheskaya, Izvestiya Akademii Nauk SSSR* 4 (1971): 41.

As the group B growth rates drew up to those of group A in 1970 and 1971, leaders began usually avoiding formulations involving "preferential" growth and used vaguer terms, describing heavy industry as the "foundation" of economic expansion or as the "basis of bases," or speaking of "accelerated" or "high" growth rates for heavy industry. This, capped by the setting of higher rates for group B than group A in the new five-year plan, led to confusion among economists and propagandists.[66] Finally, at a 29 September 1971 high-level conference on theory, Central Committee Ideology Secretary P. N. Demichev spoke of "preserving the preferential growth of subdivision I of public production as a whole" (*Pravda*, 30 September 1971), thus announcing that this formulation had superseded the old, looser talk of preferential growth of heavy industry or of group A.

The congress instructed the Council of Ministers to work on the five-year plan draft, to break it down by years, ministries, departments, and republics by 1 August, and to introduce it to the Supreme Soviet by 1 September (*Pravda*, 11 April 1971). However, the final deadlines also were not met: it was 14 October before the Politburo approved the draft (*Pravda*, 17 October), while the Central Committee approved it at a 22–23 November plenum and the Supreme Soviet finally adopted it at a 26 November 1971 session.

Despite Kosygin's marked decline in favor during 1971[67] and the attacks on consumerism by those less enthusiastic about consumer goods,[68] the final plan retained its proconsumer orientation. Kosygin, reporting on the new five-year plan at the November 1971 Supreme Soviet session, reemphasized its consumer orientation and cited Brezhnev's statement in the 24th Congress report that the new course of raising welfare was not only the main task of the new five-year plan but also the new long-range "general orientation" (*Pravda*, 25 November 1971). Kosygin identified four main features of the new plan, placing

[66] Gosplan subdepartment chief A. Dorovskikh described the confusion and conflicting interpretations among economists in an article in the September 1971 *Planovoye Khozyaystvo* (pp. 27 and 34).

[67] Kosygin dropped from number two ranking to number three—see the Postscript.

[68] Masherov, Suslov, and Shelest warned against a "consumer" approach. Masherov attacked the "cult of things and the standards of the notorious consumer society," declaring that "we are against a consumer attitude toward socialism, we are against absolutizing material incentives" and "some propagandists, not taking the trouble to think through important questions connected with the growth of the people's welfare, reduce the whole problem to satisfying material needs" (*Sovetskaya Belorussiya*, 1 June 1971). Suslov said that it "would be extremely mistaken" to approach the raising of people's welfare "in a purely consumer fashion" (*Pravda*, 30 September 1971). Noting the "much talking and writing about raising the people's welfare," Shelest complained that "in places it has become fashionable to speak exclusively about the advantages, about some sort of 'horn of plenty,' from which goods and blessings shower down all by themselves. These are harmful consumer tendencies" (*Radyanska Ukraina*, 11 November 1971). However, Brezhnev and his close allies Kirilenko and Shcherbitskiy have appeared more enthusiastic about consumer goods than Masherov, Suslov, and Shelest.

first the raising of the people's welfare (which, he said, required "redistribution" of resources, structural changes in the economy, and the raising of the share of investments in the consumer goods industry), second the further development of heavy industry, and only third agricultural growth.[69]

However, while more consumer goods and services remains the official main goal of the new plan, the precise planned investment and growth in this field remain somewhat obscure (partly because many consumer goods will be produced at heavy industrial enterprises) and, as indicated above, it appears doubtful that the lopsided relationship between heavy industry and light industry will be changed substantially by the higher growth rates for consumer goods in the new plan. Propagandists and economists can still proclaim the preferential growth rate of production of means of production.

[69] The fourth was acceleration of scientific and technical progress—a theme notably stressed by Masherov and Shelest in their 1970 election speeches (see p. 243). Kosygin and Brezhnev have also talked much about this subject, however.

POSTSCRIPT:
BREZHNEV'S RISE, 1971

Simultaneously with the victory of agriculture in the 1970 resource struggle, a significant increase in Brezhnev's power became noticeable. Following a shake-up in Agitprop and the media in the spring of 1970, he appeared to receive somewhat improved media coverage. During the April nominations for the Supreme Soviet and at anniversary ceremonies in Kazakhstan, Azerbaydzhan, and Armenia in late 1970, he received noticeably more personal attention and praise. His supporters—especially in Kazakhstan, Azerbaydzhan, and Moldavia—began building him up as a leader independent of and above the collective in their speeches at the August Kazakh anniversary, the October Azerbaydzhan anniversary, and the November Armenian anniversary, at their republic party congresses in early 1971, and finally at the 24th CPSU Congress in March–April 1971. In January 1971 Brezhnev scored a breakthrough when *Pravda* for the first time carried a local leader's statement designating him as head of the Politburo.

In the preliminaries to the 24th Congress, those cool to Brezhnev suffered minor setbacks (notably in Estonia, Georgia, the Ukraine, and the RSFSR). When the long-delayed 24th Congress finally met in March and April, the proceedings were dominated by unprecedented lavish personal praise for Brezhnev and his hand was greatly strengthened by the addition of four allies to the Politburo—including Kunayev, the initiator and leader of the Brezhnev drive. Politburo members cool to Brezhnev (Voronov, Shelest, and especially Shelepin) clearly lost ground in the congress personnel decisions. Brezhnev's power was still limited, of course, but clearly the year's delay in holding the congress was a tremendous advantage.

Brezhnev's greatest triumph, however, came shortly after the congress, when Voronov—the bitterest foe of his agricultural policies—and his allies were ousted from their posts in the RSFSR government. Voronov's fall marked the finale of the biggest agricultural dispute since Khrushchev's fall and the complete triumph of the Brezhnev–Polyanskiy–Kulakov agriculture lobby. Although Voronov still remained in the Politburo as of January 1972, his drastic demotion appeared to ensure his eventual complete retirement, and, further, may pave the way for the removal of other Politburo members hostile to Brezhnev.

Brezhnev's Build-up

Brezhnev's rise appears to date from March and April 1970[1] –the same time the crucial agricultural decisions were being debated. In early April rumors began circulating that a shake-up of Agitprop and media leaders had taken place.[2] On 25 April *Pravda* announced the removal of N. N. Mesyatsev as chairman of the Committee of Radio Broadcasting and Television[3] and his replacement with S. G. Lapin, and Lapin's removal as director of TASS and his replacement with Foreign Ministry press chief L. M. Zamyatin. Agitprop head V. I. Stepakov and Publishing Committee Chairman N. A. Mikhaylov disappeared in late March.[4]

Although no one close to Brezhnev moved into control of the media, the removal of Stepakov, Mesyatsev, and Mikhaylov appeared to somewhat improve the media's responsiveness to him. Mikhaylov's removal as chairman of the Publishing Committee appeared to coincide with the announcement of the apparently delayed publication of a two-volume collection of Brezhnev's speeches and articles[5] and a collection of his speeches on youth.[6] He delivered four speeches

[1] Events in late 1969 (especially the December 1969 Central Committee plenum) and early 1970 suggest dissension at the top, however these are still too obscure to be explained. It is clear, however, that Brezhnev's position began to improve in March and April.

[2] The French Press Agency (AFP) on 1 April, the *New York Times*, 10 and 23 April, and the London *Daily Telegraph*, 4 April.

[3] Mesyatsev, a close associate of Shelepin while Shelepin was Komsomol first secretary in the 1950's, had been appointed immediately after Khrushchev's fall (*Pravda*, 31 October 1964). He went into diplomatic exile as ambassador to Australia (announced in the 24 June 1970 *Pravda*).

[4] Stepakov was last identified in his position in the 22 March 1970 *Pravda* and Mikhaylov in the 21 March *Sovetskaya Kultura*. Stepakov's removal was only finally confirmed on 19 January 1971 when *Pravda* reported his appointment as ambassador to Yugoslavia (as of January 1972 no new Agitprop head had yet been named). According to rumor (the *New York Times*, 10 April 1970), Stepakov was scheduled to become ambassador to China, but, either because of Chinese opposition, Stepakov's refusal, or his rumored heart attack, this fell through.

The *Times* reported on 23 April 1970, after a telephone query to Mikhaylov's committee, that Mikhaylov was no longer chairman. His removal and retirement were finally announced on 24 July 1970 (*Pravda*). Mikhaylov had headed the Komsomol until 1952 and had promoted Shelepin from a local Komsomol post to his top deputy (Komsomol second secretary) and successor.

[5] Announced in *Novyye Knigi SSSR*, 20 March, and *Pravda*, 2 May. The Bulgarian translation had been issued already in late 1969. *Kommunist*, no. 1 (1970) (signed to press 30 December 1969) carried a review of the "recently" published two-volume work from the 6 December issue of the Bulgarian daily *Rabotnichesko Delo*. The first volume of the

in April (in Kharkov on 13 and 14 April, in Ulyanovsk on 16 April, and on Lenin's birthday on 21 April), all of which were especially well publicized (speeches by Kirilenko in Armenia on 14 April, by Podgornyy in Orenburg on 14 April, by Shelepin in Ulyanovsk on 16 April, and by Kosygin in Kursk on 17 April were only briefly excerpted and summarized, while Brezhnev's speeches filled the papers and were broadcast in detail). In late April when nominations for the June Supreme Soviet election began, Brezhnev was favored conspicuously over his colleagues Kosygin and Podgornyy in the TASS accounts (see the lavish praise of Brezhnev in the 25 and 26 April *Pravda*).

In the second half of 1970 Brezhnev and his supporters took advantage of a series of unusual opportunities to boost his image. He attended three republic anniversary ceremonies, garnering great publicity as the star speaker and receiving unprecedented doses of personal flattery. He was aided by the fact that two of the anniversaries were in republics run by his most outspoken supporters and they turned their ceremonies into glorification of him. The local first secretaries' lavish introductions of Brezhnev were faithfully reported in the central press, presenting to Soviet readers a much more favorable portrayal of him than they were accustomed to.

At the 28 August 50th anniversary of the Kazakh Communist Party and republic Brezhnev's protégé Kazakh First Secretary Kunayev introduced him as an "outstanding" leader not only of the party and government but of the international Communist movement as well, and as a "true Leninist who heads the Central Committee" (*Kazakhstanskaya Pravda* and *Pravda*, 29 August). Kunayev also initiated a movement to translate Brezhnev's newly published works into local languages, and on the eve of Brezhnev's arrival in Kazakhstan, a Kazakh translation of the works was announced (*Pravda*, 25 August). The representatives of several of the other republics represented at the ceremony also gave Brezhnev's Kazakh anniversary speech and/or Brezhnev personally high praise (the first secretaries of Moscow [V. V. Grishin], Azerbaydzhan [G. A. Aliyev], Armenia [A. Ye. Kochinyan], Kirgizia [T. Usubaliyev], Moldavia [I. I. Bodyul], Uzbekistan [Sh. R. Rashidov], and Tadzhikistan [D. Rasulov]).[7] After the Kazakh ceremony Brezhnev made a tour of Central Asia (31 August–9 September), receiving more publicity and appearing to campaign for support. Central Asian leaders subsequently warmly praised his visit.

On 2 October he attended the 50th Azerbaydzhan anniversary and his supporter Azerbaydzhan First Secretary Aliyev[8] lavished the same accolades on

---

original Russian collection was set in print only on 23 January 1970 and signed to press 2 April. The dates for the second volume (which included Brezhnev's April speeches) were 5 March and 24 April.

[6] *Pravda*, 24 May 1970.

[7] On the other hand, the first secretaries of Latvia (A. E. Voss), Turkmenia (M. Gapurov) and Estonia (I. G. Kebin) failed to even comment on Brezhnev's speech.

[8] Aliyev was Azerbaydzhan KGB deputy chairman until 1967, under S. K. Tsvigun. Tsvigun, who had worked under Brezhnev in Moldavia in the early 1950's, was called to

him as Kunayev had in Kazakhstan and also announced the translation of his works into Azerbaydzhani. The Azerbaydzhanis went even further, electing as an honorary presidium for the ceremony the Politburo "headed by" Brezhnev. However, this formulation, while carried in the local press (*Bakinskiy Rabochiy*, 3 October 1970), was not reported in the central press. Again, representatives of several republics also praised Brezhnev and/or his Azerbaydzhan anniversary speech (the first secretaries of Uzbekistan [Rashidov], Tadzhikistan [Rasulov], Kirgizia [Usubaliyev], Kazakhstan [Kunayev], and Turkmenia [Gapurov]).[9]

On 29 November Brezhnev attended the 50th Armenian anniversary where Armenian First Secretary Kochinyan (a frequent but not consistent admirer) also lavished praise on him. Again, such regional first secretaries as Grishin (Moscow), Aliyev (Azerbaydzhan), Bodyul (Moldavia), Usubaliyev (Kirgizia), and Rashidov (Uzbekistan) were especially laudatory toward Brezhnev, while the coolest were Estonian First Secretary Kebin, Georgian First Secretary Mzhavanadze, and Ukrainian First Secretary Shelest (Shelest was the only speaker to ignore Brezhnev entirely).

The Brezhnev build-up scored a significant breakthrough on 20 January 1971, when for the first time *Pravda* carried the formulation "the Politburo headed by General Secretary L. I. Brezhnev." On the previous four occasions when this formulation had been used, it had been mentioned only in the local press: in Kunayev's speeches at an April 1969 Kazakh Central Committee plenum (*Kazakhstanskaya Pravda*, 17 April 1969) and at the November 1969 Kazakh Congress of Kolkhozniks (*Kazakhstanskaya Pravda*, 18 November 1969), in Armenian First Secretary Kochinyan's speech at the August 1970 Kazakh 50th anniversary (*Kazakhstanskaya Pravda*, 29 August 1970), and by the Azerbaydzhanis at their 50th anniversary (*Bakinskiy Rabochiy*, 3 October 1970). On 19 January 1971 Dagestan First Secretary M.-S. I. Umakhanov at the 50th Dagestan anniversary referred to Brezhnev as head of the Politburo and this was reported in *Pravda, Sovetskaya Rossiya*, and *Selskaya Zhizn.*[10]

Umakhanov took the opportunity not only to flatter Brezhnev but to snub Voronov, who was representing the Politburo at the ceremony instead of

---

Moscow in mid-1967 to become first deputy KGB chairman in the wake of the removal of Shelepin's ally, Semichastnyy, as KGB chairman in May 1967. Aliyev succeeded him as Azerbaydzhan KGB chairman. In mid-1969 Azerbaydzhan First Secretary Akhundov was removed and, in a very unusual step, replaced by KGB Chairman Aliyev. Aliyev initiated a massive exposure of corruption and a thorough purge of Azerbaydzhan's leadership. He has advertised his support of Brezhnev by consistently obsequious praise.

[9] Brezhnev was completely ignored by the first secretaries of the Ukraine (Shelest) and Estonia (Kebin) and RSFSR First Deputy Premier Shkolnikov in their speeches.

[10] Other central papers did not carry the statement, suggesting continued contention or caution. While the shortness of the accounts of the anniversary in *Sotsialisticheskaya Industriya* and *Krasnaya Zvezda* might explain the omission in those papers, *Izvestiya, Trud, Komsomolskaya Pravda*, and *Moskovskaya Pravda* carried long versions comparable to *Pravda*'s, but without the paragraph containing the formulation. All the republic organs except those of Georgia and Belorussia carried the statement.

Brezhnev. Umakhanov thanked the Central Committee and Politburo headed by Brezhnev for their "constant fatherly attention and comprehensive help" to Dagestan after the 14-15 May 1970 earthquake. He made no mention of the fact that Voronov had been the only Politburo member who actually had taken the trouble to fly down to Dagestan, visit the stricken areas, and assure the victims of aid (reported in the 21 May 1970 *Sovetskaya Rossiya*).

At the republic party congresses in February and March 1971, the leaders of Kazakhstan, Azerbaydzhan, Moldavia, and Kirgizia continued to play up Brezhnev, stressing his special leadership role above and independent of the collective.[11] The climax of the Brezhnev buildup came at the 24th Congress, when praise for Brezhnev virtually drowned out discussion of all other issues. As usual, Brezhnev's supporters were the pacesetters, Kunayev praising Brezhnev's "skill" in uniting the ruling group and directing the work of the Central Committee, Aliyev praising Brezhnev's "huge role" in the leadership, and Bodyul and Usubaliyev acclaiming his personal leadership qualities. However, no one mentioned the Politburo "headed by" Brezhnev formulation at the congress.[12] Thus, Brezhnev's supporters were at least partially successful in changing the tone of public references to Brezhnev, making praise of Brezhnev's statements and activities a normal, acceptable and even advisable procedure for Soviet politicians.

Setbacks for Brezhnev Foes

In the preliminaries to the 24th Congress and at the congress itself Brezhnev managed to make some gains in terms of personnel also, although mainly in the negative form of dealing minor setbacks to his foes and others not cooperating in

[11] Kunayev spoke of the Politburo "headed by the outstanding figure of the international communist and workers movement comrade L. I. Brezhnev" and implied a personal executive role for Brezhnev, for instance in giving "direct orders" to Kazakhstan on irrigation (*Kazakhstanskaya Pravda*, 25 February 1971). Aliyev spoke of the Politburo "headed by" Brezhnev (*Bakinskiy Rabochiy*, 12 March), while the Kirgiz congress (the only one to do so) elected an honorary presidium consisting of the Politburo "headed by" Brezhnev (*Sovetskaya Kirgiziya*, 4 March). Kirgiz First Secretary Usubaliyev spoke of the "fatherly attention and concrete help" of the Central Committee, Politburo, and Brezhnev "personally" and praised the publication of Brezhnev's collection of speeches (*Sovetskaya Kirgiziya*, 4 March). Moldavian leader Bodyul declared that the work of the Moldavian party organizations was guided by the directives of the CPSU Central Committee, "by the everyday help of the Politburo and Secretariat of the CPSU Central Committee, and by the attention and valuable instructions of Central Committee General Secretary Comrade L. I. Brezhnev" (*Sovetskaya Moldaviya*, 26 February). In contrast, the least attention to Brezhnev was paid by Estonian leader Kebin (no one at the Estonian congress even mentioned Brezhnev) and Ukrainian leader Shelest (who made only one innocuous mention of Brezhnev).

[12] As is occasionally pointed out, Lenin objected when others attributed "nonexistent" positions to him, specifically crossing out the title of "chairman of the Politburo" (V. P. Nikolayeva, *Voprosy Istorii KPSS* 9 [1969] : 40-41).

his personal build-up. Georgian First Secretary Mzhavanadze, who has consistently remained relatively cool to Brezhnev, saw his Second Secretary P. A. Rodionov replaced with former Krasnodar Second Secretary A. N. Churkin (*Zarya Vostoka*, 2 March). The fifty-seven-year-old Rodionov—who has been the most prolific writer on the subject of collective leadership and who has oriented his writings toward a strong collective and a weak leader (i.e., against Brezhnev)—was demoted to first deputy director of the Marxism–Leninism Institute in Moscow (identified in the 11 March 1971 *Sovetskaya Rossiya*) and was not reelected a Central Committee candidate member at the 24th Congress. A Central Committee official (K. V. Lebedev, head of the Party Organizational Work Section's sector for the Baltic and Belorussia) was sent to Estonia to take over as second secretary under Kebin (*Pravda*, 12 February)—however this has had no noticeable effect so far on the behavior of the independent-minded Estonians.

Ukrainian First Secretary Shelest—who like Kebin and Mzhavanadze has been the coolest to Brezhnev—has suffered several setbacks in 1970 and 1971. His opponents from Dnepropetrovsk, led by Brezhnev protégé and Ukrainian Premier V. V. Shcherbitskiy, took over the posts of Ukrainian Central Committee cadres chief (Dnepropetrovsk City First Secretary A. A. Ulanov[13]) in late 1970 and of Ukrainian Agriculture Minister (Dnepropetrovsk Oblast Executive Committee Deputy Chairman for agriculture P. L. Pogrebnyak[14]) in February 1971. Moreover, Premier Shcherbitskiy, Shelest's long-time rival, was promoted from candidate Politburo member to full member at the 24th CPSU Congress, depriving Shelest of a considerable advantage over him and strengthening Brezhnev's faction in the Ukraine.

Podgornyy's close protégé, V. N. Titov, was removed as Kazakh second secretary in early 1971 (*Kazakhstanskaya Pravda*, 23 February) and shunted into the nonpolitical job of deputy USSR CEMA representative (see *Kazakhstanskaya Pravda*, 10 February). Titov had been CPSU Central Committee cadres secretary during the 1965 Brezhnev–Podgornyy struggle and was removed by Brezhnev and exiled to Kazakhstan to work under the supervision of Brezhnev protégé Kunayev. Podgornyy managed to protect his 1965 cadre agents Titov and P. F. Pigalev at the 24th Congress, however: Titov was reelected to the Central Com-

---

[13] First identified in the 3 October 1970 *Molod Ukrainy.*

[14] Despite Shelest's unusually harsh attack on the Dnepropetrovsk leaders for their handling of agriculture at a July 1970 Ukrainian Central Committee plenum (referring to defects in the oblast's agriculture, Shelest asked: "Can one call this effective, skilled and demanding leadership?" and he described the agricultural situation in Dnepropetrovsk as "political failure in work"—*Radyanska Ukraina*, 25 July 1970), Pogrebnyak shortly was named first deputy republic agriculture minister (identified in the 30 October 1970 *Radyanska Ukraina*) and only three months later, agriculture minister (announced in the 4 February 1971 *Radyanska Ukraina*). See also the 30 June 1970 *Radyanska Ukraina* article exposing Dnepropetrovsk agricultural failings, which served as the basis for Shelest's attack.

mittee and Pigalev was reelected to the Auditing Commission, even though their present jobs do not warrant such status.[15]

Less fortunate was Brezhnev's other 1965 rival, Shelepin, who saw several of his former subordinates and allies dropped from the new Central Committee. Not only were his already demoted subordinates dropped (S. P. Pavlov, Komsomol first secretary until 1968, now chairman of the Committee for Physical Culture and Sports; V. Ye. Semichastnyy, KGB chairman until 1967, now Ukrainian first deputy premier in charge of physical culture and transportation; D. P. Goryunov, head of TASS until 1967, now ambassador to Kenya; N. N. Mesyatsev, chairman of the Radio and Television Committee until 1970, now ambassador to Australia; and V. S. Tikunov, RSFSR MVD chief until 1966, now a Soviet diplomat in Rumania), but so were two former subordinates still in prominent positions: USSR People's Control Committee Chairman P. V. Kovanov and Central Committee Light Industry and Food Industry Section head P. K. Sizov.

Most significantly for agricultural policy, Voronov also suffered. On 2 February 1971 *Pravda* announced the pensioning off of Voronov's long-time top ally, RSFSR First Deputy Premier Pysin. Pysin was only sixty and, as if to make clear that his retirement had negative political overtones, he had been snubbed on his sixtieth birthday in December. Although he had received an Order of Lenin on his fiftieth birthday in 1960 while only a provincial secretary, in 1970 he received a lesser award (Order of the Red Banner) on his sixtieth birthday (*Pravda*, 24 December 1970). This despite the fact that the RSFSR was celebrating great agricultural successes in late 1970[16] and Pysin was the senior supervisor of RSFSR agriculture.

The political setback for Voronov was made even clearer on 19 February when Belgorod First Secretary N. F. Vasilyev was appointed Pysin's successor (*Sovetskaya Rossiya*). Vasilyev was from Dnepropetrovsk where he had worked under Brezhnev, Kirilenko, and Shcherbitskiy. He had profited indirectly from the 1964 purge of Voronov's Orenburg protégés: when Belgorod First Secretary Kovalenko was moved to Orenburg to replace Shurygin, Dnepropetrovsk Oblast Executive Committee Chairman Vasilyev replaced him in Belgorod.

Upon arriving in Belgorod, Vasilyev initiated a program of specialization which concentrated on the creation of new facilities for raising livestock rather

---

[15]Pigalev is head of the department for questions of work of soviets in Podgornyy's Supreme Soviet Presidium.

[16]The RSFSR leaders were loudly bragging about overfulfilling grain production and procurement plans in late 1970 and Voronov's favorite oblasts Volgograd and Orenburg were singled out for making the greatest contribution to this success (see RSFSR Agriculture Minister Florentyev in the 10 October 1970 *Sovetskaya Rossiya*, Voronov in the 25 November *Sovetskaya Rossiya*, and the 10 November *Sovetskaya Rossiya* editorial). On 9 February 1971 *Sovetskaya Rossiya* editorially noted that the republic had produced 113 million tons of grain instead of the targeted 110–112 million tons and had produced 62.8 million tons of wheat, as compared to only 42.3 million tons in 1969.

than on renovation or expansion of old facilities. His system was often criticized for being too expensive and for neglecting existing facilities because of its concentration of investments in new specialized farms. Voronov's subordinate, RSFSR Gosplan Deputy Chairman G. Smirnov criticized Vasilyev's system in 1969, complaining that the nonspecialized farms were being neglected and as a result the oblast as a whole was lagging behind its neighbors (*Ekonomika Selskogo Khozyaystva* 7 [1969] : p. 59). Vasilyev himself admitted that his system was very costly (*Pravda*, 25 June 1970). Furthermore, mistakes in specialization in 1968 and 1969 caused sharp setbacks to Belgorod's agriculture, and as Yuriy Chernichenko wrote in the June 1970 *Yunost*, "the Belgorod experience was never as open to criticism as at the beginning of 1970." But, according to Chernichenko, the "daring strategy" paid off as a triumph of large-scale specialization. Vasilyev's fortunes looked up in mid-1970 when the agriculture lobby won the July Central Committee plenum's approval for a costly program of building large-scale livestock complexes. Shortly before the Estonians had publicly objected to the costly new complexes.[17] Vasilyev was invited to speak at the July agricultural plenum and after the plenum Belgorod's work in creating new industrial livestock complexes began receiving more recognition. Belgorod's work was praised by Central Committee Agriculture Section deputy head N. P. Rudenko at an October livestock conference (*Ekonomika Selskogo Khozyaystva* 12 [1971] : 113-14) and *Pravda*'s 23 January 1971 editorial praised the construction of large livestock complexes and declared that Belgorod, Moscow, Penza, and Tambov were "setting the tone" for the RSFSR. Although Vasilyev's system has not been set up as the main method to follow, he is the only innovation leader singled out for promotion, implying special approval for his method. Shortly after his appointment, the Politburo further extended the big program for construction of complexes in its April 1971 decree—a decree greeted enthusiastically by the Belgoroders (see Belgorod First Secretary M. P. Trunov's 8 May 1971 *Sovetskaya Rossiya* article).

Voronov's attitude toward his new deputy's system has appeared to be unenthusiastic. Despite Voronov's frequent discussion of specialization through the years, he has failed to take note of Belgorod's work, directing attention instead to the specialization work of his own former bailiwick Orenburg Oblast.[18] Vasilyev, in turn, has failed to publicly promote Voronov's campaigns

[17]The Agriculture Ministry's insistence on expensive new complexes was criticized by Estonian First Deputy Premier E. Tynurist in the 10 April *Izvestiya*. "Big complexes certainly will play their role" and should be built, but livestock expansion is "unthinkable" without "reconstruction and reequipping of present big kolkhoz and sovkhoz [livestock] farms," wrote Tynurist. "In our view," renovated old farms "will remain the main deliverers of livestock products for a significant time" and therefore agricultural organs should aid these farms.

[18]It must be noted that Brezhnev and Polyanskiy have not publicly endorsed the Belgorod method either, and after the July Central Committee decisions Belgorod appeared to receive some attention from RSFSR authorities also. A 17 November 1970 *Sovetskaya*

(meat cattle, mechanized links)[19] and has criticized the RSFSR Agriculture Ministry for obstructing Belgorod's specialization by refusing to permit the oblast to create a joint kolkhoz-sovkhoz association for poultry production.[20]

There were further ominous signs for Voronov also. At the 24th Congress, Voronov's deputy for construction, A. Ye. Biryukov, was dropped from the Auditing Commission (Pysin was, of course, dropped from Central Committee membership). His removal as RSFSR deputy premier was announced on 21 May (*Pravda*).[21] Biryukov, as noted in Chapter VIII, had been ousted as Central Committee Construction Section head in early 1967, presumably because of opposition to the establishment of rural construction ministries—a position apparently shared by Voronov. Yet a third apparent Voronov ally on agricultural issues was removed around the time of the congress. *Sovetskaya Rossiya* editor V. P. Moskovskiy, whose paper has vigorously pushed Voronov's meat cattle and mechanized link campaigns, was retired and replaced by *Selskaya Zhizn* editor P. F. Alekseyev (*Zhurnalist* [April 1971]). In contrast to *Sovetskaya Rossiya*, *Selskaya Zhizn* had not editorially promoted links and meat cattle and Alekseyev himself had indicated his dislike of links (see *Zhurnalist* [May 1969]). Alekseyev, as *Selskaya Zhizn* editor, had led the attacks on the RSFSR government for refusing to create a rural construction ministry in 1966. *Selskaya Zhizn* has appeared to be the mouthpiece for Polyanskiy's policies. At the 24th Congress Alekseyev was promoted from member of the Auditing Commission to Central Committee candidate member. Although no clear editorial change has yet been distinguishable in *Sovetskaya Rossiya*, it seems likely that Voronov has lost its enthusiastic editorial support for his agricultural policies.

The 24th Congress appeared to completely ignore Voronov's ideas on agriculture. He himself had no opportunity to speak.[22] Even Volgograd First

Rossiya editorial praised Belgorod's specialization as one of a number of valuable innovations in the RSFSR, and Voronov in his 2 October 1970 *Komsomolskaya Pravda* interview on livestock raising praised a Belgorod kolkhoz's breeding experiment and urged wide study of this particular initiative.

[19] Although Vasilyev has failed to propagandize for Voronov's ideas, he apparently did use some of these new, more efficient methods in his oblast's complexes. In an 8 July 1971 *Selskaya Zhizn* article zoo technician M. Glinka told of a Belgorod kolkhoz's use of the untethered method of keeping cows, and in the 2 December 1971 *Pravda* Belgorod raykom secretary A. Semin told of his rayon's long-time experiments with unregulated links and noted that there would soon be 126 links in his rayon. Vasilyev's successor as oblast first secretary, M. P. Trunov, also reported Belgorod's creation of links and praised their work (*Sovetskaya Rossiya*, 8 May 1971).

[20] *Ekonomicheskaya Gazeta*, no. 29 (June 1970). On the other hand, a 16 September 1970 *Selskaya Zhizn* editorial praised the RSFSR Agriculture Ministry for creating a special unit to aid quick construction of a complex at a Belgorod sovkhoz.

[21] He was replaced with A. M. Kalashnikov, who had succeeded him in July 1964 as Moscow City construction secretary.

[22] The only Politburo members to speak were Brezhnev, Kosygin, Podgornyy, and Shelest: Brezhnev gave the main report, Kosygin reported on the five-year plan, Shelest spoke as Ukrainian chief, and Podgornyy only gave a formal opening speech, listing foreign

Secretary Kulichenko, Orenburg First Secretary Kovalenko and Altay First Secretary Georgiyev, who did speak, failed to bring up links or any other Voronov policies, and, in fact, Kovalenko even appeared mildly critical of the RSFSR government.[23]

Gains for Brezhnev at the 24th Congress

More significant than Brezhnev's improved treatment in the press and by other politicians and the minor setbacks suffered by his foes were the personnel decisions at the 24th Congress itself. The new Politburo elected at the end of the congress included four new members—two of whom were the most pro-Brezhnev candidate members (Kazakh First Secretary Kunayev and Ukrainian Premier Shcherbitskiy), while the other two appeared to be Brezhnev-supporters also (Central Committee Agriculture Secretary Kulakov has worked closely with him on agriculture; Moscow First Secretary Grishin, since his Moscow appointment in 1967, had been among those leading the praises of Brezhnev's speeches). When Brezhnev read the list of new Politburo and Secretariat members on the radio on 9 April, those coolest to Brezhnev (Shelest, Voronov, and Shelepin) wound up on the bottom of the list (except for the four new junior members), while Mzhavanadze (the senior candidate member) wound up last among candidate members.[24]

Premier Kosygin suffered a conspicuous setback in being listed in third place instead of his customary second place. Kosygin's demotion in status was confirmed in the reports of the April 1971 RSFSR Supreme Soviet nominations which also listed Podgornyy second and Kosygin only third (reversing the order in the April 1970 USSR Supreme Soviet nominations) and which gave Kosygin only the same epithets and number of nominations as Podgornyy.[25]

The most striking promotion at the congress was that of Kulakov, who had been only a Central Committee secretary while the other three new Politburo

---

delegations. RSFSR Gosplan Chairman K. M. Gerasimov spoke for Voronov's republic. Trade union secretary V. I. Prokhorov spoke for the trade unions instead of Chairman Shelepin.

[23] Kovalenko asked the RSFSR Council of Ministers and Agriculture Ministry to review their decision to allot only a little fertilizer to Orenburg on grounds that it is ineffective there (*Pravda*, 4 April 1971).

[24] The press version (*Pravda*, 10 April 1971) of Brezhnev's speech changed his hierarchical listing to an alphabetical listing. In 1966 the press also reported an alphabetical listing but did not report all Brezhnev's speech verbatim and thus did not alter the speech directly.

[25] "Prominent political and state figure." In the April 1970 nominations Kosygin had been referred to as a "true Leninist and important political and state figure," while Podgornyy had been only a "prominent figure of the Leninist Communist Party and Soviet state." *Izvestiya*, which is the organ of Podgornyy's Supreme Soviet Presidium, further compounded Kosygin's 1971 setback by deleting his epithet, while carrying Podgornyy's (*Izvestiya*, 28 April 1971).

Brezhnev's 8 April 1966
Radio Listing[a]

Brezhnev's 9 April 1971
Radio Listing[b]

Politburo

1. Brezhnev
2. Kosygin
3. Podgornyy
4. Suslov
5. Voronov
6. Kirilenko
7. Shelepin
8. Mazurov
9. Polyanskiy
10. Shelest
11. Pelshe

Candidate members

1. Demichev
2. Grishin
3. Mzhavanadze
4. Rashidov
5. Ustinov
6. Shcherbitskiy
7. Kunayev
8. Masherov

Secretariat

1. Brezhnev
2. Suslov
3. Shelepin
4. Kirilenko
5. Demichev
6. Ustinov
7. Andropov
8. Ponomarev
9. Kapitonov
10. Kulakov
11. Rudakov

Politburo

1. Brezhnev
2. Podgornyy
3. Kosygin
4. Suslov
5. Kirilenko
6. Pelshe
7. Mazurov
8. Polyanskiy
9. Shelest
10. Voronov
11. Shelepin
12. Grishin
13. Kunayev
14. Shcherbitskiy
15. Kulakov

Candidate members

1. Andropov
2. Ustinov
3. Demichev
4. Rashidov
5. Masherov
6. Mzhavanadze

Secretariat

1. Brezhnev
2. Suslov
3. Kirilenko
4. Kulakov
5. Ustinov
6. Demichev
7. Kapitonov
8. Ponomarev
9. Katushev
10. Solomentsev

[a]Also in hierarchical order in the stenographic record of the 23d Congress, vol. II, p. 292.

[b]The stenographic record of the 24th Congress carries Brezhnev's list in alphabetical order (vol. II, p. 213)—as did *Pravda*.

members had already been candidate members. Kulakov, as Central Committee Agriculture Section head since December 1964 and Central Committee agriculture secretary since September 1965, obviously had worked closely with Brezhnev and Polyanskiy in the preparation of their agricultural programs, and his promotion adds another vote for the agriculture lobby in the Politburo. It probably also strengthens Brezhnev and Polyanskiy as against Voronov in disputes over agricultural policies.

Kulakov's rising influence was also evident in the appointment of his subordinates to key posts in the agricultural field. Already in late 1970 B. A. Runov, head of a sector in the Central Committee Agriculture Section (which is headed by Kulakov), became USSR deputy agriculture minister (first identified in the 20 October 1970 *Selskaya Zhizn*). Shortly before the March–April 1971 24th congress, N. A. Zakolupin, apparently also from Kulakov's section,[26] was named chief editor of *Selskaya Zhizn* (reported in the April 1971 *Zhurnalist*). In addition, N. V. Danilenko, head of a Central Committee sector (probably of the Agriculture Section[27]) was identified as the new RSFSR first deputy agriculture minister in the 17 June 1971 *Sovetskaya Rossiya*, replacing V. K. Mesyats, who was named Kazakh second secretary in February 1971. The appointments of Central Committee officials Runov and Danilenko to the agriculture ministries are notable also in that they deviate from the normal post-Khrushchev practice of selecting deputy agriculture ministers from among regional officials.

On the other hand, Brezhnev's victory at the congress was limited. None of his foes were removed from the Politburo and no one was actually added to the pre-congress twenty-five-man ruling collective (the Politburo members and candidate members and the Secretariat). While Kunayev and Shcherbitskiy were promoted, there was little sign of improvement of the positions of Brezhnev's other closest allies (Kirilenko, Polyanskiy, and Katushev). Furthermore, Brezhnev clearly did not pack the new Central Committee: of the eighty-eight new Central Committee members and eighty-four new candidate members,[28] only a handful were clearly Brezhnev men. Three of his assistants in the Central Committee— assistant to the General Secretary G. E. Tsukanov, Central Committee Administrator of Affairs G. S. Pavlov, and head of the Central Committee's General Section K. U. Chernenko[29]—were promoted to full Central Committee member-

[26] Zakolupin, *Selskaya Zhizn* editor for rural party organizations until 1965, became a responsible official of the Central Committee in 1966 (*Zhurnalist*, no. 4 [1971]) and as such traveled with Kulakov to East Germany in November 1966 to study German agriculture (*Pravda*, 27 November 1966).

[27] He was identified as head of a sector of an unidentified section at the October 1969 Moldavian congress of kolkhozniks (*Sovetskaya Moldaviya*, 31 October 1969).

[28] The Central Committee was expanded from 195 members and 165 candidate members in 1966 to 241 members and 155 candidate members in 1971. Of the new members, 38 were just promoted from candidate membership.

[29] Tsukanov and Pavlov had worked under Brezhnev in Dnepropetrovsk; Chernenko had worked under him in Moldavia, as well as in the Supreme Soviet Presidium.

ship, while another—assistant to the General Secretary (for foreign affairs) A. M. Aleksandrov-Agentov—was added to the Auditing Commission. (On the other hand, Brezhnev's personal agricultural assistant, V. A. Golikov, was not elected to anything, and the assistants of Kosygin and Podgornyy were also elected to the leadership bodies.[30]) The three top KGB leaders with ties to Brezhnev—First Deputy Chairman S. K. Tsvigun,[31] Deputy Chairman V. M. Chebrikov,[32] and Deputy Chairman G. K. Tsinev[33]—were added to the central organs (the first

[30]The top three leaders' personal assistants were identified in the stenographic record of the 23d Congress and occasionally in the press. Kosygin's assistants, A. K. Gorchakov (head of the secretariat of the Council of Ministers) and M. S. Smirtyukov (administrator of affairs of the Council of Ministers), and Podgornyy's assistants, L. M. Shevchenko (assistant to the chairman of the Supreme Soviet Presidium) and P. F. Pigalev (head of the Supreme Soviet Presidium's department for questions of work of soviets) were elected to the Auditing Commission. Pavlov and Chernenko had been Central Committee candidate members in 1966; Tsukanov and Pigalev had been on the Auditing Commission.

[31]In the early 1950's Tsvigun was deputy Moldavian security chief under then Moldavian First Secretary Brezhnev and then Moldavian First Deputy Premier (now USSR MVD chief) Shchelokov and held candidate membership in the Moldavian Central Committee (elected 1952 and 1954). From the post of Azerbaydzhan KGB chairman, Tsvigun was called to Moscow in June 1967 to become first deputy KGB chairman in the wake of the removal of Shelepin's protégé, Semichastnyy, as KGB chairman. By 1970 the other first deputy chairman, Shelepin-Semichastnyy appointee N. S. Zakharov, had faded from the scene and apparently been removed. Zakharov failed to sign the obituary of deceased Ukrainian KGB First Deputy Chairman B. S. Shulzhenko, even though other USSR KGB deputy chairmen did so: S. K. Tsvigun, V. M. Chebrikov, A. M. Malygin, and L. I. Pankratov (*Radyanska Ukraina*, 6 June 1970). In June 1970 he was not reelected a Supreme Soviet deputy (his former boss and patron, Semichastnyy, also was dropped from the Supreme Soviet in June 1970). Zakharov's last identification was at a seminar of leaders of Shelepin's trade unions in early 1970 (*Trud*, 25 March 1970).

[32]Chebrikov was Dnepropetrovsk Oblast secretary from 1963 to 1965 under First Secretary Shcherbitskiy and was promoted to oblast second secretary by Shcherbitskiy in 1965. In late 1967, not long after Tsvigun was called to Moscow, Chebrikov left the Ukraine and became chief of the KGB cadres administration, apparently to supervise the purge of Shelepin–Semichastnyy appointees. Later, in September 1968, he was promoted to KGB deputy chairman (*Bolshaya Sovetskaya Entsiklopediya* yearbook for 1971).

[33]Tsinev's early career is closely tied to Brezhnev's protégé, present MVD chief Shchelokov, as well as to Brezhnev. (The best account of Tsinev's early career appeared in the 11 May 1971 *Leningradskaya Pravda* account of his nomination for the RSFSR Supreme Soviet.) Tsinev graduated from the Dnepropetrovsk Metallurgical Institute in 1934; Shchelokov graduated from the same institute in 1933; while Brezhnev graduated from the metallurgical institute in the neighboring town of Dneprodzerzhinsk in 1935. After their graduations, all three worked as engineers in metallurgical plants in Dnepropetrovsk Oblast, and in 1939 Brezhnev became a Dnepropetrovsk Oblast secretary, Tsinev a Dnepropetrovsk City secretary, and Shchelokov the chairman of the Dnepropetrovsk City Executive Committee. They worked together until 1941 when all three went into the army. Tsinev remained in the army after World War II, becoming deputy high commissioner in Austria, while Brezhnev (in 1950) and Shchelokov (in 1951) moved from party work in the Ukraine to Moldavia where they became Central Committee first secretary and first deputy premier, respectively.

two as Central Committee candidate members and Tsinev as an Auditing Commission member)—the only police leaders so favored except for KGB Chairman Yu. V. Andropov and MVD chief N. A. Shchelokov themselves, who were re-elected Central Committee members. Other Brezhnev supporters added to the Central Committee are Azerbaydzhan First Secretary G. A. Aliyev, Ivano-Frankovsk First Secretary V. F. Dobryk,[34] Gorkiy First Secretary N. I. Maslennikov,[35] Komsomol First Secretary Ye. M. Tyazhelnikov,[36] and Dagestan First Secretary M.-S. I. Umakhanov.[37] Among the new candidate members, in addition to KGB leaders Tsvigun and Chebrikov, the clearest Brezhnev beneficiary is First Secretary I. L. Furs of Brezhnev's home town, Dneprodzerzhinsk. A Katushev protégé from Gorkiy, Central Committee Construction Section head

---

In September 1966 Moldavian Second Secretary Shchelokov was selected to become head of the new USSR Ministry for Defense of Public Order (later renamed MVD)—in preference to Shelepin protégé, RSFSR Minister for Defense of Public Order V. S. Tikunov (he was deputy KGB chairman under KGB Chairman Shelepin 1959-61).

Tsinev's first public association with the KGB was shortly after Tsvigun and Chebrikov had taken over in 1967: identified only as a colonel general, he wrote an article on the 50th KGB anniversary for the 20 December 1967 *Sovetskaya Rossiya.* He was appointed KGB deputy chairman in July 1970 (according to the 1971 yearbook) and was first publicly identified in this post in the 3 December 1970 *Pravda.*

Thus, KGB deputy chairmen Chebrikov and Tsinev and MVD chief Shchelokov all hail from Dnepropetrovsk, while KGB First Deputy Chairman Tsvigun is also a Ukrainian. Brezhnev men clearly dominate the security forces' leadership. Brezhnev likewise relied on an especially close associate from Dnepropetrovsk to be political watchdog for the army units around Moscow. K. S. Grushevoy graduated from the Dneprodzerzhinsk Metallurgical Institute in 1934 (Brezhnev graduated in 1935), worked as an engineer in Dneprodzerzhinsk's Dzerzhinskiy metallurgical plant 1934-38 (where Brezhnev also was engineer 1935-37), became Dneprodzerzhinsk city first secretary in 1938 (while Brezhnev was city executive committee chairman), was Dnepropetrovsk Obkom second secretary 1939-41 (Brezhnev was obkom secretary 1939-41), entered the army in 1941 (as did Brezhnev), became a political officer in 1953 (under army political administration deputy chief Brezhnev 1953-54), and in December 1965, after Brezhnev established his supremacy, became chief of the political administration of the Moscow military district (*Bolshaya Sovetskaya Entsiklopediya* yearbook for 1971). Grushevoy was elected a Central Committee candidate member at both 1966 and 1971 congresses.

[34] As first secretary of Brezhnev's home town of Dneprodzerzhinsk, he had been favored with Central Committee candidate membership at the 1966 congress—the only provincial city first secretary so honored, except for Leningrad's secretary. Dobryk was the only one at the 1971 Ukrainian party congress to lavish personal attention on Brezhnev.

[35] A protégé of Brezhnev's protégé, former Gorkiy first secretary and now Central Committee Secretary K. F. Katushev. Maslennikov was quite solicitous toward Brezhnev in his 24th Congress speech.

[36] Chosen to replace Shelepin's protégé, S. P. Pavlov, as Komsomol leader in 1968. He has been especially solicitous toward Brezhnev and has cleaned out almost all the old Shelepin-Semichastnyy-Pavlov clique in the Komsomol.

[37] One of the few leaders to label Brezhnev head of the Politburo—see *Pravda*, 20 January 1971.

I. N. Dmitriyev, was added to the Auditing Commission. In addition, one could count several officials from the strongly pro-Brezhnev areas of Kazakhstan, Azerbaydzhan, and Moldavia who were added to the central organs.

One reason for the small number of obvious Brezhnev men among the additions to the Central Committee is that he has not been able to manipulate local cadre changes to his advantage in most cases. As he explained in his 24th Congress report: In selecting new republic and provincial first secretaries "the Central Committee has consistently followed the line of advancing local officials" and "sending people to these posts from the center has been done only by way of exception" (*Pravda*, 31 March 1971). And, in fact, almost all RSFSR oblast first secretaries (most of whom are on the Central Committee) appointed since the 1966 congress were previously local executive committee chairmen, oblast second secretaries, city first secretaries, etc. This is considerably different than the cadre pattern from late 1964 to early 1966 when Brezhnev and Kirilenko were running the RSFSR Bureau.[38]

Voronov's Fall

Despite the failure of the 24th Congress to purge Brezhnev's Politburo foes, a major shake-up did occur shortly after the congress. In the most drastic move against a Politburo member since Khrushchev's fall,[39] Voronov was removed from his post as RSFSR premier and named to the minor post of USSR People's Control Committee chairman in late July.[40] The reason action was taken against him rather than Shelepin or some other Brezhnev foe apparently lay in his almost open opposition to the mid-1970 agricultural decisions, his use of his RSFSR post to promote his own policies, and his probably bitter clashes with Brezhnev and Polyanskiy. His acts and statements had come perilously close to staking out a personal position distinct from the collective anonymity of the Politburo. While as RSFSR government leader he was able to initiate policies in his own bailiwick, in his new post as USSR people's control leader he had only the functions of checking on the fulfillment of government and party orders and on eliminating waste and corruption.[41]

[38] See the footnote in Chapter VII, p. 160.

[39] Brezhnev foe Shelepin was demoted from Central Committee secretary to trade union chairman in 1967, but—in contrast to Voronov's new post—Shelepin's trade union post entitled him to at least Politburo candidate membership and, in fact, he remained a full Politburo member. Mikoyan and Shvernik were retired from the Presidium (Politburo) at the 1966 congress, but both were in their seventies and were retired with honor and no hint of criticism (although Mikoyan's relatively liberal positions probably prompted his colleagues to retire him).

[40] *Pravda*, 23 and 24 July 1971. He replaced former Shelepin subordinate Kovanov, who was retired at sixty-four.

[41] After Shelepin had apparently attempted to expand the powers of his Party-State Control Committee to censure party officials as well as government officials, local party

The politically alert had been warned of Voronov's increasing isolation by his low rankings and the snub on his August 1970 birthday, as well as by the early 1971 removal of his key allies, RSFSR First Deputy Premier Pysin, RSFSR Deputy Premier Biryukov, and *Sovetskaya Rossiya* editor Moskovskiy. At the 28 July 1971 RSFSR Supreme Soviet session Brezhnev himself nominated Voronov's successor and his only comment on the change was that "as is known" Voronov had held this post for nine years but "now he has been appointed chairman of the USSR People's Control Committee" (*Pravda*, 29 July 1971). No praise was given.

Voronov's successor as premier was Central Committee Heavy Industry Secretary M. S. Solomentsev—the lowest ranking among the twenty-five members of the Politburo and Secretariat (see Brezhnev's listing on p. 262). Solomentsev was not an obvious Brezhnev protégé,[42] although as heavy industry

---

organizations' control over party-state control organs was reasserted in the fall of 1965 and at the December 1965 plenum the committee was reduced to a People's Control Committee. At the spring 1966 party congress the Party Control Committee was strengthened and Latvian First Secretary Pelshe was appointed its chairman and made a Politburo member. The people's control organs, however, remained weak, with no power over party organs and under close party control.

Although the 1971 appointment of Politburo member Voronov might suggest that people's control was being strengthened in a parallel fashion to party control, this was clearly not the case. At the 1971 congress (and afterward) there was no campaign to strengthen the people's control committees and, in fact, the power of primary party organizations to check the work of their institutions and organizations was expanded, suggesting less rather than more room for operation of people's control organs. When the late 1971 elections of local people's control groups and posts began, editorials (*Pravda* and *Sovetskaya Rossiya*, 15 September 1971) stressed that they should be run directly by local party organs.

The political insignificance of Voronov's new post was clear from the committee's tasks in late 1971. In August the Council of Ministers ordered the committee to intensify checking on correct use of power and fuel (*Izvestiya*, 19 August), and in October the committee carried out a check on waste of cement (*Pravda*, 29 October).

[42] Solomentsev rose to Kazakh second secretary in late 1962 during the purge of Brezhnev's Kazakh appointees and he was removed as soon as Brezhnev became Central Committee first secretary and restored his protégés (Kunayev, Beysebayev, etc.) to power in Kazakhstan in December 1964. Solomentsev was transferred to another important post (first secretary of Rostov), but became involved in political infighting. In late 1965 the RSFSR Bureau (Chairman Brezhnev, First Deputy Chairman Kirilenko) discussed his obkom's lag in construction of light industry and food industry enterprises and condemned the obkom leaders for not eliminating the "harmful attitudes" that light industry was of secondary importance and that heavy industry should be favored. The Bureau's complaints against the Rostov leaders were spelled out in detail in a 14 September 1965 *Sovetskaya Rossiya* editorial. Whether this really reflected Brezhnev's disapproval of Solomentsev's work is hard to say, however, since Brezhnev himself was the loudest advocate of heavy industrial priority in 1965 and 1966.

Solomentsev came under fire again in 1966, when he was being considered for the post of Central Committee secretary. Central Committee Heavy Industry Secretary Rudakov entered a hospital with heart disease on 8 April 1966 and died on 10 July, suggesting that

secretary since 1966 he had worked closely with Brezhnev and Kirilenko and presumably had won their favor.

The Politburo still appears to be operating cautiously, however, limiting Brezhnev's moves against Voronov. As of January 1972 Voronov still had not been further demoted—the only Central Committee plenum in the second half of 1971 (22-23 November 1971) failed to remove him from the Politburo. Most of his remaining protégés (including RSFSR First Deputy Premier Shkolnikov) were reappointed to the RSFSR government in late July 1971. Voronov's successor Solomentsev (not as clear a Brezhnev man as other possible candidates for the post) was raised only to Politburo *candidate* member at the November 1971 plenum. What is more, there have been no direct attacks on Voronov or his policies.[43] But the Voronov shake-up is still uncompleted. His new status clearly does not justify his remaining in the Politburo. His protégés in the RSFSR government (Shkolnikov, Florentyev, etc.) presumably will sooner or later be retired. No successor to Solomentsev as Central Committee heavy industry sec-

---

the question of his successor arose in the Politburo in the spring and summer of 1966. A lengthy 25 May 1966 *Pravda* article attacked the Rostov Obkom for poor leadership of scientific institutions and cited Solomentsev himself as admitting that the obkom's work could be improved. On 5 June, however, Solomentsev wrote an article in *Pravda* appearing to defend his leadership, citing positive examples of how his obkom had corrected local leaders' errors—and ignoring the 25 May article. Nevertheless, *Pravda*'s criticisms were later acknowledged as correct by Solomentsev's deputy, oblast Secretary M. K. Fomenko in the 17 October *Pravda*. On 17 November *Sovetskaya Rossiya* announced Solomentsev's removal as Rostov first secretary in connection with his appointment as Central Committee Heavy Industry Section head. At the 13 December 1966 Central Committee plenum he was elected a Central Committee secretary.

[43] Although indirect attacks surfaced at a 4-9 October 1971 Kiev all-union rural construction conference, where the RSFSR was singled out for criticism for its poor work in rural construction and its negative attitude toward the program to reorganize villages. Initial accounts of the conference ignored the attacks on the RSFSR, but *Selskaya Zhizn*'s construction editor P. B. Vaynshteyn, who was loudest in defending Polyanskiy's rural construction program in 1967 and 1968, wrote a long account in the 13 October 1971 *Selskaya Zhizn* revealing the criticisms of RSFSR rural construction policies—policies in line with RSFSR Premier Voronov's footdragging and resistance to expenditures. Vaynshteyn claims the RSFSR planned poorly for many model villages, delayed construction (beginning only 64 model farm villages instead of the planned 130), and failed to provide financing and material resources ("financing was not arranged properly—the RSFSR Agriculture Ministry entrusted it to local organs" and special material resources were not planned for construction of the model villages). "The impermissibility of such an attitude toward this important matter was stressed" at the conference, according to Vaynshteyn. Judging from his account, the RSFSR was the only area criticized at the conference and RSFSR Gosstroy Chairman D. Basilov and RSFSR Rural Construction Deputy Minister M. Pilipchuk were forced to concede shortcomings in the RSFSR's work. In contrast, Vaynshteyn praises the Belorussian officials (who developed the prototype village reorganization plan in 1965-67).

Perhaps it is a measure of the importance of the controversy over rural construction policy that the three top RSFSR leaders removed in 1971 (Premier Voronov, First Deputy Premier for agriculture Pysin, and Deputy Premier for construction Biryukov) were precisely the top RSFSR leaders with most responsibility for rural construction.

retary has been chosen—a touchy decision, since it means introducing a new man into the twenty-five-man Politburo-Secretariat leadership collective (something even the 24th Congress did not do). The very limited decisions of the November 1971 Central Committee plenum (only to promote Solomentsev to Politburo candidate member) suggest that important changes are still coming.

APPENDIXES

APPENDIX 1

KHRUSHCHEV ERA PRESIDIUM

Jan. 1960–May 1960	May 1960–Oct. 1961	Oct. 1961–Oct. 1962	Nov. 1962–Nov. 1964
Khrushchev[a]	Khrushchev[a]	Khrushchev[a]	Khrushchev[a](–Oct. '64)
Mikoyan	Mikoyan	Mikoyan	Mikoyan
Kozlov	Kozlov[a]	Kozlov[a]	Kozlov[a](–Nov. '64)
Suslov[a]	Suslov[a]	Suslov[a]	Suslov[a]
Brezhnev[a]	Brezhnev	Brezhnev	Brezhnev[a]
Voroshilov	Voroshilov (–July '60)		
Kirichenko[a](–May)			
Belyayev (–May)			
Aristov[a]	Aristov (–Oct. '61)		
Ignatov[a]	Ignatov (–Oct. '61)		
Furtseva[a]	Furtseva (–Oct. '61)		
Mukhitdinov[a]	Mukhitdinov[a](–Oct. '61)		
Shvernik	Shvernik	Shvernik	Shvernik
Kuusinen[a]	Kuusinen[a]	Kuusinen[a]	Kuusinen[a](–May '64)[b]
	(May–) Polyanskiy	Polyanskiy	Polyanskiy
	(May–) Podgornyy	Podgornyy	Podgornyy[a]
	(May–) Kosygin	Kosygin	Kosygin
		(Oct.–) Voronov	Voronov
			(Apr. '62–) Kirilenko

Candidate Members

Polyanskiy (–May)			
Podgornyy (–May)			
Kosygin (–May)			
Mazurov	Mazurov	Mazurov	Mazurov
Mzhavanadze	Mzhavanadze	Mzhavanadze	Mzhavanadze
Kirilenko	Kirilenko (–Oct. '61)		
Pospelov[a]	Pospelov (–Oct. '61)		
Korotchenko	Korotchenko (–Oct. '61)		
Kalnberzin	Kalnberzin (–Oct. '61)		
Pervukhin	Pervukhin (–Oct. '61)		
	(Jan. '61–) Voronov (–Oct. '61)		
	(Jan. '61–) Grishin	Grishin	Grishin
		(Oct.–) Rashidov	Rashidov
		(Oct.–) Shcherbitskiy	Shcherbitskiy[c]
			(Nov. '62–) Yefremov (–Nov. '64)

[a]Also Central Committee secretaries.
[b]Died.
[c]In December 1963 Shcherbitskiy was replaced as candidate member by Shelest. In November 1964 Shelest was promoted to full member.

POST-KHRUSHCHEV POLITBURO[a]

Nov. 1964–Feb. 1965	Mar. 1965–Mar. 1966	Apr. 1966–Mar. 1971	Apr. 1971–
Brezhnev[b]	Brezhnev[b]	Brezhnev[b]	Brezhnev[b]
Kosygin	Kosygin	Kosygin	Kosygin
Podgornyy[b]	Podgornyy[b]	Podgornyy	Podgornyy
Suslov[b]	Suslov[b]	Suslov[b]	Suslov[b]
Mikoyan	Mikoyan (–Mar. '66)		
Shvernik	Shvernik (–Mar. '66)		
Polyanskiy	Polyanskiy	Polyanskiy	Polyanskiy
Voronov	Voronov	Voronov	Voronov
Kirilenko	Kirilenko	Kirilenko[b]	Kirilenko[b]
(Nov.–) Shelepin[b]	Shelepin[b]	Shelepin	Shelepin
(Nov.–) Shelest	Shelest	Shelest	Shelest
	(Mar.–) Mazurov	Mazurov	Mazurov
		(Apr.–) Pelshe	Pelshe
			(Apr.–) Grishin
			(Apr.–) Shcherbitskiy
			(Apr.–) Kunayev
			(Apr.–) Kulakov[b]

Candidate Members

Mazurov (–Mar. '65)			
Mzhavanadze	Mzhavanadze	Mzhavanadze	Mzhavanadze
Grishin	Grishin	Grishin (–Apr. '71)	
Rashidov	Rashidov	Rashidov	Rashidov
Yefremov	Yefremov (–Mar. '66)		
(Nov.–) Demichev[b]	Demichev[b]	Demichev[b]	Demichev[b]
	(Mar.–) Ustinov[b]	Ustinov[b]	Ustinov[b]
	(Dec. '65–) Shcherbitskiy	Shcherbitskiy (–Apr. '71)	
		(Apr.–) Kunayev (–Apr. '71)	
		(Apr.–) Masherov	Masherov
		(Jun. '67–) Andropov	Andropov

[a]The Presidium was renamed the Politburo at the 22d Congress in March–April 1966.
[b]Also Central Committee secretaries.

APPENDIX 2

KHRUSHCHEV ERA SECRETARIAT

Jan. 1960–May 1960	May 1960–Oct. 1961	Nov. 1961–Oct. 1962	Nov. 1962–Nov. 1964
Khrushchev[a]	Khrushchev[a]	Khrushchev[a]	Khrushchev[a](–Oct. '64)
Suslov[a]	Suslov[a]	Suslov[a]	Suslov[a]
Brezhnev[a]	Brezhnev[a](–Jul. '60)		
Kirichenko[a](–May)			
Aristov[a](–May)			
Ignatov[a](–May)			
Pospelov[a](–May)			
Furtseva[a](–May)			
Kuusinen[a]	Kuusinen[a]	Kuusinen[a]	Kuusinen[a](–May '64)[b]
Mukhitdinov[a]	Mukhitdinov[a](–Oct. '61)		
	(May–) Kozlov[a]	Kozlov[a]	Kozlov[a](–Nov. '64)
		(Nov.–) Ilichev	Ilichev
		(Nov.–) Shelepin	Shelepin
		(Nov.–) Ponomarev	Ponomarev
		(Nov.–) Demichev	Demichev
		(Nov.–) Spiridonov (–Apr. '62)	
			(Nov.–) Rudakov
			(Nov.–) Andropov
			(Nov.–) Titov
			(Nov.–) Polyakov (–Nov. '64)
			(Jun. '63–) Brezhnev[a]
			(Jun. '63–) Podgornyy[a]

[a] Also member of Presidium.
[b] Died.

POST-KHRUSHCHEV SECRETARIAT

Nov. 1964–Feb. 1965	Mar. 1965–Mar. 1966	Apr. 1966–Mar. 1971	Apr. 1971–
Brezhnev[a]	Brezhnev[a]	Brezhnev[a]	Brezhnev[a]
Suslov[a]	Suslov[a]	Suslov[a]	Suslov[a]
Podgornyy[a]	Podgornyy[a](–Dec. '65)		
Shelepin[a]	Shelepin[a]	Shelepin[a](–Sep. '67)	
Demichev[b]	Demichev[b]	Demichev[b]	Demichev[b]
Ponomarev	Ponomarev	Ponomarev	Ponomarev
Andropov	Andropov	Andropov (–June '67)	
Rudakov	Rudakov	Rudakov (–July '66)[c]	
Ilichev (–Mar. '65)			
Titov	Titov (–Sep. '65)		
(Mar. '65–)	Ustinov[b]	Ustinov[b]	Ustinov[b]
(Sep. '65–)	Kulakov	Kulakov	Kulakov[a]
(Dec. '65–)	Kapitonov	Kapitonov	Kapitonov
	(Apr. '66–)	Kirilenko[a]	Kirilenko[a]
	(Dec. '66–)	Solomentsev	Solomentsev
	(Apr. '68–)	Katushev	Katushev

[a] Also member of Politburo.
[b] Also candidate member of Politburo.
[c] Died.

CENTRAL COMMITTEE BUREAU FOR THE RSFSR[a]

	1956-1957	1958	1959	1960	1961
Chairman	Khrushchev	Khrushchev	Khrushchev	Khrushchev	Khrushchev
Dep. chairman	Belyayev	Aristov	Aristov	Aristov	Voronov
Dep. chairman		Brezhnev			Churayev
Members:					
CC secretary	Aristov[b]				
CC secretary	Pospelov[b]	Pospelov	Pospelov	Pospelov	
RSFSR cadre chief	Churayev	Churayev	Churayev	M. Yefremov	
CC cadre chief				Churayev	
RSFSR agri. chief	Mylarshchikov	Mylarshchikov	Vorobyev		
RSFSR premier	Yasnov	Kozlov	Polyanskiy	Polyanskiy	Polyanskiy
First dep. premier	Puzanov	Yasnov	Yasnov	Yasnov	Yasnov
President					
Moscow sec.	Kapitonov	Kapitonov	Demichev	Demichev	Demichev
Leningrad sec.	Kozlov		Spiridonov	Spiridonov	Spiridonov
Gorkiy sec.	Ignatov		L. Yefremov	Yefremov	Yefremov
Sverdlovsk sec.	Kirilenko				
Others					M. Yakovlev

[a]Since the Bureau was not an elective body like the Presidium or Secretariat its membership was rarely announced (exceptions include the announcement of its original establishment in 1956 [*Spravochnik Partiynogo Rabotnika*, 1st edition, 1957]), the announcement after the 22d Congress [*Pravda*, 1 November 1961], and the listings in the *Bolshaya Sovetskaya Entsiklopediya* yearbooks for 1964 and 1965). Therefore, this table is based mainly on press identifications and biographies. Holding certain RSFSR posts (such as that of RSFSR president) did not assure automatic membership in the Bureau, and often when a member joined the Presidium or Secretariat he would drop out of the Bureau even though still holding a leading post in the RSFSR (for example, Kirilenko in 1957 or Spiridonov in 1961).

[b]Added to the Bureau by a 14 March 1956 Central Committee decree (see *Spravochnik Partiynogo Rabotnika*, 1st edition [1957]).

CENTRAL COMMITTEE BUREAU FOR THE RSFSR (continued)

	1961–62	1962	1963	1964	1965
Chairman	Khrushchev	Khrushchev	Khrushchev	Khrushchev	Brezhnev
First deputy	Voronov	Voronov	L. Yefremov	Yefremov	
First deputy		Kirilenko	Kirilenko	Kirilenko	Kirilenko
Deputy	Lomako				
Members:					
CC secretary					
RSFSR cadre chief					Kapitonov
RSFSR agri. chief					Karlov
RSFSR premier	Polyanskiy	Polyanskiy	Voronov	Voronov	Voronov
First deputy	Yasnov	Yasnov	Yasnov	Yasnov	Yasnov
President	Organov	Organov	Ignatov	Ignatov	Ignatov
Moscow sec.	Abramov	Abramov	Yegorychev	Yegorychev	Yegorychev
Leningrad sec.		Tolstikov	Tolstikov	Tolstikov	Tolstikov
Gorkiy sec.	Yefremov	Yefremov			
Sverdlovsk sec.	Kirilenko				
Others	Churayev	Churayev	(Abramov)	(Abramov)	(Abramov)
	Romanov	Romanov		Yenyutin	Yenyutin

The dates in the headings refer to the following exact periods:

1956–57–from the Bureau's creation by a 27 February 1956 decree until December 1957;

1958–from January 1958 until spring 1959;

1959–from mid-1959 until early 1960;

1960–from mid-1960 until February 1961;

1961–from March 1961 until the 22d Party Congress in October 1961;

1961–62–from October 1961 (including appointments to the Bureau shortly before the 22d Congress in late October, as well as the new Bureau announced in the 1 November 1961 *Pravda*) until March 1962;

1962–from April 1962 until December 1962;

1963–from January 1963 until December 1963;

1964–from January 1964 until Khrushchev's fall in October 1964;

1965–from Khrushchev's fall in October 1964 until the Bureau was abolished at the 23d Party Congress in April 1966.

Members of the RSFSR Bureau

Abramov, G. G.: became Moscow Oblast first secretary in mid-1960, but was first identified as a Bureau member in the 1 November 1961 *Pravda*. The 1962 *Bolshaya Sovetskaya Entsiklopediya* yearbook lists him as a member starting in 1961, but it is unclear whether he replaced Demichev in the Bureau in early 1961 or only in late 1961. In January 1963 he was not reelected Moscow Oblast first secretary and was demoted to first deputy chairman of the Moscow Sovnarkhoz (identified in the 15 August 1964 *Pravda*). The yearbooks for 1964 and 1965 continue to list him as a member of the Bureau, although the accuracy of this may be questioned because of his demotion and virtual disappearance from the press.

Aristov, A. B.: while Central Committee secretary he was added to the Bureau by a 14 March 1956 Central Committee decree (along with Central Committee Secretary Pospelov) only two weeks after the Bureau's creation and after its original composition had already been announced. After Bureau Deputy Chairman Belyayev was transferred to Kazakhstan as first secretary in December 1957, Aristov became Bureau deputy chairman (first identified in the 28 December 1958 *Pravda*, although the 1962 and 1966 yearbooks of the *Bolshaya Sovetskaya Entsiklopediya* list Aristov as deputy chairman starting 1957). In May 1960 he and Pospelov were dropped as Central Committee secretaries in order "to concentrate their attention on work in the Central Committee's RSFSR Bureau" (*Pravda*, 5 May 1960). Aristov remained the lone Bureau deputy chairman until the January 1961 plenum (last identified as such in the 27 December 1960 *Pravda*), when he was replaced with Voronov. On 6 February 1961 *Pravda* announced his appointment as ambassador to Poland.

Belyayev, N. I.: was named the sole deputy chairman of the Bureau when it was originally established in February 1956. He was also a Central Committee secretary, and in June 1957 he was added to the Presidium. In December 1957 he became first secretary of Kazakhstan, surrendering his Bureau post about that time or sometime in 1958.

Brezhnev, L. I.: was identified by the 1966 yearbook and volume 4 of the new *Bolshaya Sovetskaya Entsiklopediya* (issued in 1971) as deputy chairman of the RSFSR Bureau during 1958, while he also was Central Committee secretary (1956–60). However, other sources have not mentioned this and the accuracy of this identification may be questioned. Brezhnev succeeded Khrushchev as Bureau chairman in November 1964 (volume 4 of the new *Bolshaya Sovetskaya Entsiklopediya*) and headed the Bureau until its abolition in April 1966.

Churayev, V. M.: as head of the Central Committee's Party Organs Section for the RSFSR he was named a Bureau member when the Bureau was created in February 1956. In the fall of 1959 he was promoted from RSFSR cadres chief to national cadres chief (head of the Central Committee Party Organs Section for the Union Republics—first identified in the 21 October 1959 *Izvestiya*), but he retained membership in the Bureau (see his identifications in the 4 October 1960 and 20 November 1960 *Pravda*s). Despite the fall of his chief, Aristov, in February 1961, Churayev was promoted to Bureau deputy chairman in February 1961 (see the 1962 and 1966 yearbooks; first identified in the 12 February 1961 *Pravda*). However, he surrendered his key cadre post at that time and remained Bureau deputy chairman only until October 1961. In the new Bureau announced after the 22d Congress (*Pravda*, 1 November 1961) he was listed only as a member. He was dropped from the Bureau in 1962 (yearbook for 1966), apparently in late 1962. After the RSFSR Party-State Control Committee was established on 17 December 1962, Churayev became its first deputy chairman (identified in the 19 March 1963 *Leninskoye Znamya*), a considerable demotion.

Demichev, P. N.: was elected Moscow Oblast first secretary in March 1959 and soon was identified as a Bureau member (*Sovetskaya Rossiya*, 19 July 1959). He was transferred to Moscow City first secretary in July 1960, but apparently remained in the Bureau until sometime in 1961 (the 1966 yearbook lists him as a Bureau member 1959-61). On 31 October 1961 he was elected a Central Committee secretary and he was not included in the Bureau listed in the 1 November 1961 *Pravda*.

Ignatov, N. G.: was named a member of the Bureau when it was created in February 1956. He was elected to the Presidium in mid-1957 and Central Committee Secretariat in December 1957. When he surrendered his post as Gorkiy Oblast first secretary to take up his post as Central Committee secretary in December 1957, he apparently dropped out of the Bureau (the 1966 yearbook lists him as a Bureau member 1956-57). He became RSFSR president for a short time in 1959, but apparently did not rejoin the Bureau. In December 1962 he lost his posts as USSR deputy premier, chairman of the State Committee for Procurements and chairman of the USSR Agriculture Committee, and was demoted to RSFSR president again. He became a Bureau member in late 1962 (yearbook for 1966; first identification, *Pravda*, 6 January 1963) and remained in the Bureau until its abolition in April 1966 (yearbooks for 1964, 1965, and 1966).

Kapitonov, I. V.: as Moscow Oblast first secretary was named to the Bureau when it was originally created in February 1956. When he was removed as Moscow leader in March 1959, he also lost his Bureau membership (the 1966 yearbook lists him as a Bureau member 1956-59; he was identified as such as late as 21 February 1959 in *Sovetskaya Rossiya*). Kapitonov staged a comeback later in 1959 but did not rejoin the Bureau until late 1964 (*Pravda*, 7 December 1965). In December 1964 he left his post as Ivanovo Oblast first secretary to become head of the Central Committee Party Organs Section for the RSFSR (first identified in the 26 January 1965 *Pravda*). On 17 March 1965 *Pravda* identified him as a Bureau member. In December 1965 he gave up his RSFSR posts to become a Central Committee secretary and head of the Central Committee's Party Organizational Work Section (the 1966 yearbook identifies him as a Bureau member 1964-65).

Karlov, V. A.: left his post of Uzbek second secretary in March 1965 (*Pravda Vostoka*, 4 March 1965) to become a member of the RSFSR Bureau (identified in the 9 March 1965 *Pravda*). He remained in the Bureau until its abolition in

April 1966, whereupon he became first deputy head of the Central Committee's Agriculture Section (see the 1966 yearbook and the 15 June 1966 *Pravda* identification of him).

Khrushchev, N. S.: chairman of the Bureau from its creation in February 1956 until his removal as Central Committee first secretary in October 1964.

Kirilenko, A. P.: as Sverdlovsk first secretary he was named a member of the Bureau in February 1956 when it was created. When he became a Presidium candidate member in mid-1957, he gave up his Bureau membership (the 1962 and 1966 yearbooks list him as a Bureau member 1956–57). In October 1961 he lost his candidate membership in the Presidium and returned to his lower status as a Bureau member (he was listed as a member of the new Bureau in *Pravda*, 1 November 1961; the 1966 yearbook lists him as a Bureau member 1961–April 1966). In April 1962 he left his post as Sverdlovsk first secretary to become a Presidium member and first deputy chairman of the Bureau (first identified in the 28 April 1962 *Pravda*; the 1966 yearbook lists him as Bureau first deputy chairman 1962–66).

Kozlov, F. R.: as Leningrad Oblast first secretary he was named a member of the Bureau when it was created in February 1956. He became a Presidium candidate member in February 1957 and a full member in June 1957, apparently surrendering his Bureau membership at that time. In December 1957 he became RSFSR premier and resumed his membership in the Bureau (the 1962 yearbook lists him as a Bureau member 1956–57 and from January 1958 until November 1958). In March 1958 he became USSR first deputy premier and left his post as RSFSR premier.

Lomako, P. F.: was deputy chairman of the Bureau 1961–62 (see the 1966 yearbook), apparently being added to the Bureau shortly before the 22d Congress (he was last identified as chairman of the Krasnoyarsk Sovnarkhoz in the 28 July 1961 *Pravda* and first identified as Bureau deputy chairman in the 16 October 1961 *Pravda*) and apparently being dropped in November 1962 when he was named USSR deputy premier and Gosplan chairman. Ironically, Lomako replaced Churayev as deputy chairman. During the campaign against localism in mid-1959 Sovnarkhoz Chairman Lomako was severely censured by the RSFSR Bureau (Deputy Chairman Aristov) for violations of state discipline and Aristov's deputy, Churayev, attacked Lomako by name for this in the 14 August 1959 *Pravda* (also see the editorial in *Partiynaya Zhizn* 15 [1959]: 3–5).

Mylarshchikov, V. P.: as head of the Central Committee's Agriculture Section for the RSFSR he was named to the Bureau when it was created in February 1956. In the spring of 1959 he was removed as Agriculture Section head (he was last identified as such in the 19 March 1959 *Izvestiya*; his successor was first identified in the 28 April 1959 *Sovetskaya Rossiya*) and as Bureau member (last identified as such in the 18 January 1959 *Pravda*). He was demoted to director of the specialized trust of potato and vegetable growing sovkhozes in Moscow Oblast (identified in the 26 December 1959 *Pravda*).

Organov, N. N.: was RSFSR deputy premier 1958–59 and RSFSR president from November 1959 until December 1962, but was a Bureau member only in

1961–62 (1966 yearbook). He was first identified as a Bureau member in the 6 October 1961 *Sovetskaya Rossiya* and was in the new Bureau announced in the 1 November 1961 *Pravda*. He apparently remained in the Bureau until he was removed as RSFSR president in December 1962, and appointed ambassador to Bulgaria in January 1963.

Polyanskiy, D. S.: was added to the Bureau after becoming RSFSR Premier in March 1958 (the 1966 yearbook lists him as a member 1958– 62). He was included in the new Bureau announced in the 1 November 1961 *Pravda*, but apparently was dropped when he became USSR deputy premier in November 1962.

Pospelov, P. N.: while Central Committee secretary he was added to the Bureau by the 14 March 1956 Central Committee decree. Although the biographies in the 1962 and 1966 yearbooks completely ignore Pospelov's membership in the Bureau and his biographies in the 1962 *Deputaty Verkhovnogo Soveta SSSR* and the *Sovetskaya Istoricheskaya Entsiklopediya* cite him as a member starting only in 1960, he appears to have been a member between 1956 and 1960 as well. He acted as representative of the RSFSR Bureau on numerous occasions: in December 1958 he delivered greetings to the RSFSR writers union congress from the RSFSR Bureau (*Pravda*, 8 December 1958); in May 1959 he presented the RSFSR· agricultural banner to the Tatar Republic (*Pravda*, 10 May 1959); in August 1959 he supervised an RSFSR education conference called by the RSFSR Bureau (*Sovetskaya Rossiya*, 2 August 1959); at the November 1959 RSFSR Supreme Soviet session he proposed that RSFSR President Ignatov be released so he could concentrate on his work as Central Committee secretary (*Pravda*, 27 November 1959); in January 1960 he installed Belyayev as Stavropol first secretary (*Pravda*, 29 January 1960); and in March 1960 he attended a conference of *Sovetskaya Rossiya* correspondents, along with RSFSR leaders Aristov and Polyanskiy (*Sovetskaya Rossiya*, 9 March 1960). He was not identified as a Bureau member on any of these occasions, however. In May 1960, along with Aristov, Pospelov was released as Central Committee secretary in order to concentrate on his work in the RSFSR Bureau (*Pravda*, 5 May 1960). On 19 June 1960 *Pravda* specifically identified Pospelov as a member of the RSFSR Bureau. Pospelov appears to have dropped out of the Bureau when he became director of the Marxism–Leninism Institute in early 1961 (identified in the 4 March 1961 *Sovetskaya Rossiya*) and he was not in the new Bureau announced in the 1 November 1961 *Pravda*.

Puzanov, A. M.: as RSFSR first deputy premier he was named to the original Bureau in February 1956. But he was a member only in 1956–57 (yearbook, 1966), and in 1957 he became ambassador to North Korea.

Romanov, A. V.: was still deputy head of the Central Committee's Agitprop Section in late August 1961 (*Pravda*, 30 August 1961), but was identified as a Bureau member in the 8 October 1961 *Pravda*. He was a member only in 1961–62 (yearbook, 1966), being last identified in the 6 May 1962 *Moskovskaya Pravda*. The 6 January 1963 *Pravda* identified him as first deputy head of the Central Committee's new Ideology Section.

Spiridonov, I. V.: although becoming Leningrad Oblast first secretary in December 1957, he became a Bureau member only in 1959 (the 1966 yearbook lists him as a member 1959–61; *Pravda* first identified him as such on 9 April 1959). When he was elected a Central Committee secretary in October 1961, he dropped out of the Bureau (he was not in *Pravda*'s 1 November 1961 listing).

Tolstikov, V. S.: elected Leningrad Oblast first secretary in May 1962 (*Pravda*, 4 May 1962) and soon joined the Bureau (first identified in the 21 June 1962 *Leningradskaya Pravda*). He remained in the Bureau until its abolition in 1966 (yearbooks for 1964, 1965, and 1966).

Vorobyev, G. I.: became head of the Central Committee's Agriculture Section for the RSFSR in the spring of 1959 (identified in the 28 April 1959 *Sovetskaya Rossiya*), but was transferred to first secretary of Krasnodar in June 1960 (elected, *Pravda*, 10 June 1960). The 1962 yearbook lists him as a Bureau member 1959–61, although he presumably became inactive after June 1960.

Voronov, G. I.: replaced Aristov as Bureau deputy chairman after the 10–18 January 1961 plenum (released as Orenburg first secretary on 26 January 1961; first identified as Bureau deputy chairman in the 1 February 1961 *Pravda*; listed as deputy chairman from January 1961 to October 1961 in the 1966 yearbook). He became first deputy chairman after the 22d Congress (in the new Bureau announced in the 1 November 1961 *Pravda*), but dropped to ordinary member after the November 1962 plenum, when he replaced Polyanskiy as RSFSR premier (the 1966 yearbook lists him as first deputy chairman from October 1961 to November 1962; he was listed as a member in the 1964 and 1965 yearbooks).

Yakovlev, M. D.: was RSFSR deputy premier and foreign minister until August 1960, when he was appointed ambassador to the Congo. After being expelled from the Congo (September 1960) he returned to the USSR and soon became a member of the Bureau (identified in the 4 March 1961 *Sovetskaya Rossiya* and 14 July 1961 *Pravda*). However, in September 1961 he was named Ambassador to Iraq and dropped out of the Bureau.

Yasnov, M. A.: as RSFSR Premier he was named a Bureau member when it was created in February 1956 and remained a member until it was abolished in 1966 (yearbooks for 1962, 1964 and 1965). He was demoted to RSFSR first deputy premier in December 1957.

Yefremov, L. N.: as Gorkiy Oblast first secretary (1958–62) he joined the Bureau in 1959 (yearbook, 1966), although his first press identification as a member occurred only in the 30 January 1960 *Pravda*. In December 1962 he left Gorkiy (*Pravda*, 8 December 1962) and became Bureau first deputy chairman (first identified in the 21 December 1962, *Sovetskaya Rossiya*). After Khrushchev's fall, he was demoted to Stavropol first secretary (*Sovetskaya Rossiya*, 3 December 1964) and dropped from Bureau membership (the 1966 yearbook lists him as a Bureau member from 1959 to January 1965).

Yefremov, M. T.: succeeded Churayev as head of the Central Committee's Party Organs Section for the RSFSR in late 1959 (first identified as section head in the 30 December 1959 *Pravda*; last identified as Kuybyshev Oblast first secretary in the 6 September 1959 *Pravda*) and became a Bureau member (the 1966 yearbook lists him as a member 1959–61; he was first identified in the 14 January 1960 *Sovetskaya Rossiya*). He was removed shortly after the demotion of his boss, Aristov, becoming first secretary of Chelyabinsk in March 1961 (he was last identified as Bureau member and section head in the 16 February 1961 *Pravda*; *Pravda* on 17 March 1961 reported his election in Chelyabinsk).

Yegorychev, N. G.: was elected Moscow City first secretary in November 1962 (*Pravda*, 27 November 1962) and immediately became a Bureau member (the 1966 yearbook lists him as a member from 1962 until the Bureau's abolition in April 1966; however, he was first identified in the press only in the 28 January 1964 *Leningradskaya Pravda*).

Yenyutin, G. V.: was named chairman of the RSFSR Party-State Control Committee when it was established in December 1962 (*Pravda*, 19 December 1962) and presumably became a Bureau member at that time also, although he was not identified as a member until 29 October 1964 (*Pravda*). He was listed as a member in the 1964 and 1965 yearbooks.

APPENDIX 4

CENTRAL COMMITTEE SECTION HEADS, 1959–71

	Jan. 1959	Mid-1959	1960
Adm. of Affairs	Pivovarov	Pivovarov	Pivovarov
Adm. Organs		Mironov[a]	Mironov
Agriculture	Doroshenko[b]	Denisov	Denisov[c]
Bloc Relations	Andropov	Andropov	Andropov
Construction	Grishmanov	Grishmanov	Grishmanov[d]
Culture	Polikarpov	Polikarpov	Polikarpov
Defense Industry	Serbin	Serbin	Serbin
Foreign Cadres	(Orlov)[e]	Panyushkin	Panyushkin
General	Malin	Malin	Malin
Heavy Industry	Rudakov	Rudakov	Rudakov
International	Ponomarev	Ponomarev	Ponomarev
Light Industry	Lubennikov	Lubennikov[f]	Melnikov
Machine Building	Frolov	Frolov	Frolov
Party Organs	(none)	Semichastnyy[g,h]	Churayev[i]
Propaganda	Ilichev	Ilichev	Ilichev
Science	Kirillin	Kirillin	Kirillin
Trade	Kabkov	Kabkov	Kabkov
Transport			

[a]Leningrad KGB chief N. R. Mironov was appointed head of the Administrative Organs Section (which supervises the police) in 1959 (yearbook, 1962), and was first identified as such in the 8 August 1959 *Pravda*.

[b]P. Ye. Doroshenko was last identified as section head in the 19 June 1959 *Sovetskaya Estoniye* and was elected first secretary of Chernigov Oblast in September (*Pravda Ukrainy*, 11 September 1959) G. A. Denisov was last identified as Saratov first secretary in the 11 July 1959 *Sovetskaya Rossiya* and first identified as section head in the 22 August 1959 *Pravda*.

[c]Denisov was named ambassador to Bulgaria in May 1960 (*Pravda* 25 May 1960), but a new section head was not immediately appointed.

[d]I. A. Grishmanov was appointed chairman of the USSR Gosstroy in January 1961 (*Pravda*, 2 January 1961).

[e]In view of A. L. Orlov's involvement in foreign affairs, he probably was Panyushkin's predecessor although the section he headed was never named. *Pravda* on 24 July 1959 reported Orlov's appointmen as deputy foreign minister. A. S. Panyushkin became head of this section (which controls those working or traveling abroad) in 1959 (yearbook, 1962).

[f]L. I. Lubennikov was elected Kemerovo first secretary in February 1960 (*Pravda*, 13 Februar 1960). He was succeeded by N. A. Melnikov (identified as deputy head of this section in the 6 April 196 *Pravda Ukrainy*; the 1962 edition of the *Deputaty Verkhovnogo Soveta SSSR* lists him as deputy head then head of a section).

[g]V. Ye. Semichastnyy was released as Komsomol first secretary in March 1959 (*Pravda*, 26 Marc 1959) and first appeared as section head in the 22 April 1959 *Pravda*. No one had headed this sectio since section head Shelepin left to become KGB chairman in December 1958.

[h]Semichastnyy was still identified as section head in the 28 July 1959 *Pravda*, but in early Augu he was elected Azerbaydzhan second secretary (*Pravda*, 13 August 1959). V. M. Churayev was fir identified as section head in the 21 October 1959 *Izvestiya*.

[i]Churayev was appointed deputy chairman of the RSFSR Bureau in February 1961 (yearbool 1962) and left the section.

CENTRAL COMMITTEE SECTION HEADS

	1961	1962	1963
Adm. of Affairs	Pivovarov[a]	Chernyayev	Chernyayev
Adm. Organs	Mironov	Mironov	Mironov
Agriculture	Karlov[b,c]	Polyakov	Polyakov
Agri. Processing	–	–	Lushin[d]
Bloc Economic Ties	–	–	Miroshnichenko[e]
Bloc Relations	Andropov	Andropov	Andropov
Chemical Industry	–	–	(apparently none)[f]
Construction	(apparently none)	Abyzov[g]	Abyzov
Culture	Polikarpov	Polikarpov[h]	–
Defense Industry	Serbin	Serbin	Serbin
Foreign Cadres	Panyushkin	Panyushkin	Panyushkin
General	Malin	Malin	Malin
Heavy Industry	Rudakov	Rudakov	Rudakov
International	Ponomarev	Ponomarev	Ponomarev
Light Industry	Melnikov[i]	Maksimov	Maksimov
Machine Building	Frolov	Frolov	Frolov
Party Organs	Titov[j]	Titov	Titov
Propaganda	Ilichev	Ilichev[k]	Ilichev
Science	Kirillin	Kirillin[l]	–
Trade	Kabkov	Kabkov[m]	–
Transport		Simonov[n]	Simonov
Unnamed section	Doluda[o]		

[a]V. V. Pivovarov was still identified as administrator of affairs in the 3 November 1961 *Pravda*. K. P. Chernyayev first appeared as administrator of affairs in the 10 October 1962 *Pravda*.

[b]V. A. Karlov was released as Kalinin first secretary in September 1960 (*Pravda*, 30 September 1960), but was identified as section head only in the 27 January 1961 *Pravda*. The 1962 yearbook lists him as joining the Central Committee apparatus in 1960.

[c]Karlov was identified as section head in the 14 December 1961 *Selskaya Zhizn*, but by March 1962 he was demoted to Central Committee inspector (first identified in the 21 March 1962 *Pravda*). *Selskaya Zhizn* editor V. I. Polyakov took over leadership of the section (first identified in the 10 March 1962 *Sovetskaya Rossiya*).

[d]A short-lived Section for Industry Which Processes Agricultural Raw Material appeared in 1963. The first and only mention of it appeared in the 29 June 1963 *Radyanska Ukraina*, which also identified M. G. Lushin (former deputy chairman of the Poltava Sovnarkhoz) as its head.

[e]A Section for Economic Collaboration with Socialist Countries appeared in 1963 and 1964. B. P. Miroshnichenko, deputy head of the Section for Trade, Financial and Planning Organs (*Kommunist*, 14 September 1961), was identified as head of this section in the 8 January 1964 *Moskovskaya Pravda* and also in the 12 August 1963 *New York Times*, and also as head of an unnamed section as early as 26 January 1963 (*Pravda*).

[f]A Chemical Industry Section was first mentioned in the 3 March 1963 *Zarya Vostoka*, but no head was identified until August 1965.

[g]V. P. Abyzov was still first deputy head of the section in November 1961 (see the Stenographic record of the 22d Party Congress), but he was identified as section head for the first time in the 11 August 1962 *Ekonomicheskaya Gazeta*, p. 3.

(*Table notes continued on page 286*)

[h]In Khrushchev's late 1962 reorganization, the Culture Section was combined with Agitprop to form the new Ideological Section. Polikarpov became deputy head of the new Ideological Section (first identified in the 21 March 1963 *Sovetskaya Rossiya*).

[i]Melnikov was elected Moldavian second secretary in May 1961 (*Sovetskaya Moldaviya*, 30 May 1961). P. I. Maksimov, head of a sector in this section (identified in the 19 March 1960 *Sovetskaya Belorussiya*), was first identified as section head in the 20 February 1962 *Pravda*.

[j]V. N. Titov was released as Kharkov first secretary in March 1961 (*Pravda*, 3 March 1961) and was identified as section head in the 16 March 1961 *Pravda* (the 1962 yearbook lists him as section head since February 1961).

[k]In late 1962 the Propaganda and Agitation Section was reorganized into an Ideological Section (first mentioned in the 6 January 1963 *Pravda*).

[l]In late 1962 the Section for Science, Higher Educational Institutions and Schools was combined with the Agitprop and Culture sections to form the new Ideological Section. V. A. Kirillin became deputy head of the new section (identified as such in the 22 January 1963 *Pravda*), but soon was elected vice president of the Academy of Sciences (*Moskovskaya Pravda*, 6 February 1963).

[m]When the Party-State Control Committee was created in late 1962 Ya. I. Kabkov left his post as head of the Section for Trade, Financial, and Planning Organs (see the 1966 yearbook) and became head of a section of the new committee (identified in the 2 June 1964 *Izvestiya*). The section was abolished about this time. The trade functions were shifted to the Light Industry and Food Industry Section, which now became the Light Industry, Food Industry, and Trade Section (identified in the 13 June 1963 *Pravda*). The planning and financial organs part eventually became an independent section.

[n]K. S. Simonov, chief of the Gorkiy Railroad 1961–62 (yearbook, 1966), became deputy head of the section (identified in the 10 May 1962 *Pravda*) and then head (first identified in the 4 August 1962 *Ekonomicheskaya Gazeta*; the 1966 yearbook lists him as head since June 1962).

[o]A. K. Doluda was twice identified as head of an unnamed section in late 1961 (*Pravda*, 16 October 1961 and 10 November 1961).

CENTRAL COMMITTEE SECTION HEADS

	1964	Mid-1965	Late 1965
Admin. of Affairs	Chernyayev	Chernyayev[a] (–late '65)	Pavlov (Dec. '65–)
Adm. Organs	Mironov[b] (–Oct. '64)	(none)	(none)
Agriculture	Polyakov[c] (–Nov. '64)	Kulakov (Nov. '64–)	Kulakov
Agri. Processing	Lushin[d]		–
Bloc Economic Ties	Miroshnichenko[e]		–
Bloc Relations	Andropov	Andropov	Andropov
Chemical Industry	(apparently none)	Bushuyev[f] (May '65–)	Bushuyev
Construction	Biryukov[g] (July '64–)	Biryukov	Biryukov
Culture	–	Polikarpov[h] (spring '65–Nov. '65)	Shauro[i] (Nov. '65–)
Defense Industry	Serbin	Serbin	Serbin
Foreign Cadres	Panyushkin	Panyushkin	Panyushkin
General	Malin (–mid-'65)	Chernenko[j] (July '65–)	Chernenko
Heavy Industry	Rudakov	Rudakov	Rudakov[k] (–July '66)
Information	–	–	Shevlyagin[l] (Oct. '65–)
International	Ponomarev	Ponomarev	Ponomarev
Light Industry	Maksimov	Maksimov	Sizov[m] (Oct. '65–)
Machine Building	Frolov	Frolov	Frolov
Party Organs	Titov[n] (–Apr. '65)	–	Kapitonov[o] (Dec. '65–)
Propaganda	Ilichev (–Mar. '65)	Stepakov[p] (May '65–)	Stepakov
Science	–	Trapeznikov[q] (May '65–)	Trapeznikov
Trade	–	Kabkov[r] (June '65–)	Kabkov
Transport	Simonov	Simonov	Simonov

[a]Chernyayev was last identified as administrator of affairs in the 26 July 1965 *Vechernyaya Moskva*; he later became deputy chairman of the State Committee for Science and Technology. G. S. Pavlov, an old Brezhnev associate from Dneprodzerzhinsk, worked in the Party-State Control Committee until its abolition in December 1965. At that time (yearbook, 1966) he became administrator of affairs (he was first identified in the press in the 7 January 1966 *Pravda*).

[b]Mironov died in a plane crash (obituary in the 22 October 1964 *Pravda*). No one succeeded him until 1968.

(*Table notes continued on page 288*)

cPolyakov was removed as Central Committee secretary (and presumably also as section head) at the November 1964 Central Committee plenum (*Pravda*, 17 November 1964). F. D. Kulakov was first secretary of Stavropol until the beginning of December 1964. He was appointed head of the section in November 1964 (yearbook, 1966).

dLushin apparently still headed this section in December 1964 when he, along with Light Industry Section head Maksimov, signed the obituary of a dairy industry official (*Pravda*, 27 December 1964). On 7 December 1965, however, *Izvestiya* identified Lushin as first deputy minister of the meat and dairy industry. The section was abolished, apparently in 1965.

eMiroshnichenko was still identified as a section head in the 13 April 1965 *Pravda*, but *Ekonomicheskaya Gazeta* (no. 52) in December 1965 identified him as rector of the Institute of International Relations. This section has not been mentioned since then.

fV. M. Bushuyev was still listed as first deputy head in the 10 December 1964 *Pravda*, and was first identified as head in the 3 August 1965 *Pravda*. The 1966 yearbook states that he became head in May 1965.

gA. Ye. Biryukov was released as Moscow City secretary in July 1964 "in connection with [his] confirmation as head of the Central Committee Construction Section" (*Pravda*, 30 July 1964).

hThe Culture Section was restored in the spring of 1965 when the Ideological Section was broken up. Ideological Section deputy head D. A. Polikarpov became head of the new section and remained head until his death in November 1965 (see his obituary in the 3 November 1965 *Pravda*).

iV. F. Shauro was last identified as Belorussian Central Committee ideology secretary on 13 November 1965 (*Sovetskaya Belorussiya*) and first identified as a section head in the 12 December 1965 *Pravda*. According to the 1966 yearbook, he was appointed in November 1965.

jV. N. Malin had been replaced as section head by October 1965 when he was first identified as rector of the Academy of Social Sciences (*Pravda*, 5 October 1965). K. U. Chernenko, head of the Moldavian Agitprop Section under Moldavian First Secretary Brezhnev in the early 1950's and assistant to Brezhnev during Brezhnev's 1960–64 term as Soviet president (identified as head of the secretariat of the Presidium of the Supreme Soviet in the 19 July 1961 and 6 September 1963 *Pravda*s), became head of the General Section (i.e., assistant to the Central Committee first secretary) in July 1965 (yearbook, 1966).

kA. P. Rudakov died in July 1966 (*Pravda*, 11 July 1966).

lD. P. Shevlyagin, deputy head of the International Section, was identified as head of a section in the 12 December 1965 *Pravda*. Later, this was identified as the Section for Information (*Pravda*, 30 August 1966). The 1966 yearbook indicates that he became head of the section in October 1965.

mP. K. Sizov, head of the Section for Light Industry, Food Industry, and Trade for the RSFSR, became head of the Central Committee's Light Industry and Food Industry Section in October 1965 (yearbook, 1966; first identified in the 18 January 1966 *Pravda*), and his RSFSR section was abolished in the 1966 reorganization. His predecessor, Maksimov, was demoted to deputy minister of light industry (identified in the May 1966 *Ekonomicheskaya Gazeta*, no. 19, p. 8).

nTitov was transferred to Kazakhstan as second secretary in April 1965 (*Pravda*, 6 April 1965) and at the same time the Party Organs Section was renamed the Party Organizational Work Section (the first mention of this title was in the 27 May 1965 *Pravda*).

oI. V. Kapitonov, head of the Party Organs Section for the RSFSR, was named head of the Central Committee's Party Organizational Work Section and Central Committee secretary in December 1965 (*Pravda*, 7 December 1965).

pL. F. Ilichev was removed as Central Committee secretary (and presumably as section head) at the March 1965 Central Committee plenum and demoted to deputy foreign minister. After his removal, the Ideological Section was broken up into Propaganda and Agitation, Culture, and Science and Educational Institutions sections in May 1965. The first mention of the old propaganda and agitation title occurred in the 11 June 1965 *Pravda Ukrainy*; in mid-1966 its title was shortened to Propaganda Section (first mentioned in the 17 May 1966 *Pravda*). *Izvestiya* chief editor V. I. Stepakov replaced Ilichev as Agitprop head in May 1965 (yearbook, 1966).

qThe Section for Science and Educational Institutions was created when the Ideological Section was broken up in May 1965. S. P. Trapeznikov, a Brezhnev associate in Moldavia and deputy rector of the Higher Party School 1960–65, became head of the new section in May 1965 (yearbook, 1966).

rThis section was reestablished in mid-1965 and Kabkov returned from the Party-State Control Committee in June 1965 to become head of it (yearbook, 1966). The new section's title—Section for Trade and Everyday Services—was first mentioned when Kabkov was first identified as head in the 14 January 1966 *Pravda Ukrainy*. Similar sections were reestablished in several republic central committees, starting with Belorussia's (first identified in the 10 July 1965 *Sovetskaya Belorussiya*). In the Central Committee (and also in several republics) the Light Industry, Food Industry, and Trade Section reverted to its old title of Light Industry and Food Industry (first mentioned in the 16 January 1966 *Pravda*). At the same time several republic central committees dismantled their agricultural processing industry sections.

CENTRAL COMMITTEE SECTION HEADS

	1966	1969	1971
Adm. of Affairs	Pavlov	Pavlov	Pavlov
Adm. Organs	(none)	Savinkin[a] (spring '68-)	Savinkin
Agriculture	Kulakov	Kulakov	Kulakov
Bloc Relations	Andropov (-mid-'67)	Rusakov[b] (Mar. '68-)	Rusakov
Chemical Industry	Bushuyev	Bushuyev	Bushuyev
Construction	Biryukov (-Apr. '67)	Dmitriyev[c] (mid-'69-)	Dmitriyev
Culture	Shauro	Shauro	Shauro
Defense Industry	Serbin	Serbin	Serbin
Foreign Cadres	Panyushkin	Panyushkin	Panyushkin
General	Chernenko	Chernenko	Chernenko
Heavy Industry	Solomentsev[d] (Nov. '66-)	Solomentsev	Solomentsev
Information	Shevlyagin[e] (-Feb. '68)		
International	Ponomarev	Ponomarev	Ponomarev
Light Industry	Sizov	Sizov	Sizov
Machine Building	Frolov	Frolov	Frolov
Party Organs	Kapitonov	Kapitonov	Kapitonov
Planning-Finance[f]			
Propaganda	Stepakov	Stepakov[g] (-spring '70)	(none)
Science	Trapeznikov	Trapeznikov	Trapeznikov
Trade	Kabkov	Kabkov	Kabkov
Transport	Simonov	Simonov	Simonov
Unnamed Section		Organov[h] (Mar. '67-)	Organov

[a]N. I. Savinkin was still identified as first deputy head of the section in the 15 February 1968 *Izvestiya*, but was cited as head by the 5 May 1968 *Pravda*.

[b]Yu. V. Andropov left to become KGB chairman in May 1967. K. V. Rusakov was still listed as first deputy head of the section in the 5 March 1968 *Pravda*, but was identified as head in the 4 April 1968 *Pravda*.

[c]Biryukov was transferred to RSFSR deputy premier in April 1967. The post remained vacant until mid-1969. I. N. Dmitriyev was still identified as Gorkiy Oblast construction secretary in the 14 March 1969 *Pravda*, but was identified as a section head in the 16 July 1969 *Moskovskaya Pravda*.

[d]M. S. Solomentsev was released as Rostov first secretary on 16 November 1966 "in connection with [his] confirmation as head of the Heavy Industry Section of the CPSU Central Committee" (*Sovetskaya Rossiya*, 17 November 1966).

[e]Shevlyagin was exiled to Algeria as Soviet ambassador in February 1968 and the section apparently was abolished.

[f]The head of this section has never been identified (except for a mistaken identification of B. I. Gostev as head in the 20 April 1967 *Trud*). It apparently is administered by first deputy head Gostev,

who was first identified as deputy head of this section in the 17 January 1967 *Moskovskaya Pravda* (this was also the first mention of this section). Gostev had been cited as deputy head of an unnamed section already in the 18 January 1966 *Pravda*.

[g]Stepakov was removed as section head in March–April 1970 (last identified as section head in the 22 March 1970 *Pravda*) and no successor had been chosen as of January 1972.

[h]N. N. Organov was released as ambassador to Bulgaria in 1967 and became head of an unnamed section in 1967 (*Deputaty Verkhovnogo Soveta SSSR*, 8th convocation, 1970, p. 328; he was first identified as section head in the 22 March 1967 *Vedomosti Verkhovnogo Soveta SSSR*, p. 160).

APPENDIX 5

HEADS OF CENTRAL COMMITTEE SECTIONS FOR THE RSFSR

	Early 1959	Mid-1959–60	1961	1962
Adm. Organs		Tishchenko[a]	Tishchenko	Dyakov[b] (Feb. '62–)
Agitprop	Moskovskiy	Moskovskiy[c] (–Oct. '60)	Stepakov (Feb. '61–)	Stepakov
Agriculture	Mylarshchikov[d] (–spring '59)	Vorobyev[e] (Apr. '59–June '60)	Pankin (Feb. '61–)	Pankin
Ind.-Transpt.	Baskakov	Baskakov	Baskakov	Baskakov
Party Organs	Churayev[f] (– fall '59)	Yefremov[g] (late '59–Mar. '61)	Polekhin (spring '61–)	Polekhin
Science –Culture	Kazmin	Kazmin	Kazmin[h]	Chekharin[i]

[a]V. I. Tishchenko, formerly deputy head of the section, was first identified as head of the Administrative and Trade-Financial Organs Section in the 4 February 1960 *Komsomolskaya Pravda*.

[b]Tishchenko was still head of the section in July 1961 (*Leningradskaya Pravda*, 15 July 1961). V. A. Dyakov was released as first secretary of a Moscow City raykom in February 1962 (*Moskovskaya Pravda*, 15 February 1962) and first appeared as a section head on 28 February (*Moskovskaya Pravda*, 1 March 1962).

[c]V. P. Moskovskiy was appointed RSFSR deputy premier in October 1960 (*Sovetskaya Rossiya*, 28 October 1960). V. I. Stepakov was released from his post of Moscow City second secretary in February 1961 "in connection with [his] confirmation as head of the Central Committee's Propaganda and Agitation Section for the RSFSR" (*Pravda*, 28 February 1961).

[d]V. P. Mylarshchikov was last identified as section head in the 19 March 1959 *Izvestiya*. Udmurt First Secretary G. I. Vorobyev was first identified as section head in the 28 April 1959 *Sovetskaya Rossiya*.

[e]Vorobyev was elected Krasnodar first secretary in June 1960 (*Pravda*, 10 June 1960). I. S. Pankin was released as Stalingrad Oblast Executive Committee chairman on 30 January 1961 and was first identified as section head in the 11 February 1961 *Pravda*.

[f]V. M. Churayev was still identified as head of the RSFSR Party Organs Section in the 14 August 1959 *Pravda*, but was identified as head of the Central Committee's Party Organs Section for the Union Republics in the 21 October 1959 *Izvestiya*. M. T. Yefremov was last identified as Kuybyshev first secretary in the 6 September 1959 *Pravda* and first identified as RSFSR Party Organs Section head in the 30 December 1959 *Pravda*.

[g]Yefremov was last identified as section head in the 16 February 1961 *Pravda*; *Pravda* on 17 March 1961 reported his election as Chelyabinsk first secretary. M. A. Polekhin was still identified as deputy head of the section in the 12 April 1961 *Sovetskaya Rossiya*, but on 7 May 1961 *Pravda* cited him as head for the first time.

[h]N. D. Kazmin was identified as section head as late as 5 April 1961 (*Sovetskaya Rossiya*), but later was removed and semi-retired (appointed director of the Central Lenin Museum—see his obituary in the 31 October 1963 *Pravda*). His successor, Ye. M. Chekharin, was first identified as a section head in the 20 May 1962 *Pravda*.

[i]In the late 1962 reorganization, the Science, Schools, and Culture Section was merged with Agitprop into the new RSFSR ideological sections. Chekharin became first deputy head of the new Ideological Section for Industry (first identified in the 9 April 1963 *Sovetskaya Kultura*).

HEADS OF CENTRAL COMMITTEE SECTIONS FOR THE RSFSR

	1963	1964	1965[a]
Adm. Organs	Dyakov[b] (-Mar. '63)	Laputin (spring '63-)	Laputin
Agriculture	Pankin	Pankin[c]	(apparently none)
Agri. Processing	Tyasto[d]	Tyasto[e]	
Chemical Industry		Belyayev[f]	Belyayev[g]
Construction	Gladyrevskiy[h]	Gladyrevskiy	Gladyrevskiy
Heavy Industry	Baskakov[i]	Baskakov	Baskakov
Ideology–Agri.[j]	Stepakov	Stepakov[k] (-Oct. '64)	Khaldeyev
Ideology–Ind.	Khaldeyev	Khaldeyev	
Light Industry	Sizov[l]	Sizov	Sizov[m] (-Oct. '65)
Mach. Building	Kozlov[n]	Kozlov	Kozlov
Party Organs–Agri.[o]	Polekhin	Polekhin[p]	Kapitonov (Dec. '64-Dec. '65)
Party Organs–Ind. Science[q]	Voronovskiy	Voronovskiy	

[a]After the abolition of the RSFSR Bureau at the 23d Congress in March–April 1966, the Central Committee sections for the RSFSR were merged into the regular Central Committee sections. In the merger, RSFSR section heads Laputin, Gladyrevskiy, Baskakov, and Kozlov became deputy heads of the corresponding Central Committee sections; Khaldeyev became editor of *Partiynaya Zhizn*; while Sizov and Kapitonov had become heads of the corresponding Central Committee sections already in late 1965.

[b]Dyakov was last identified as section head in the 9 February 1963 *Moskovskaya Pravda* and was appointed RSFSR deputy premier on 5 March 1963 (*Sovetskaya Rossiya*, 7 March 1963). Former deputy section head V. I. Laputin was first identified as section head in the 12 April 1963 *Sovetskaya Rossiya*.

[c]Pankin was last identified as section head in the 18 March 1964 *Sovetskaya Rossiya* and was not mentioned after his patron Voronov came under attack in the spring of 1964. V. A. Karlov apparently took over responsibility for the RSFSR Agriculture Section when he was appointed a member of the RSFSR Bureau in March 1965; however, he was never identified as section head.

[d]A short-lived Section for Processing Agricultural Raw Material and Trade appeared in 1963 (first mentioned in the 24 July 1963 *Sovetskaya Rossiya*, when A. I. Tyasto was identified as head).

[e]This section was apparently merged back into the RSFSR Section for Light Industry, Food Industry, and Trade in 1964 or 1965 (*Moskovskaya Pravda* on 2 June 1966, shortly after the abolition of the RSFSR sections, identified Tyasto as former deputy head of the RSFSR Section for Light Industry, Food Industry, and Trade–a post he presumably took in 1964 or 1965).

[f]The RSFSR Chemical Industry Section was first identified in the 22 September 1964 *Moskovskaya Pravda*, when V. D. Belyayev was identified as head, although it may well have been established in 1963 along with the regular Central Committee Chemical Industry Section. Belyayev, as first deputy chairman of the Nizhne Volzhskiy Sovnarkhoz, showed Khrushchev around the Volzhskiy Chemical Combine during his September 1963 visit to Volgograd (*Pravda*, 18 and 19 September 1963) and wrote an article on the chemical industry in the Volga area in the 21 December 1963 *Moscow News*.

[g]Belyayev had been transferred by February 1966, when he was identified as deputy minister of the chemical industry USSR (*Vedomosti Verkhovnogo Soveta RSFSR*, 10 February 1966, p. 112), and

(Table notes continued on page 294)

the 27 March 1966 *Izvestiya* reported his appointment as chief of the Main Administration for the USSR Microbiological Industry.

[h]The Construction Section was first mentioned in the 5 October 1962 *Pravda*, when A. V. Gladyrevskiy was first identified as section head.

[i]The Section for Heavy Industry, Transport, and Communications was first mentioned in the 7 March 1963 *Izvestiya*, when S. A. Baskakov was identified as head. Its predecessor, the Industry-Transport Section, was broken up into separate sections for construction, chemistry, light industry and food industry, machine building, and this heavy industry-transportation-communications section, apparently during 1962 when these sections first began appearing.

[j]The Propaganda and Agitation Section was split into Ideological Sections for Agriculture and for Industry after Khrushchev's November 1962 reorganization. M. I. Khaldeyev was released as a Moscow City raykom first secretary in January 1963 (*Vechernyaya Moskva*, 24 January 1963) and was first identified as head of the Ideological Section for Industry in the 10 March 1963 *Moskovskaya Pravda*. Stepakov was first identified as head of the Ideological Section for Agriculture in the 7 March 1963 *Izvestiya*.

[k]After Khrushchev's fall, the ideological sections were recombined and renamed the Propaganda and Agitation Section (first mentioned in the 6 February 1965 *Vechernyaya Moskva*, when Khaldeyev was identified as head of the new combined section). Stepakov became chief editor of *Izvestiya* immediately after Khrushchev's fall (first identified in the 25 October 1964 *Izvestiya*), replacing Khrushchev's son-in-law, Adzhubey.

In all republics except the RSFSR the separate ideological and party organs sections for industry and agriculture established in December 1962 and January 1963 were recombined between April and July 1963—implicitly casting doubt on the wisdom of Khrushchev's November 1962 plan to divide party units into agricultural and industrial units. The RSFSR retained separate agricultural and industrial sections through 1964 (the last identification—of the Ideological Section for Industry—was in the 31 December 1964 *Vedomosti Verkhovnogo Soveta RSFSR*).

[l]The Section for Light Industry, Food Industry, and Trade was first mentioned in the 24 April 1963 *Vedomosti Verkhovnogo Soveta SSSR*. Sector head P. K. Sizov was first identified as section head in the 17 May 1963 *Sovetskaya Rossiya*.

[m]Sizov became head of the Central Committee's Light Industry and Food Industry Section in October 1965 (yearbook, 1966).

[n]The Machine Building Section was first mentioned in the 28 September 1962 *Vedomosti Verkhovnogo Soveta SSSR*, p. 896. I. I. Kozlov, identified as deputy head of an unnamed Central Committee section in the 1 April 1962 *Pravda*, was first cited as head of the RSFSR Machine Building Section in the 31 October 1963 *Pravda*.

[o]After Khrushchev's November 1962 reorganization, the RSFSR Party Organs Section was split into separate Party Organs Sections for Agriculture and Industry. RSFSR Party Organs Section head Polekhin became head of the section for agriculture (first identified in the 15 January 1963 *Komsomolskaya Pravda*) and RSFSR Party Organs Section deputy head N. A. Voronovskiy became head of the section for industry (first identified in the 7 March 1963 *Sovetskaya Rossiya*).

[p]After Khrushchev's fall, the party organs sections were recombined (first indicated in the 26 January 1965 *Pravda*) and later renamed the Party Organizational Work Section (first indicated in the 27 May 1965 *Pravda*). I. V. Kapitonov was replaced as Ivanovo first secretary in December 1964 (*Sovetskaya Rossiya*, 23 December 1964) and was first identified as section head in the 26 January 1965 *Pravda*. Polekhin and Voronovskiy became his deputies. In December 1965 Kapitonov became head of the Central Committee's Party Organization Work Section and Central Committee secretary.

[q]The Science and Educational Institutions Section was established during the break-up of the RSFSR Agitprop Section in the spring of 1965 (first mention of this section was in the 11 March 1965 *Vedomosti Verkhovnogo Soveta RSFSR*). No one had yet been identified as head when the section was merged with the regular Central Committee Science and Educational Institutions Section in early 1966.

APPENDIX 6

EDITORS OF LEADING NEWSPAPERS 1960–71

	Pravda	*Izvestiya*	*Sovetskaya Rossiya*	*Selskaya Zhizn*	*Komsomolskaya Pravda*
1960	P. A. Satyukov	A. I. Adzhubey	I. S. Pustovalov (–Mar. '61)	A. M. Sirotin (–spring '60)	Yu. P. Voronov
1961	Satyukov	Adzhubey	K. I. Zarodov (Mar. '61–)	V. I. Polyakov (Apr. '60–)	Voronov
1962	Satyukov	Adzhubey	Zarodov	Polyakov (–Dec. '62)	Voronov
1963	Satyukov (–Nov. '64)	Adzhubey (–Oct. '64)	Zarodov	P. F. Alekseyev (Dec. '62–)	Voronov
1964	A. M. Rumyantsev (Nov. '64– Sep. '65)	V. I. Stepakov (Oct. '64– May '65)	Zarodov (–Oct. '65)	Alekseyev	Voronov (–fall '65)
1965	M. V. Zimyanin (Sep. '65–)	L. N. Tolkunov (Oct. '65–)	V. P. Moskovskiy (Oct. '65–)	Alekseyev	B. D. Pankin (fall '65–)
1966	Zimyanin	Tolkunov	Moskovskiy	Alekseyev	Pankin
1967	Zimyanin	Tolkunov	Moskovskiy	Alekseyev	Pankin
1968	Zimyanin	Tolkunov	Moskovskiy	Alekseyev	Pankin
1969	Zimyanin	Tolkunov	Moskovskiy	Alekseyev	Pankin
1970	Zimyanin	Tolkunov	Moskovskiy (–spring '71)	Alekseyev (–spring '71)	Pankin
1971	Zimyanin	Tolkunov	P. F. Alekseyev (spring '71–)	N. A. Zakolupin (spring '71–)	Pankin

APPENDIX 7

USSR AGRICULTURE MINISTRY LEADERS

	1960	1961	1962	1963
Minister:	Matskevich[a]	Olshanskiy[b]	Pysin[c]	Volovchenko
First Deputy:	Volchenko[d]	Pysin	Levykin[e]	Levykin[f]
Deputies:	Petrov	Petrov	Petrov	Petrov
	Borkov[g]			
	Chekmenev[h]			
	Kuchumov[i]			
		Nazarenko[j]	Nazarenko	Nazarenko
		Mozgov[k]	Mozgov	
				Savelyev[l]

[a]V. V. Matskevich removed as minister and transferred to Tselinnyy Kray as executive committee chairman; VASKhNIL Vice President M. A. Olshanskiy appointed minister on 29 December 1960 (*Pravda*, 30 December 1960).

[b]Olshanskiy demoted to president of VASKhNIL on 5 April 1962 (*Pravda*, 6 April 1962); First Deputy Minister K. G. Pysin appointed minister on 25 April 1962 (*Pravda*, 26 April 1962).

[c]Pysin removed as minister and replaced with sovkhoz director I. P. Volovchenko on 8 March 1963 (*Pravda*, 9 March 1963).

[d]Ya. S. Volchenko released as first deputy minister for reasons of health on 8 March 1961 and Altay First Secretary K. G. Pysin appointed to replace him (*Sobraniye Postanovleniy Pravitelstva SSSR*, no. 6 [1961]).

[e]Pysin was succeeded as first deputy minister by the director of the All-Union Institute for Mechanization of Agriculture, N. I. Levykin, who was first identified as first deputy minister in the 30 September 1962 *Sovetskaya Rossiya*.

[f]Levykin was last identified as deputy minister in the 14 March 1964 *Izvestiya*, on which occasion he was attacked for opposing Khrushchev on production of a tractor. He later (*Moskovskaya Pravda*, 17 April 1965) was again identified as director of the All-Union Institute for Mechanization of Agriculture.

[g]G. A. Borkov was last identified as deputy minister in the 29 November 1960 *Literaturnaya Gazeta*.

[h]Ye. M. Chekmenev was released as deputy minister and appointed deputy chairman of the State Committee on Procurements in early 1961 (*Sobraniye Postanovleniy Pravitelstva SSSR*, no. 7 [1961]). He was criticized by Khrushchev in an 8 March 1961 speech.

[i]P. S. Kuchumov was transferred to head of the new All-Union Agricultural Equipment Association on 20 February 1961 (*Pravda*, 21 February 1961).

[j]Chairman of the State Commission for Testing Varieties K. S. Nazarenko was appointed deputy minister in early 1961 (*Sobraniye Postanovleniy Pravitelstva SSSR*, no. 6 [1961]).

[k]I. Ye. Mozgov was appointed deputy minister in early 1961 (*Sobraniye Postanovleniy Pravitelstva SSSR*, no. 7 [1961]).

[l]Director of the All-Union Poultry Raising Institute I. K. Savelyev was first identified as deputy minister in the 9 January 1963 *Izvestiya*.

USSR AGRICULTURE MINISTRY LEADERS

	1964	1965	1966	1971
Minister:	Volovchenko	Matskevich[a]	Matskevich	Matskevich
First Deputies:	Morozov[b,c]	Volovchenko[d]	Volovchenko	Volovchenko
	Sidak[e,f]			
Deputies:		Morozov[g]	Morozov	Morozov
		Sidak[h]	Sidak	Sidak
	Petrov	Petrov	Petrov	Petrov
	Nazarenko	Nazarenko	Nazarenko	Nazarenko
	Savelyev[i]			
		Kardapoltsev[j]	Kardapoltsev	Kardapoltsev
		Balyasinskiy[k,l]		
			Vorobyev[m,n]	
			Dubrovin[o]	Dubrovin
				Runov[p]
				Chubarov[q]

[a]Volovchenko was removed and replaced by Matskevich on 17 February 1965 (*Pravda*, 18 February 1965).

[b]P. I. Morozov was released as Amur Oblast first secretary in April 1964 and first identified as first deputy minister in the 15 May 1964 *Izvestiya*.

[c]Morozov was last identified as first deputy minister in the 16 April 1965 *Trud*, after which he was demoted to deputy minister.

[d]Volovchenko was appointed first deputy minister on 17 February 1965, being demoted from minister (*Pravda*, 18 February 1965).

[e]R. N. Sidak, director of the Lgovskaya experimental selection station, was first identified as first deputy minister in the 15 June 1964 *Pravda*.

[f]Sidak was last identified as first deputy minister in the 1 April 1965 *Radyanska Ukraina*, after which he was identified only as deputy minister.

[g]Morozov was demoted from first deputy minister to deputy minister (first identified as deputy minister in the 25 August 1965 *Selskaya Zhizn*).

[h]Sidak was demoted from first deputy minister to deputy minister about the same time as Morozov. In reporting a 30 March 1965 Agriculture Ministry conference, the 1 April 1965 *Radyanska Ukraina* (and some other regional papers) referred to Sidak as first deputy minister, while the central agricultural organ *Selskaya Zhizn* (which reported the conference only on 4 April) identified him only as a deputy minister. *Selskaya Zhizn* turned out to be correct, since all subsequent identifications have been as deputy minister.

[i]Savelyev was last identified as deputy minister in the 31 May 1964 *Pravda*. He became deputy chief of the All-Union Poultry-raising Administration (*Ptitseprom*)—identified in the 20 February 1968 *Selskaya Zhizn*.

[j]A. V. Kardapoltsev was first secretary of the Chelyabinsk Agricultural Obkom until the agricultural and industrial obkoms were reunited in December 1964, following the November 1964 reversal of Khrushchev's 1962 division of party organs into agricultural and industrial. He was first identified as deputy minister in the 2 July 1965 *Sovetskaya Latviya*.

[k]I. G. Balyasinskiy was first secretary of the Kuybyshev Agricultural Obkom (last identified in the 15 December 1964 *Izvestiya*) until the agricultural and industrial obkoms were reunited in December 1964. He was first identified as deputy minister in the 18 September 1965 *Moskovskaya Pravda*.

(*Table notes continued on page 298*)

[l]On 13 March 1966 *Izvestiya* reported Balyasinskiy's appointment as first deputy chairman of the State Committee for Procurements.

[m]G. I. Vorobyev was released as Krasnodar first secretary on 12 January 1966 in connection with his appointment as deputy minister (*Pravda*, 13 January 1966).

[n]*Pravda* on 29 May 1970 reported Vorobyev's appointment as chairman of the State Committee on Forestry.

[o]A. F. Dubrovin, still identified as deputy chairman of the Moscow Sovnarkhoz in the 4 November 1965 *Moskovskaya Pravda*, was first identified as deputy minister in the 31 March 1966 *Vedomosti Verkhovnogo Soveta RSFSR.*

[p]B. A. Runov, apparently a subordinate of Central Committee agriculture chief Kulakov (the 17 September 1969 *Sovetskaya Moldaviya* identified him as head of a Central Committee sector—presumably of the Agriculture Section—while he attended the 1969 Moldavian Congress of Kolkhozniks), was first identified as deputy minister in the 20 October 1970 *Selskaya Zhizn.*

[q]A. P. Chubarov, Kirgiz second secretary until March 1971 (formally replaced at the 5 March 1971 Kirgiz party congress), was first identified as deputy minister in a June 1971 *Ekonomicheskaya Gazeta* (no. 23, p. 18).

APPENDIX 8

IDENTIFICATION OF PERIODICAL SOURCES

Central newspapers:

Ekonomicheskaya Gazeta, economic weekly of the Central Committee
Izvestiya, organ of the USSR Supreme Soviet Presidium
Komsomolskaya Pravda, organ of the Komsomol Central Committee
Krasnaya Zvezda, central organ of the Ministry of Defense
Literaturnaya Gazeta, main organ of the USSR Writers Union
Literaturnaya Rossiya, weekly of the RSFSR Writers Union and the Moscow Writers Organization
Pravda, main organ of the Central Committee
Selskaya Zhizn, newspaper of the Central Committee specializing in agriculture
Sotsialisticheskaya Industriya, newspaper of the Central Committee specializing in industry
Sovetskaya Kultura, organ of the Ministry of Culture
Sovetskaya Rossiya, newspaper of the Central Committee specializing in RSFSR affairs (until 1966 organ of the RSFSR Bureau, RSFSR Supreme Soviet, and RSFSR Council of Ministers)
Trud, organ of the Central Council of Trade Unions

Republic newspapers:

Bakinskiy Rabochiy, organ of the Azerbaydzhan Central Committee
Kazakhstanskaya Pravda, organ of the Kazakh Central Committee
Kommunist, organ of the Armenian Central Committee
Kommunist Tadzhikistana, organ of the Tadzhik Central Committee
Molod Ukrainy, Ukrainian language organ of the Ukrainian Komsomol Central Committee
Pravda Ukrainy, Russian language organ of the Ukrainian Central Committee
Pravda Vostoka, organ of the Uzbek Central Committee
Radyanska Ukraina, Ukrainian language organ of the Ukrainian Central Committee
Sovetskaya Belorussiya, Russian language organ of the Belorussian Central Committee
Sovetskaya Estoniya, organ of the Estonian Central Committee
Sovetskaya Kirgiziya, organ of the Kirgiz Central Committee
Sovetskaya Latviya, organ of the Latvian Central Committee
Sovetskaya Litva, organ of the Lithuanian Central Committee
Sovetskaya Moldaviya, organ of the Moldavian Central Committee
Turkmenskaya Iskra, organ of the Turkmen Central Committee
Zarya Vostoka, organ of the Georgian Central Committee
Zvyazda, Belorussian language organ of the Belorussian Central Committee

Local newspapers:

Leningradskaya Pravda, organ of Leningrad Oblast and City
Leninskoye Znamya, organ of Moscow Oblast
Moskovskaya Pravda, organ of Moscow City
Vechernyaya Moskva, organ of Moscow City

Journals:

Agitator, biweekly journal of the Central Committee

Biologiya v Shkole, scientific journal of the USSR Education Ministry

Botanicheskiy Zhurnal, monthly journal of the Academy of Sciences and All-Union Botanical Society, published in Leningrad

Druzhba Narodov, monthly journal of the USSR Writers Union

Ekonomika Selskogo Khozyaystva, monthly journal of the USSR Agriculture Ministry

Filosofskiye Nauki, bimonthly journal of the Ministry of Higher and Secondary Specialized Education USSR

Grani, Russian émigré journal published in Frankfurt-am-Main, Germany

Kommunist, leading theoretical and political journal of the Central Committee

Kommunist Belorussii, main political journal of the Belorussian Central Committee

Kommunist Estonii, main political journal of the Estonian Central Committee

Narodnoye Khozyaystvo Kazakhstana, monthly journal of the Kazakh Gosplan

Nash Sovremennik, monthly literary journal of the RSFSR Writers Union

Nauka i Zhizn, monthly popular science journal of the "Znaniye" Society

Neva, monthly literary journal of the RSFSR Writers Union and Leningrad Writers Organization

Novyy Mir, monthly literary journal of the USSR Writers Union

Ogonek, weekly popular picture magazine

Oktyabr, monthly literary journal of the RSFSR Writers Union

Partiynaya Zhizn, journal of the Central Committee

Planovoye Khozyaystvo, monthly political-economic journal of Gosplan

Politicheskoye Samoobrazovaniye, monthly political education journal of the Central Committee

Prostor, monthly literary journal of the Kazakh Writers Union

Selskoye Khozyaystvo Rossii, monthly journal of the RSFSR Agriculture Ministry

Seriya Ekonomicheskaya, Izvestiya Akademii Nauk SSSR, bimonthly economic series published by the USSR Academy of Sciences

Sibirskiye Ogni, monthly literary journal of the USSR Writers Union for west Siberia

Sotsialisticheskaya Zakonnost, organ of the USSR Prosecutor's Office and the USSR Supreme Court

Sovetskaya Pechat (renamed *Zhurnalist* in January 1967)

Sovetskoye Gosudarstvo i Pravo, monthly organ of the Institute of State and Law of the Academy of Sciences

Sovety Deputatov Trudyashchikhsya, monthly journal of the newspaper *Izvestiya*

Ural, monthly literary journal of the RSFSR Writers Union for west Siberia

Vedomosti Verkhovnogo Soveta RSFSR, announcements of the RSFSR Supreme Soviet

Vedomosti Verkhovnogo Soveta SSSR, announcements of the USSR Supreme Soviet

Vestnik Akademii Nauk SSSR, monthly journal of the USSR Academy of Sciences

Vestnik Moskovskogo Universiteta, journal of Moscow University

Vestnik Selskokhozyaystvennoy Nauki, monthly journal of the All-Union Academy of Agricultural Sciences (VASKhNIL)

Volga, monthly literary journal of the RSFSR Writers Union and the Saratov Writers Organization

Voprosy Ekonomiki, monthly journal of the Institute of Economics of the Academy of Sciences

Voprosy Filosofii, monthly journal of the Institute of Philosophy of the Academy of Sciences

Voprosy Istorii KPSS, monthly party history journal of the Marxism–Leninism Institute

Voprosy Literatury, monthly literary journal of the USSR Writers Union

Yunost, monthly literary-youth journal of the USSR Writers Union

Zhivotnovodstvo, monthly zootechnical journal of the USSR Agriculture Ministry

Zhurnalist, monthly journal of the Journalists Union

Zvezda, monthly literary journal of the USSR Writers Union, published in Leningrad

INDEX OF NAMES

Kuznetsov, I. N., 198
Kvasnikov, V., 74

Lalayants, A. M., 192, 193
Lanshin, I. A., 201
Lapidus, M., 188n
Lapin, S. G., 253
Laptev, I. D., 78, 81
Laptev, N. V., 30n, 31, 39, 61, 61n
Laputin, V. I., 293, 293n
Larionov, A. N., 11, 35, 36, 37, 40, 40n,
  41, 42n, 60
Laskovaya, L., 111n
Latsis, V. T., 18
Latunov, I. S., 39
Lavrentyev, M. A., 47
Lebedev, K. V., 257
Lebedev, M. M., 119, 129
Lemeshev, M. Ya., 194n
Lenin, V. I., 141n, 230, 238, 242, 249, 254,
  256n
Lerner, I. M., 65n
Lerner, N., 23n
Lesechko, M. A., 110
Levykin, N. I., 100, 101, 296, 296n
Ligachev, Ye. K., 160n
Lisavenko, M. A., 59
Lisichkin, G., 145, 208n
Lobanov, P. P., 31, 59, 65, 137, 138n, 140,
  143, 144, 145, 147, 154
Lobashev, M. Ye., 129, 129n, 130, 133, 141
Logvinov, L., 249
Lomakin, V. P., 161n
Lomako, P. F., 115n, 116, 277, 280
Loza, G. M., 70
Lubennikov, L. I., 284, 284n
Lukich, L. Ye., 172n
Lukyanenko, P. P., 75, 131
Lushin, M. G., 285, 285n, 287, 288n
Lutak, I. K., 173n
Lutsenko, M. N., 150, 154
Lysenko, T. D., 2, 7, 8, 8n, 9, 11, 20, 26,
  27, 28, 28n, 29, 30, 30n, 31, 32, 43, 44,
  44n, 45, 46, 46n, 47, 47n, 48, 51, 54, 56,
  56n, 57, 58, 58n, 59, 59n, 63, 64, 64n,
  65, 66, 67, 68, 68n, 69, 69n, 70, 70n,
  71, 72n, 73, 74, 74n, 75, 76, 77, 78, 78n,
  79, 80, 81, 82, 83, 92, 98, 103, 111, 117,
  118, 119, 119n, 120, 121, 122, 122n,
  126, 126n, 127n, 128, 129, 129n, 130,
  130n, 131, 132, 133, 133n, 135, 136,
  137, 138, 138n, 139, 140, 141, 141n,
  145, 146, 154, 156

Makarov, V. I., 106
Makeyev, P. A., 213
Makhmudov, M., 210

Maksimov, L. I., 38, 85, 101, 119, 150, 151,
  152, 153
Maksimov, P. I., 285, 286n, 287, 288n
Malakhovskiy, A., 52n
Malenkov, G. M., 1, 2, 8, 22, 25n, 27, 44,
  45, 74n, 127n, 142
Malin, V. N., 284, 285, 287, 288n
Malinovskiy, B. A., 122n
Maltsev, T. S., 27, 28, 30n, 31, 45, 58, 60,
  71, 73n, 74n, 76, 113, 113n, 117, 121,
  122, 137, 145, 145n, 146, 152
Malygin, A. M., 264n
Malygin, V., 50
Masherov, P. M., 151n, 229, 232n, 243,
  243n, 250n, 262, 273
Maslennikov, N. I., 265, 265n
Matsepuro, M. Ye., 80, 135, 136, 137, 138,
  138n
Matskevich, V. V., 11, 20, 20n, 28, 29,
  30, 31, 32, 33, 34, 43, 46, 48, 56, 56n,
  57, 57n, 58, 59, 60n, 61, 65, 104, 105,
  106, 136, 139, 139n, 140, 143, 144, 145,
  147, 148, 150, 151, 153, 153n, 154,
  154n, 155, 183, 184, 185, 188, 194n,
  202, 207, 210, 213, 233, 296, 296n, 297,
  297n
Matyushkin, D. M., 20, 21, 105
Mayat, A. S., 158n
Mayer, V., 247n
Mazurov, K. T., 33, 35, 75, 80, 81, 86, 143,
  143n, 150, 150n, 151n, 153, 154, 155,
  157, 160, 161, 168, 170, 173, 174n,
  176n, 178, 179, 179n, 183, 186, 203,
  218, 219n, 232n, 236, 242, 251n, 262,
  272, 273
Medvedev, R. A., 137, 137n
Medvedev, Zh. A., 8n, 59n, 65, 65n, 66,
  66n, 67, 68, 68n, 69, 70, 71, 73, 73n, 74,
  79, 82, 126, 126n, 127, 127n, 128, 129n,
  130, 132, 133, 136, 137n, 150n
Melentyev, V., 52, 52n, 157n
Melnik, G. A., 107, 108, 109, 112, 145n
Melnikov, N. A., 284, 284n, 285, 286n
Memnonov, V. V., 100
Mendel, Gregor, 83, 133
Mesyats, V. K., 144, 263
Mesyatsev, N. N., 253, 253n, 258
Metelev, V. Ya., 78, 78n, 147
Michurin, I. V., 67, 74
Mikhaylov, N. A., 253, 253n
Mikheyev, V., 77n, 78
Mikoyan, A. I., 10, 11, 11n, 12, 85, 110,
  132n, 161, 173, 266n, 272, 273
Minkovich, I., 186, 186n
Mironov, N. R., 284, 284n, 285, 287, 287n
Miroshnichenko, B. P., 285, 285n, 287,
  288n
Mitin, M. B., 127n

THE JOHNS HOPKINS UNIVERSITY PRESS

This book was composed in Press Roman text and Columna and
Univers Bold Extended display type by Jones Composition Company, Inc.
from a design by Victoria Dudley. It was printed on
60-lb. Sebago stock and bound in Joanna Arrestox cloth by
The Maple Press Company.

Library of Congress Cataloging in Publication Data

Hahn, Werner G
    The politics of Soviet agriculture, 1960–1970.

    Includes bibliographical references.
    1. Agriculture and state—Russia. 2. Agriculture—Economic aspects—Russia. I. Title.
HD1993.H33 1972   338.1'0947   72–151
ISBN 0–8018–1359–X